Its to·空·

YUUKI IINUMA

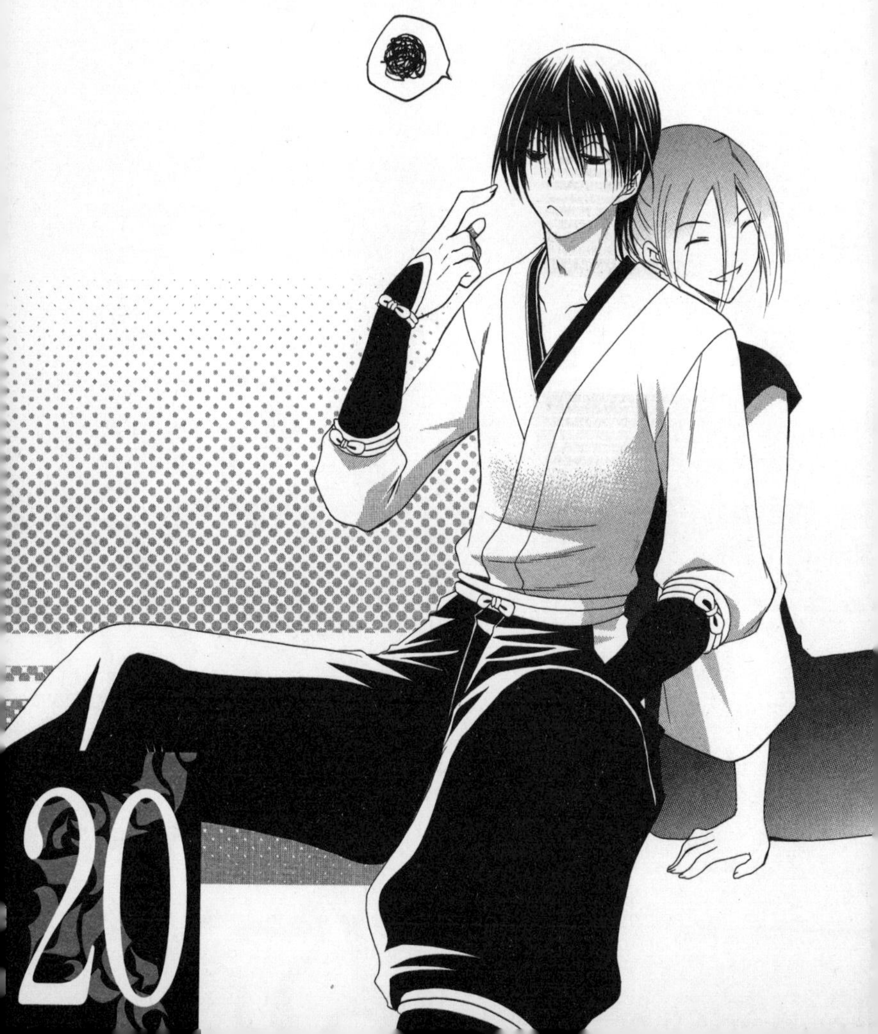

20

Contents

Chapter 188 Don't Let Me Die 3

Chapter 189 Protecting 21

Chapter 190 I Won't Kill 39

Chapter 191 Battle at the Old Tower 57

Chapter 192 Serious 75

Chapter 193 Nearer the Truth 93

Chapter 194 Two with Vision 111

Chapter 195 Liars and Honest People 129

Chapter 196 Promise 147

Chapter 197 The Course of Fate Ends 167

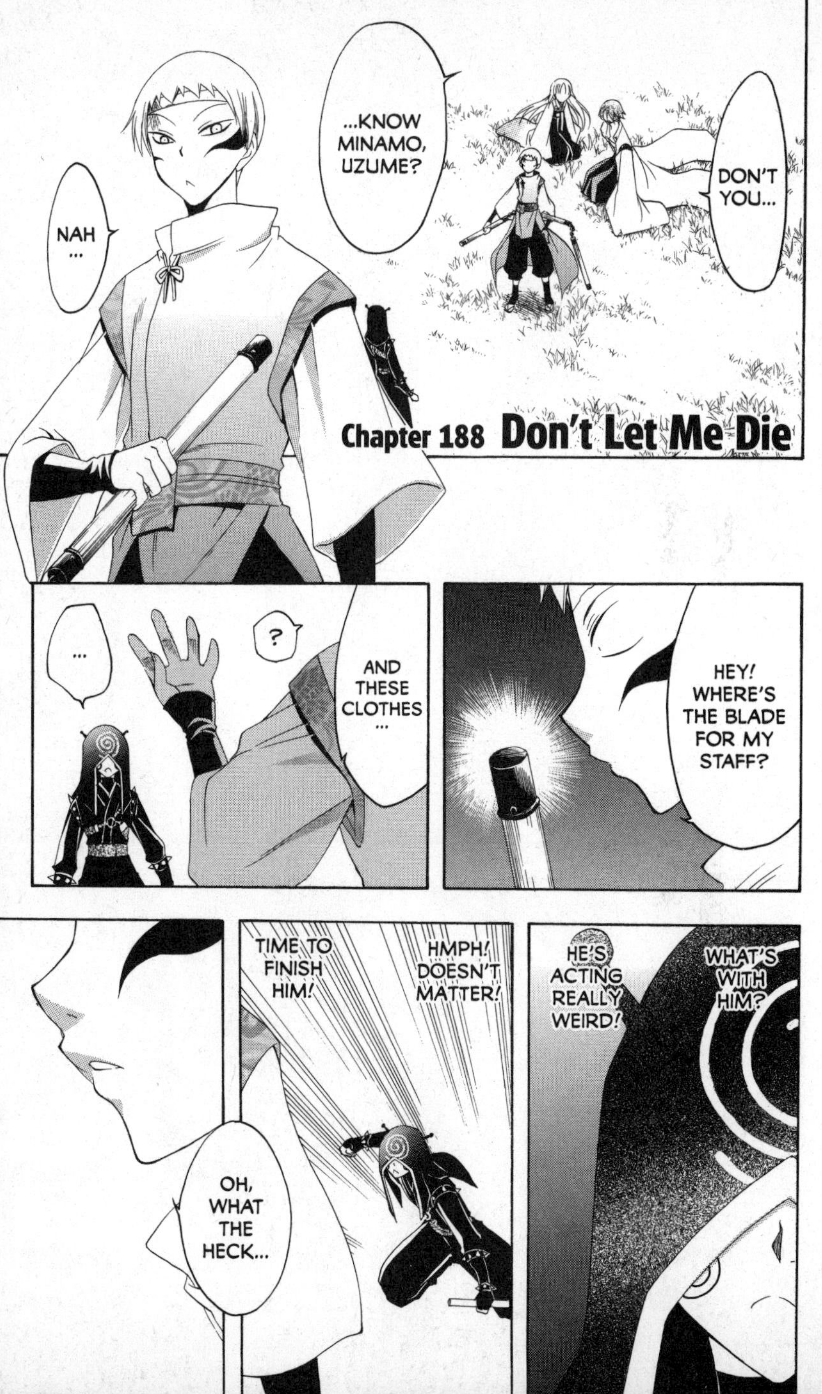
DON'T YOU...
...KNOW MINAMO, UZUME?
NAH...
Chapter 188 Don't Let Me Die
HEY! WHERE'S THE BLADE FOR MY STAFF?
AND THESE CLOTHES...
?
...
WHAT'S WITH HIM?
HE'S ACTING REALLY WEIRD!
HMPH! DOESN'T MATTER!
TIME TO FINISH HIM!
OH, WHAT THE HECK...

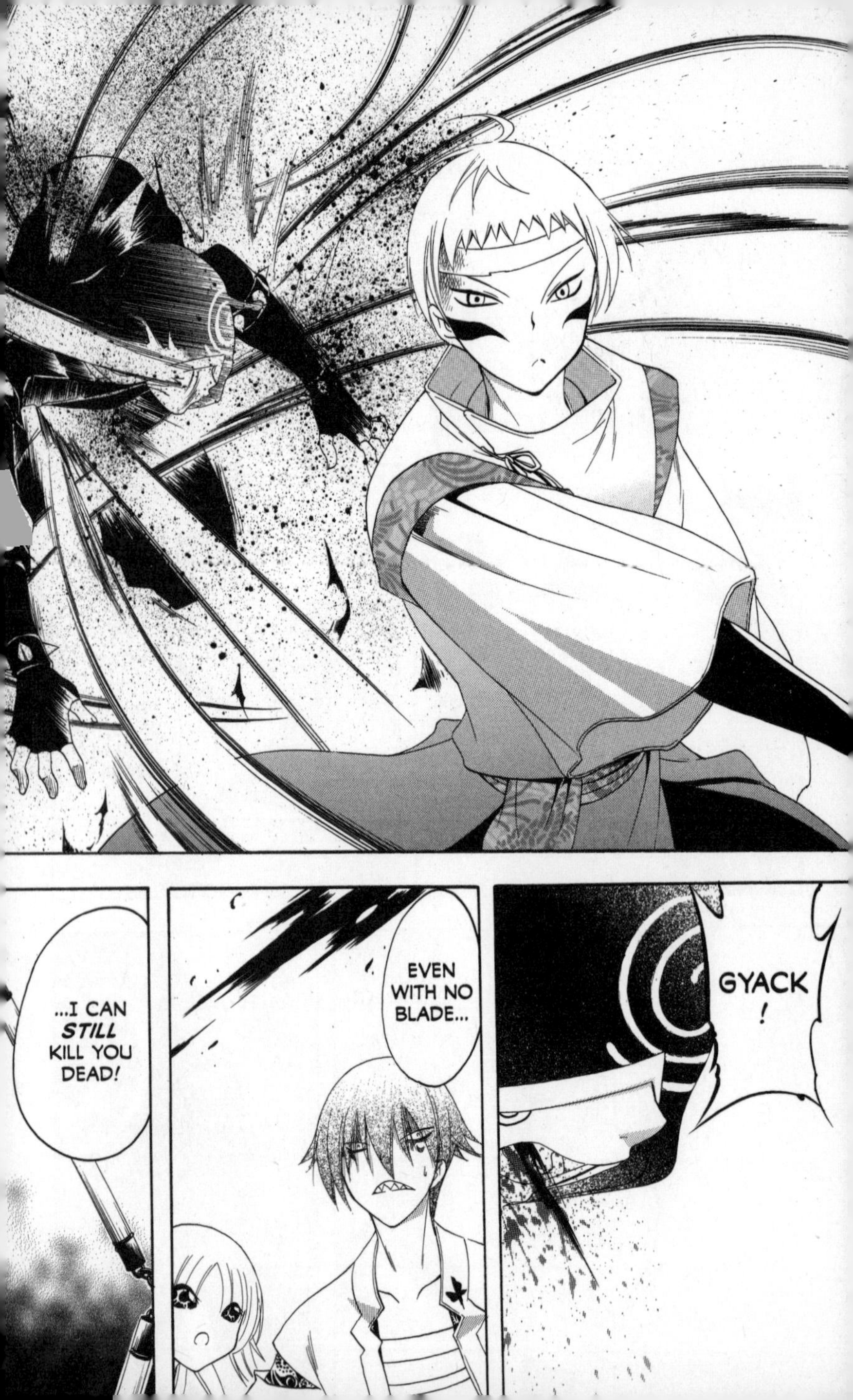
GYACK!
EVEN WITH NO BLADE...
...I CAN *STILL* KILL YOU DEAD!

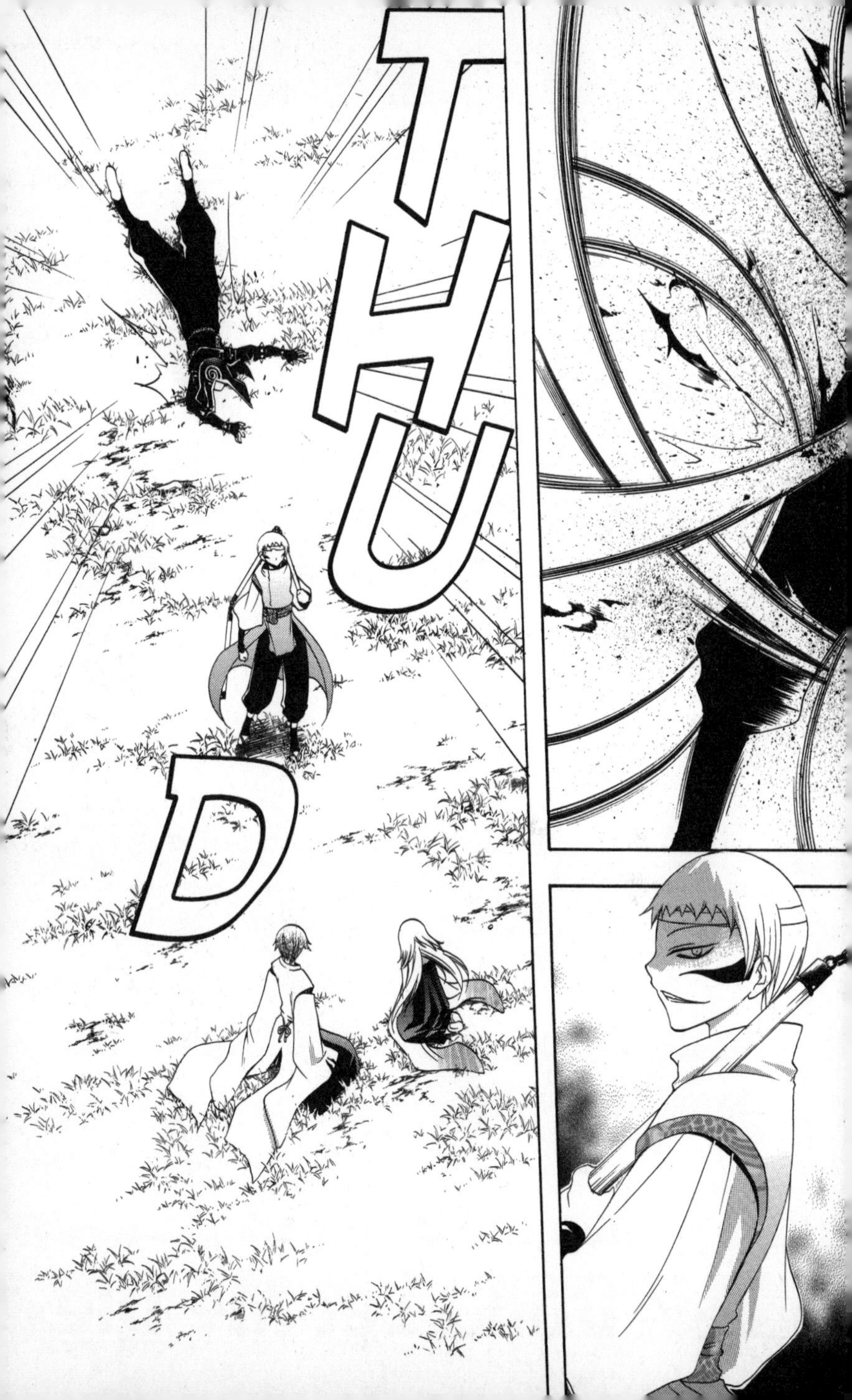
THUD

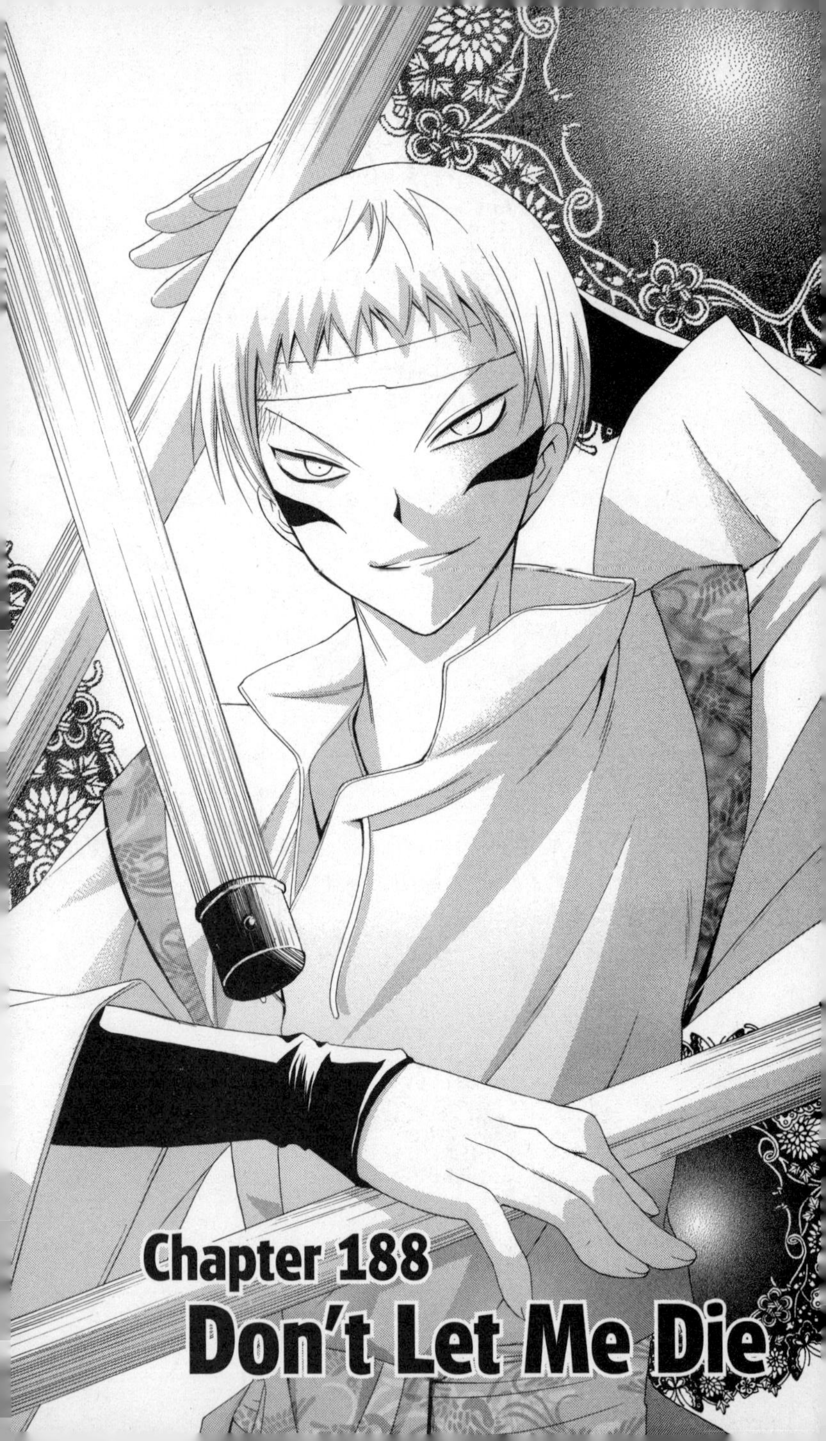
Chapter 188
Don't Let Me Die

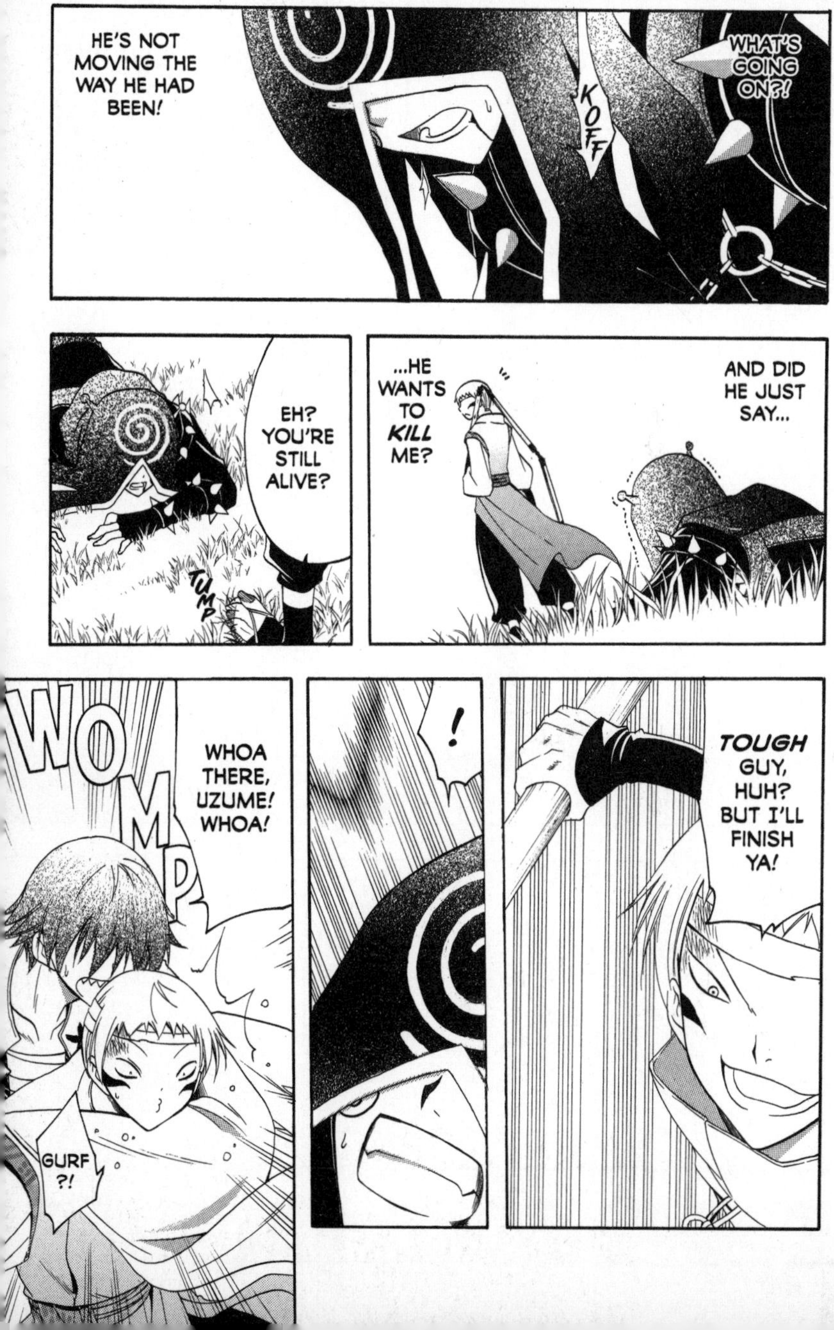
WHAT'S GOING ON?!
KOFF
HE'S NOT MOVING THE WAY HE HAD BEEN!
AND DID HE JUST SAY...
...HE WANTS TO *KILL* ME?
EH? YOU'RE STILL ALIVE?
TUMP
TOUGH GUY, HUH? BUT I'LL FINISH YA!
!
WOMP
WHOA THERE, UZUME! WHOA!
GURF ?!

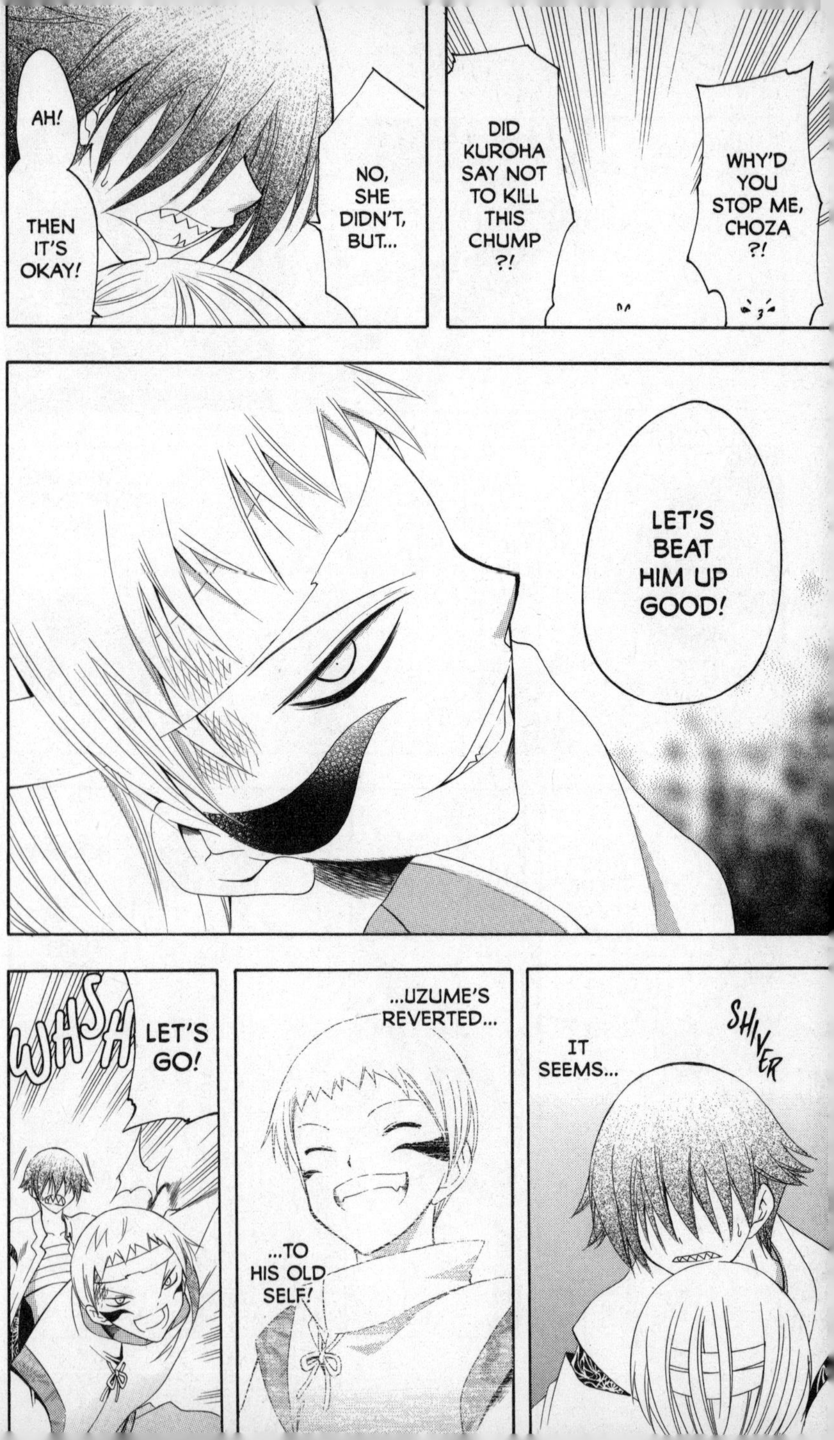
WHY'D YOU STOP ME, CHOZA?!
DID KUROHA SAY NOT TO KILL THIS CHUMP?!
NO, SHE DIDN'T, BUT...
AH!
THEN IT'S OKAY!
LET'S BEAT HIM UP GOOD!
SHIVER
IT SEEMS...
...UZUME'S REVERTED...
...TO HIS OLD SELF!
WHSH
LET'S GO!

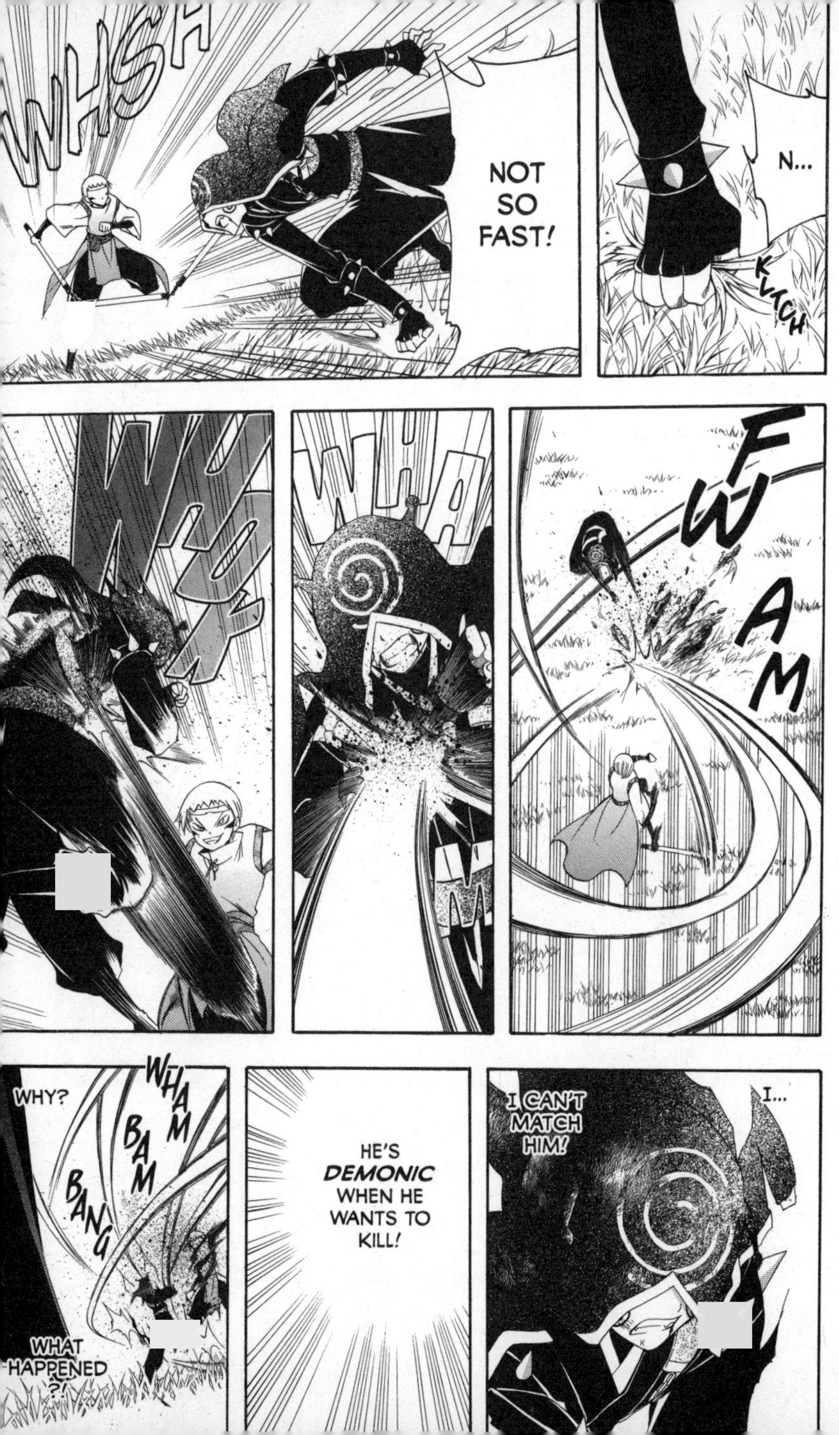
N...
KLATCH
NOT SO FAST!
WHISH
WHAM
I...
I CAN'T MATCH HIM!
HE'S *DEMONIC* WHEN HE WANTS TO KILL!
WHY?
WHAM
BAM
BANG
WHAT HAPPENED ?!

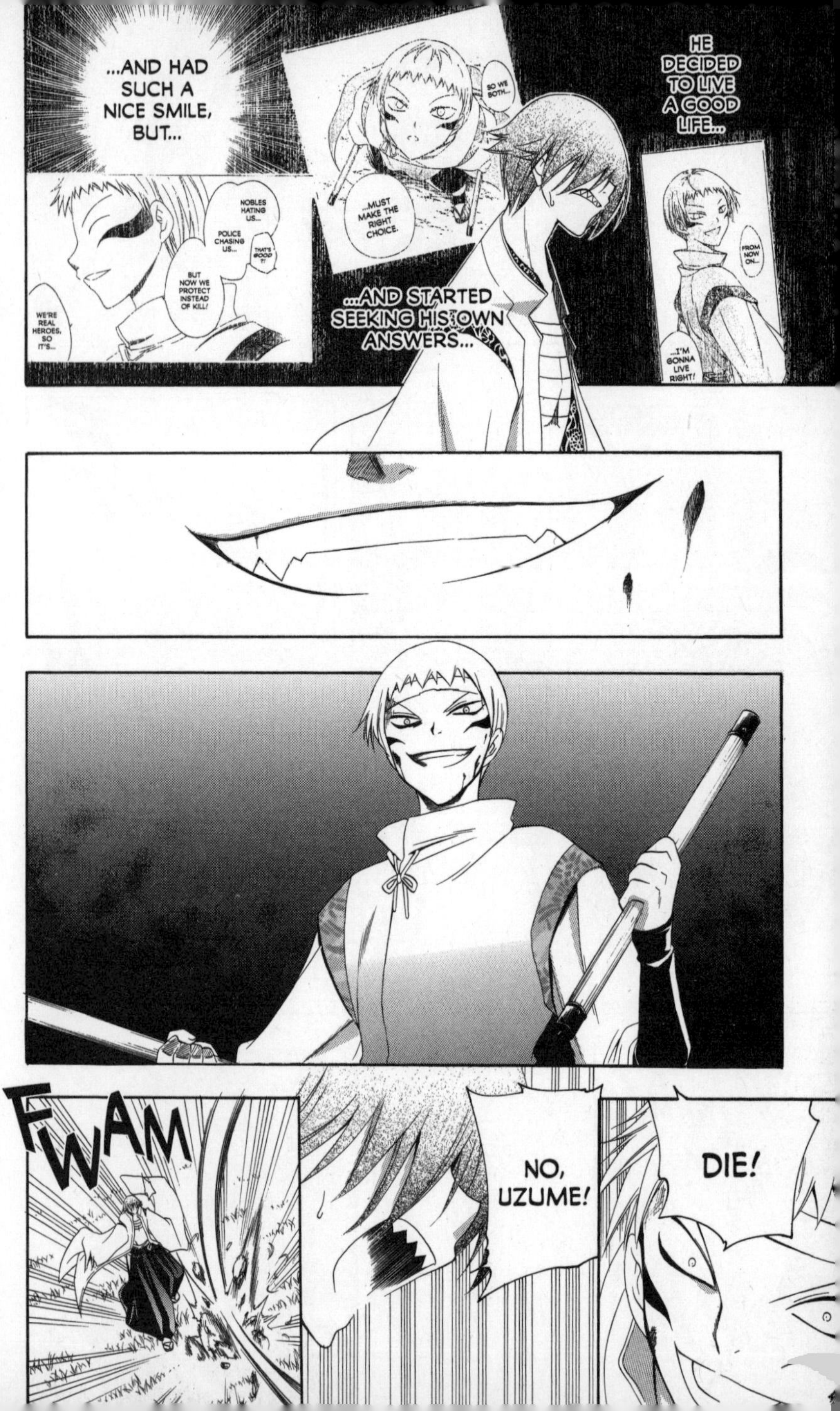
HE DECIDED TO LIVE A GOOD LIFE...
FROM NOW ON...
...I'M GONNA LIVE RIGHT!
...AND STARTED SEEKING HIS OWN ANSWERS...
SO WE BOTH...
...MUST MAKE THE RIGHT CHOICE.
...AND HAD SUCH A NICE SMILE, BUT...
NOBLES HATING US...
POLICE CHASING US...
THAT'S GOOD?!
BUT NOW WE PROTECT INSTEAD OF KILL!
WE'RE REAL HEROES, SO IT'S...
DIE!
NO, UZUME!
FWAM

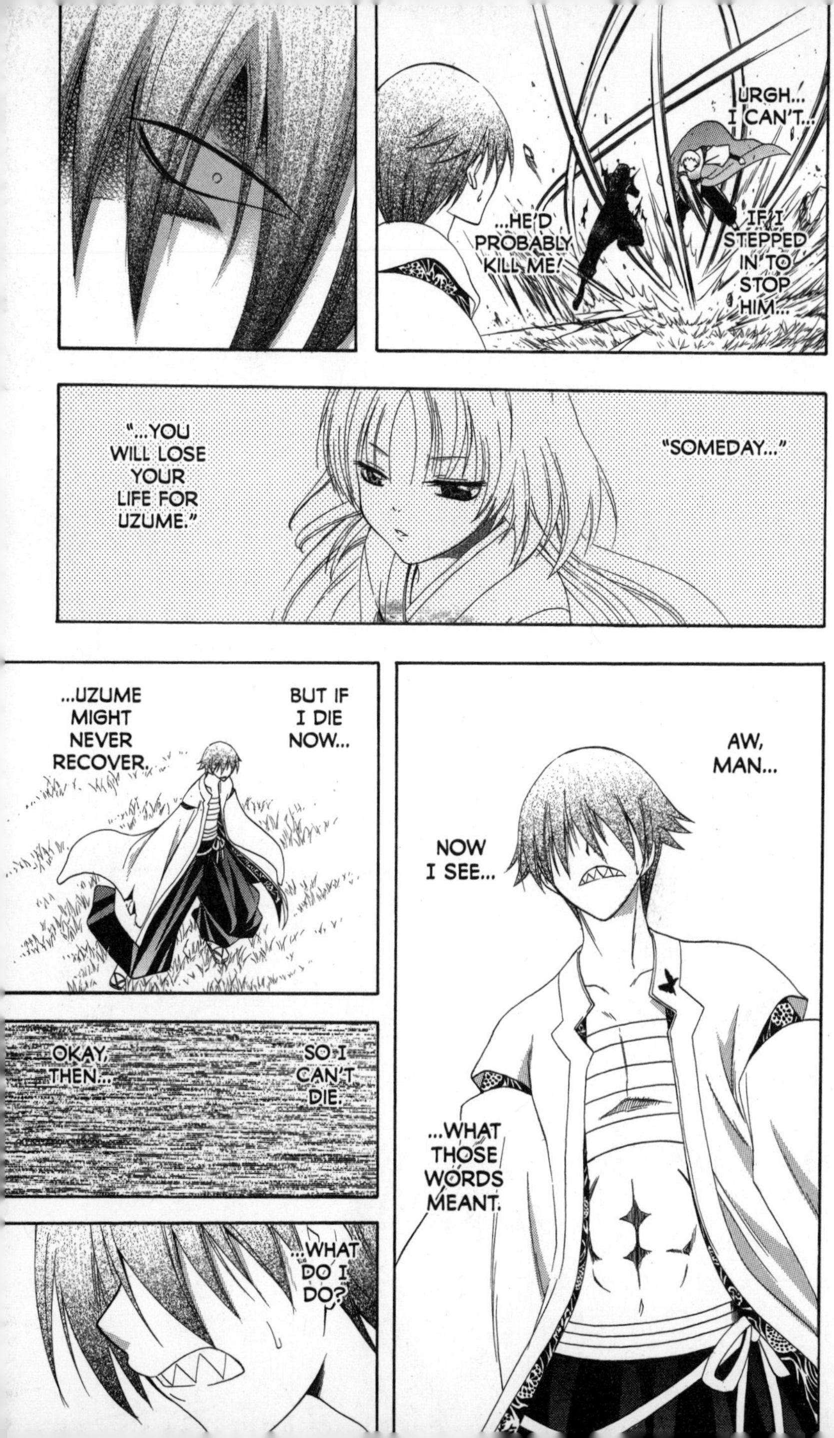
URGH... I CAN'T...
IF I STEPPED IN TO STOP HIM...
...HE'D PROBABLY KILL ME!
"SOMEDAY..."
"...YOU WILL LOSE YOUR LIFE FOR UZUME."
AW, MAN...
NOW I SEE...
...WHAT THOSE WORDS MEANT.
BUT IF I DIE NOW...
...UZUME MIGHT NEVER RECOVER.
SO I CAN'T DIE.
OKAY, THEN...
...WHAT DO I DO?

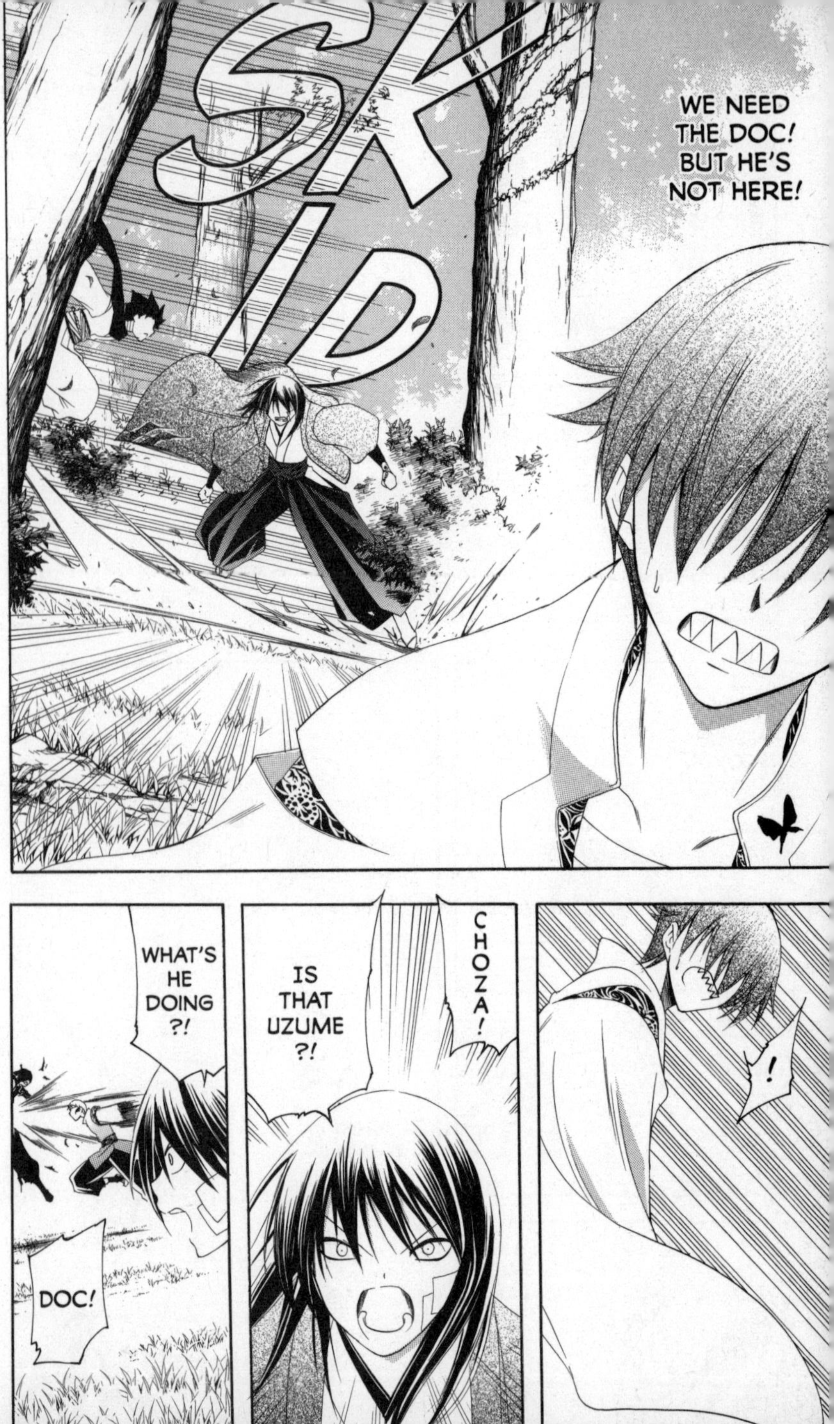
WE NEED THE DOC! BUT HE'S NOT HERE!
SKID
!
CHOZA!
IS THAT UZUME ?!
WHAT'S HE DOING ?!
DOC!

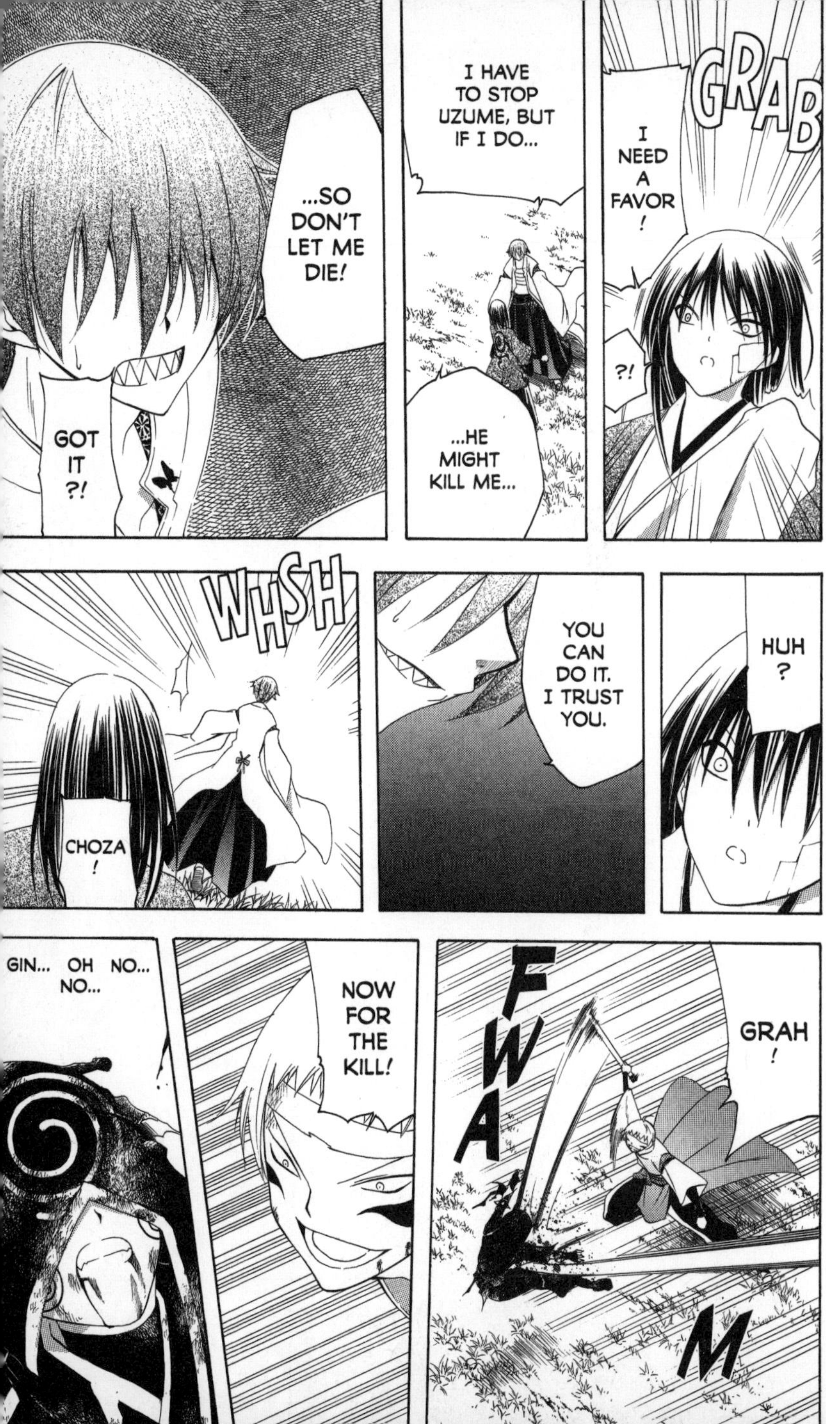
GRAB
I NEED A FAVOR!
?!
I HAVE TO STOP UZUME, BUT IF I DO...
...HE MIGHT KILL ME...
...SO DON'T LET ME DIE!
GOT IT ?!
HUH ?
YOU CAN DO IT. I TRUST YOU.
WHSH
CHOZA!
GRAH!
FWAM
NOW FOR THE KILL!
GIN... OH NO... NO...

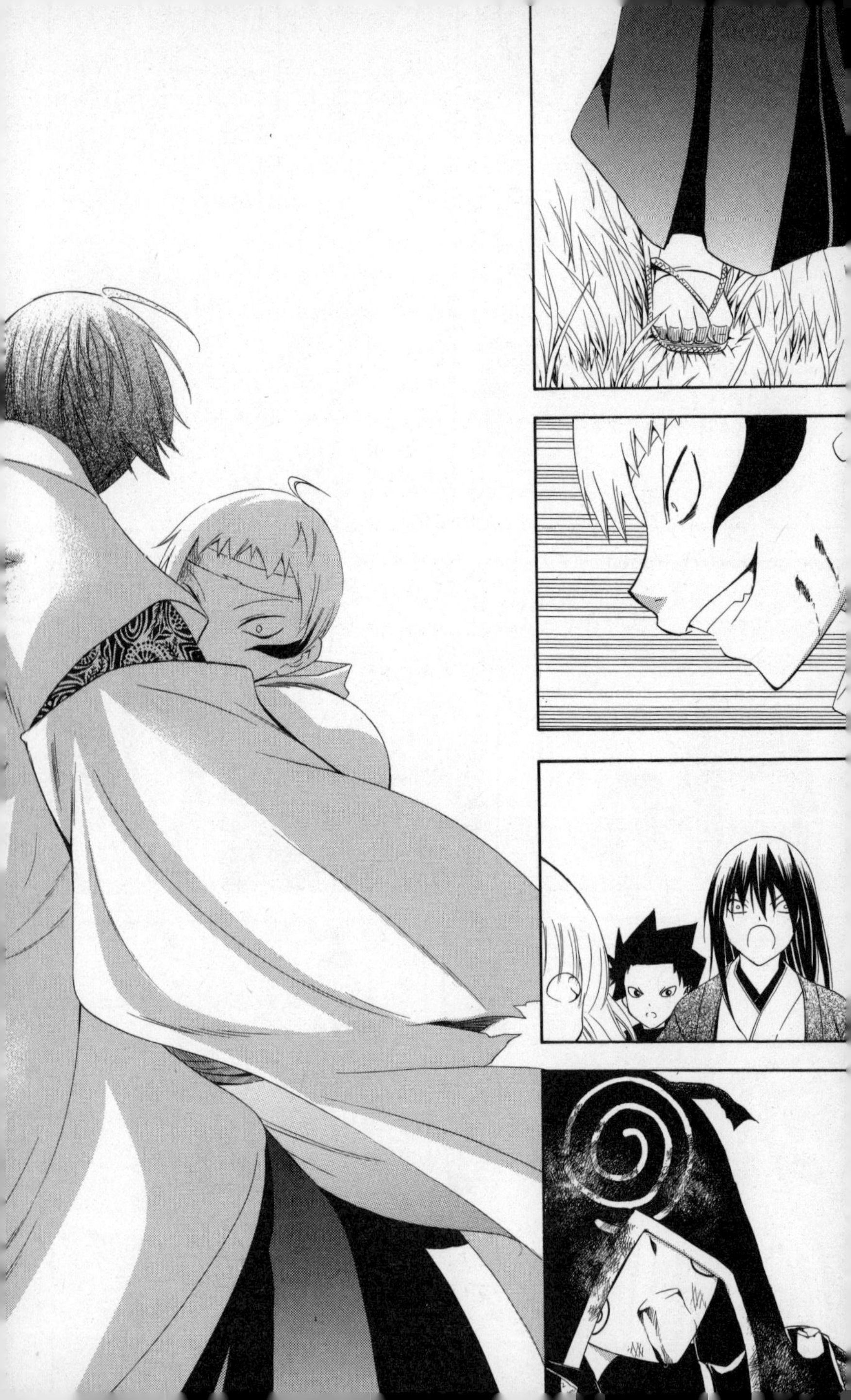

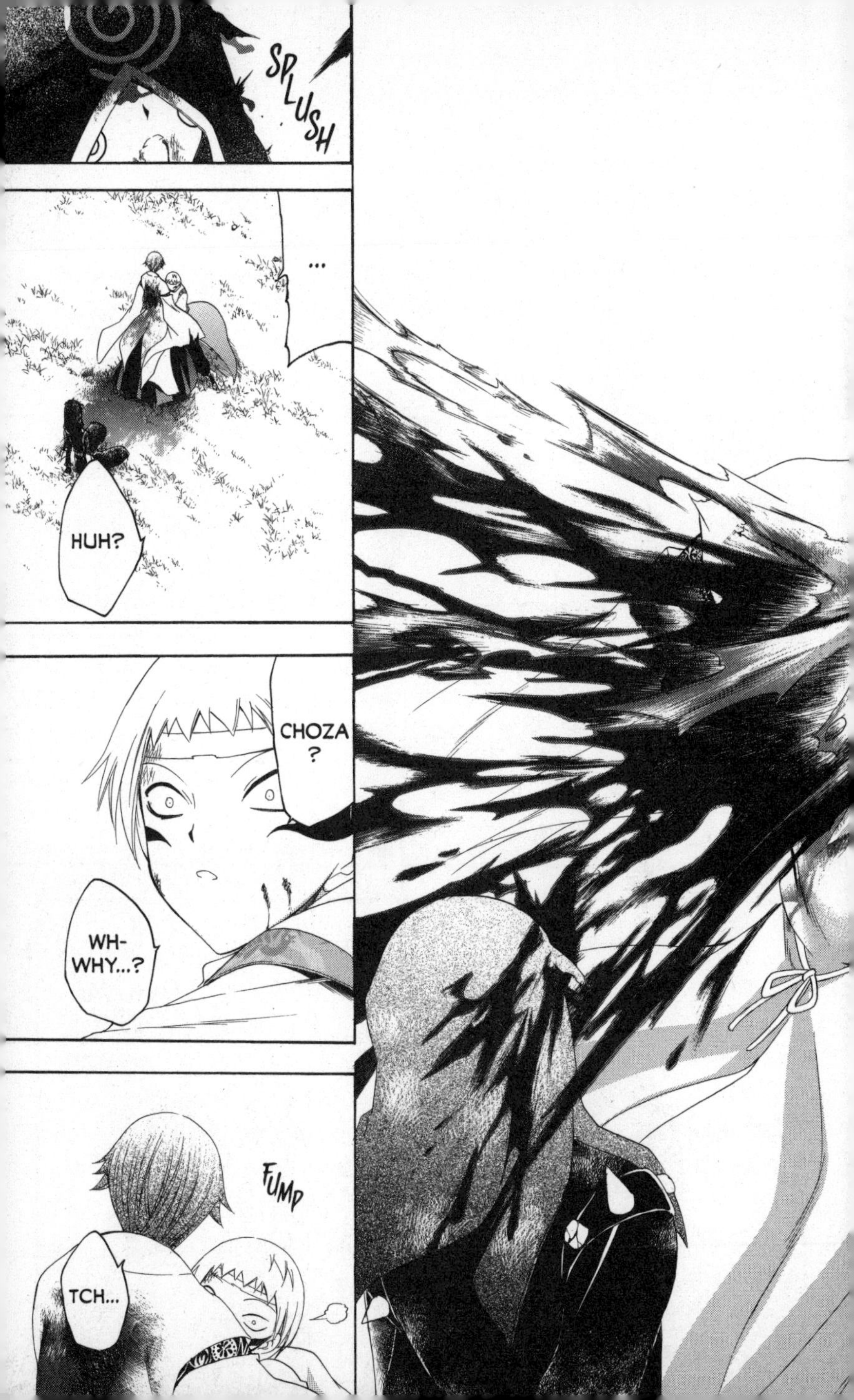
SPLUSH
...
HUH?
CHOZA?
WH-WHY...?
FUMP
TCH...

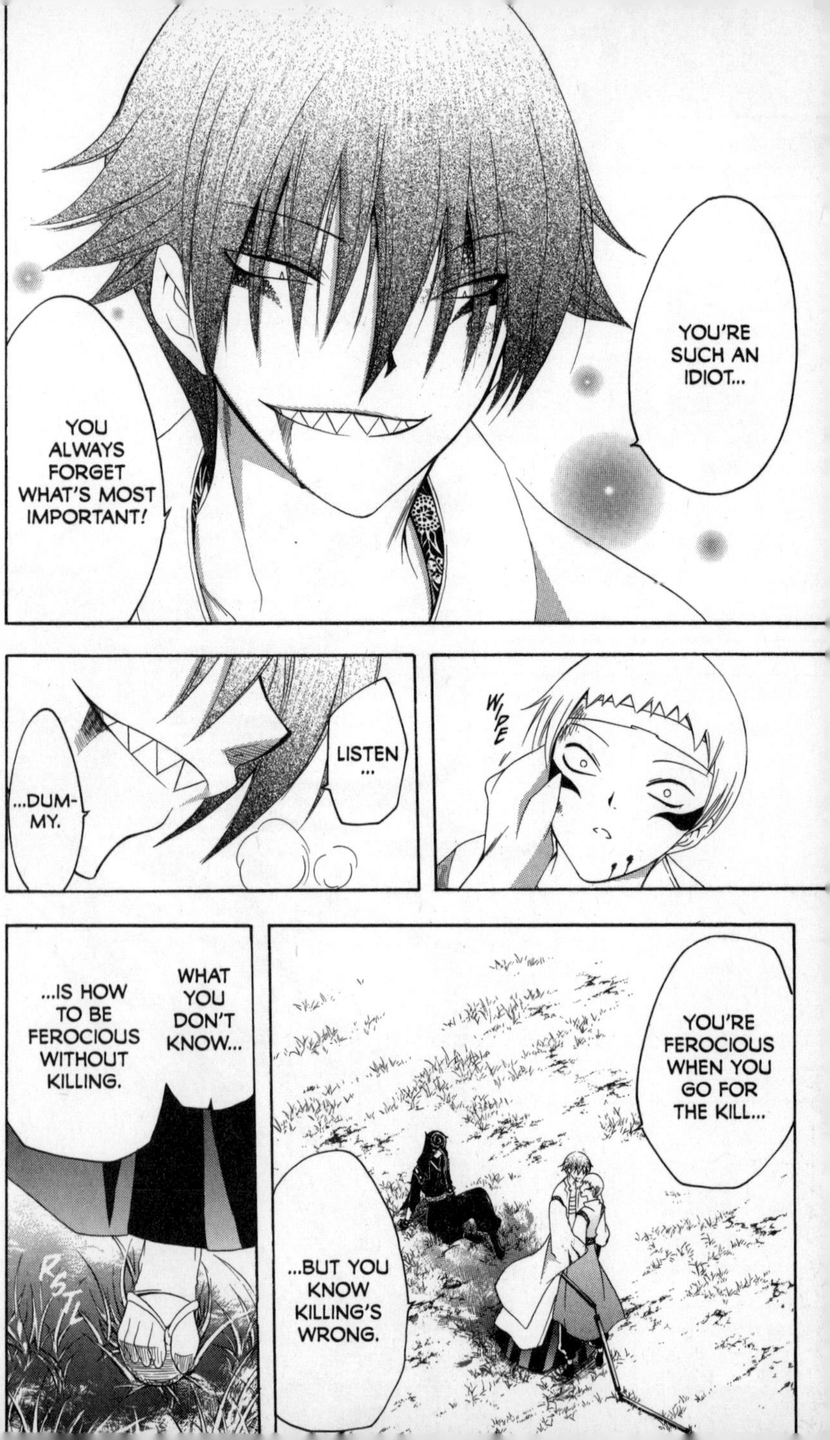
YOU'RE SUCH AN IDIOT...
YOU ALWAYS FORGET WHAT'S MOST IMPORTANT!
WIPE
LISTEN...
...DUM-MY.
YOU'RE FEROCIOUS WHEN YOU GO FOR THE KILL...
...BUT YOU KNOW KILLING'S WRONG.
WHAT YOU DON'T KNOW...
...IS HOW TO BE FEROCIOUS WITHOUT KILLING.
RSTL

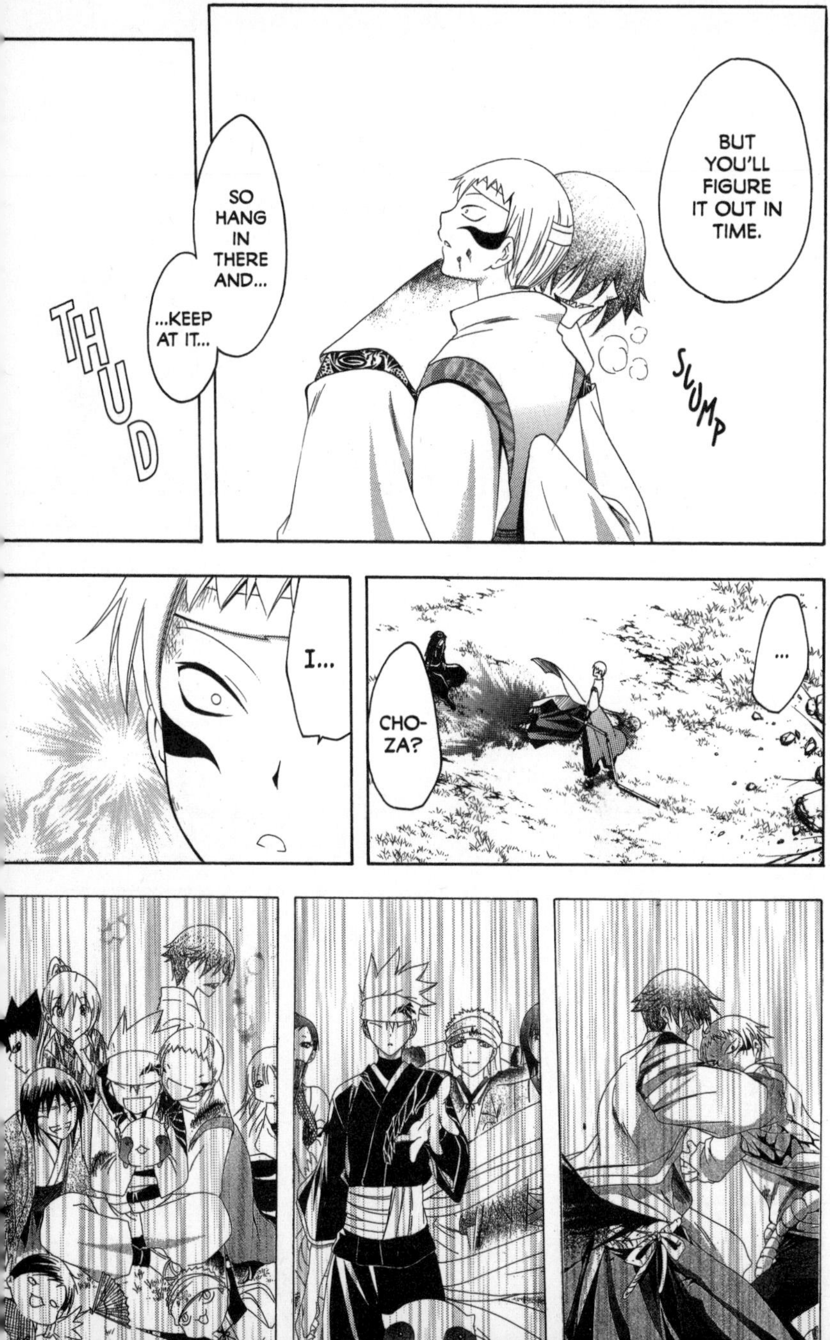
BUT YOU'LL FIGURE IT OUT IN TIME.
SUUMP
SO HANG IN THERE AND...
...KEEP AT IT...
THUD
...
CHO-ZA?
I...

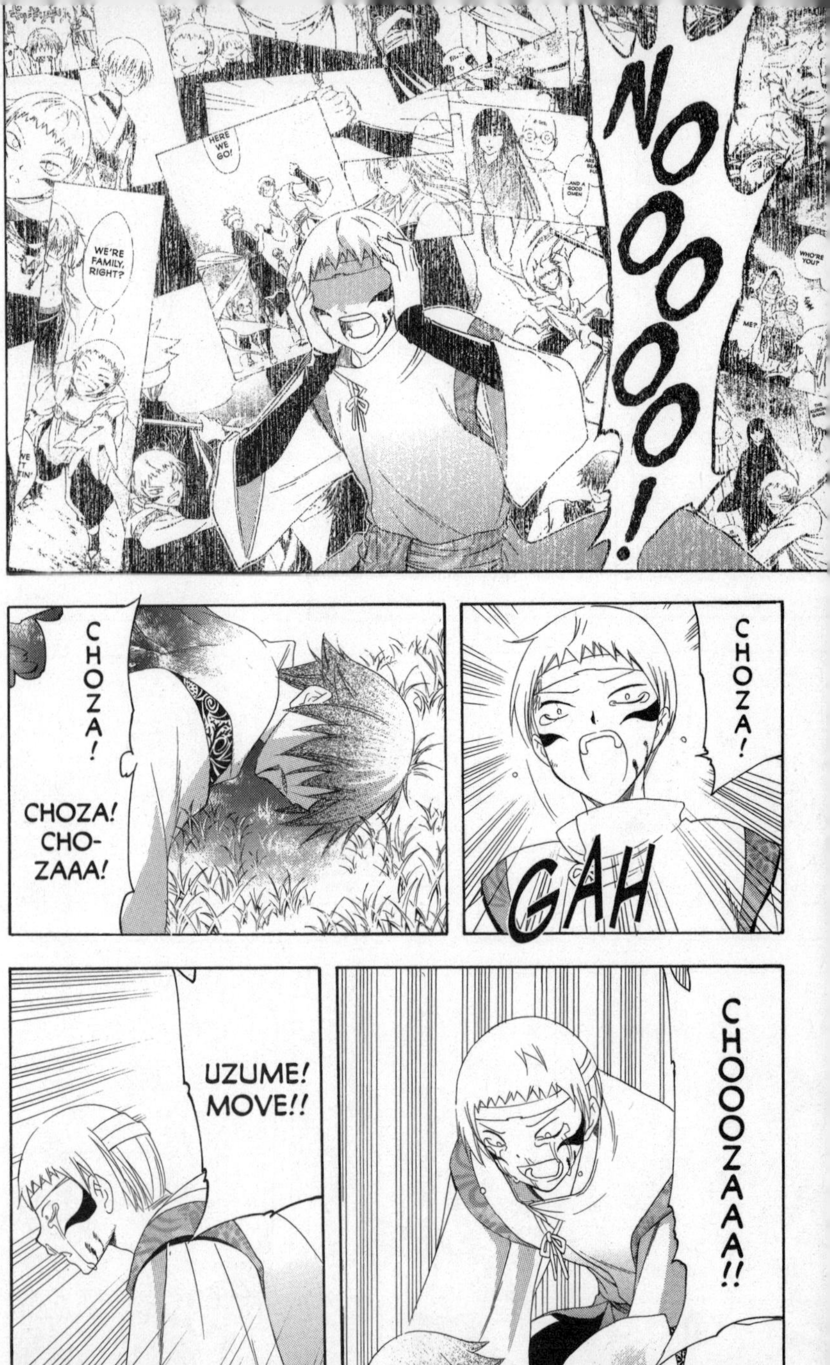
WHO'RE YOU?
ME?
NOOOOO!
...AND A GOOD OMEN.
HERE WE GO!
WE'RE FAMILY, RIGHT?
CHOZA!
GAH
CHOZA!
CHOZA! CHO-ZAAA!
CHOOOZAAAA!!
UZUME! MOVE!!

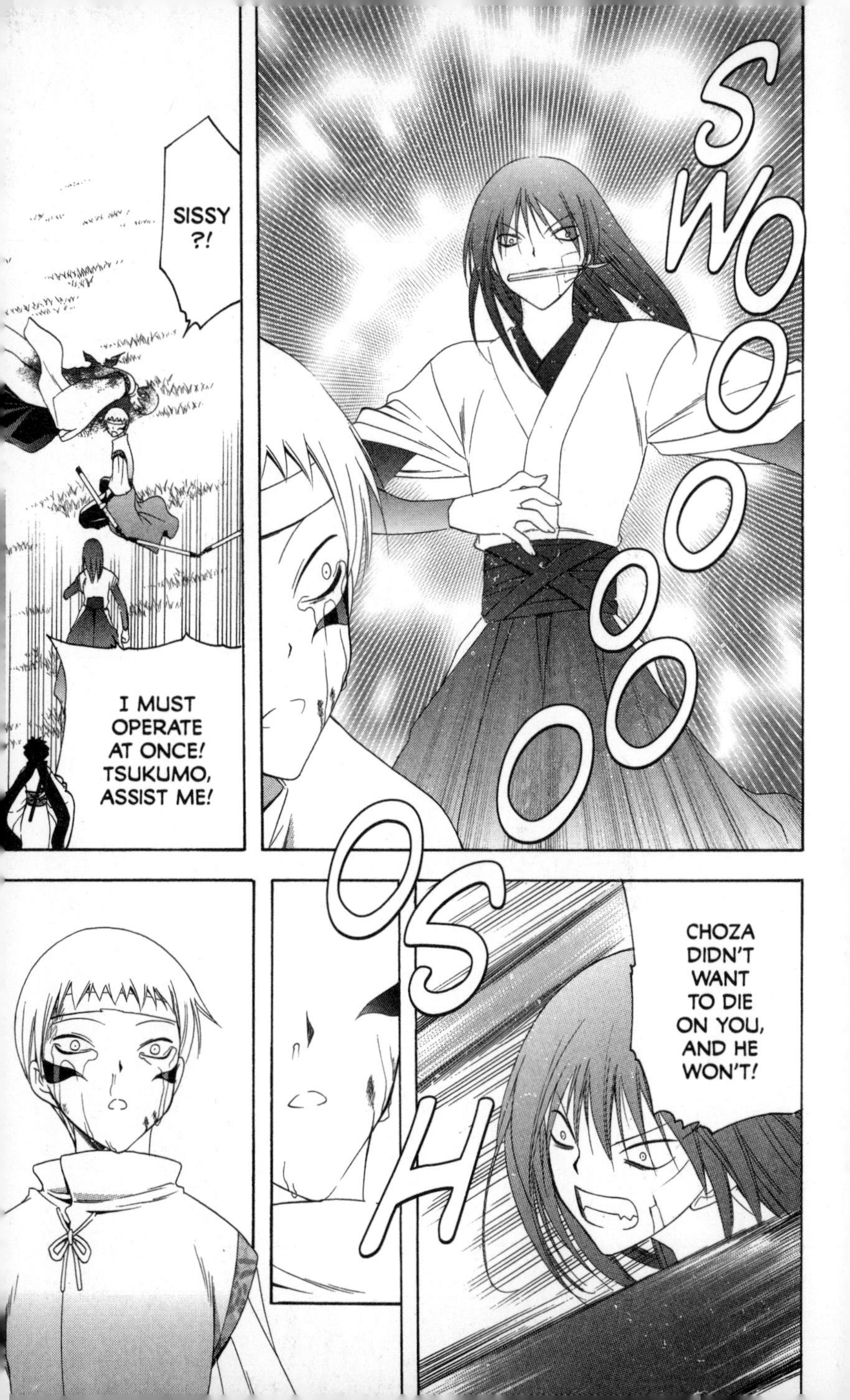
SWOOOOOOOOO
SISSY ?!
I MUST OPERATE AT ONCE! TSUKUMO, ASSIST ME!
OOSH
CHOZA DIDN'T WANT TO DIE ON YOU, AND HE WON'T!

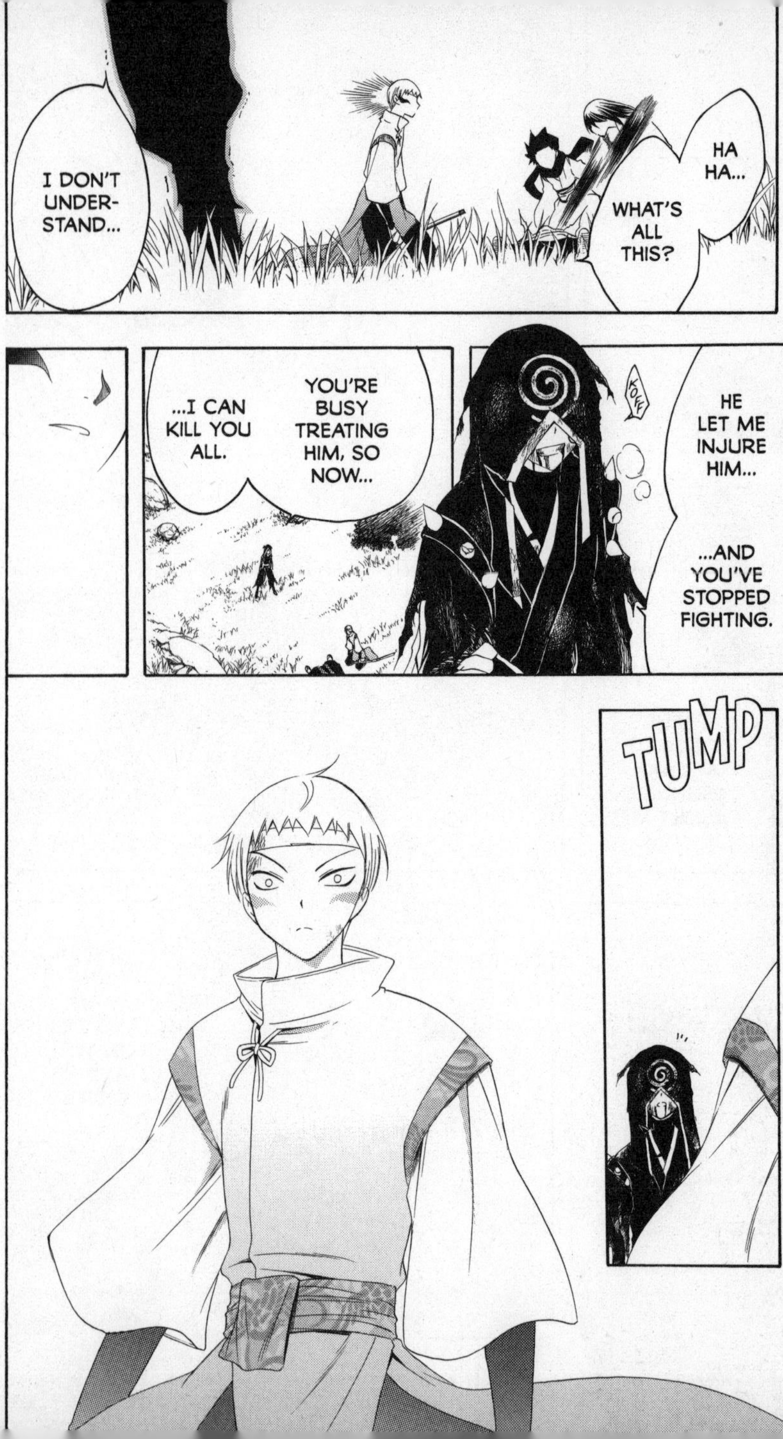
HA HA...
WHAT'S ALL THIS?
I DON'T UNDER-STAND...
KOFF
HE LET ME INJURE HIM...
...AND YOU'VE STOPPED FIGHTING.
YOU'RE BUSY TREATING HIM, SO NOW...
...I CAN KILL YOU ALL.
TUMP

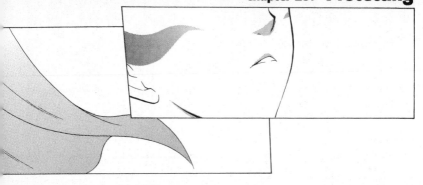

HE'S... CHANGED AGAIN...

WHAT NOW?

TUMP

...

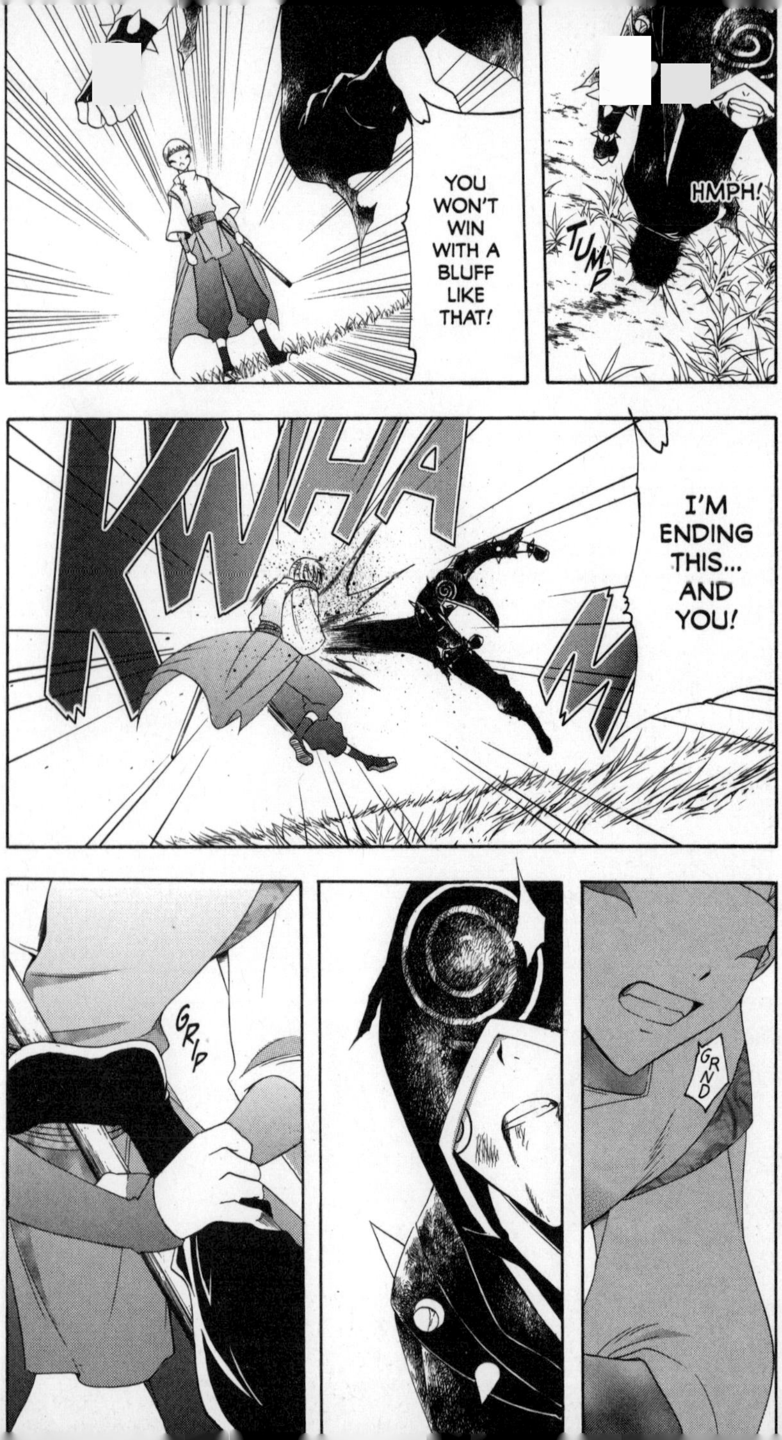
HMPH!
TUMP
YOU WON'T WIN WITH A BLUFF LIKE THAT!
I'M ENDING THIS... AND YOU!
KWHAM
GRND
GRIP

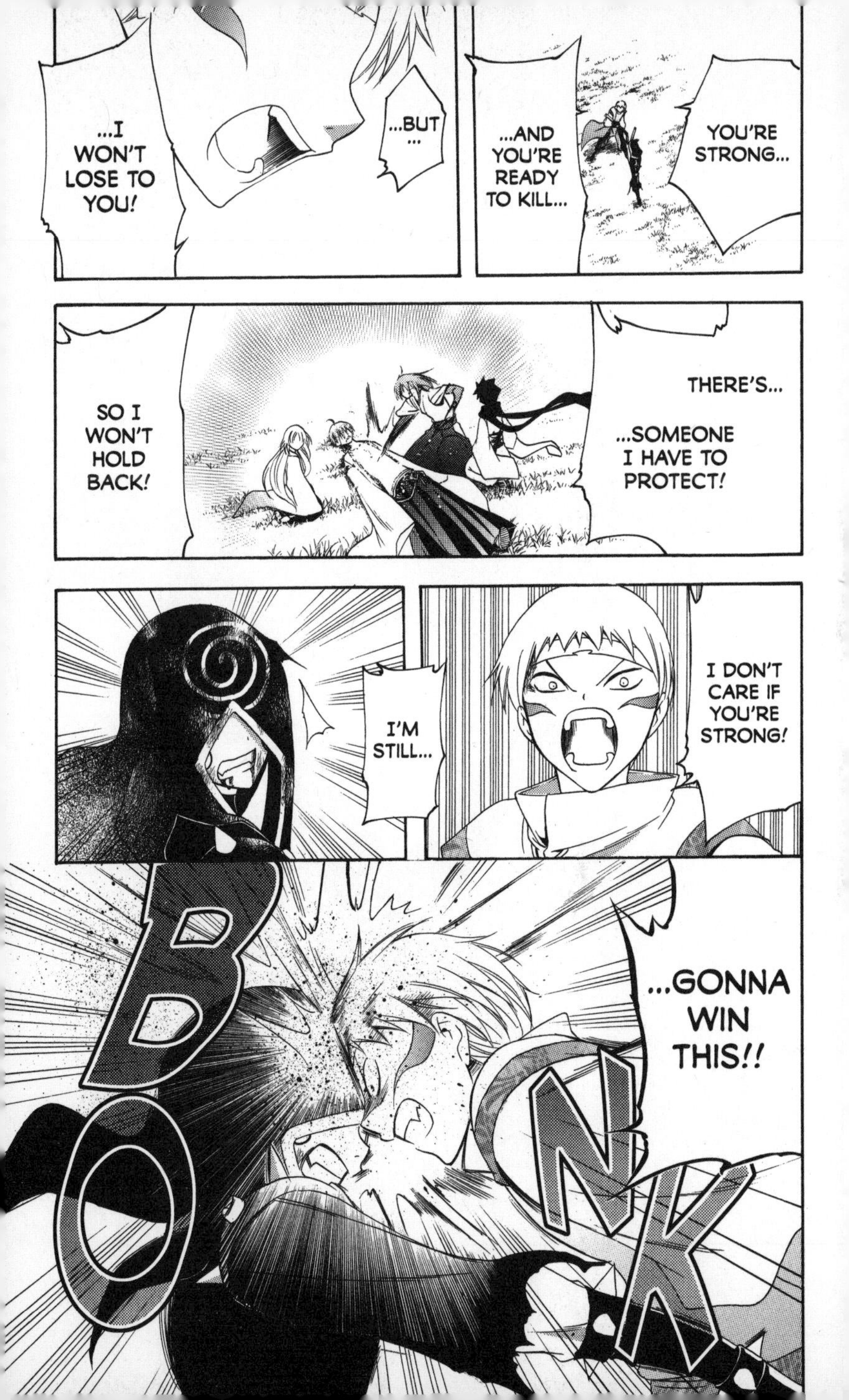
YOU'RE STRONG...
...AND YOU'RE READY TO KILL...
...BUT ...
...I WON'T LOSE TO YOU!
THERE'S...
...SOMEONE I HAVE TO PROTECT!
SO I WON'T HOLD BACK!
I DON'T CARE IF YOU'RE STRONG!
I'M STILL...
...GONNA WIN THIS!!
BONK

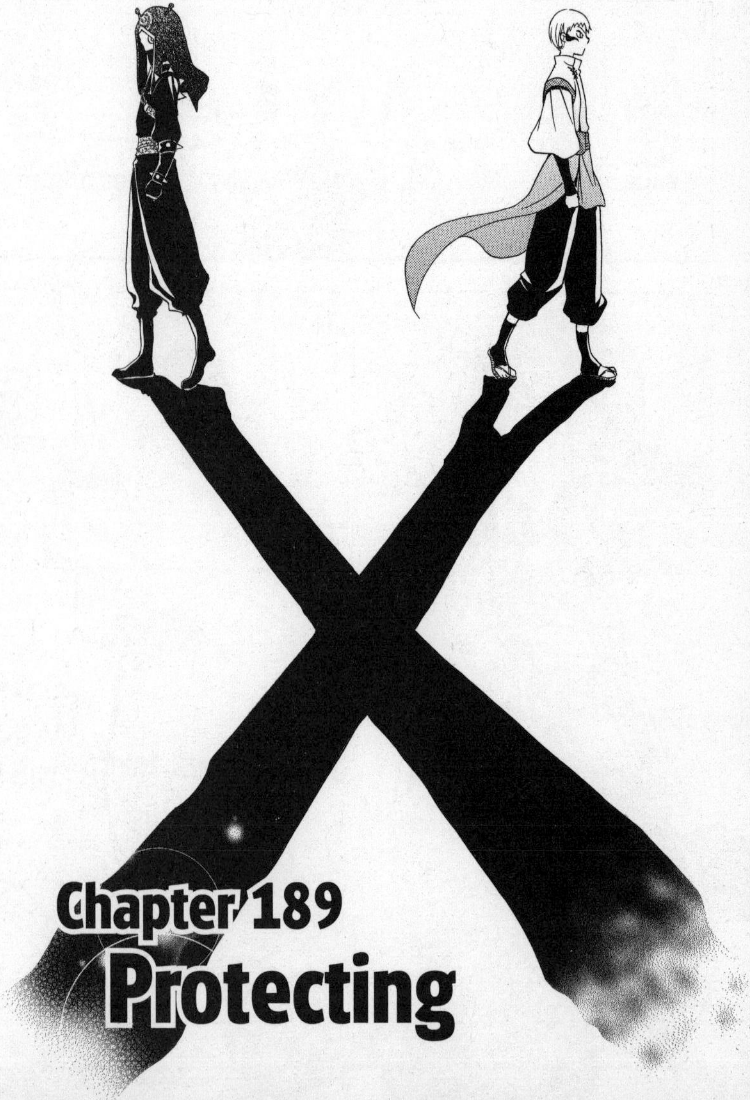

Chapter 189
Protecting

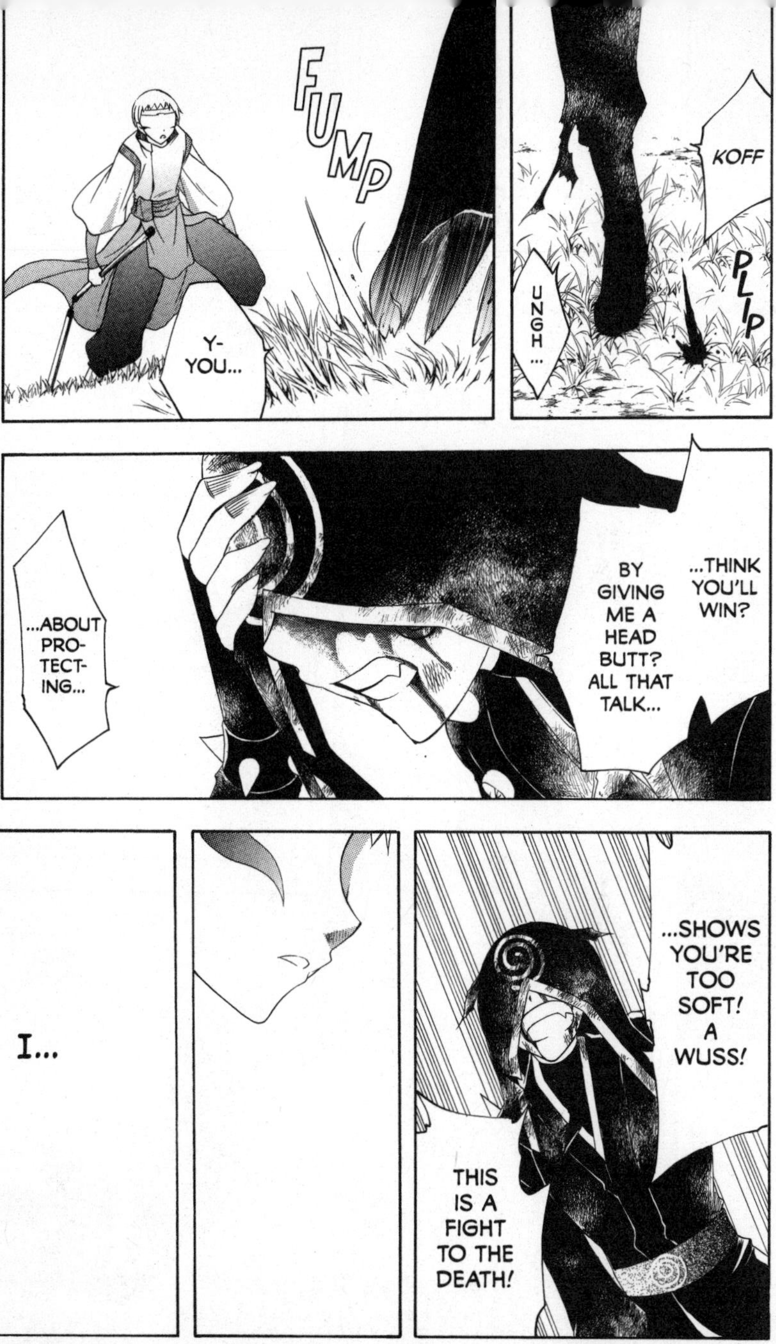
KOFF
PLIP
UNGH...
FUMP
Y-YOU...
...THINK YOU'LL WIN?
BY GIVING ME A HEAD BUTT? ALL THAT TALK...
...ABOUT PROTECTING...
...SHOWS YOU'RE TOO SOFT! A WUSS!
THIS IS A FIGHT TO THE DEATH!
I...

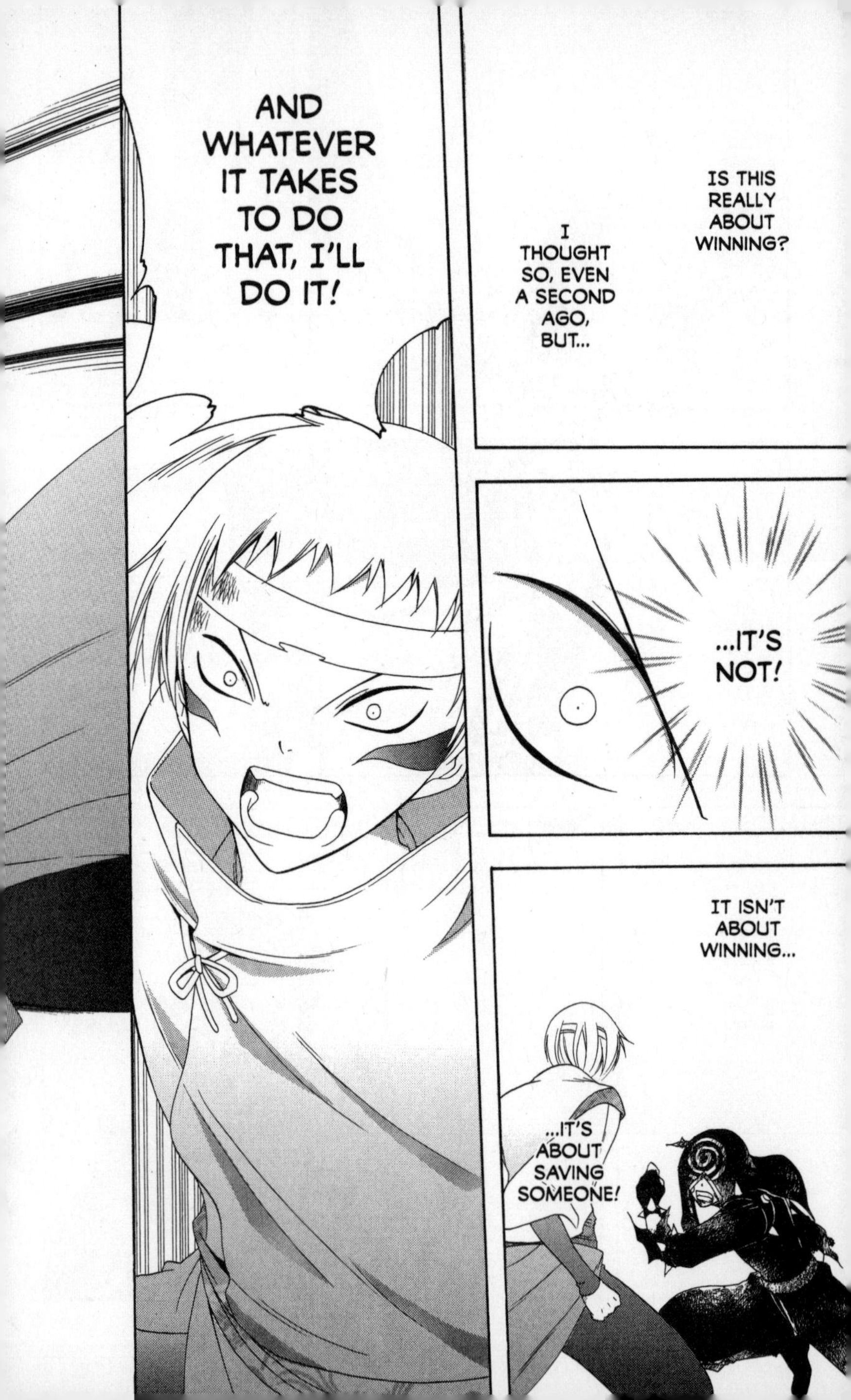
IS THIS REALLY ABOUT WINNING?
I THOUGHT SO, EVEN A SECOND AGO, BUT...
...IT'S NOT!
IT ISN'T ABOUT WINNING...
...IT'S ABOUT SAVING SOMEONE!
AND WHATEVER IT TAKES TO DO THAT, I'LL DO IT!

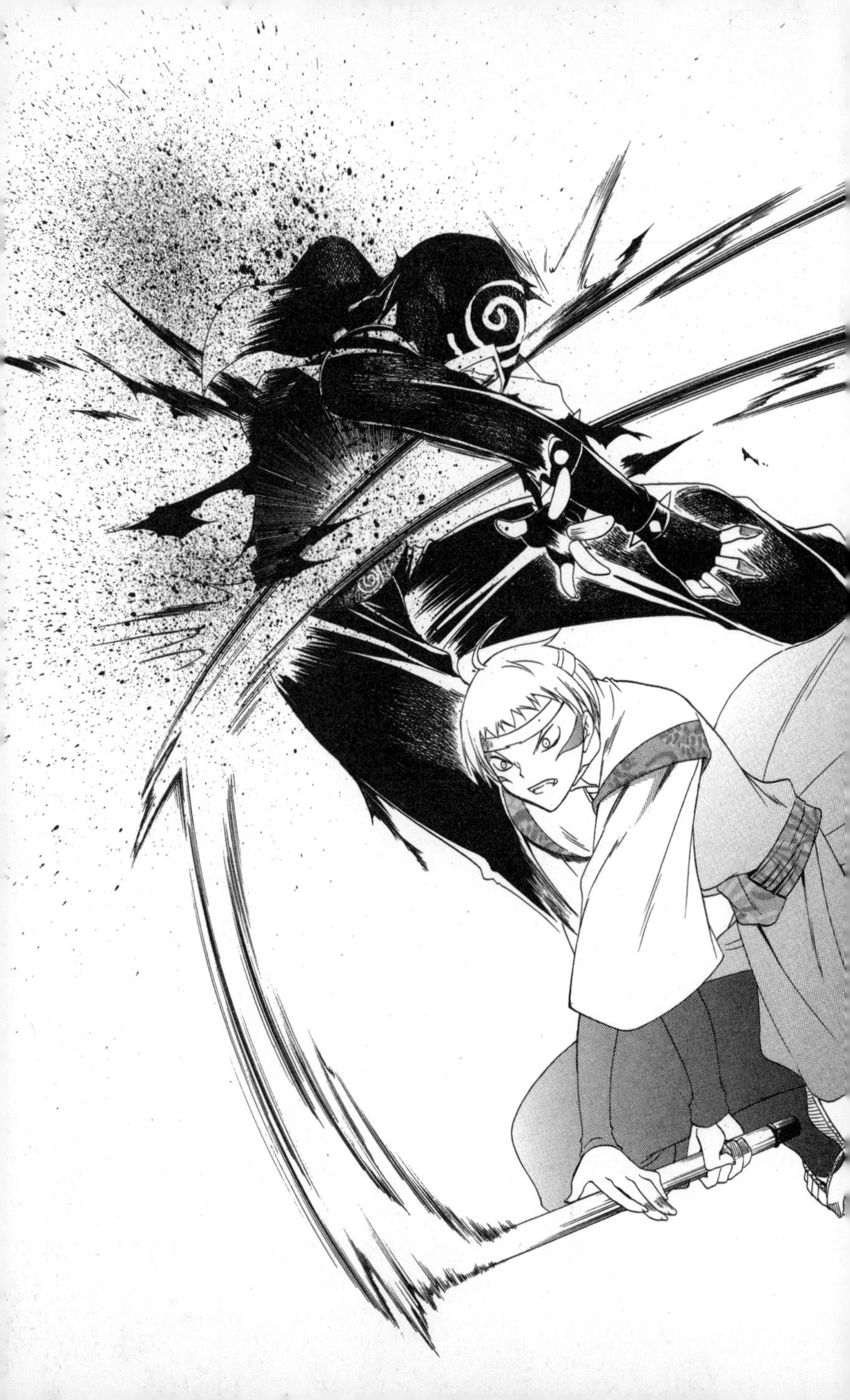

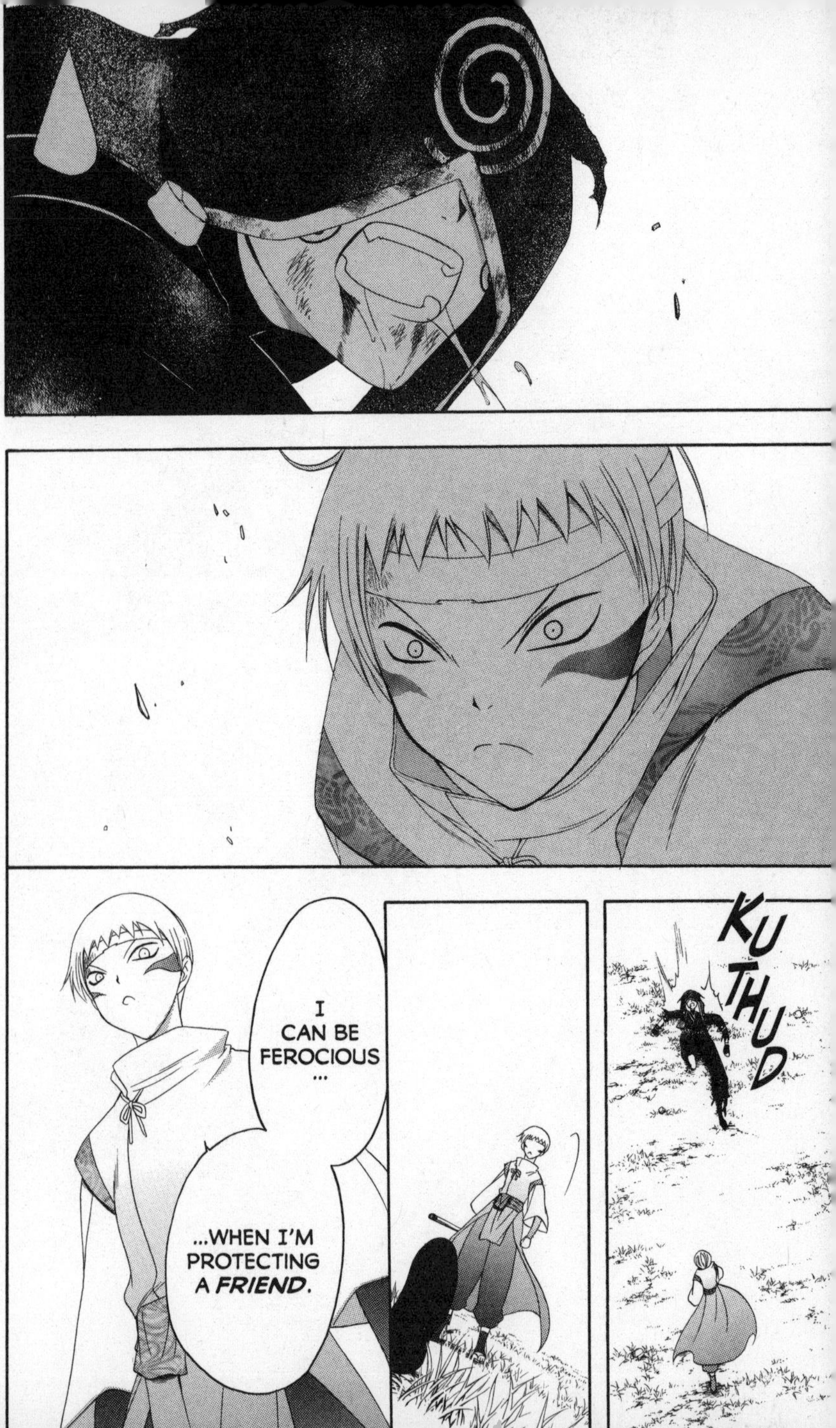
KUTHUD
I CAN BE FEROCIOUS...
...WHEN I'M PROTECTING A *FRIEND*.

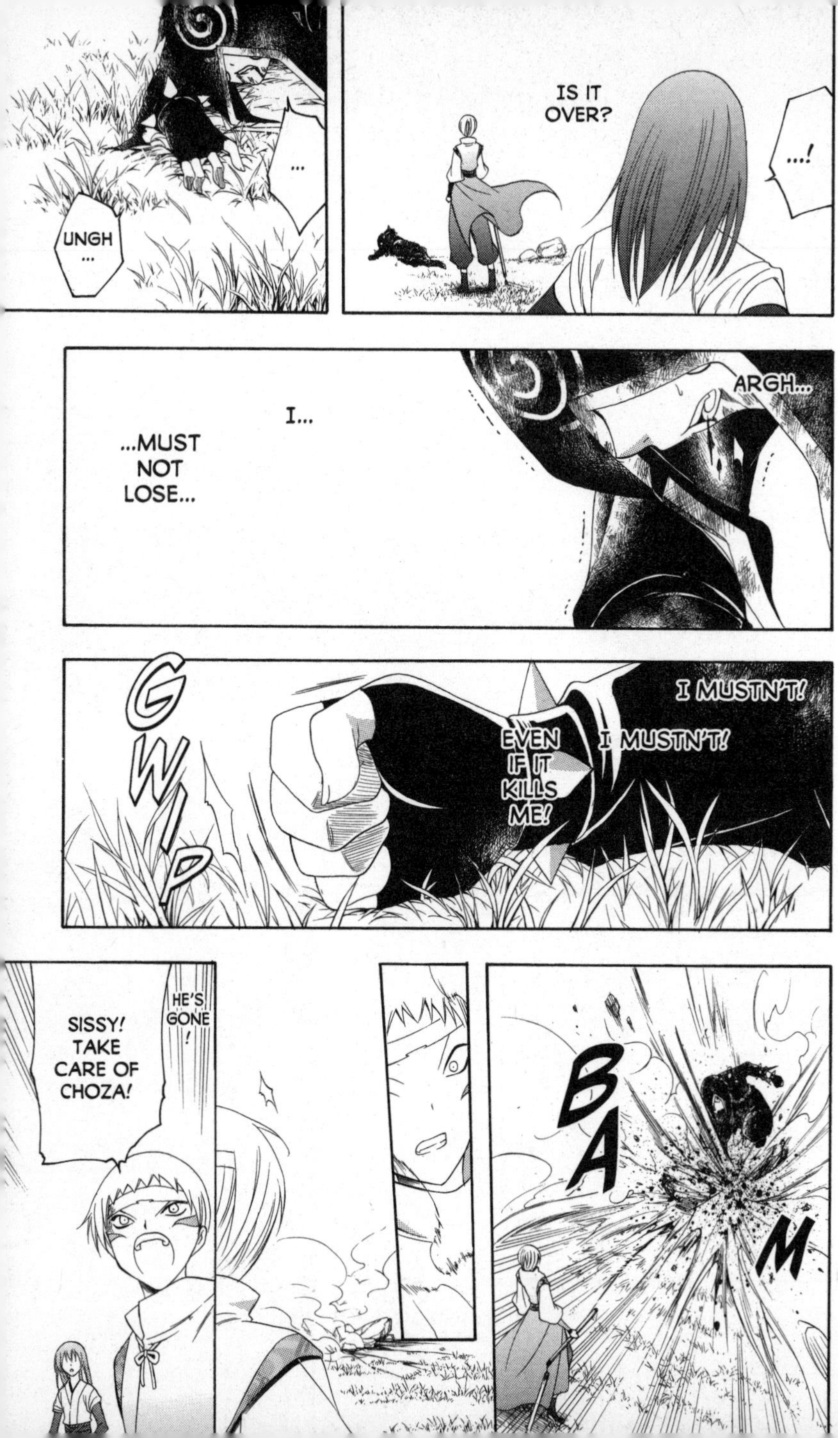
IS IT OVER?
...!
...
UNGH ...
ARGH...
I...
...MUST NOT LOSE...
I MUSTN'T!
I MUSTN'T!
EVEN IF IT KILLS ME!
GWIP
BAM
HE'S GONE!
SISSY! TAKE CARE OF CHOZA!

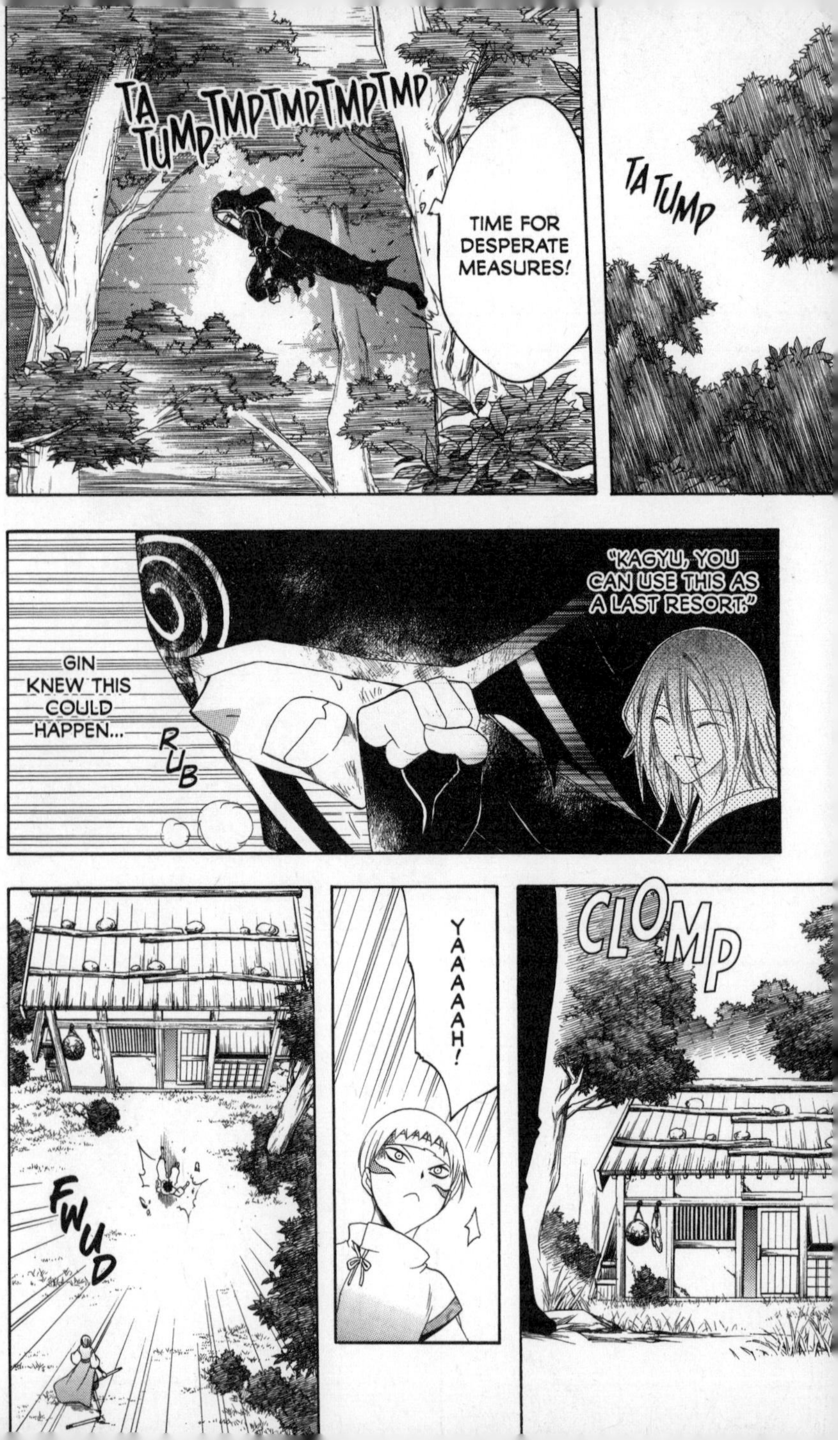
TA TUMP
TIME FOR DESPERATE MEASURES!
TA TUMP TMPTMPTMPTMP
"KAGYU, YOU CAN USE THIS AS A LAST RESORT."
GIN KNEW THIS COULD HAPPEN...
RUB
CLOMP
YAAAAAAH!
FWUD

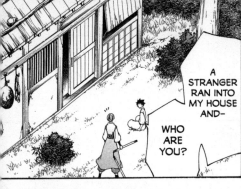

I DON'T BELIEVE THIS!
WHAT'S WRONG ?!
A STRANGER RAN INTO MY HOUSE AND–
WHO ARE YOU?
TUMP
HEY! WHAT'S GOING ON?!
NAH...
...I'M LYING.
IT'S JUST A SHED FULL OF SAKE. I ONLY HAVE...
...A LITTLE ACID...
DRIP
...BUT AS HE DOESN'T SUSPECT IT'S ME, I'LL...
YOU...

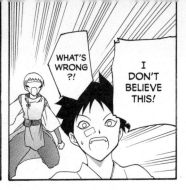

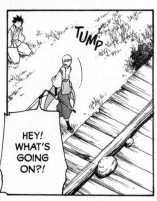

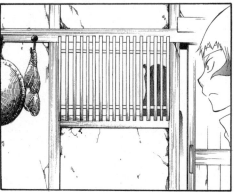

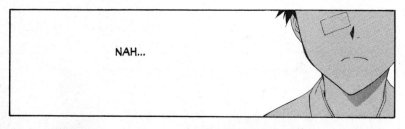

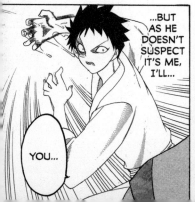

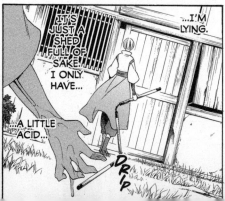

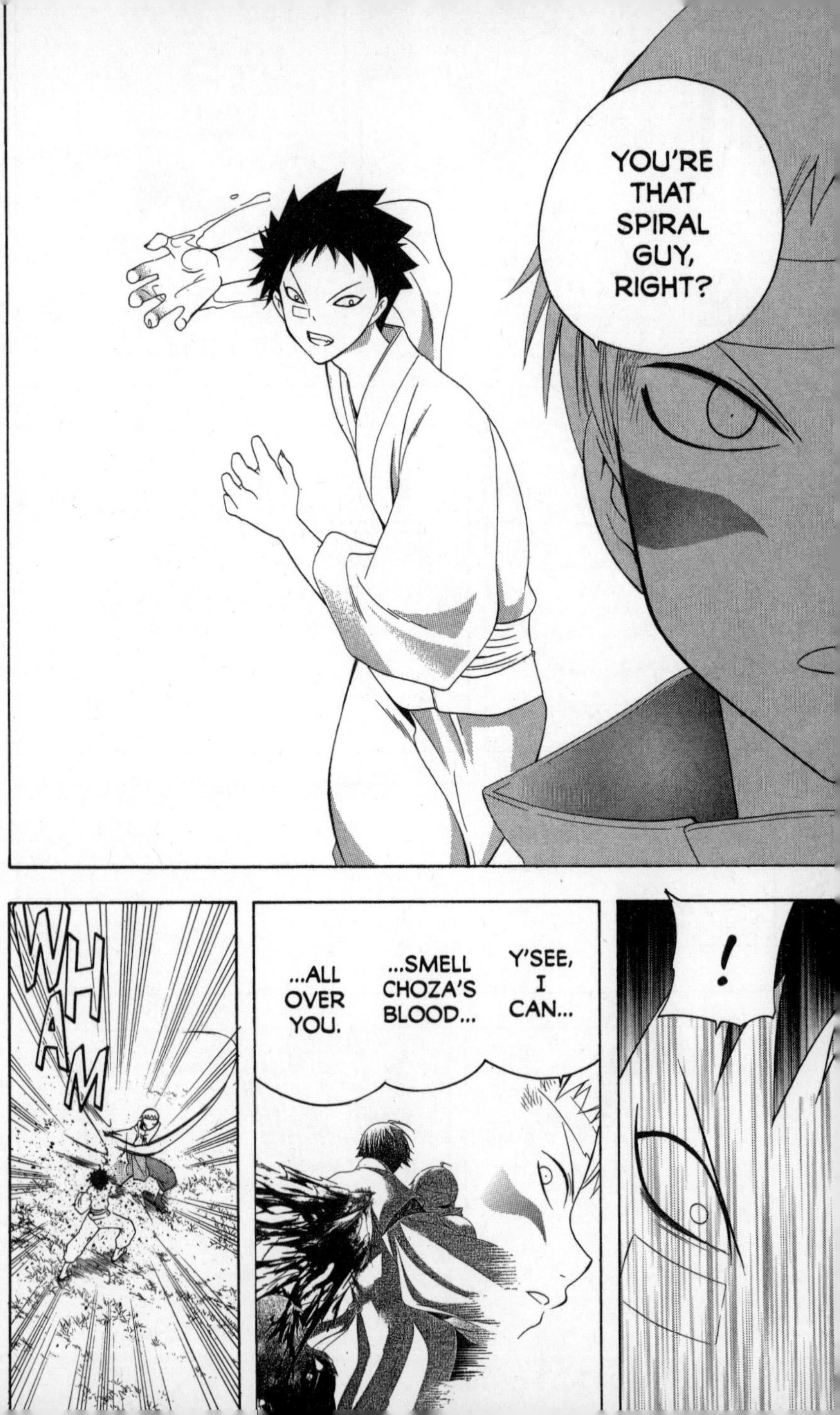
YOU'RE THAT SPIRAL GUY, RIGHT?
!
Y'SEE, I CAN...
...SMELL CHOZA'S BLOOD...
...ALL OVER YOU.
WHAM

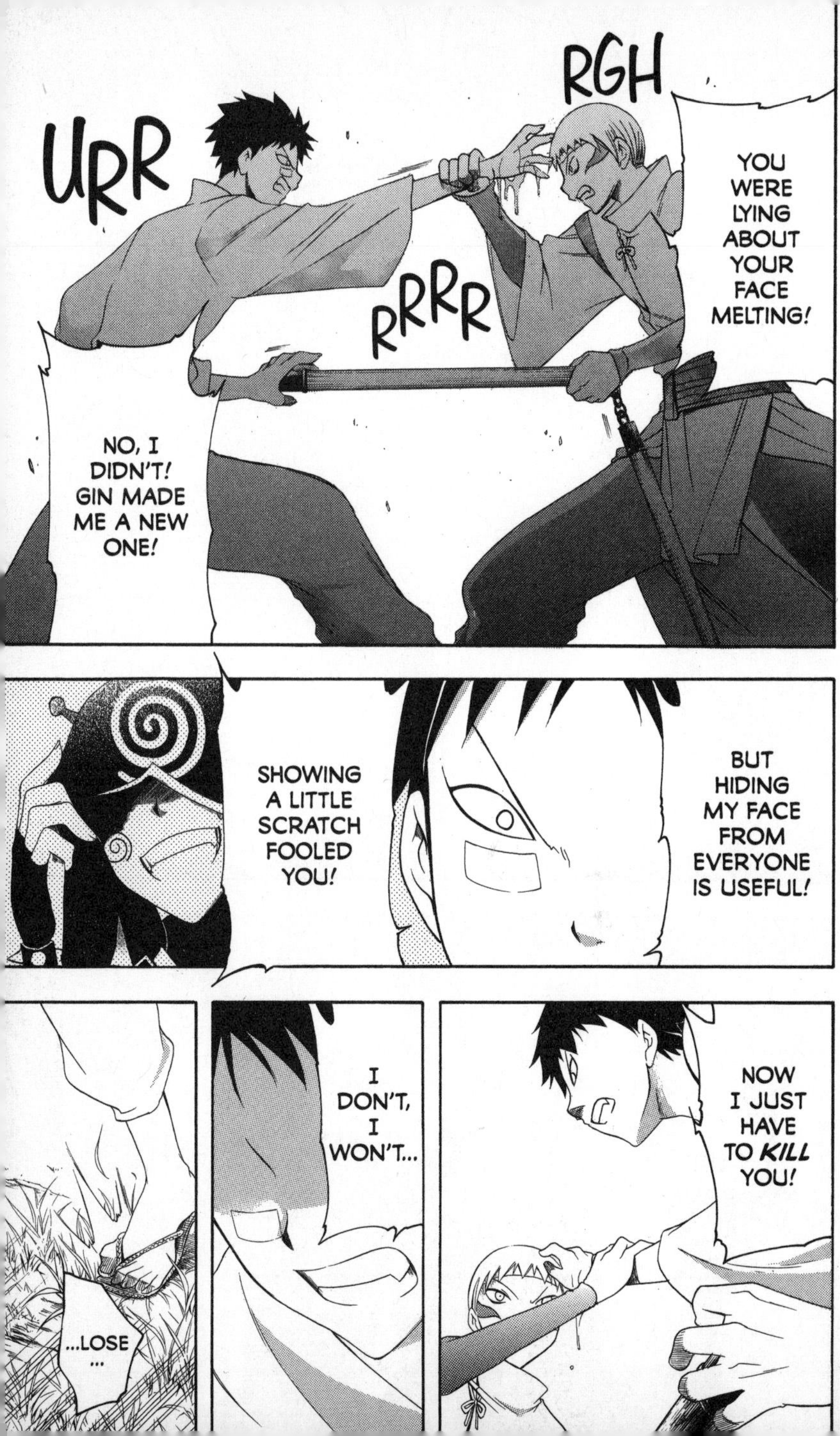

RGH
YOU WERE LYING ABOUT YOUR FACE MELTING!
URR
RRRR
NO, I DIDN'T! GIN MADE ME A NEW ONE!
BUT HIDING MY FACE FROM EVERYONE IS USEFUL!
SHOWING A LITTLE SCRATCH FOOLED YOU!
NOW I JUST HAVE TO KILL YOU!
I DON'T, I WON'T...
...LOSE ...

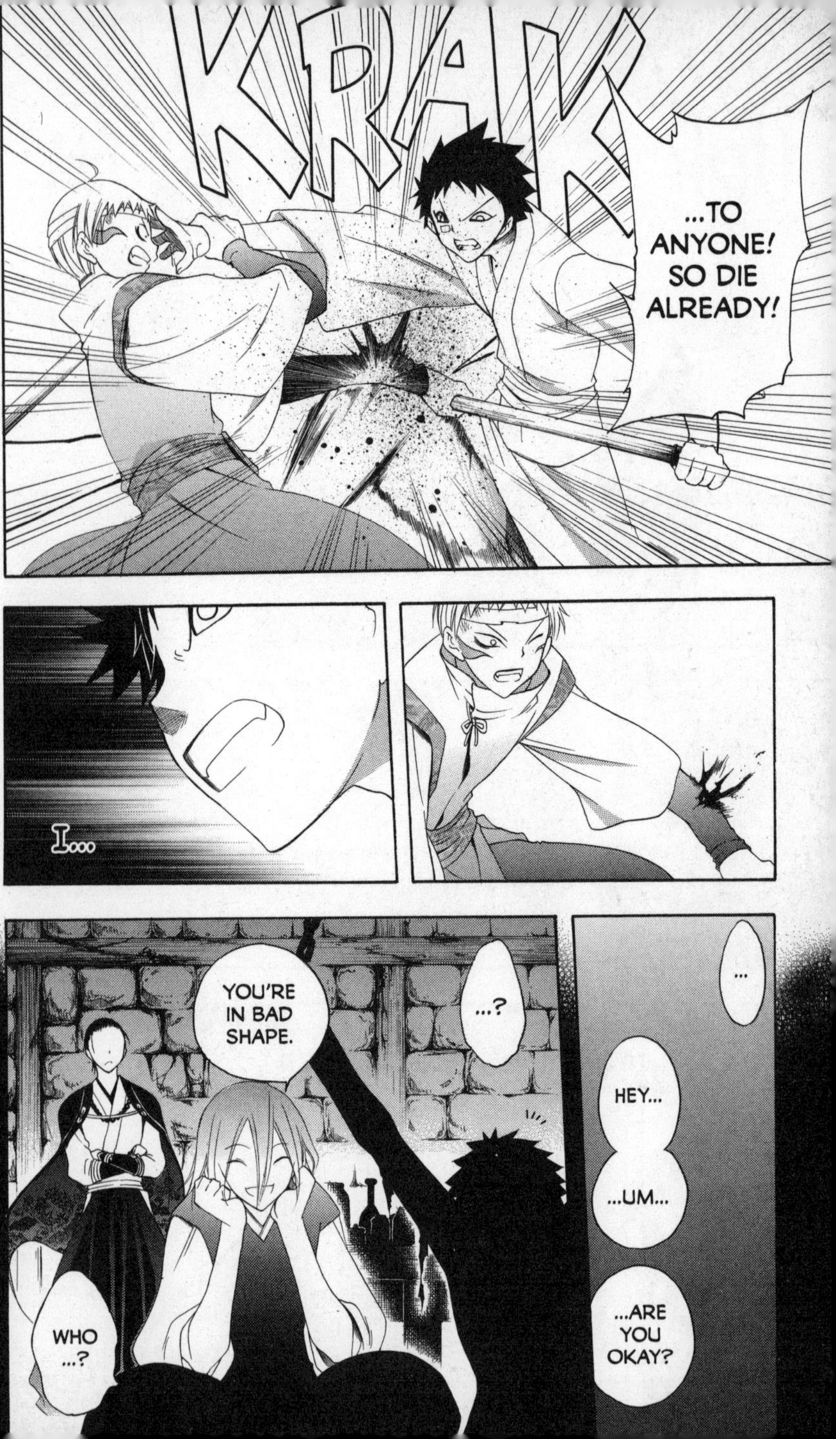
KRAK
...TO ANYONE! SO DIE ALREADY!
I...
...
HEY...
...UM...
...ARE YOU OKAY?
...?
YOU'RE IN BAD SHAPE.
WHO ...?

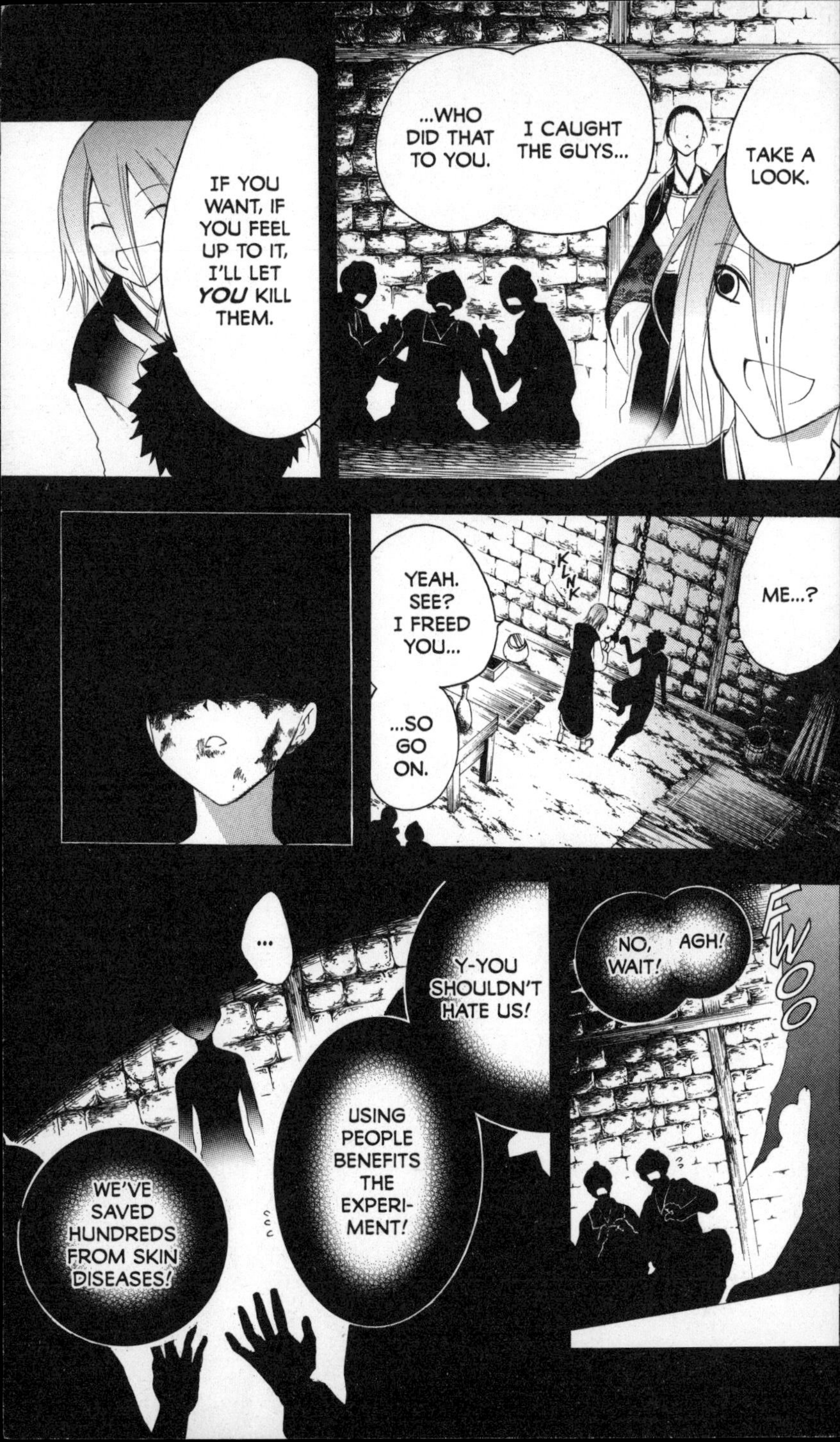
TAKE A LOOK.
I CAUGHT THE GUYS...
...WHO DID THAT TO YOU.
IF YOU WANT, IF YOU FEEL UP TO IT, I'LL LET *YOU* KILL THEM.
ME...?
YEAH. SEE? I FREED YOU...
KLINK
...SO GO ON.
FWOO
AGH!
NO, WAIT!
...
Y-YOU SHOULDN'T HATE US!
USING PEOPLE BENEFITS THE EXPERIMENT!
WE'VE SAVED HUNDREDS FROM SKIN DISEASES!

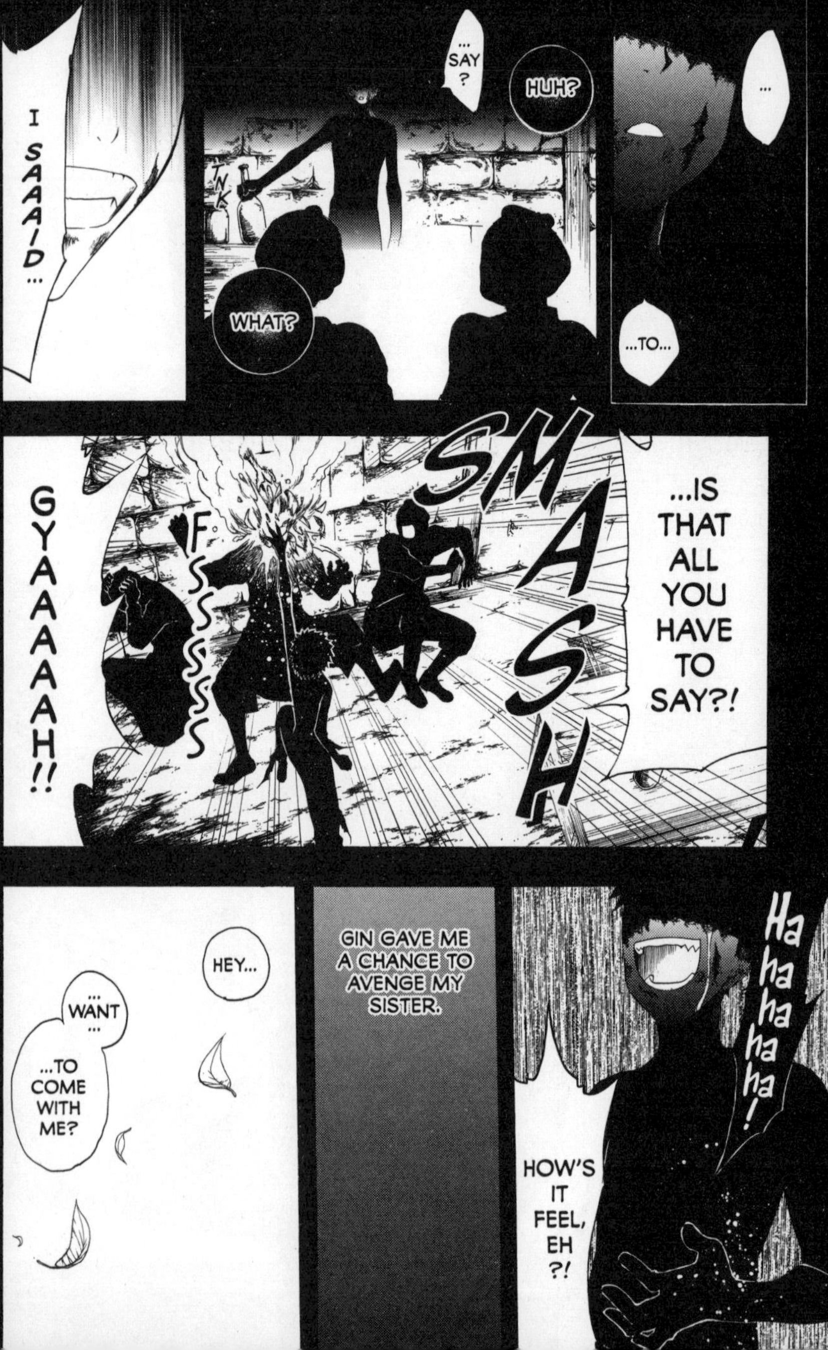
...
...TO...
...SAY?
HUH?
TNK
WHAT?
I SAAAID...
SMASH
...IS THAT ALL YOU HAVE TO SAY?!
FSSSSSS
GYAAAAAAH!!
Hahahahaha!
HOW'S IT FEEL, EH?!
GIN GAVE ME A CHANCE TO AVENGE MY SISTER.
HEY...
...WANT...
...TO COME WITH ME?

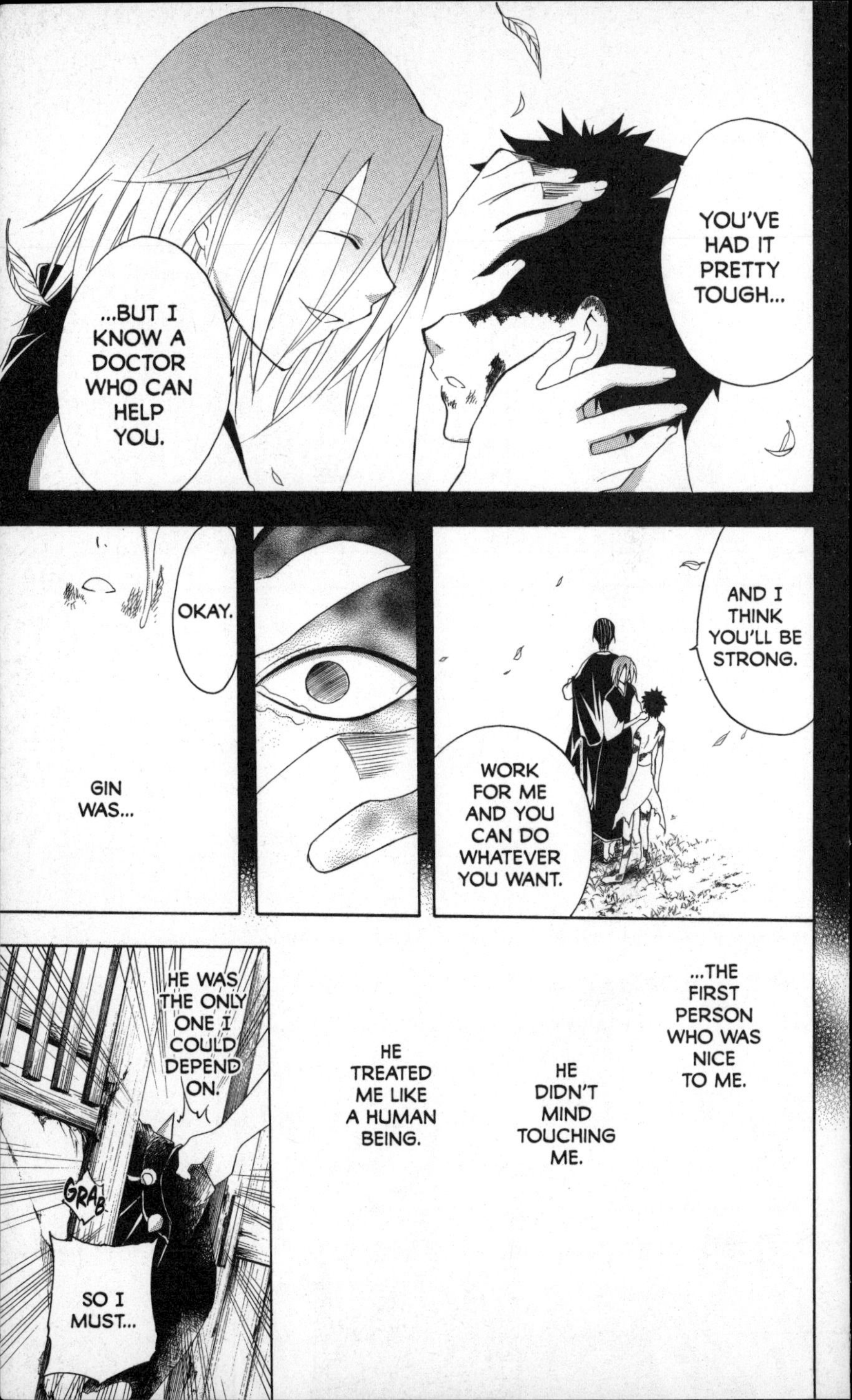
YOU'VE HAD IT PRETTY TOUGH...
...BUT I KNOW A DOCTOR WHO CAN HELP YOU.
AND I THINK YOU'LL BE STRONG.
WORK FOR ME AND YOU CAN DO WHATEVER YOU WANT.
OKAY.
GIN WAS...
...THE FIRST PERSON WHO WAS NICE TO ME.
HE DIDN'T MIND TOUCHING ME.
HE TREATED ME LIKE A HUMAN BEING.
HE WAS THE ONLY ONE I COULD DEPEND ON.
GRAB
SO I MUST...

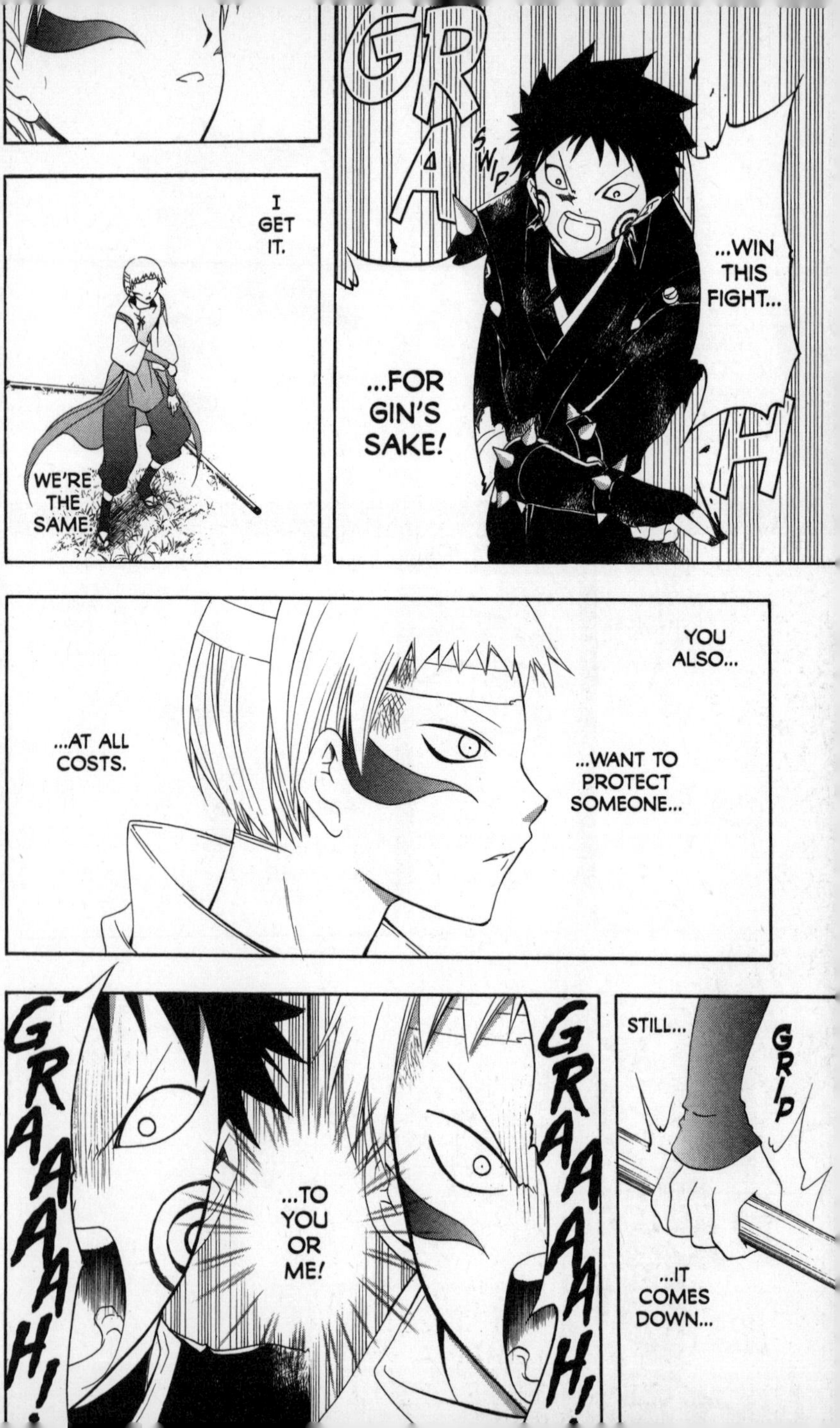
GR
A
SWIP
H
...WIN THIS FIGHT...
...FOR GIN'S SAKE!
I GET IT.
WE'RE THE SAME.
YOU ALSO...
...WANT TO PROTECT SOMEONE...
...AT ALL COSTS.
STILL...
GRIP
...IT COMES DOWN...
GRAAAAH!
...TO YOU OR ME!
GRAAAAH!

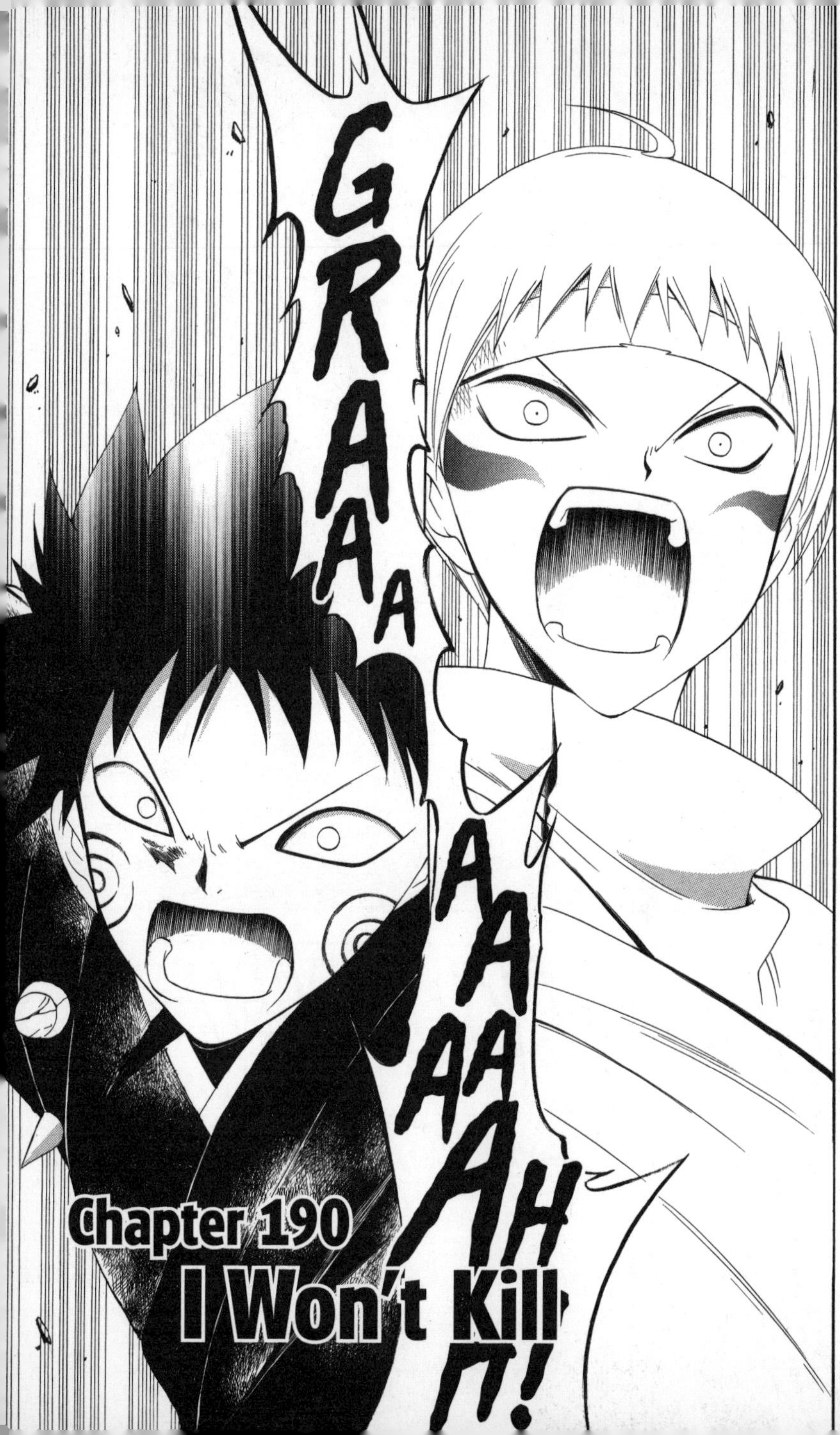
GRAAAA
AAAAAHH!
Chapter 190
I Won't Kill

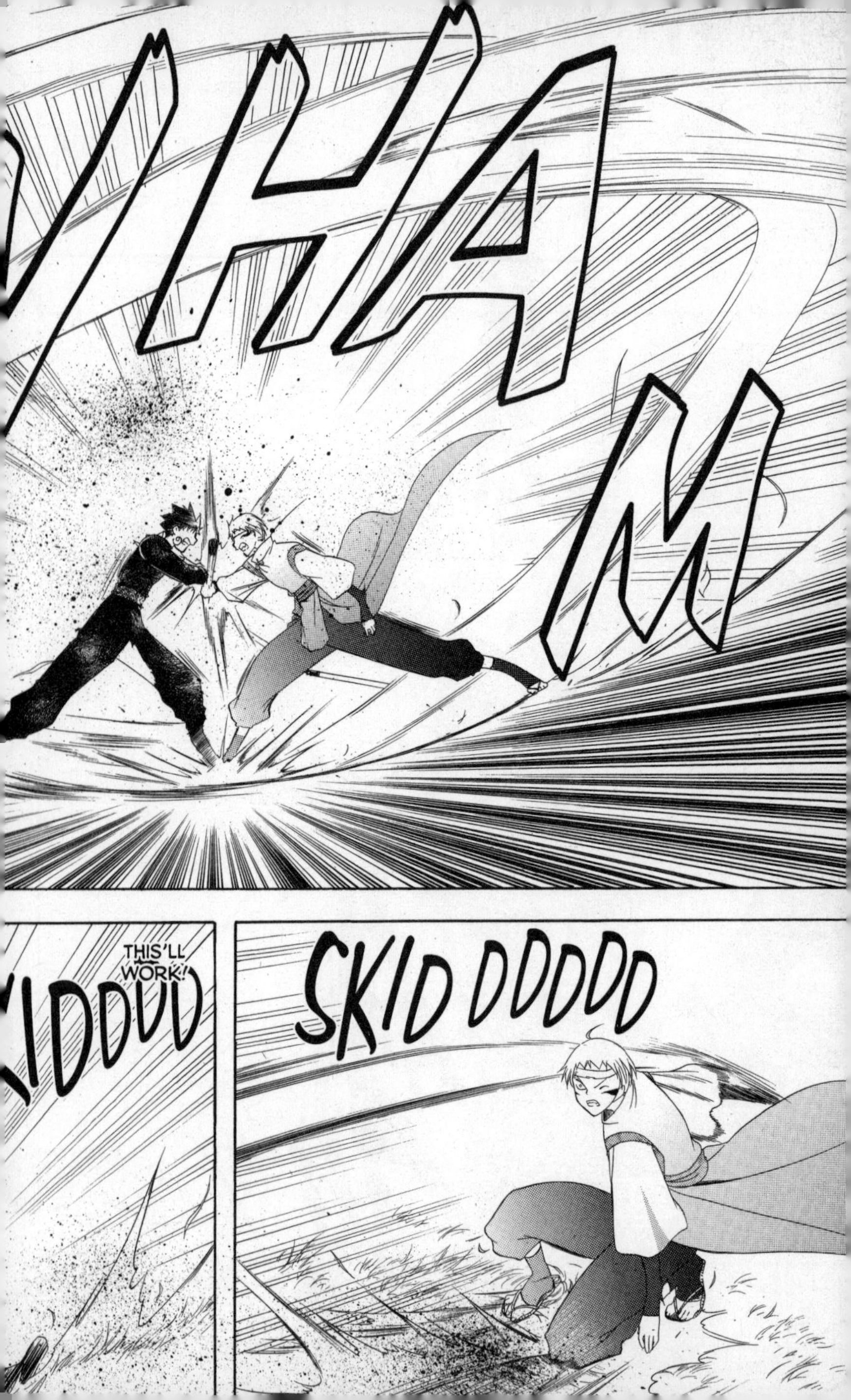
HAM
SKID DDDDD
THIS'LL WORK!
IDDDD

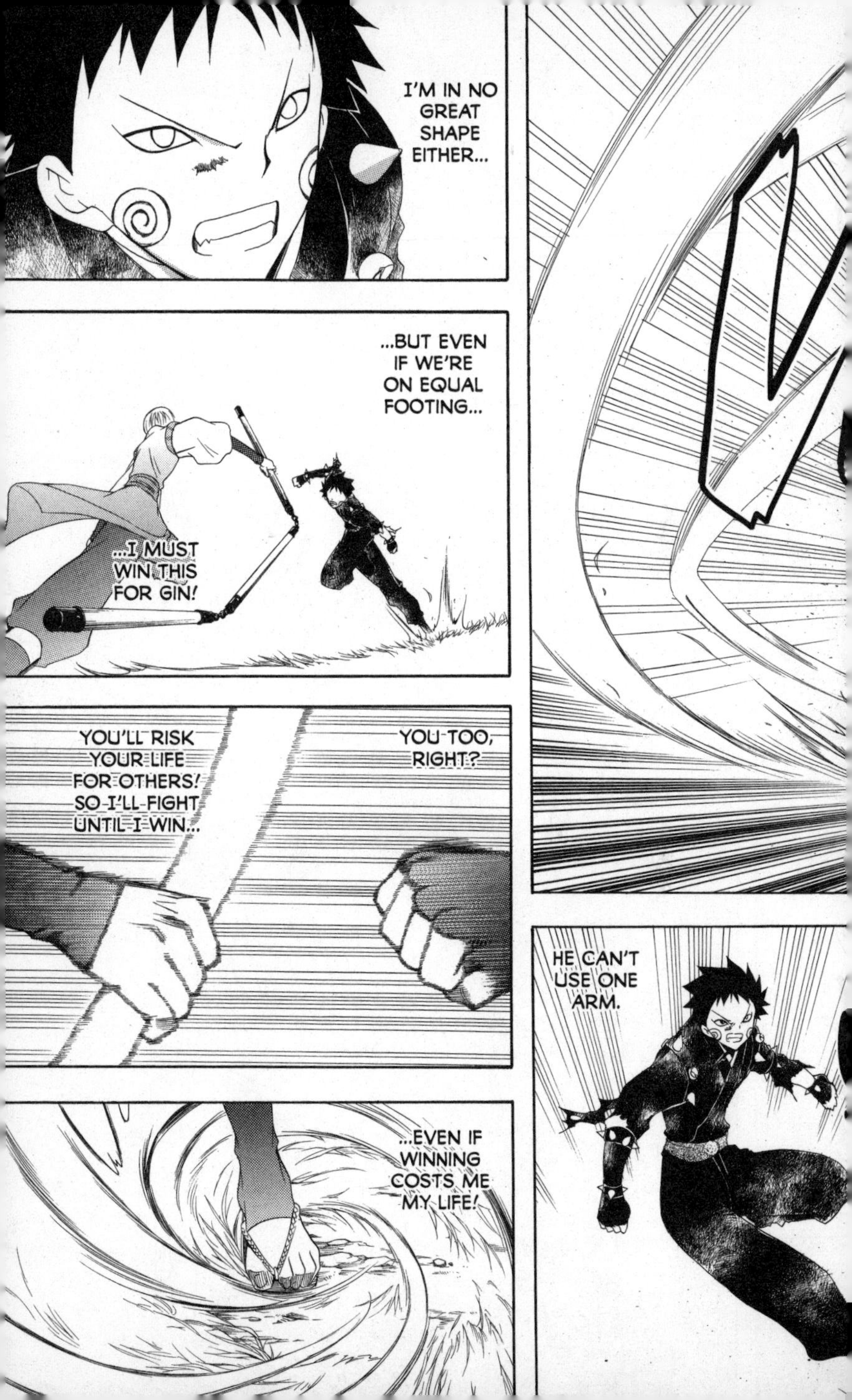
I'M IN NO GREAT SHAPE EITHER...
...BUT EVEN IF WE'RE ON EQUAL FOOTING...
...I MUST WIN THIS FOR GIN!
YOU TOO, RIGHT?
YOU'LL RISK YOUR LIFE FOR OTHERS! SO I'LL FIGHT UNTIL I WIN...
...EVEN IF WINNING COSTS ME MY LIFE!
HE CAN'T USE ONE ARM.

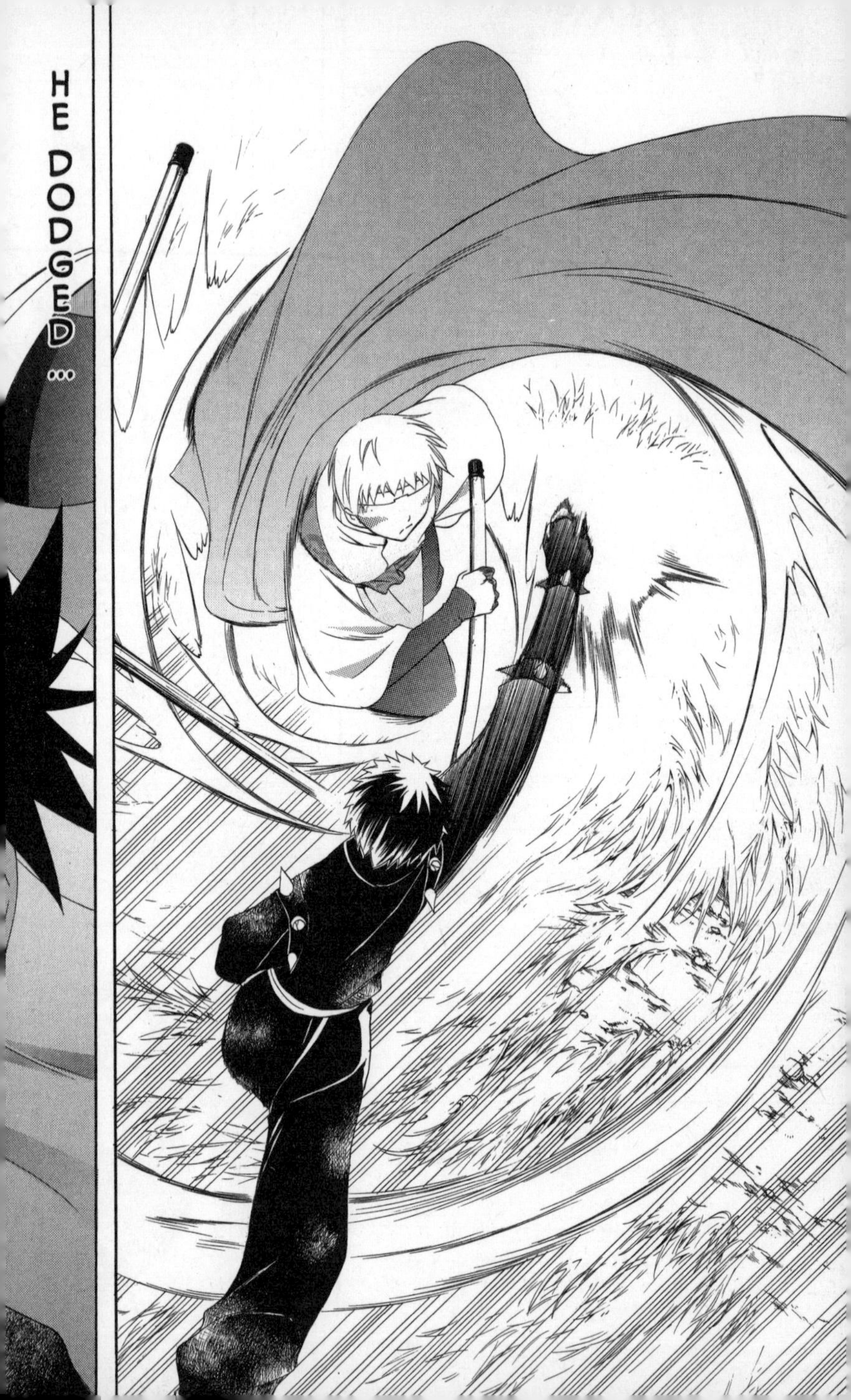
HE DODGED...

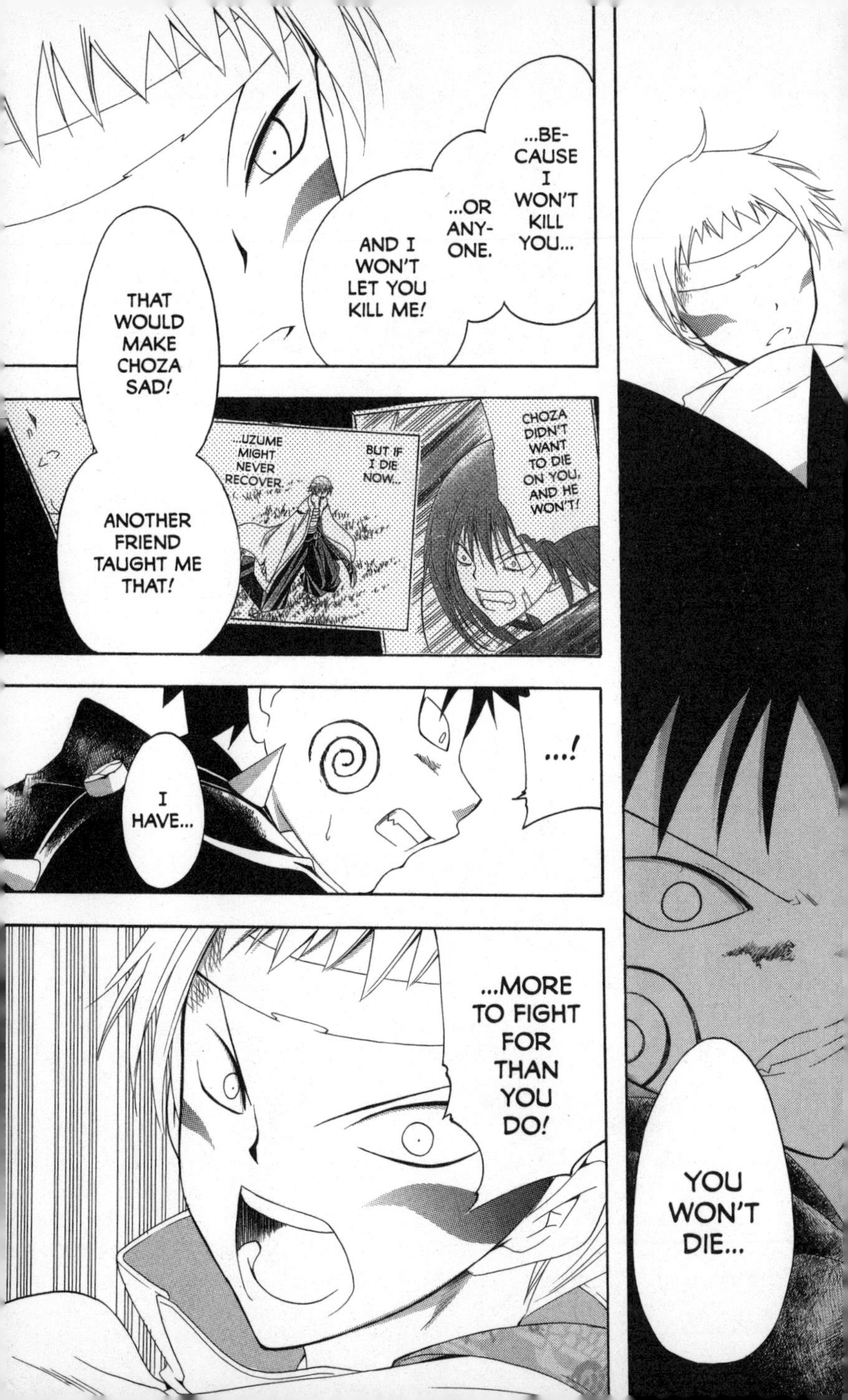
YOU WON'T DIE...
...BECAUSE I WON'T KILL YOU...
...OR ANYONE.
AND I WON'T LET YOU KILL ME!
THAT WOULD MAKE CHOZA SAD!
CHOZA DIDN'T WANT TO DIE ON YOU, AND HE WON'T!
BUT IF I DIE NOW...
...UZUME MIGHT NEVER RECOVER.
ANOTHER FRIEND TAUGHT ME THAT!
...!
I HAVE...
...MORE TO FIGHT FOR THAN YOU DO!

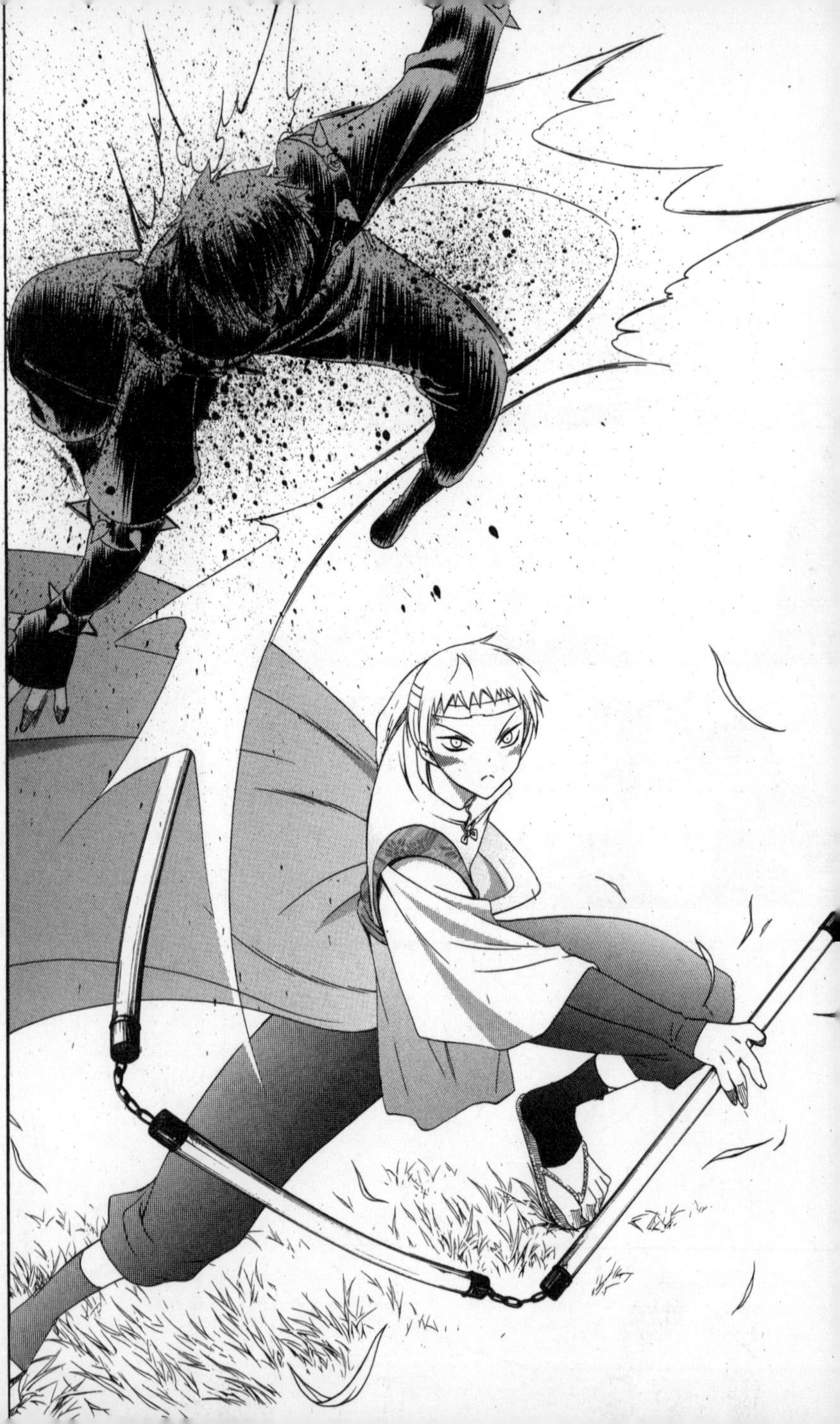

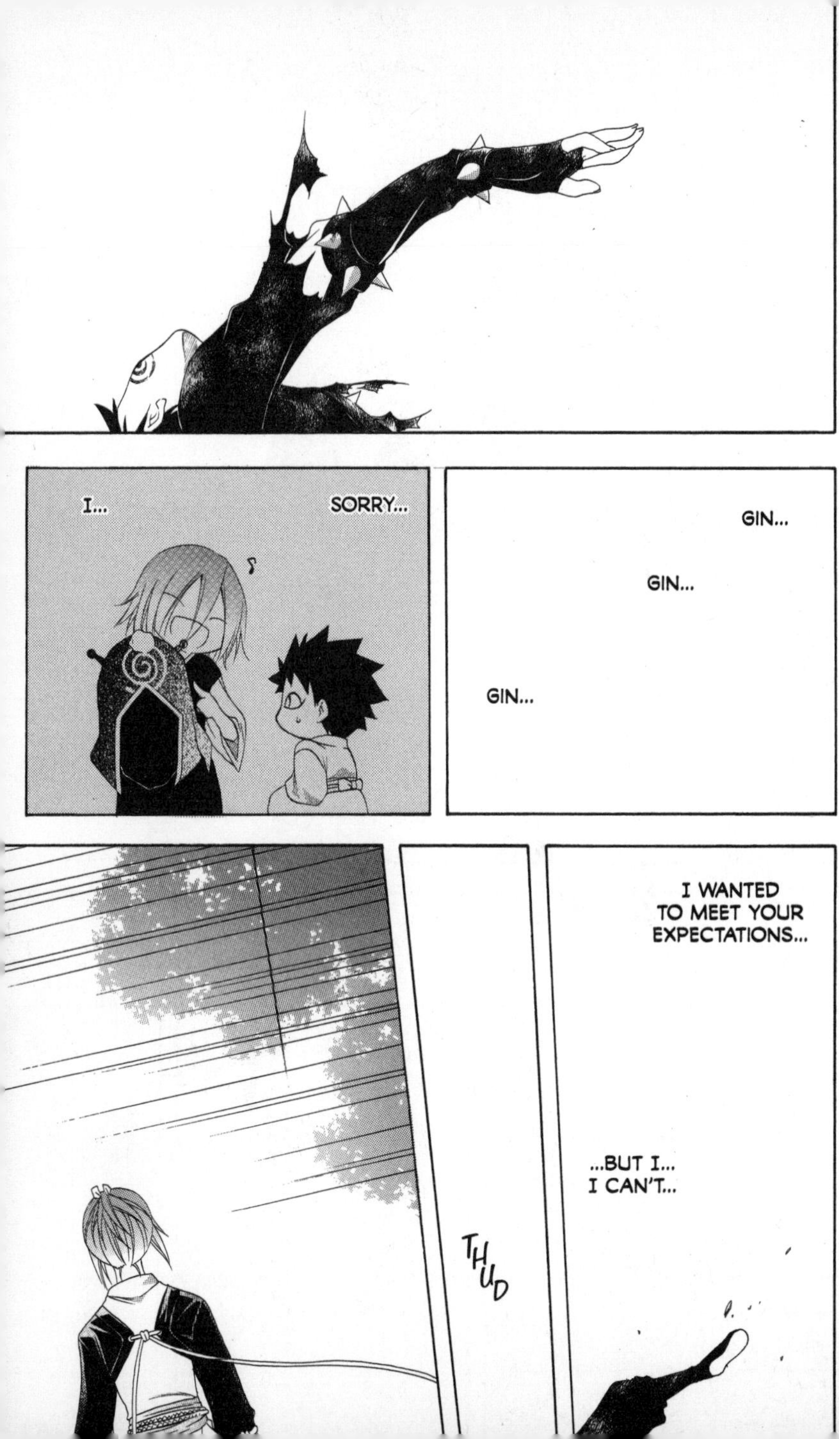
GIN...
GIN...
GIN...
SORRY...
I...
I WANTED TO MEET YOUR EXPECTATIONS...
...BUT I... I CAN'T...
THUD

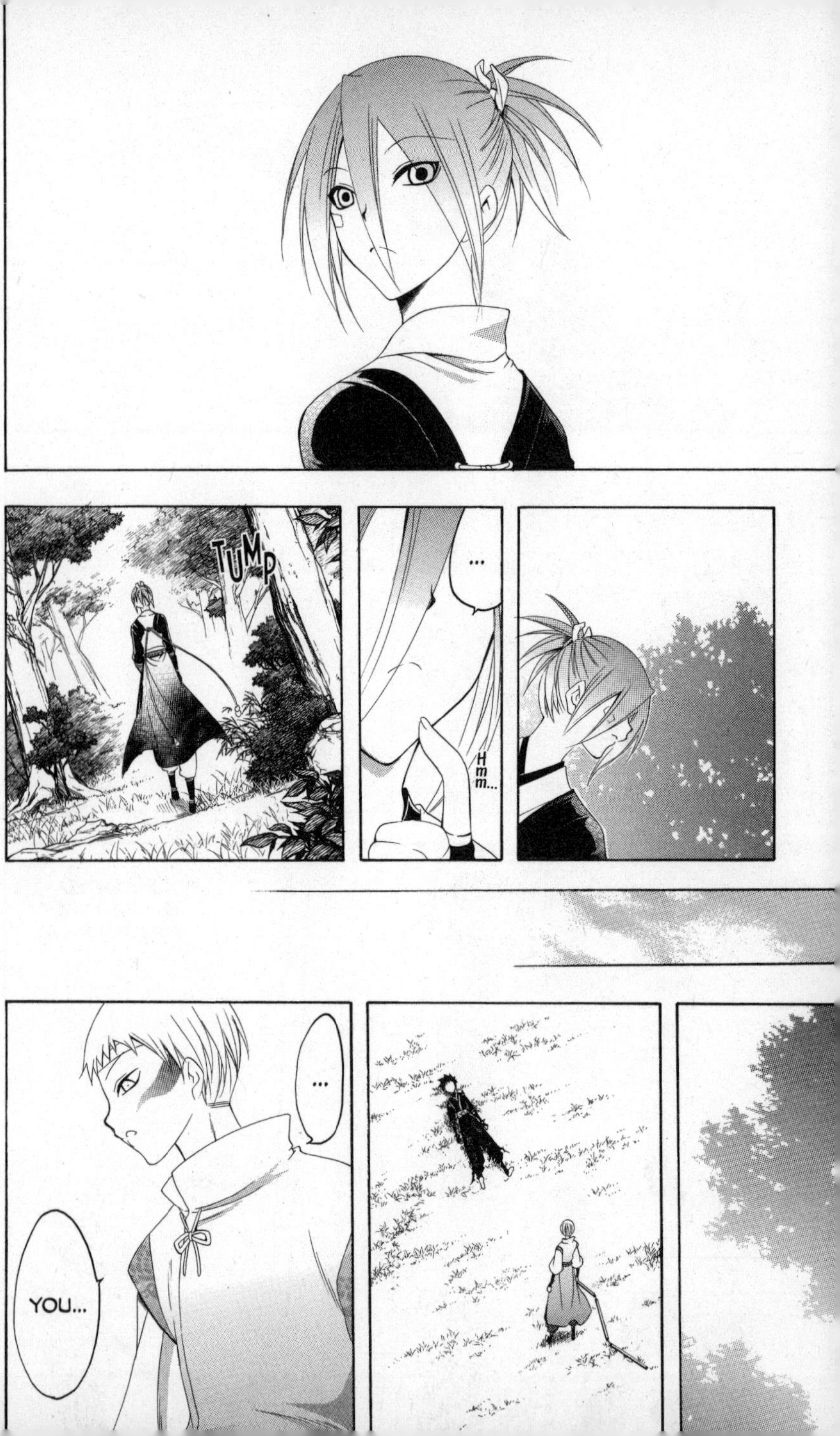
...
Hmm...
TUMP
...
YOU...

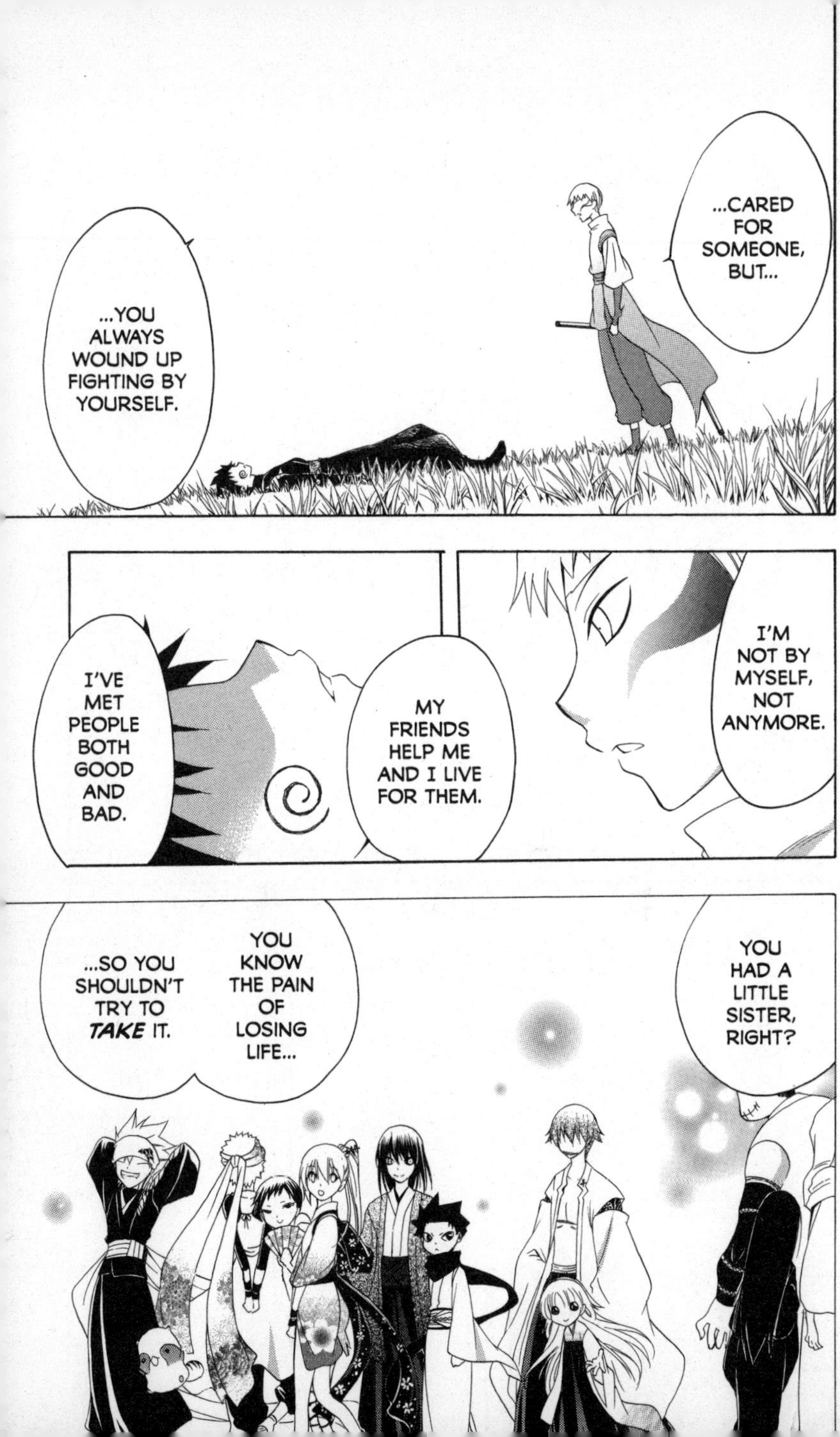
...CARED FOR SOMEONE, BUT...
...YOU ALWAYS WOUND UP FIGHTING BY YOURSELF.
I'M NOT BY MYSELF, NOT ANYMORE.
MY FRIENDS HELP ME AND I LIVE FOR THEM.
I'VE MET PEOPLE BOTH GOOD AND BAD.
YOU HAD A LITTLE SISTER, RIGHT?
YOU KNOW THE PAIN OF LOSING LIFE...
...SO YOU SHOULDN'T TRY TO *TAKE* IT.

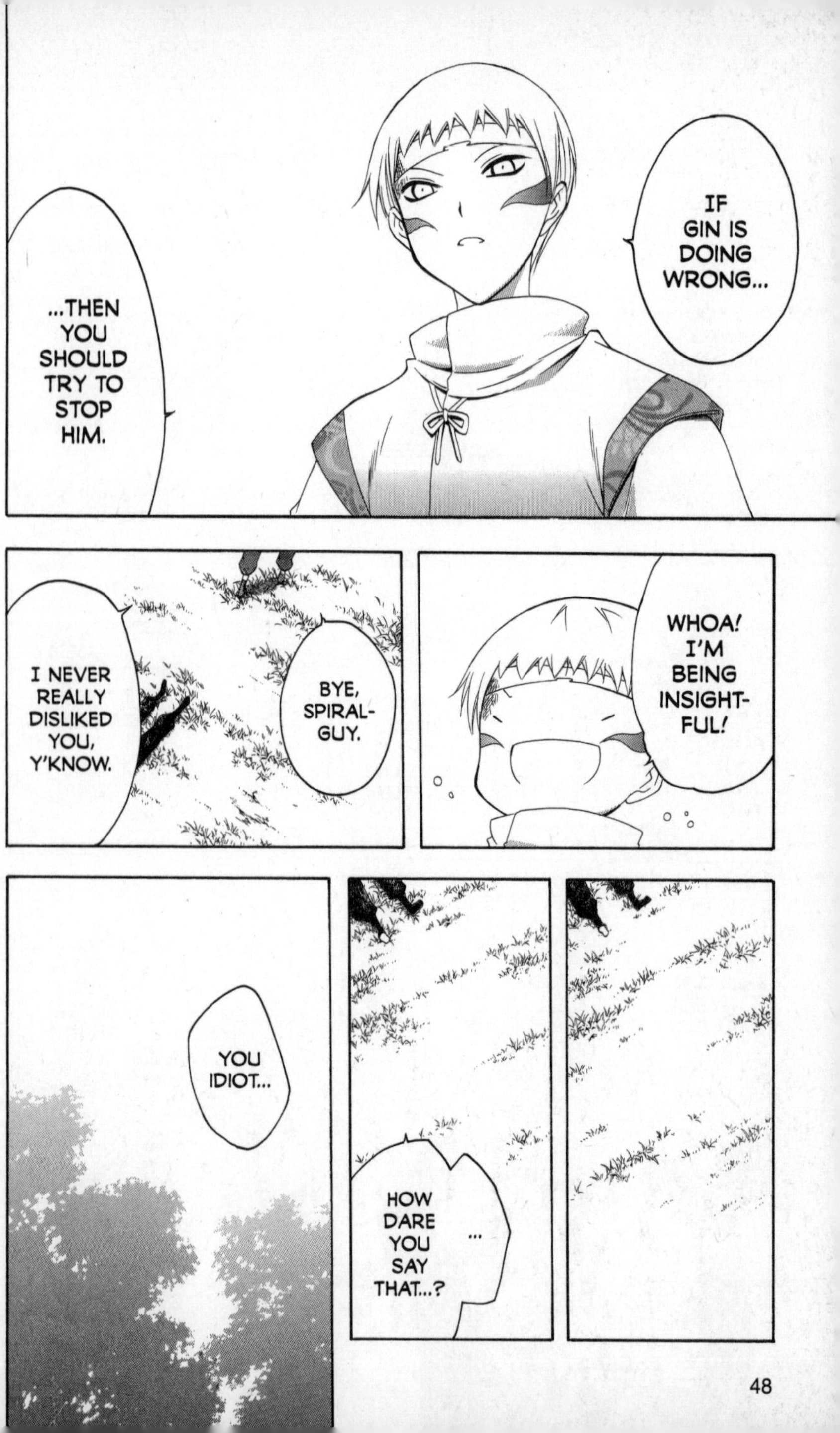
IF GIN IS DOING WRONG...
...THEN YOU SHOULD TRY TO STOP HIM.
WHOA! I'M BEING INSIGHTFUL!
BYE, SPIRAL-GUY.
I NEVER REALLY DISLIKED YOU, Y'KNOW.
...
HOW DARE YOU SAY THAT...?
YOU IDIOT...

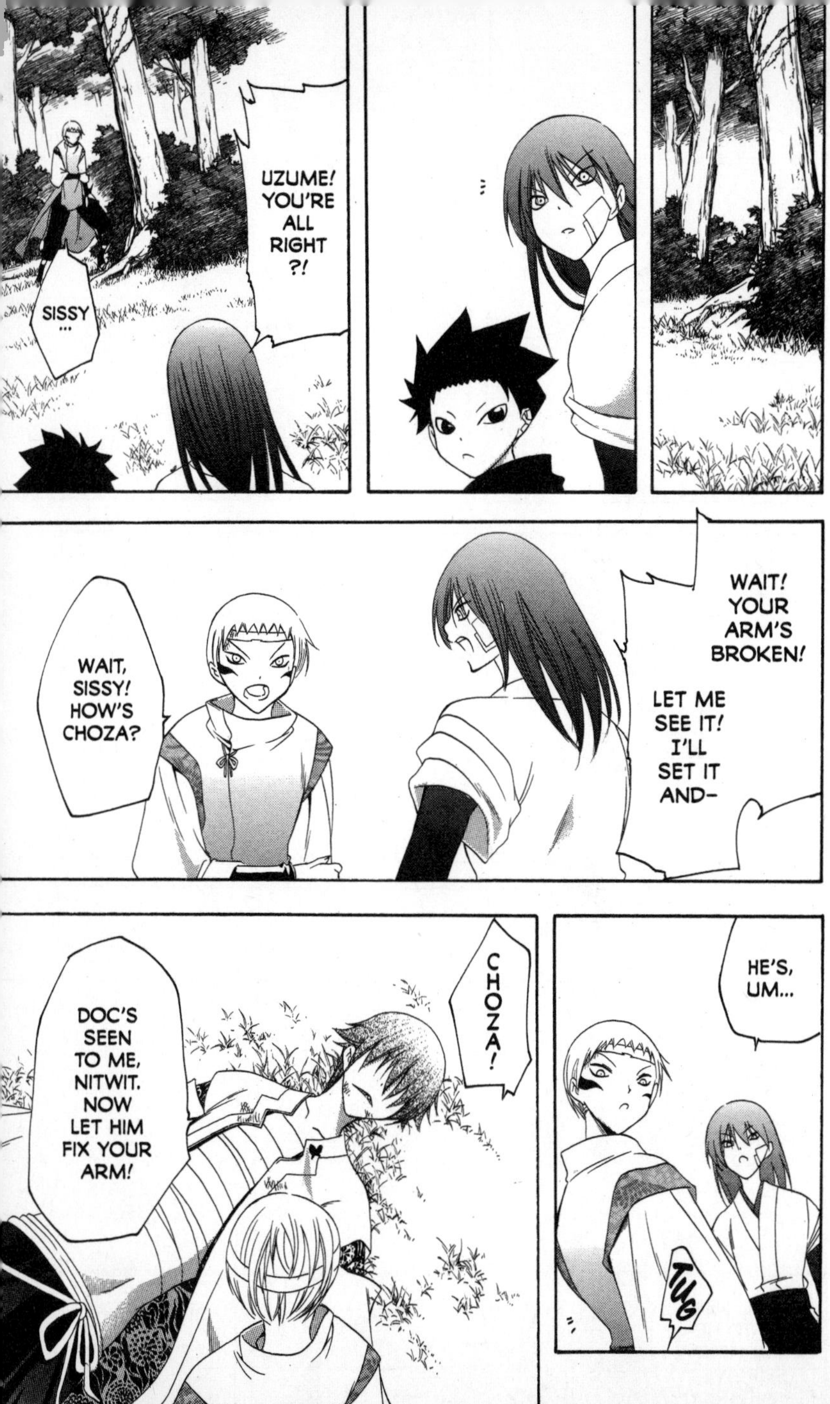
UZUME! YOU'RE ALL RIGHT?!
SISSY...
WAIT! YOUR ARM'S BROKEN!
LET ME SEE IT! I'LL SET IT AND–
WAIT, SISSY! HOW'S CHOZA?
HE'S, UM...
TUG
CHOZA!
DOC'S SEEN TO ME, NITWIT. NOW LET HIM FIX YOUR ARM!

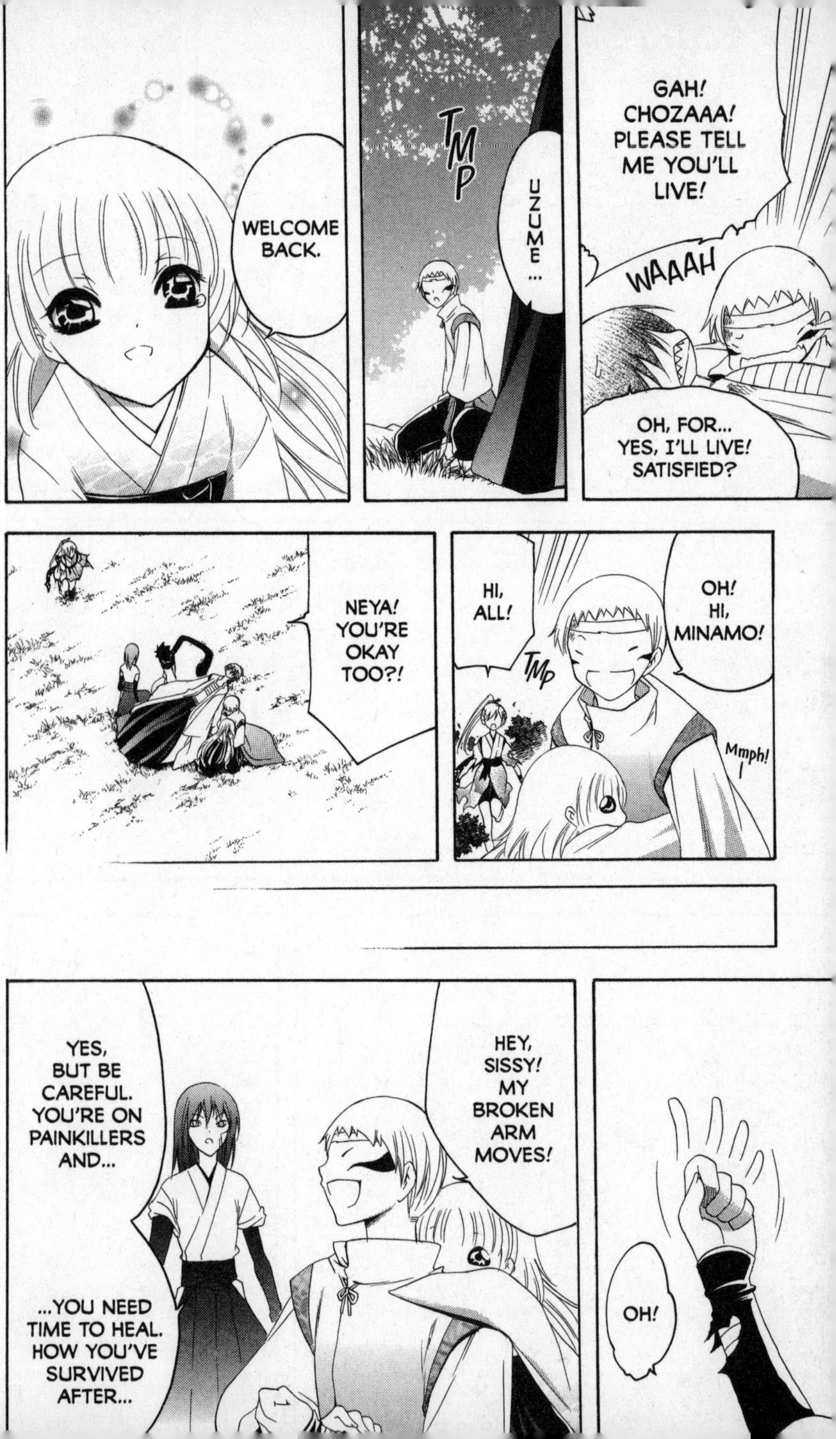
GAH! CHOZAAA! PLEASE TELL ME YOU'LL LIVE!
WAAAH
OH, FOR... YES, I'LL LIVE! SATISFIED?
TMP
UZUME...
WELCOME BACK.
OH! HI, MINAMO!
HI, ALL!
TMP
Mmph!
NEYA! YOU'RE OKAY TOO?!
OH!
HEY, SISSY! MY BROKEN ARM MOVES!
YES, BUT BE CAREFUL. YOU'RE ON PAINKILLERS AND...
...YOU NEED TIME TO HEAL. HOW YOU'VE SURVIVED AFTER...

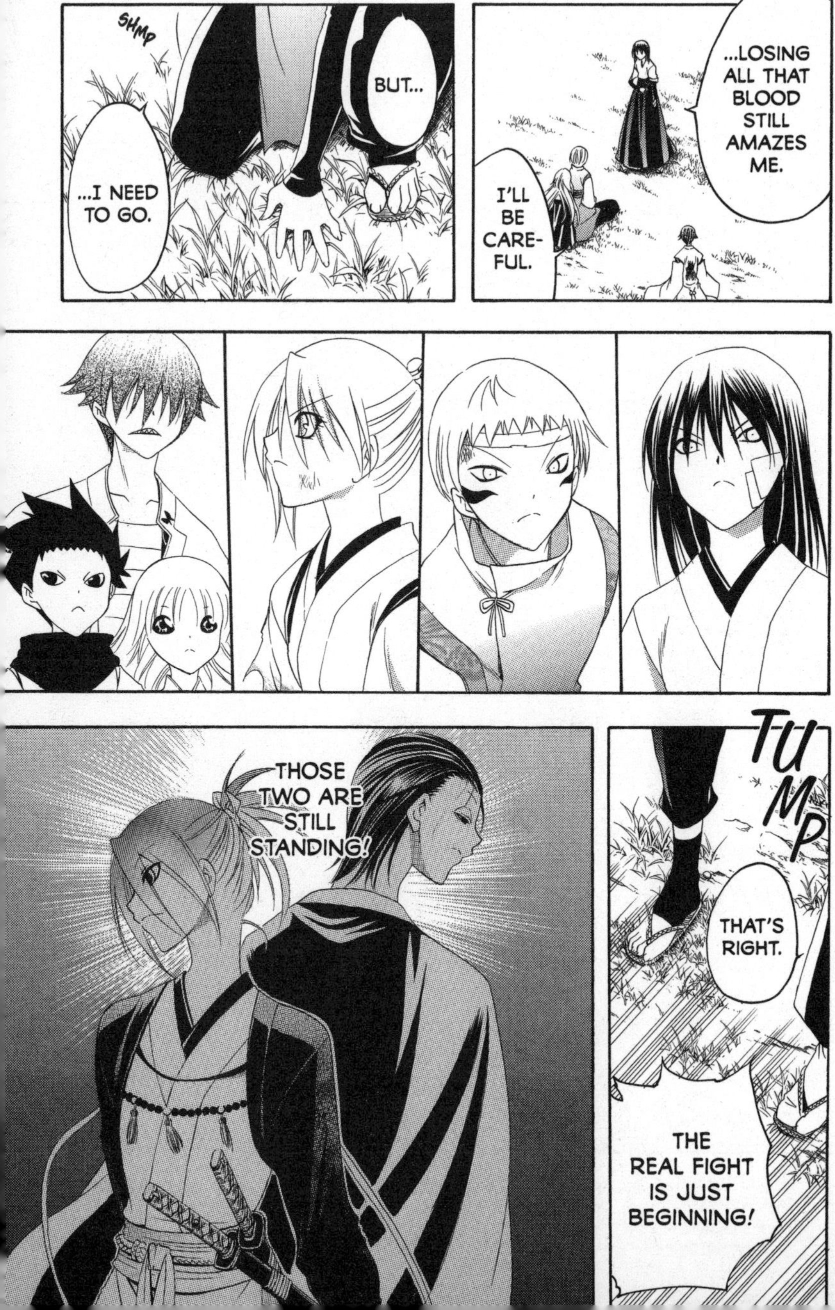
...LOSING ALL THAT BLOOD STILL AMAZES ME.
I'LL BE CAREFUL.
SHMP
BUT...
...I NEED TO GO.
TUMP
THAT'S RIGHT.
THE REAL FIGHT IS JUST BEGINNING!
THOSE TWO ARE STILL STANDING!

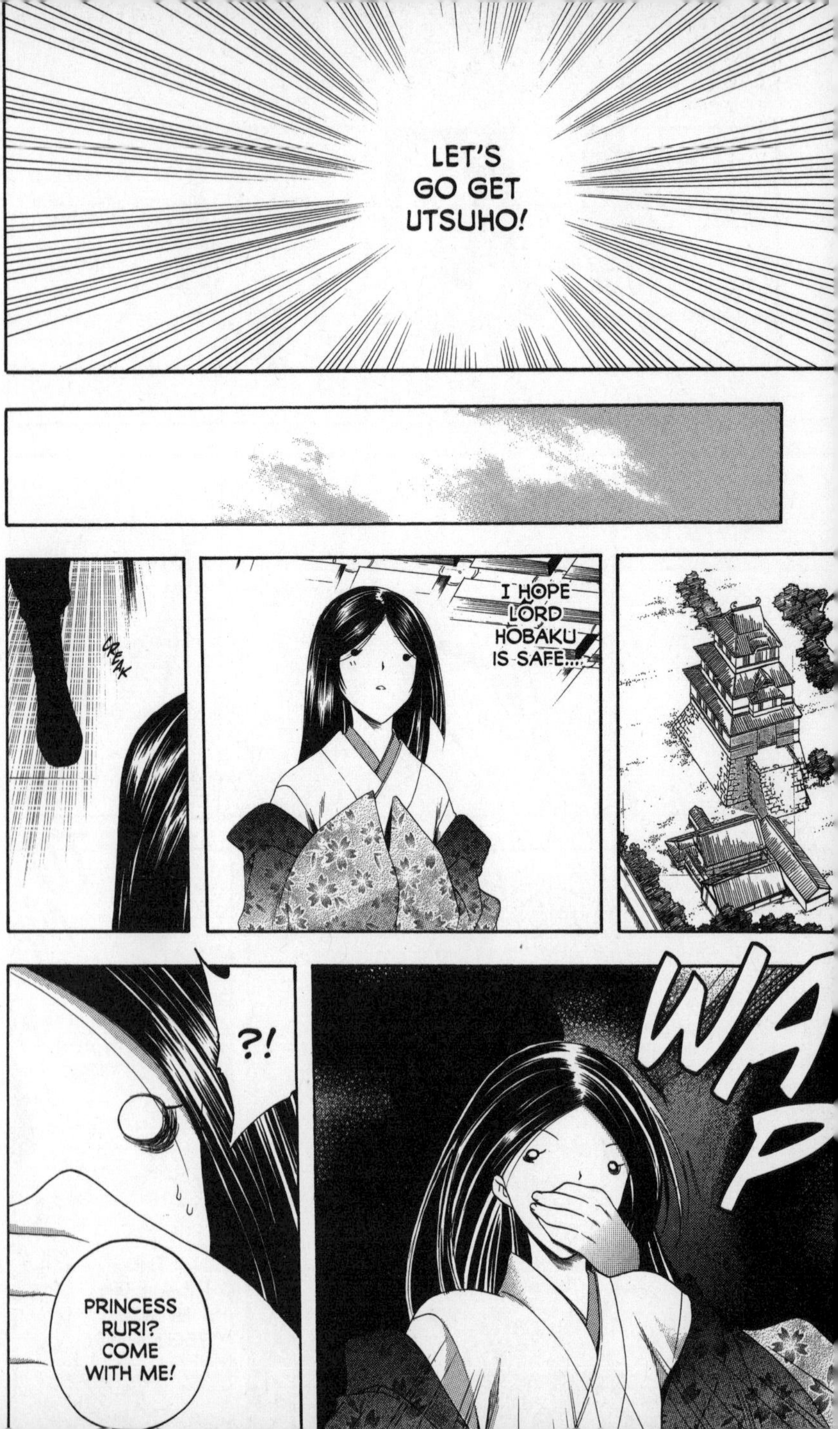
LET'S GO GET UTSUHO!
I HOPE LORD HOBAKU IS SAFE....
CREAK
WAP
?!
PRINCESS RURI? COME WITH ME!

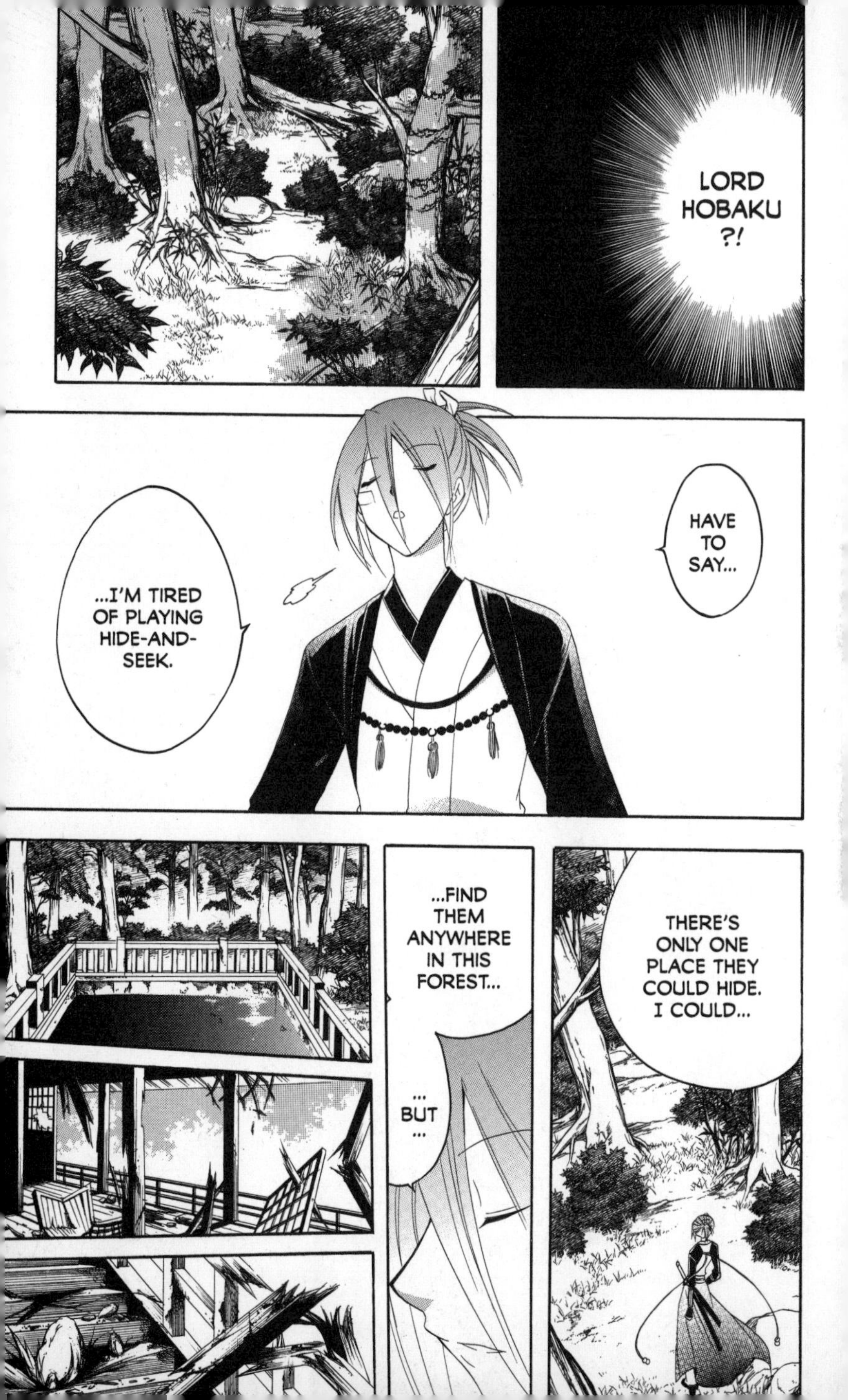
LORD HOBAKU ?!
HAVE TO SAY...
...I'M TIRED OF PLAYING HIDE-AND-SEEK.
THERE'S ONLY ONE PLACE THEY COULD HIDE. I COULD...
...FIND THEM ANYWHERE IN THIS FOREST...
...BUT...

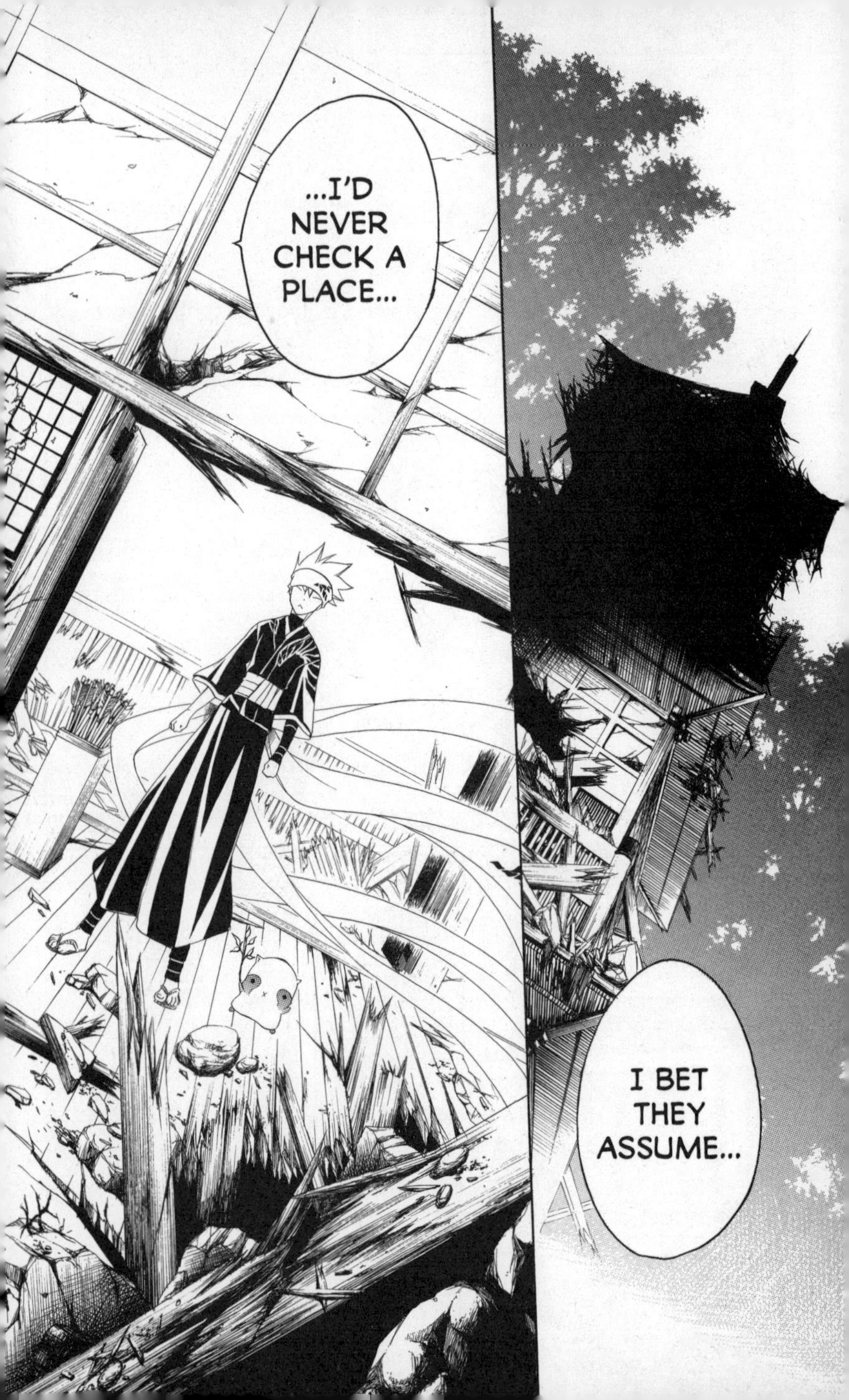
I BET THEY ASSUME...
...I'D NEVER CHECK A PLACE...

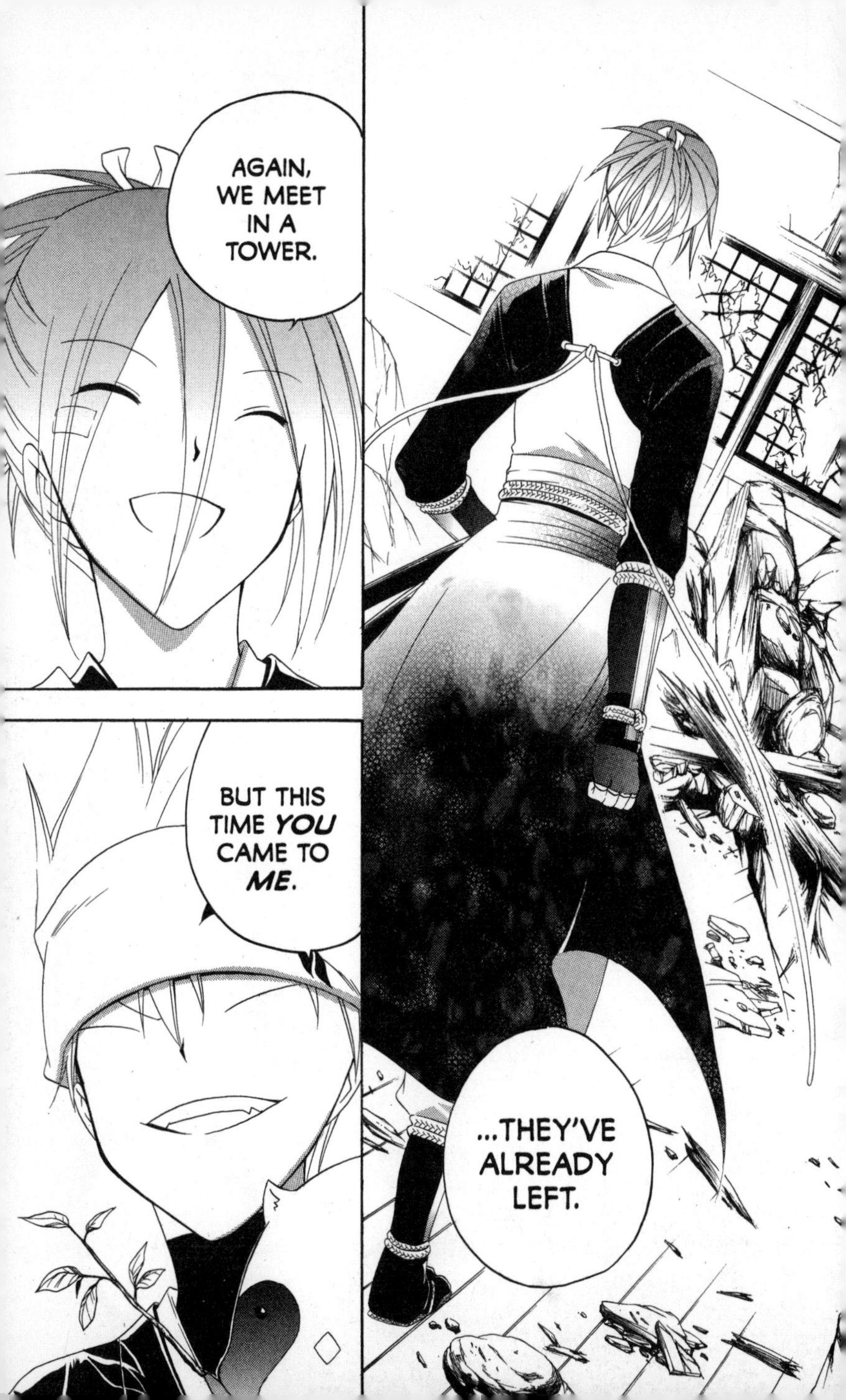
...THEY'VE ALREADY LEFT.
AGAIN, WE MEET IN A TOWER.
BUT THIS TIME *YOU* CAME TO ***ME***.

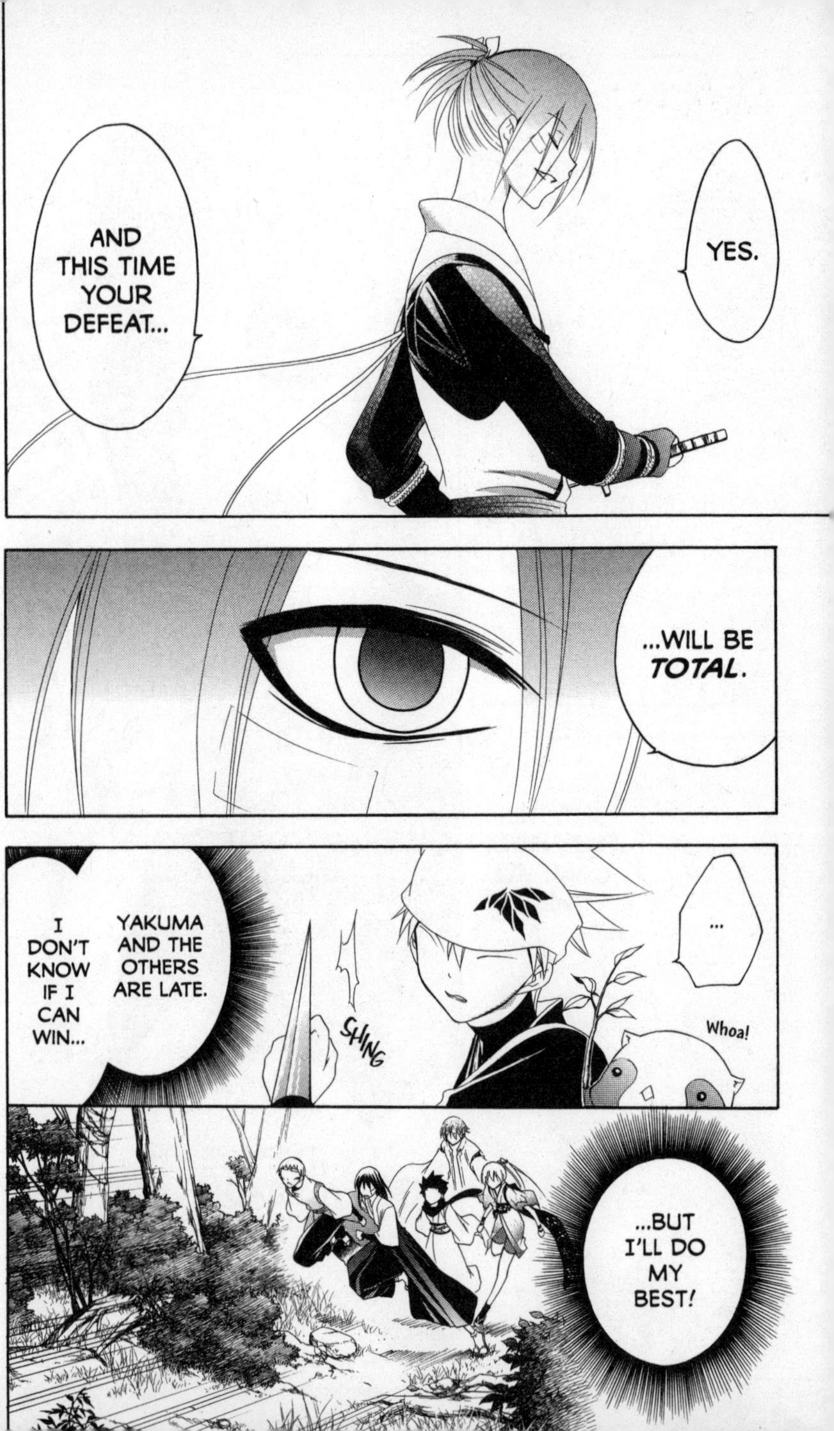
YES.
AND THIS TIME YOUR DEFEAT...
...WILL BE *TOTAL*.
...
Whoa!
SHING
YAKUMA AND THE OTHERS ARE LATE.
I DON'T KNOW IF I CAN WIN...
...BUT I'LL DO MY BEST!

Chapter 191
Battle at the Old Tower

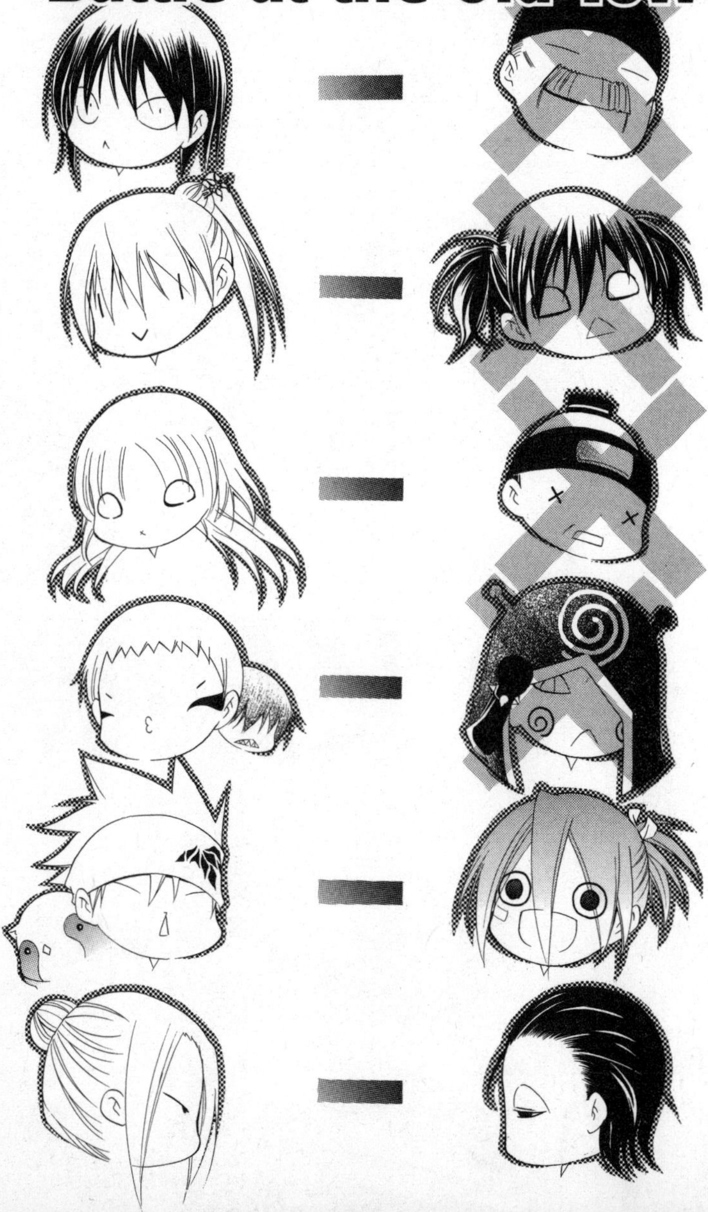

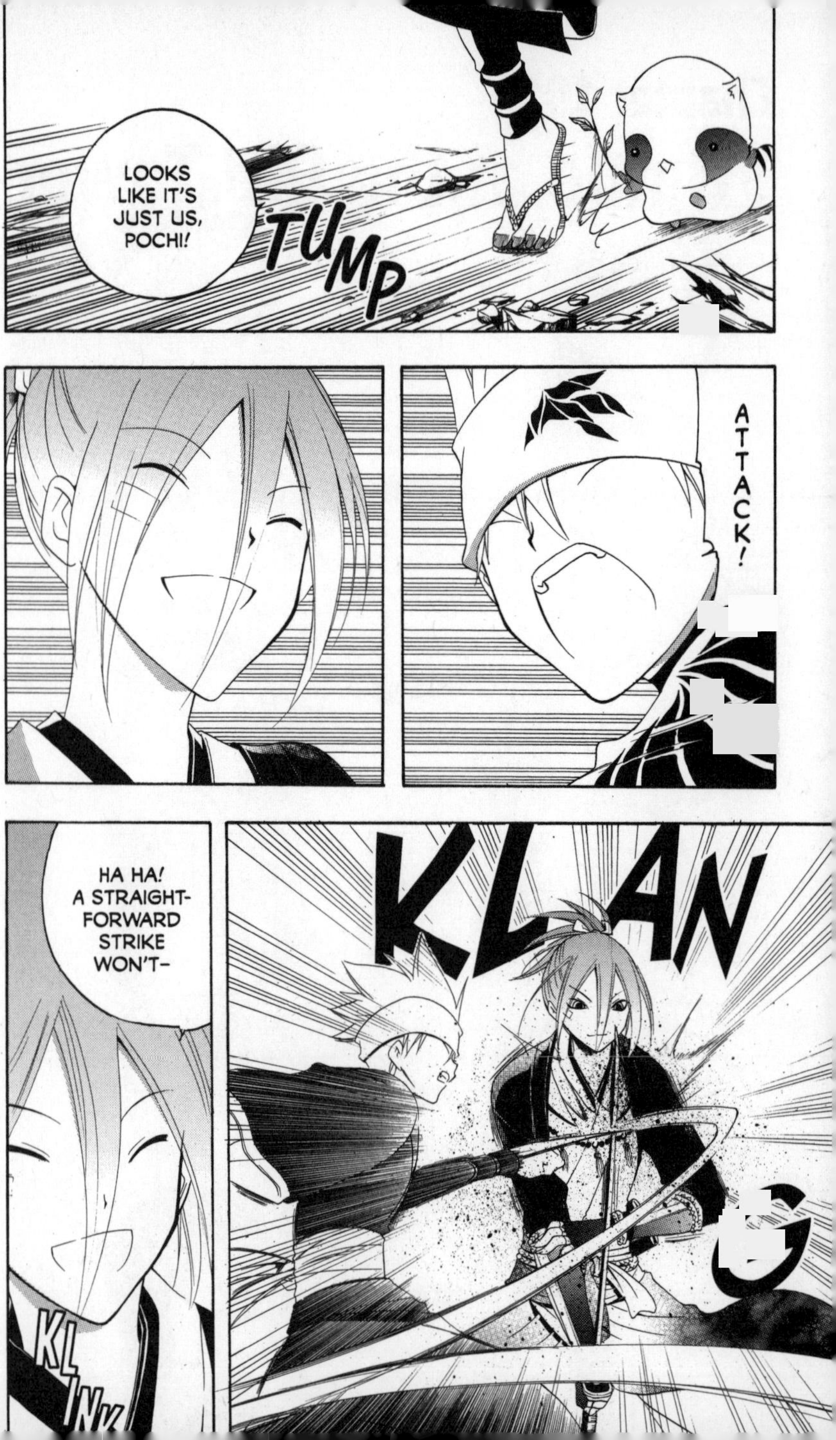
LOOKS LIKE IT'S JUST US, POCHI!
TUMP
ATTACK!
KLAN
HA HA! A STRAIGHT-FORWARD STRIKE WON'T-
KLINK

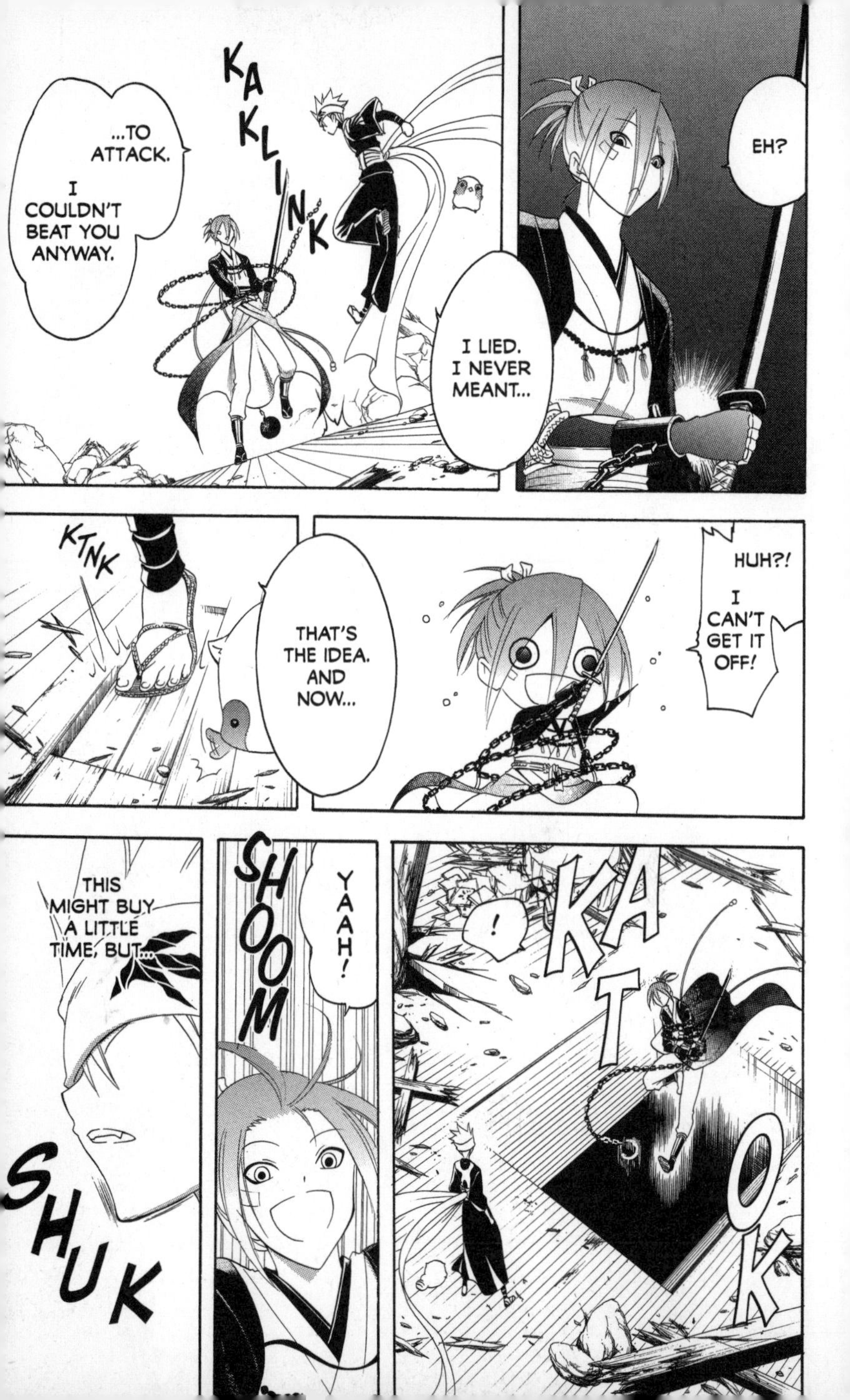
EH?
I LIED. I NEVER MEANT...
KAKLINK
...TO ATTACK.
I COULDN'T BEAT YOU ANYWAY.
HUH?!
I CAN'T GET IT OFF!
THAT'S THE IDEA. AND NOW...
KTNK
!
KATOK
YAAAH!
SHOOOM
THIS MIGHT BUY A LITTLE TIME, BUT...
SHUK

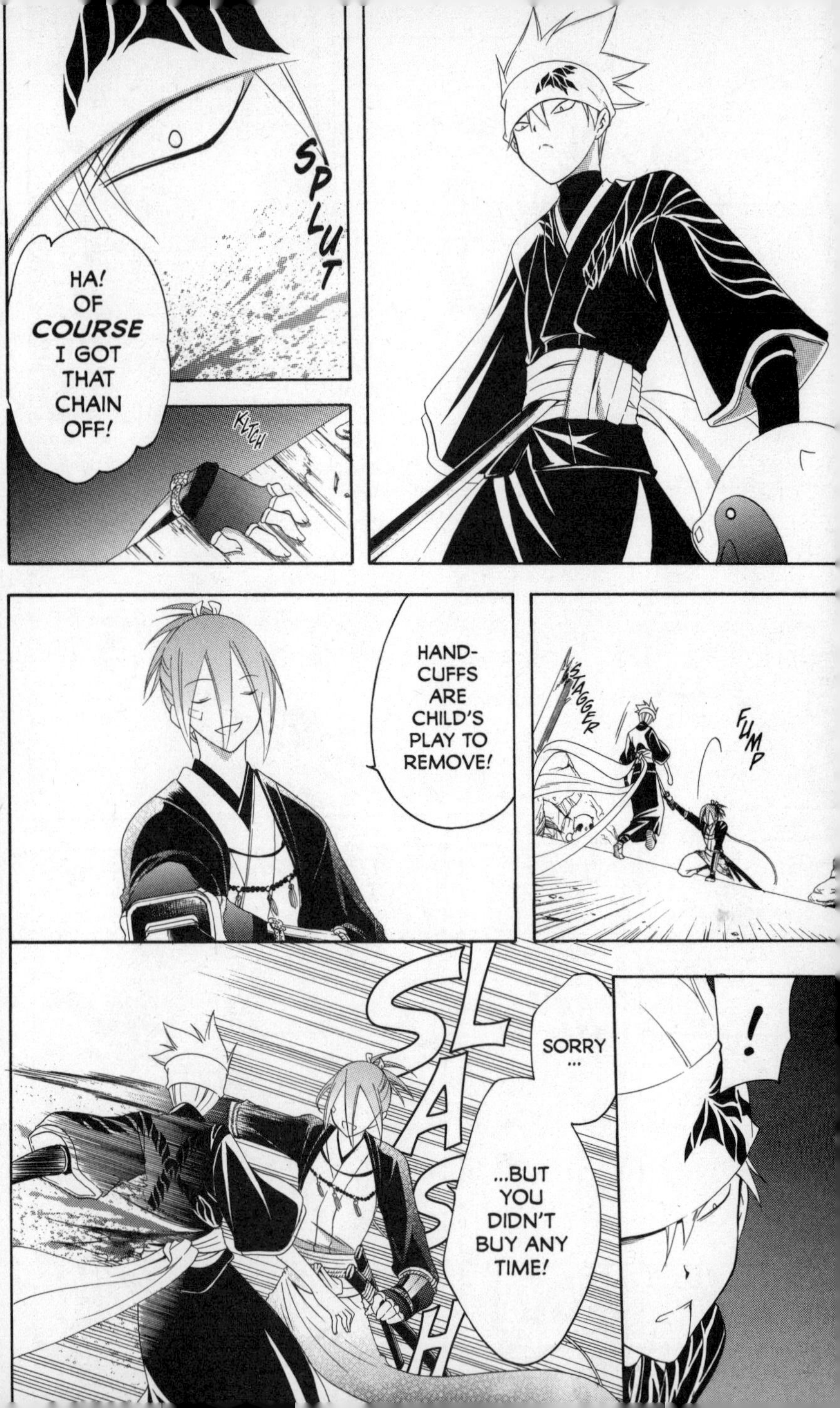
SPLUT
HA! OF *COURSE* I GOT THAT CHAIN OFF!
KLTCH
STAGGER
FUMP
HAND-CUFFS ARE CHILD'S PLAY TO REMOVE!
!
SORRY...
...BUT YOU DIDN'T BUY ANY TIME!
SLASH

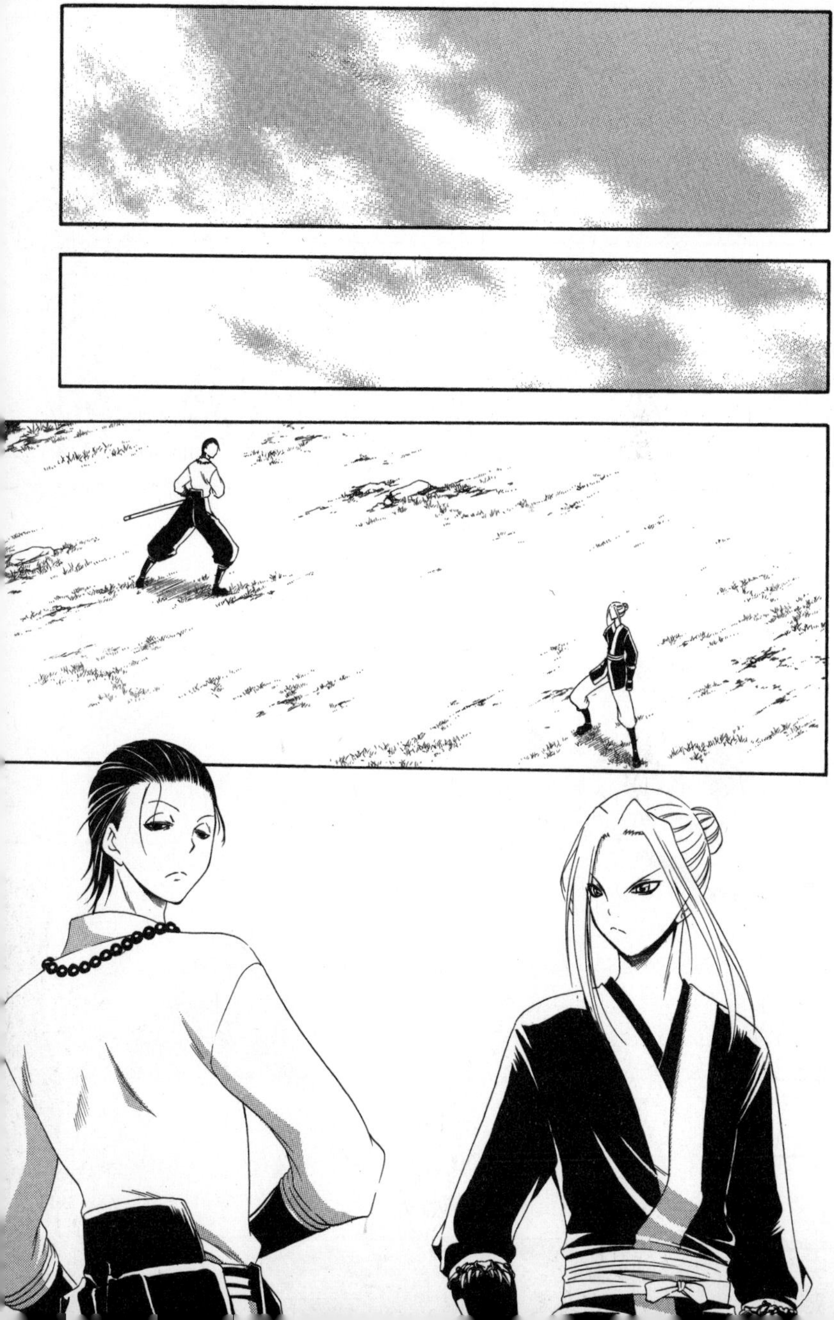

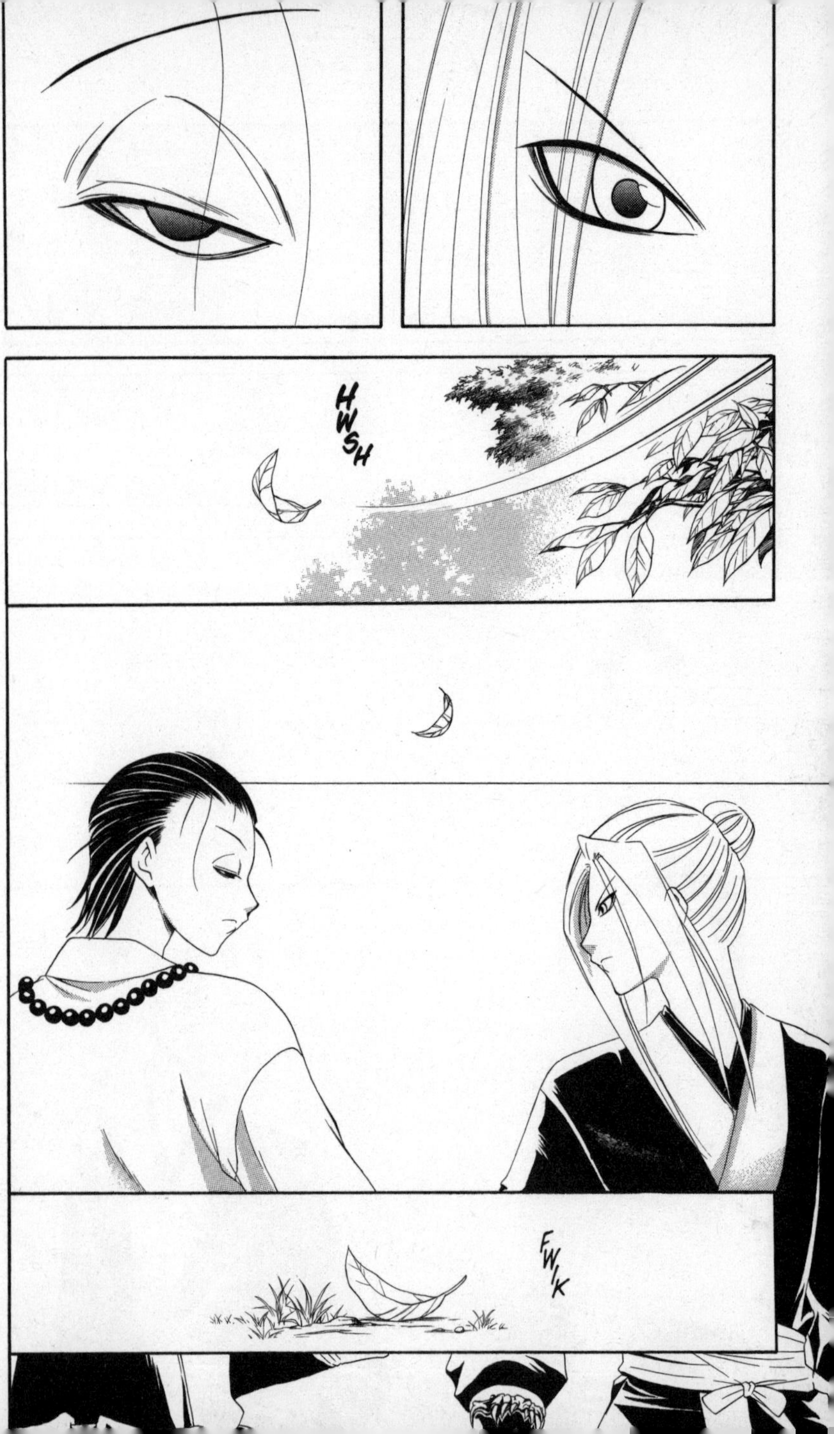
HWSH
FWIK

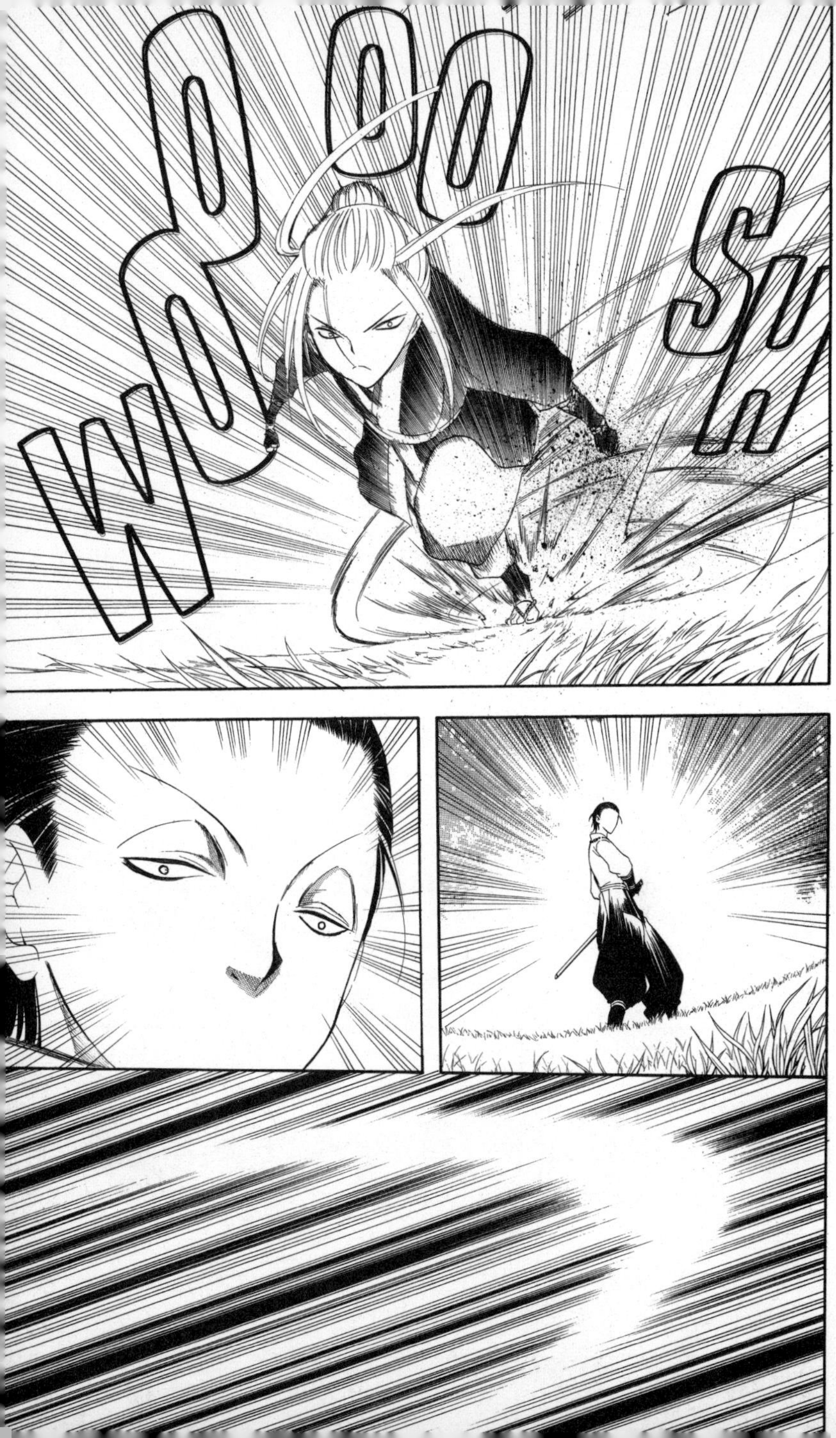
WOOOSH

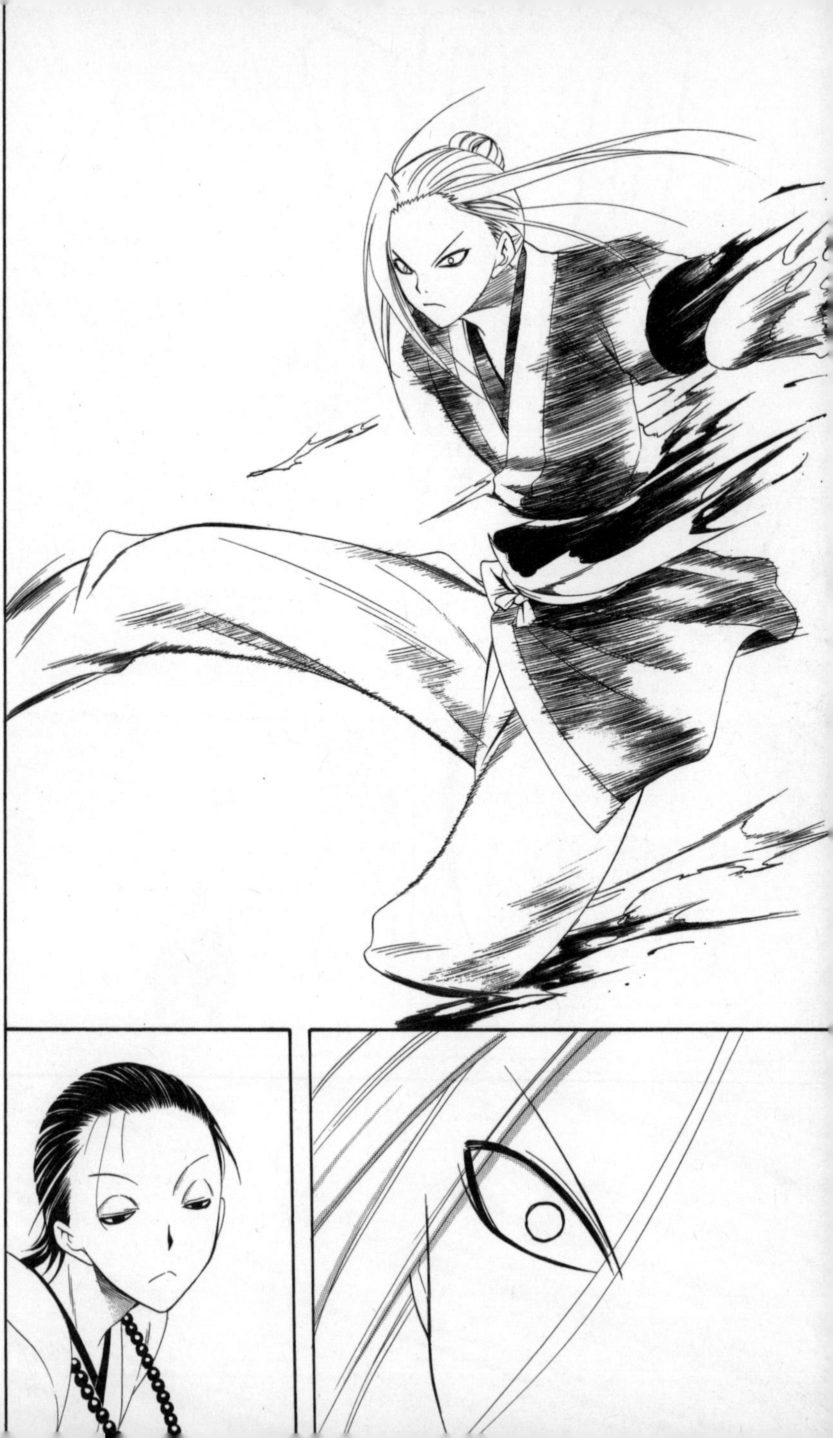

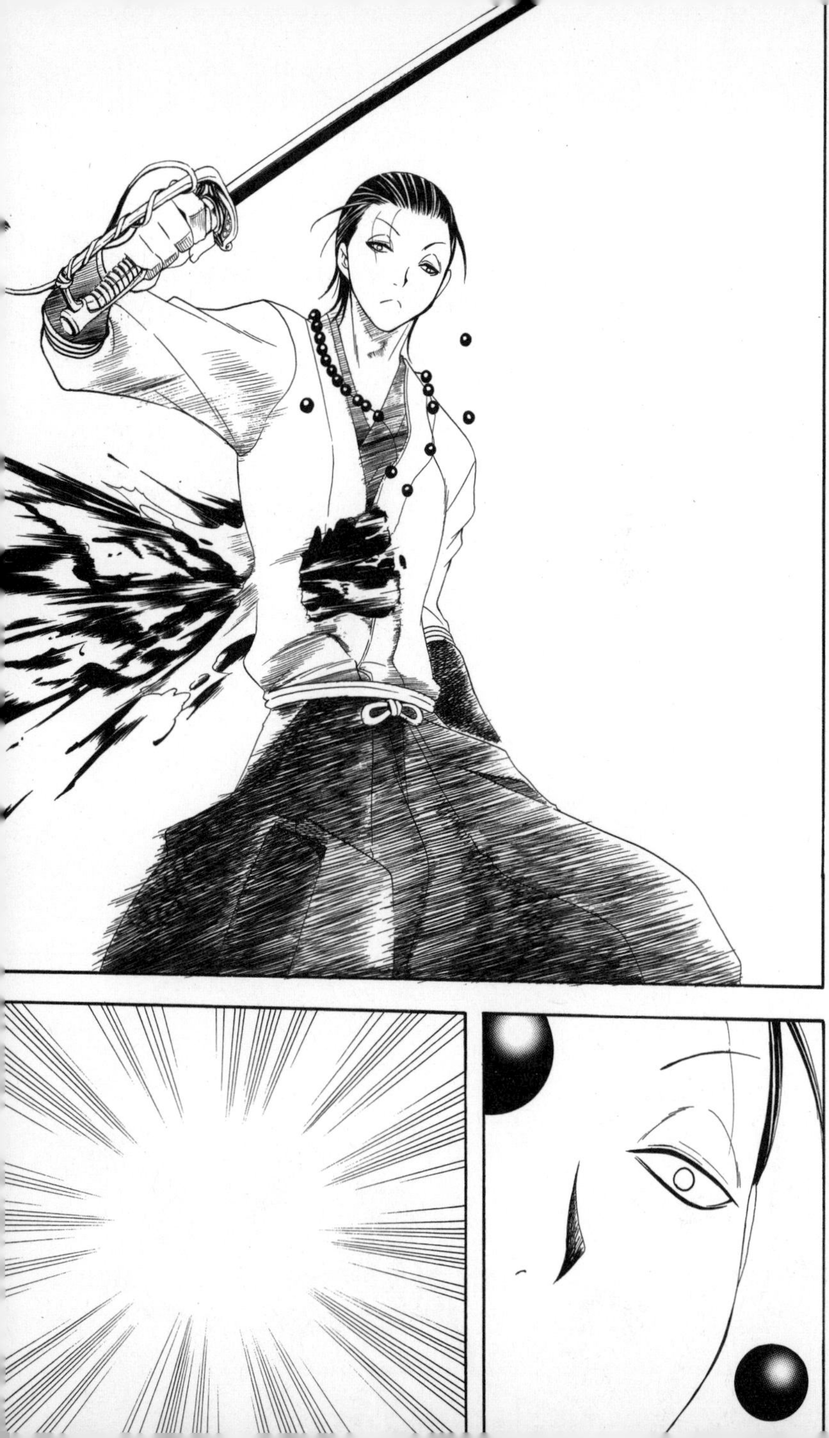

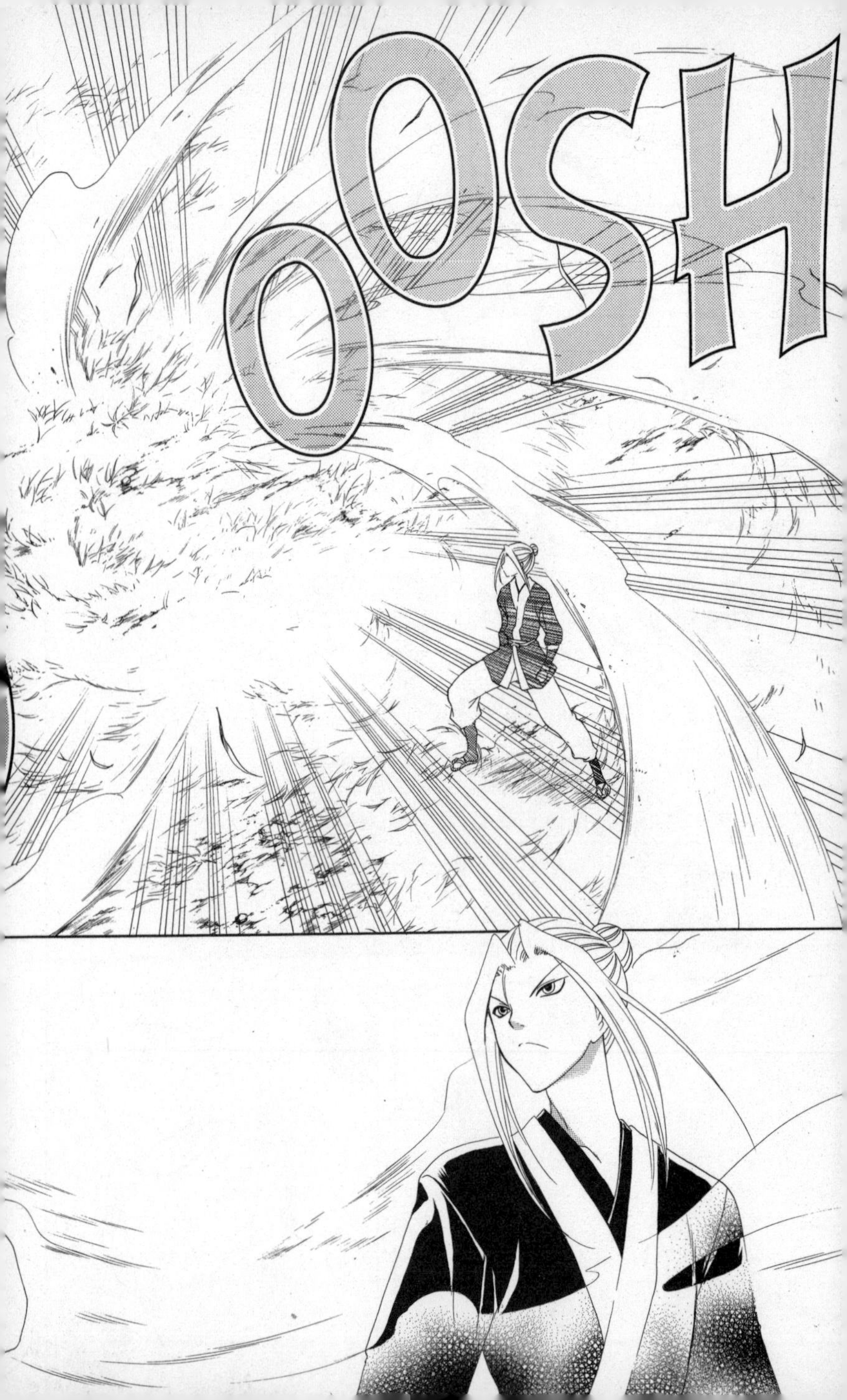
WOOSH

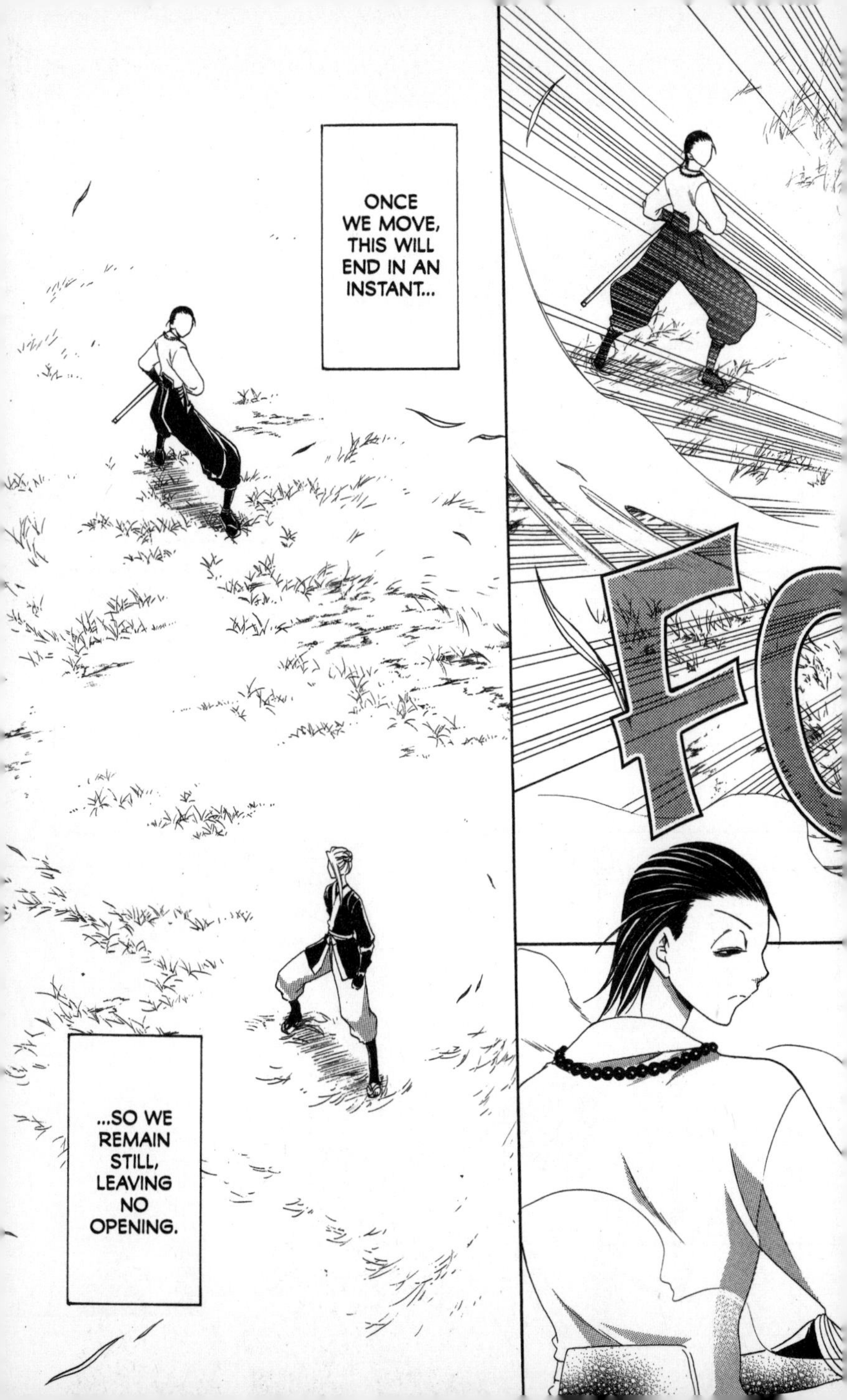
FO
ONCE WE MOVE, THIS WILL END IN AN INSTANT...
...SO WE REMAIN STILL, LEAVING NO OPENING.

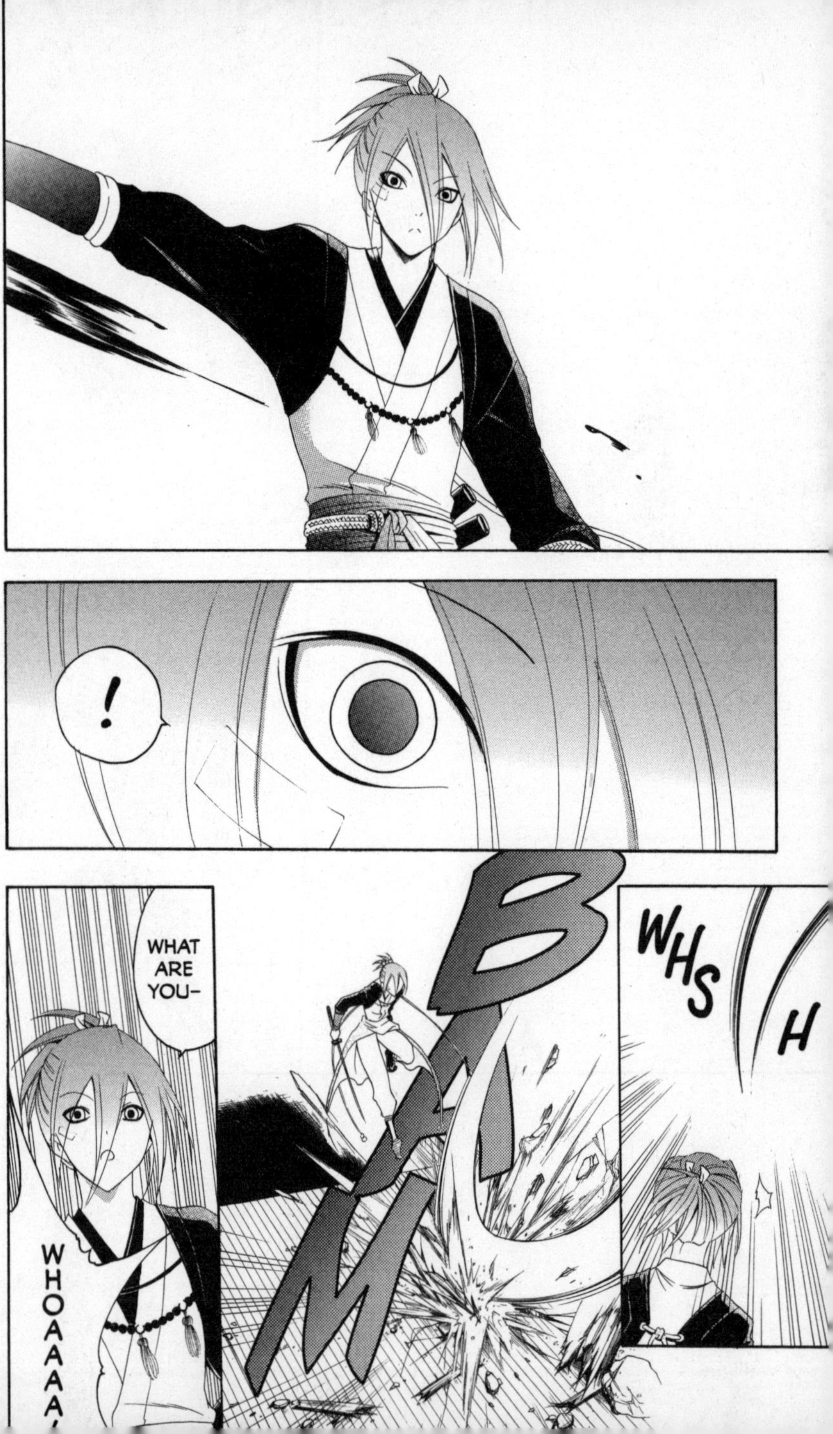
!
WHSH
BAM
WHAT ARE YOU-
WHOAAAA

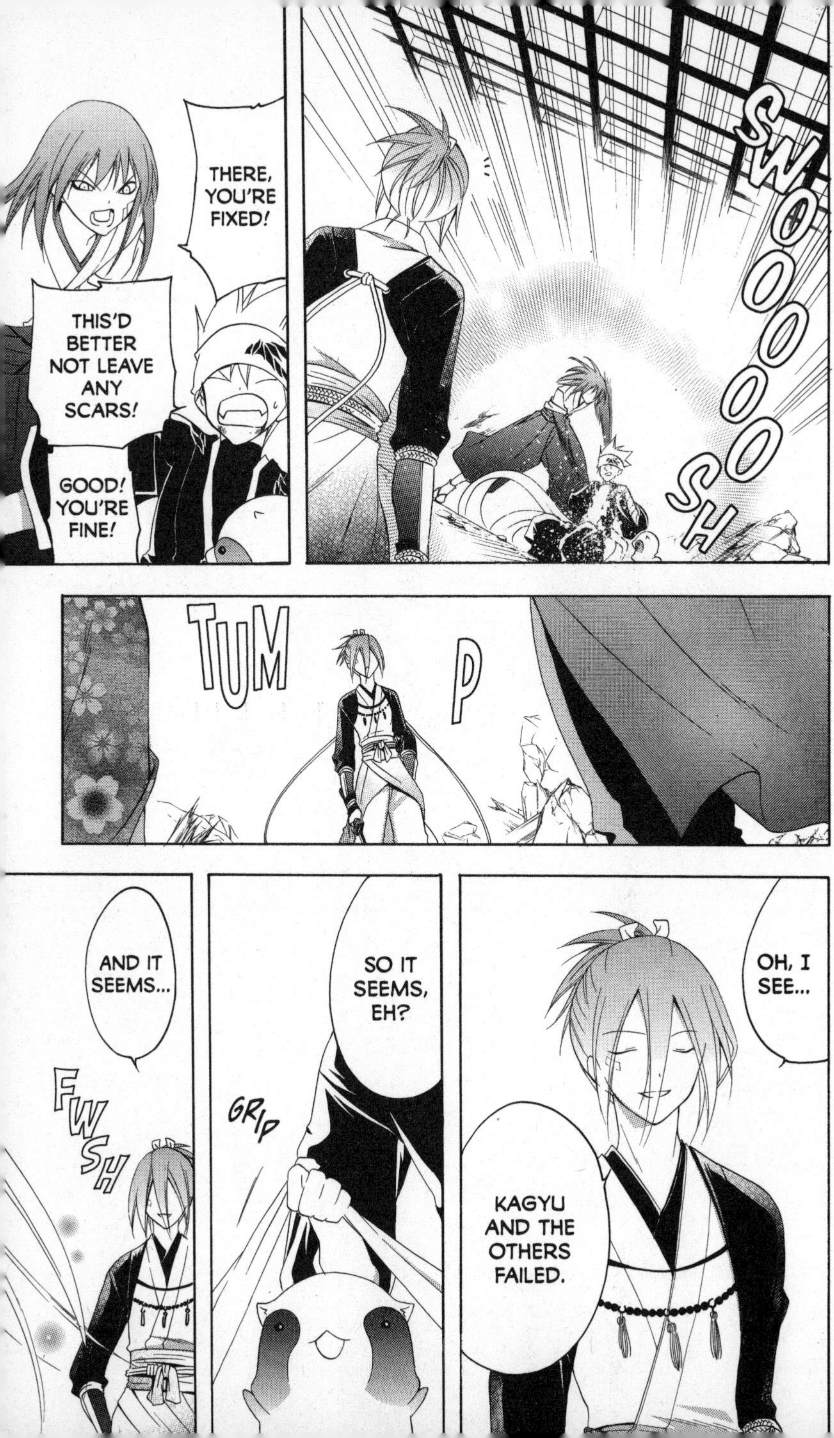
SWOOOOOOSH
THERE, YOU'RE FIXED!
THIS'D BETTER NOT LEAVE ANY SCARS!
GOOD! YOU'RE FINE!
TUMP
OH, I SEE...
KAGYU AND THE OTHERS FAILED.
SO IT SEEMS, EH?
GRIP
AND IT SEEMS...
FWSH

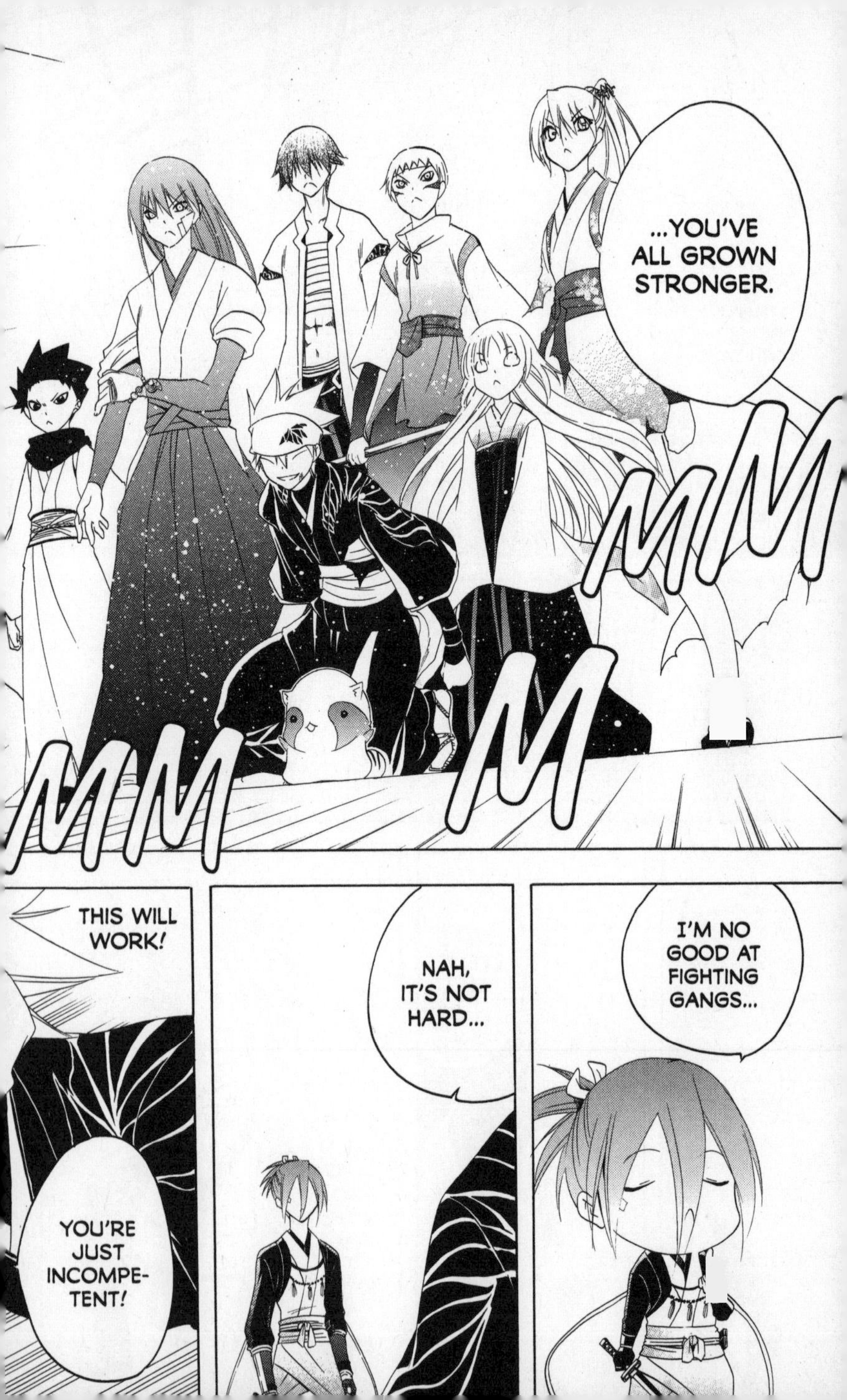
...YOU'VE ALL GROWN STRONGER.
MMMMMM
I'M NO GOOD AT FIGHTING GANGS...
NAH, IT'S NOT HARD...
THIS WILL WORK!
YOU'RE JUST INCOMPE-TENT!

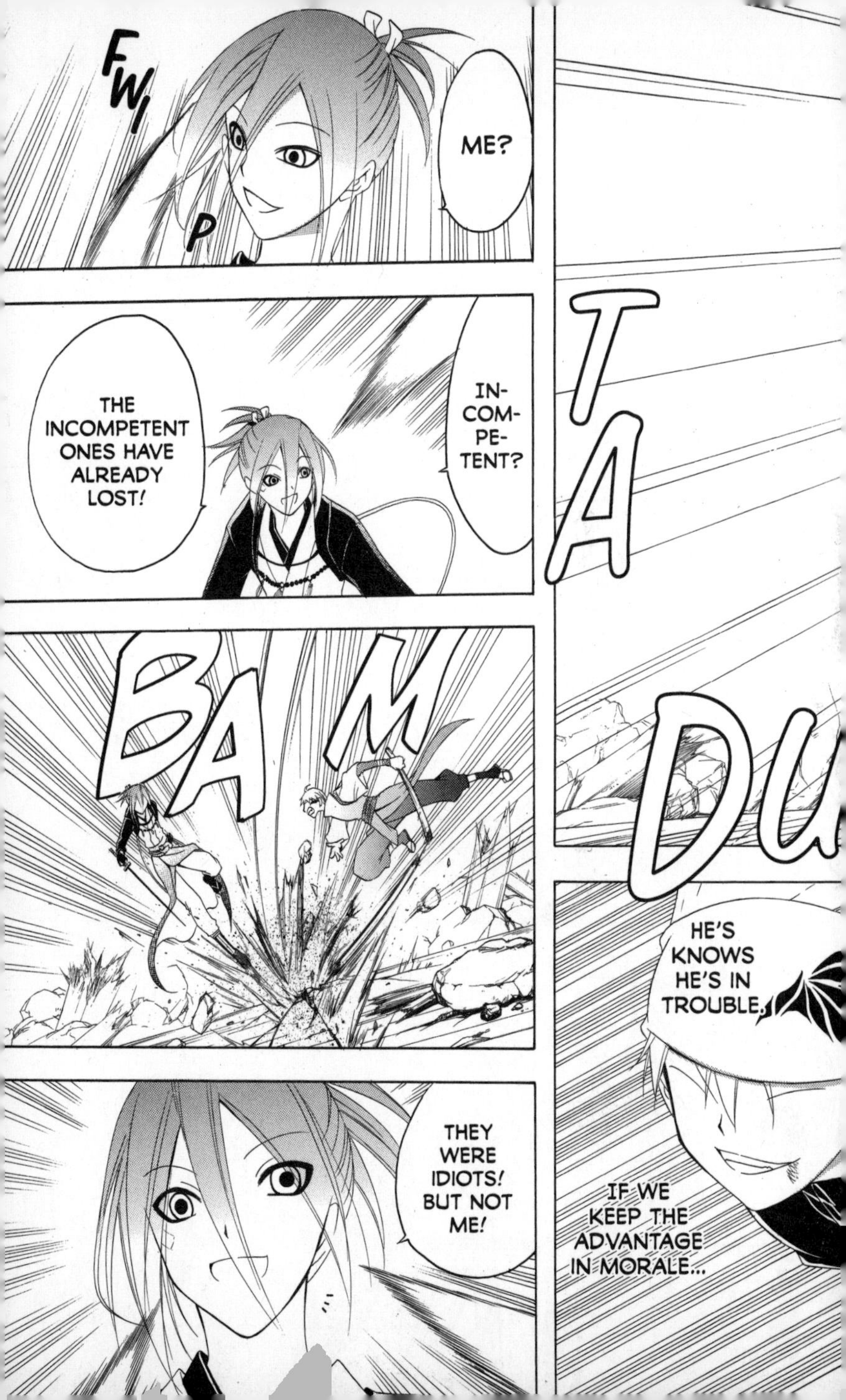
ME?
FWIP
TA
IN-COMPETENT?
THE INCOMPETENT ONES HAVE ALREADY LOST!
DU
BAM
HE'S KNOWS HE'S IN TROUBLE.
IF WE KEEP THE ADVANTAGE IN MORALE...
THEY WERE IDIOTS! BUT NOT ME!

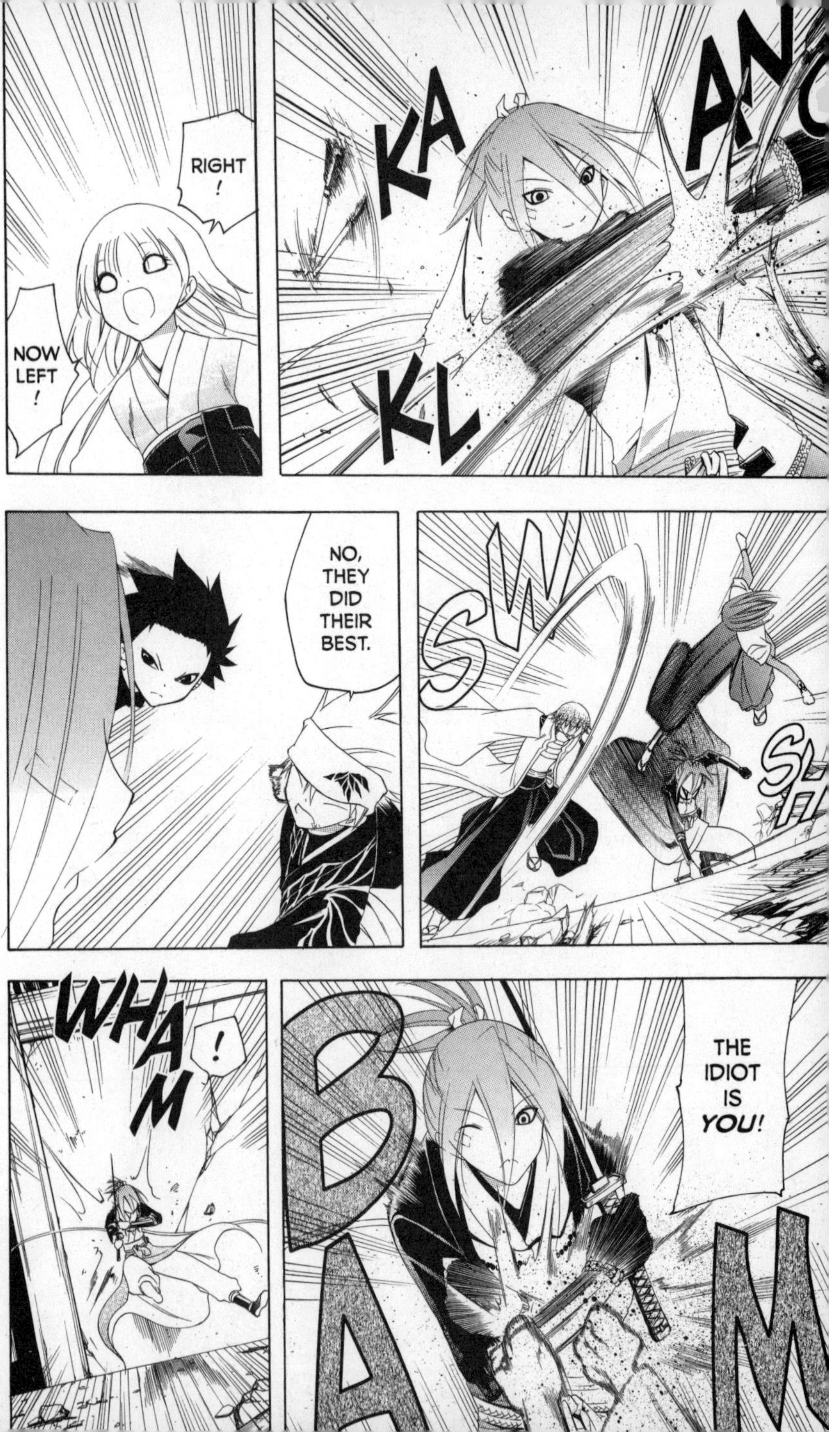

KA
AN
KL
RIGHT!
NOW LEFT!
SW
SH
NO, THEY DID THEIR BEST.
THE IDIOT IS *YOU*!
BAM
WHAM
!

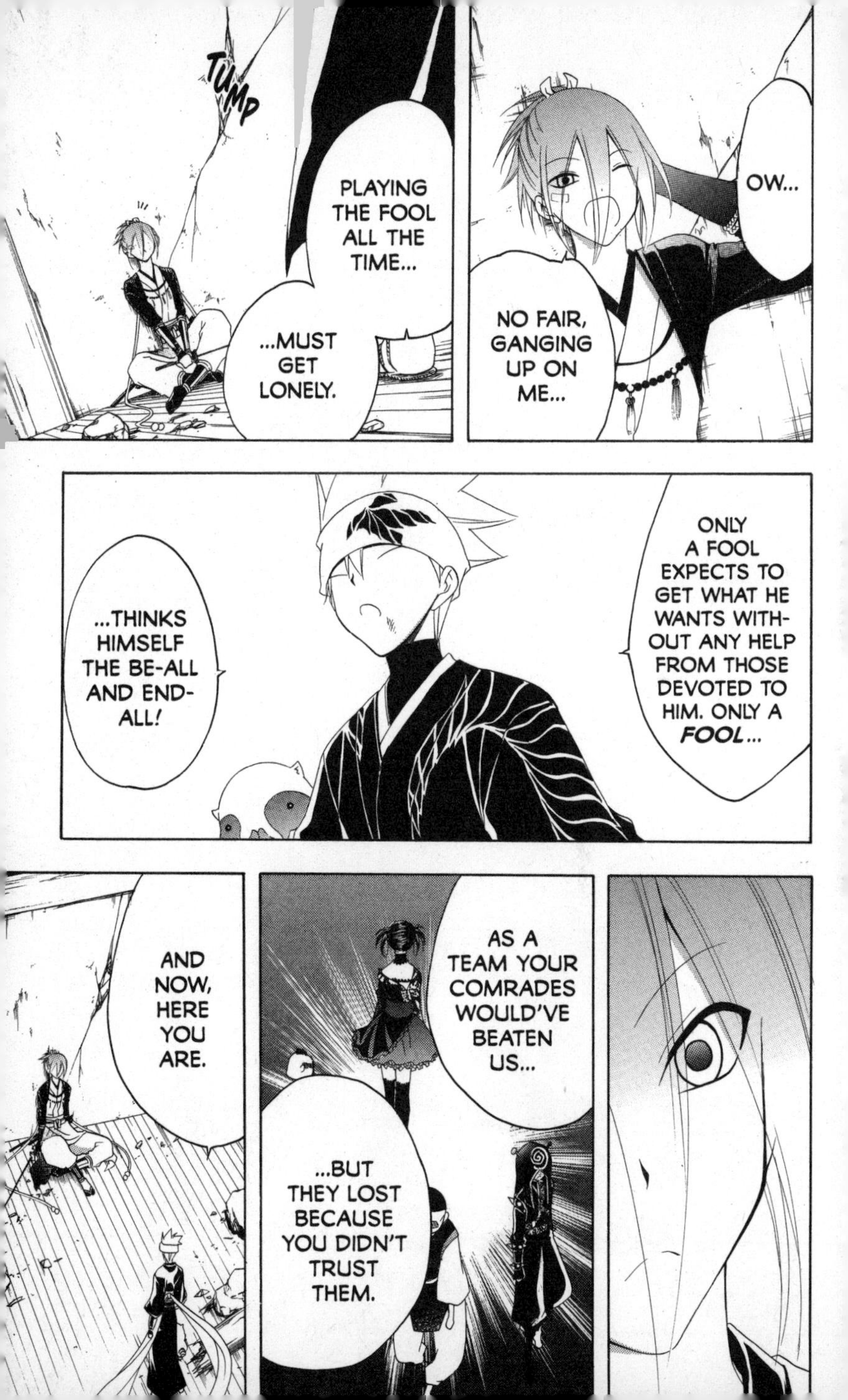
OW...
NO FAIR, GANGING UP ON ME...
PLAYING THE FOOL ALL THE TIME...
...MUST GET LONELY.
TUMP
ONLY A FOOL EXPECTS TO GET WHAT HE WANTS WITH-OUT ANY HELP FROM THOSE DEVOTED TO HIM. ONLY A ***FOOL***...
...THINKS HIMSELF THE BE-ALL AND END-ALL!
AS A TEAM YOUR COMRADES WOULD'VE BEATEN US...
...BUT THEY LOST BECAUSE YOU DIDN'T TRUST THEM.
AND NOW, HERE YOU ARE.

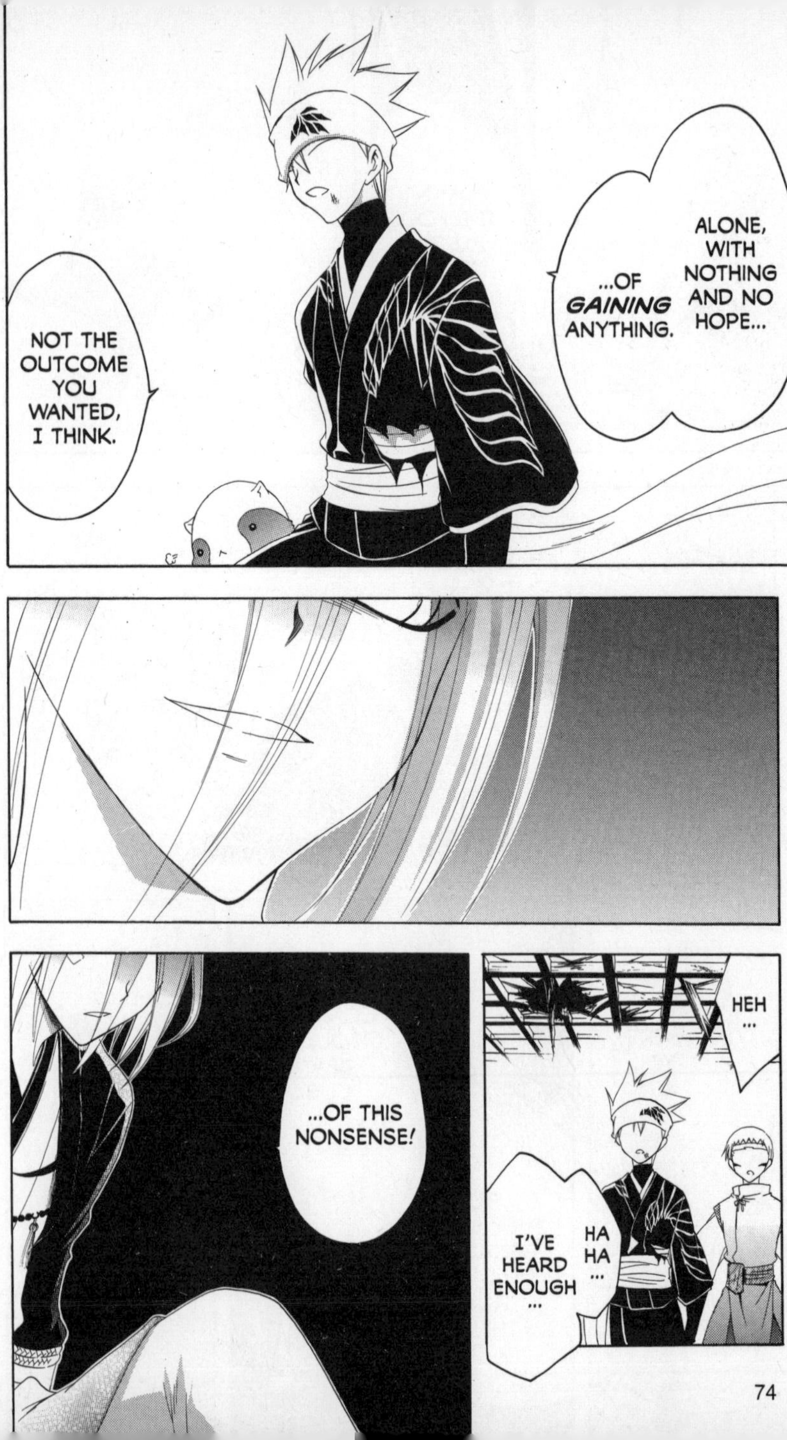
ALONE, WITH NOTHING AND NO HOPE...
...OF *GAINING* ANYTHING.
NOT THE OUTCOME YOU WANTED, I THINK.
HEH ...
HA HA ...
I'VE HEARD ENOUGH ...
...OF THIS NONSENSE!

Chapter 192
Serious

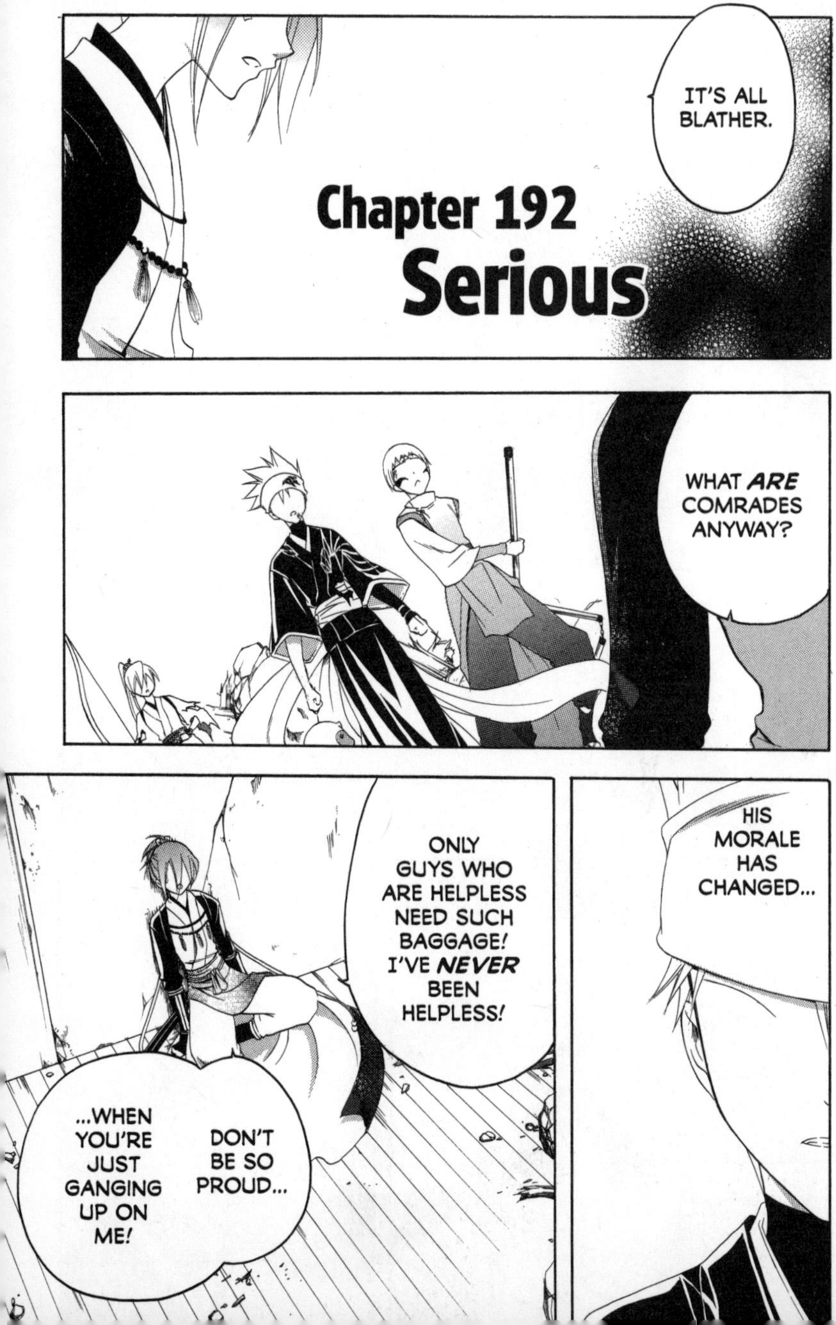
IT'S ALL BLATHER.
WHAT *ARE* COMRADES ANYWAY?
HIS MORALE HAS CHANGED...
ONLY GUYS WHO ARE HELPLESS NEED SUCH BAGGAGE! I'VE *NEVER* BEEN HELPLESS!
DON'T BE SO PROUD...
...WHEN YOU'RE JUST GANGING UP ON ME!

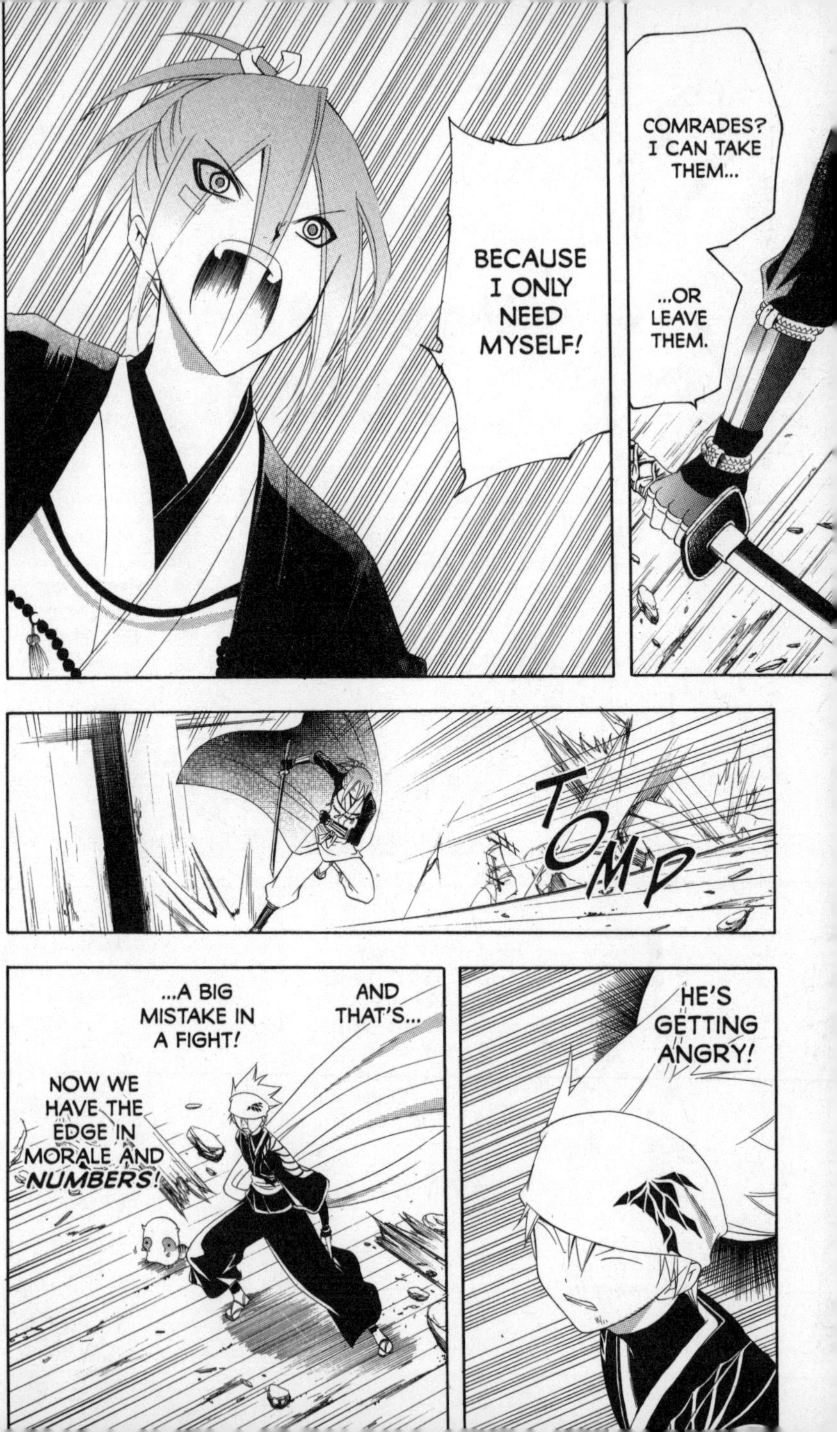
COMRADES? I CAN TAKE THEM...
...OR LEAVE THEM.
BECAUSE I ONLY NEED MYSELF!
TOMP
HE'S GETTING ANGRY!
AND THAT'S...
...A BIG MISTAKE IN A FIGHT!
NOW WE HAVE THE EDGE IN MORALE AND NUMBERS!

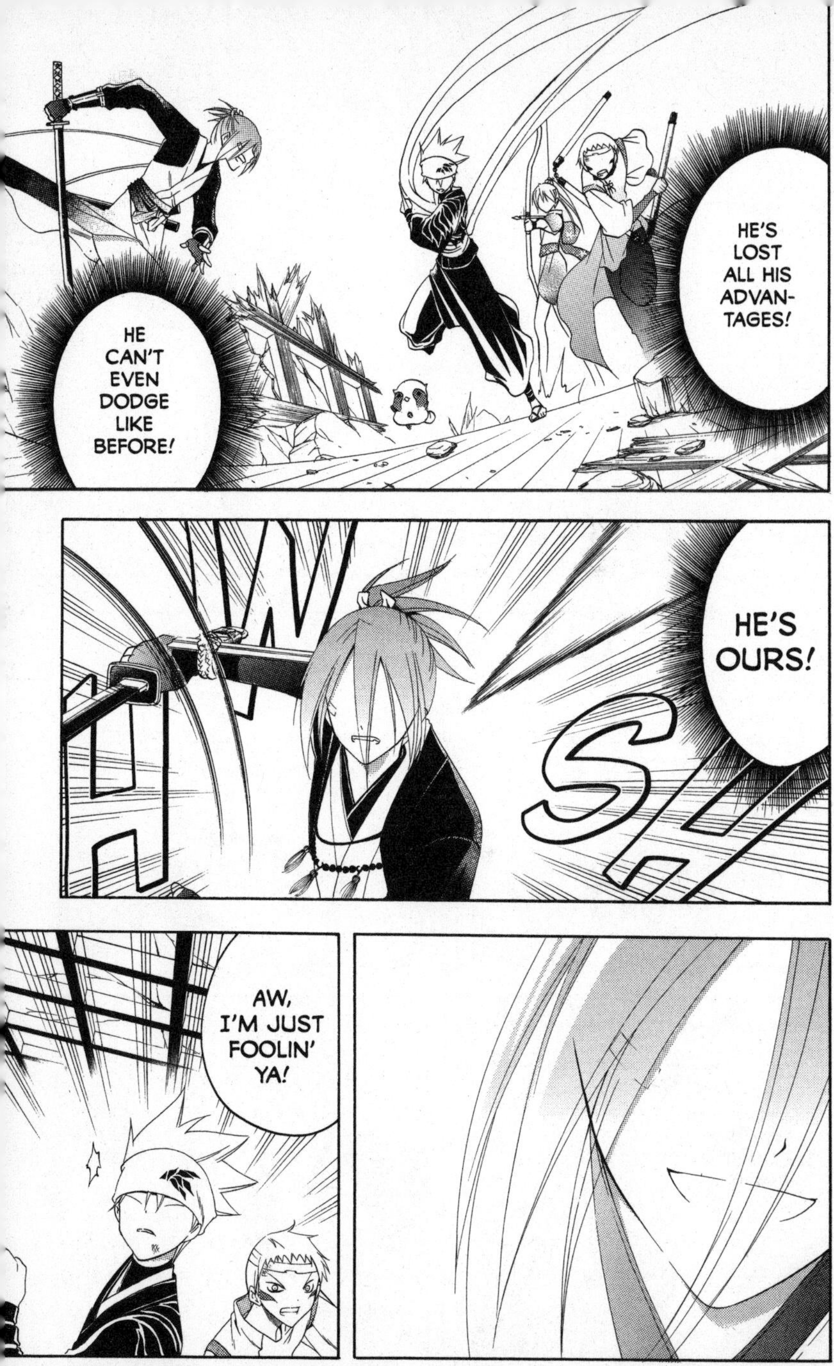
HE'S LOST ALL HIS ADVAN-TAGES!
HE CAN'T EVEN DODGE LIKE BEFORE!
HE'S OURS!
AW, I'M JUST FOOLIN' YA!

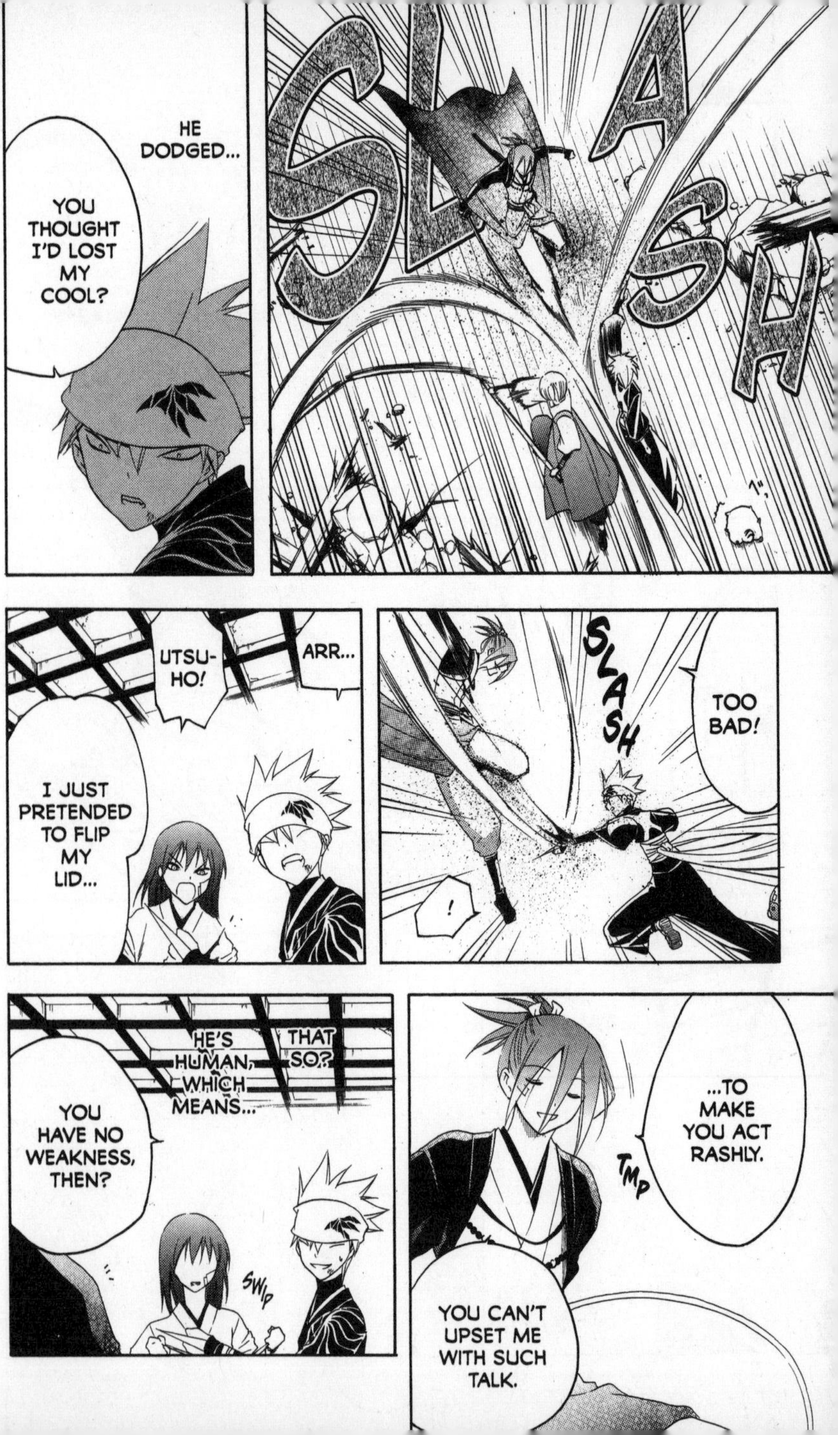
SLASH
HE DODGED...
YOU THOUGHT I'D LOST MY COOL?
SLASH
TOO BAD!
!
ARR...
UTSU-HO!
I JUST PRETENDED TO FLIP MY LID...
...TO MAKE YOU ACT RASHLY.
TMP
YOU CAN'T UPSET ME WITH SUCH TALK.
THAT SO?
HE'S HUMAN, WHICH MEANS...
YOU HAVE NO WEAKNESS, THEN?
SWIP

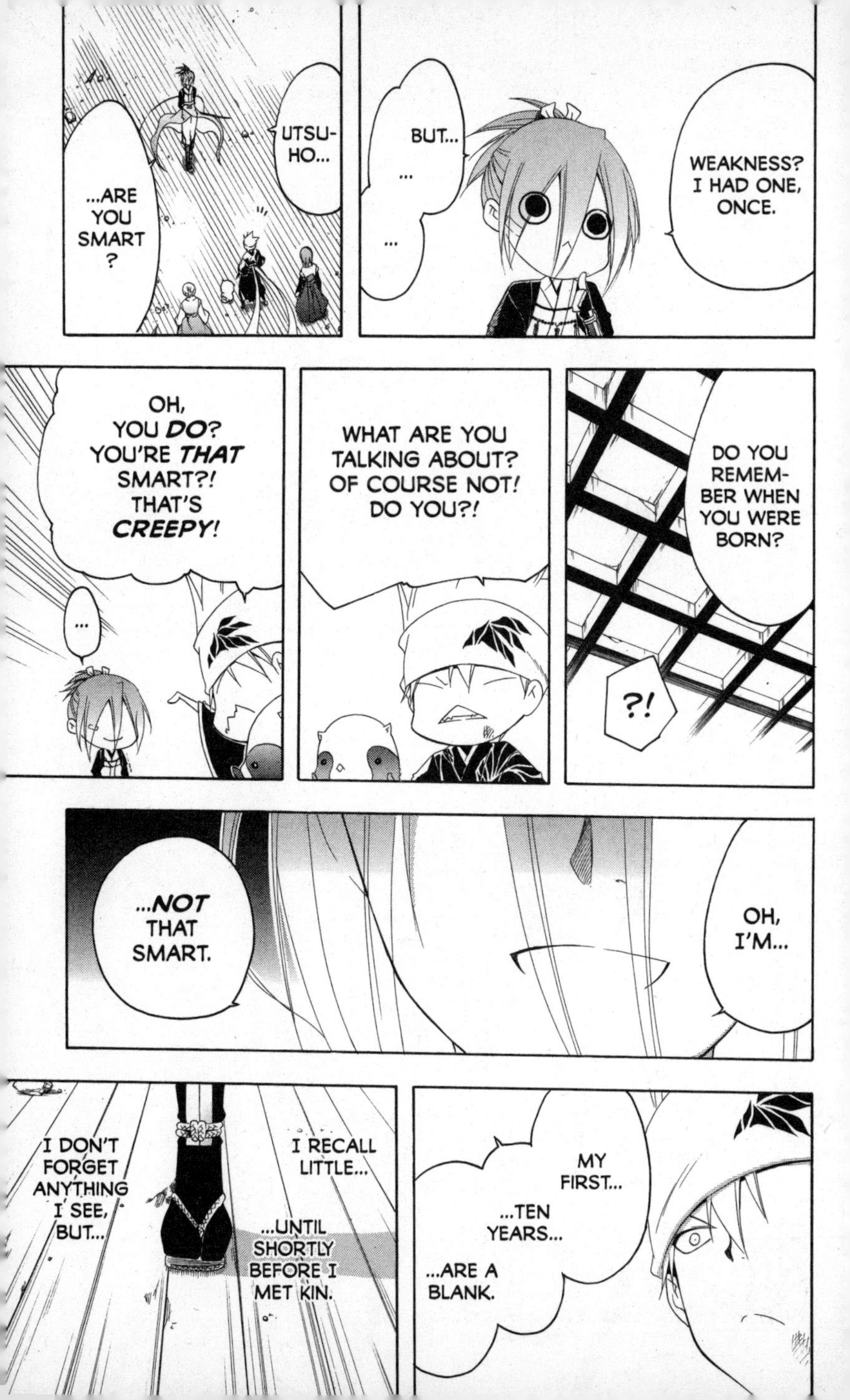
WEAKNESS? I HAD ONE, ONCE.
BUT...
...
...
UTSU-HO...
...ARE YOU SMART?
DO YOU REMEMBER WHEN YOU WERE BORN?
?!
WHAT ARE YOU TALKING ABOUT? OF COURSE NOT! DO YOU?!
OH, YOU *DO*? YOU'RE *THAT* SMART?! THAT'S *CREEPY*!
...
OH, I'M...
...*NOT* THAT SMART.
MY FIRST...
...TEN YEARS...
...ARE A BLANK.
I DON'T FORGET ANYTHING I SEE, BUT...
I RECALL LITTLE...
...UNTIL SHORTLY BEFORE I MET KIN.

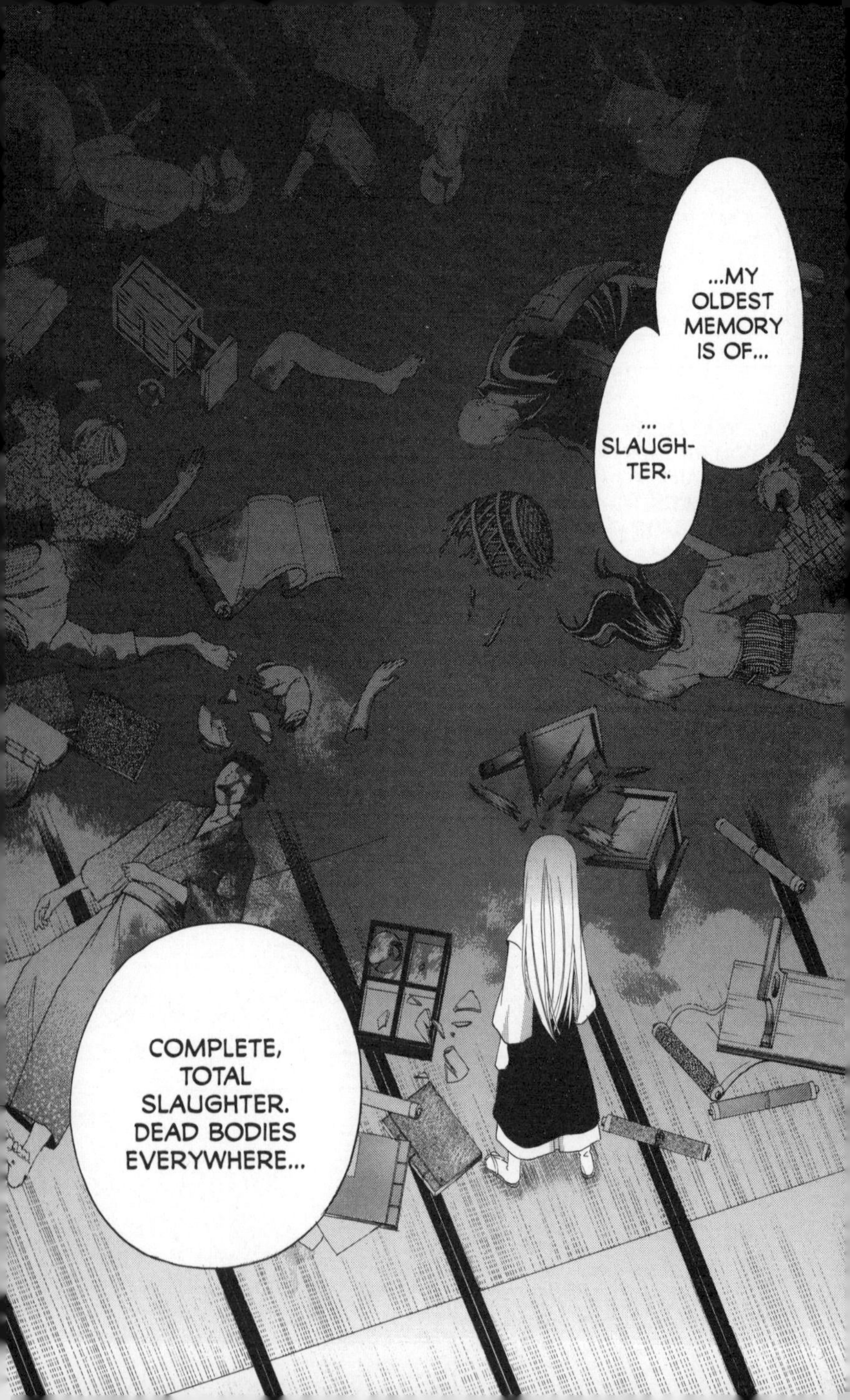
...MY OLDEST MEMORY IS OF...
... SLAUGH-TER.
COMPLETE, TOTAL SLAUGHTER. DEAD BODIES EVERYWHERE...

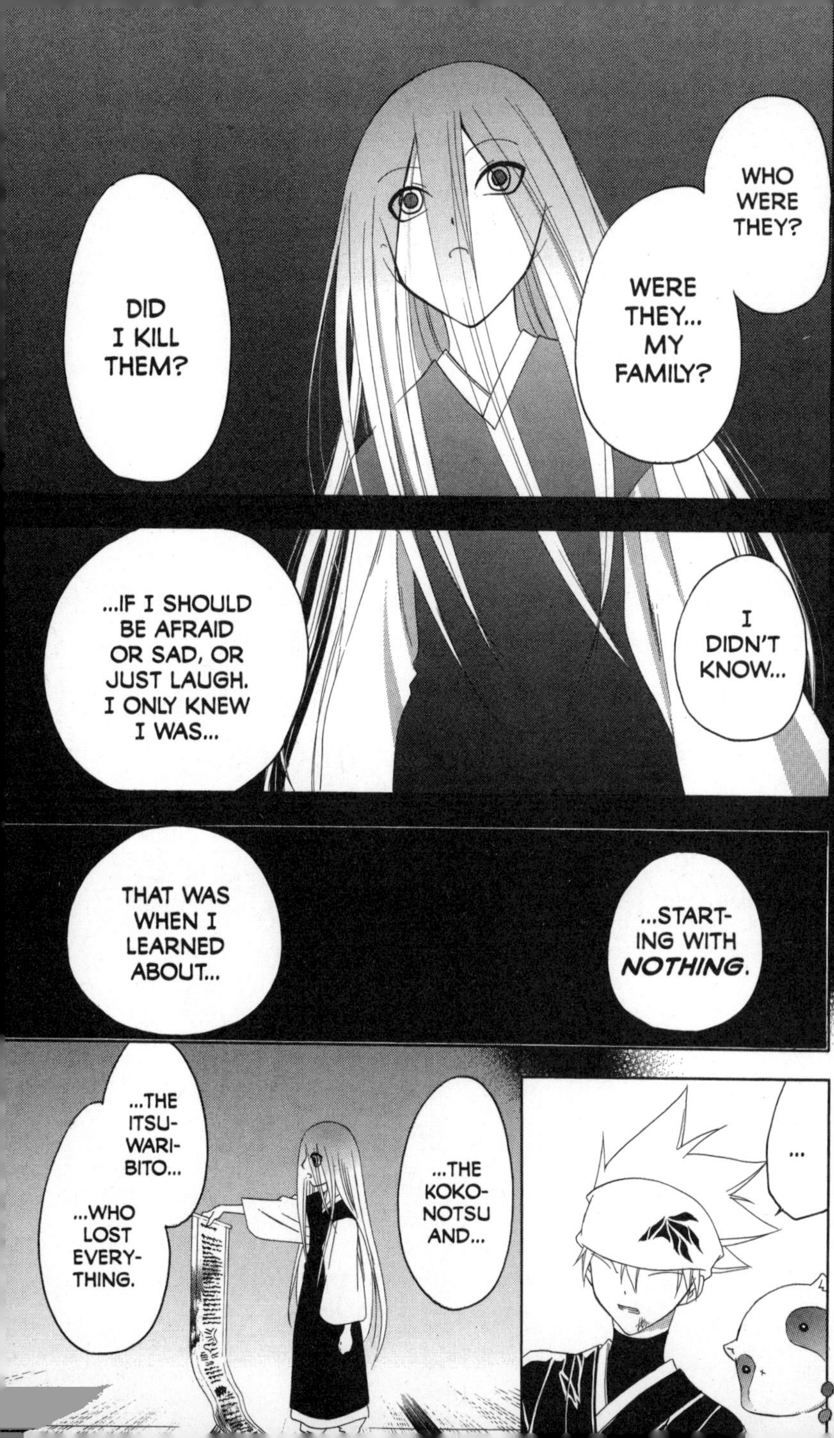
WHO WERE THEY?
WERE THEY... MY FAMILY?
DID I KILL THEM?
I DIDN'T KNOW...
...IF I SHOULD BE AFRAID OR SAD, OR JUST LAUGH. I ONLY KNEW I WAS...
...START-ING WITH ***NOTHING***.
THAT WAS WHEN I LEARNED ABOUT...
...
...THE KOKO-NOTSU AND...
...THE ITSU-WARI-BITO...
...WHO LOST EVERY-THING.

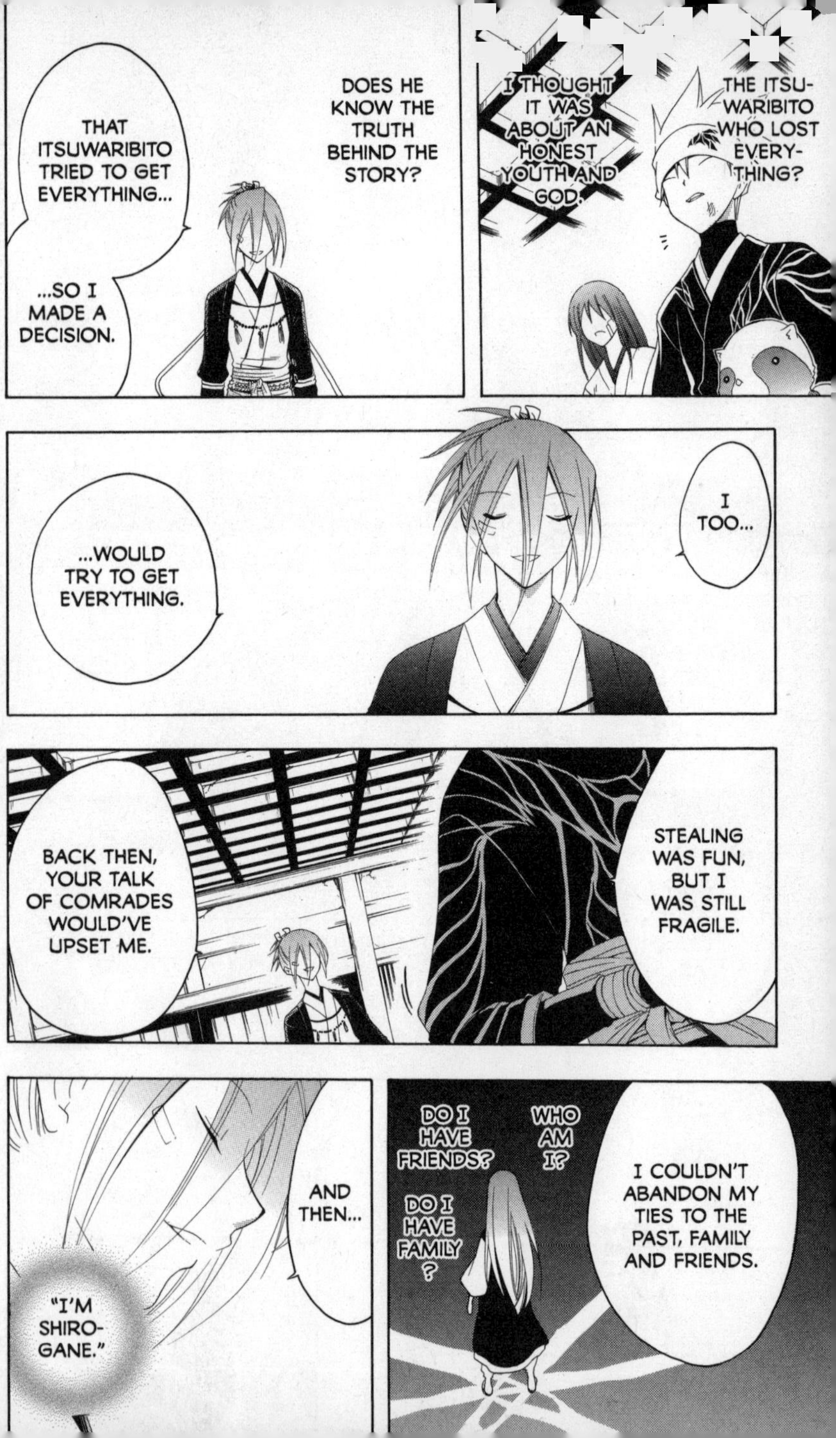
THE ITSU-WARIBITO WHO LOST EVERY-THING?
I THOUGHT IT WAS ABOUT AN HONEST YOUTH AND GOD.
DOES HE KNOW THE TRUTH BEHIND THE STORY?
THAT ITSUWARIBITO TRIED TO GET EVERYTHING...
...SO I MADE A DECISION.
I TOO...
...WOULD TRY TO GET EVERYTHING.
STEALING WAS FUN, BUT I WAS STILL FRAGILE.
BACK THEN, YOUR TALK OF COMRADES WOULD'VE UPSET ME.
I COULDN'T ABANDON MY TIES TO THE PAST, FAMILY AND FRIENDS.
WHO AM I?
DO I HAVE FRIENDS?
DO I HAVE FAMILY?
AND THEN...
"I'M SHIRO-GANE."

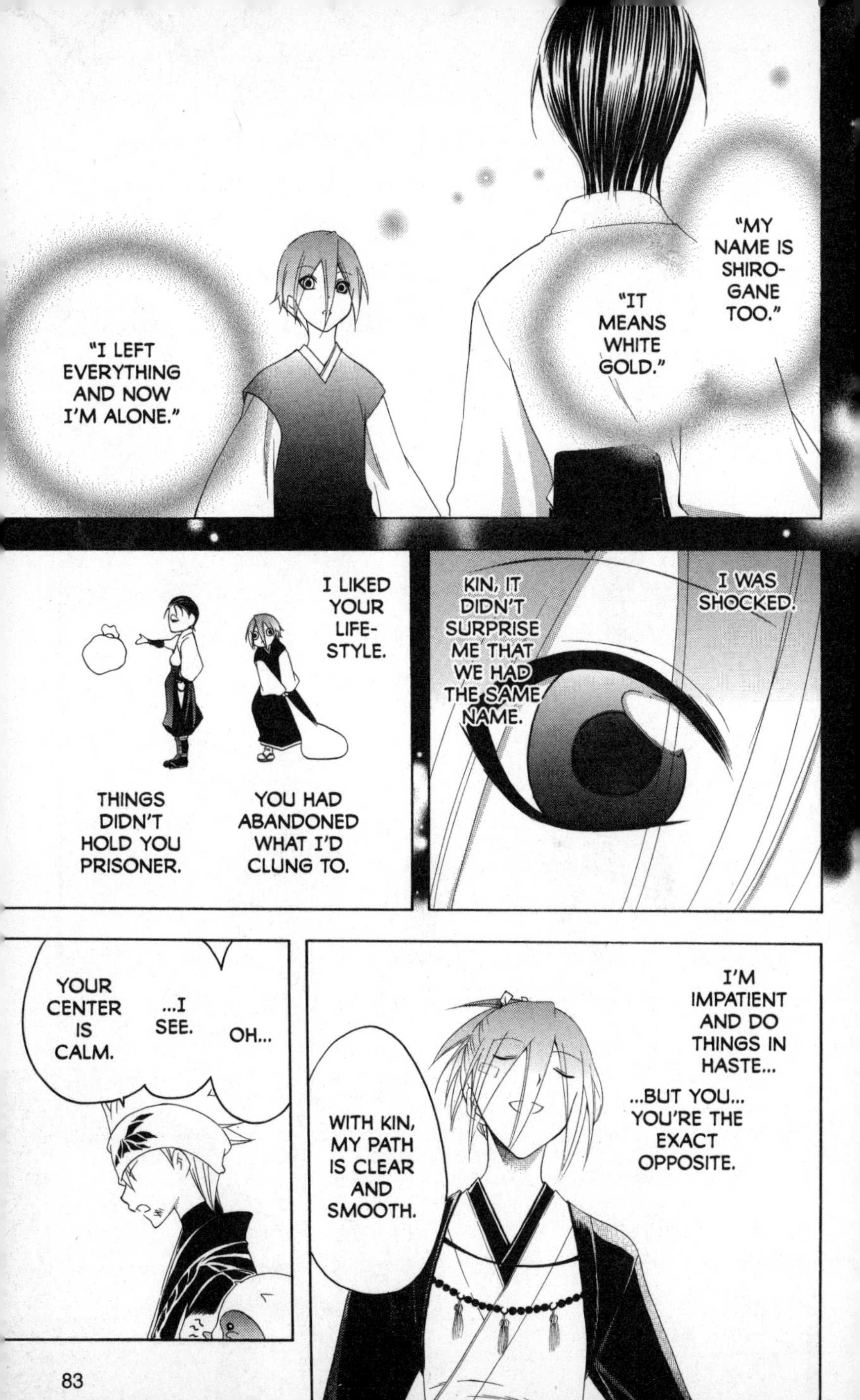
"MY NAME IS SHIROGANE TOO."
"IT MEANS WHITE GOLD."
"I LEFT EVERYTHING AND NOW I'M ALONE."
I WAS SHOCKED.
KIN, IT DIDN'T SURPRISE ME THAT WE HAD THE SAME NAME.
I LIKED YOUR LIFE-STYLE.
YOU HAD ABANDONED WHAT I'D CLUNG TO.
THINGS DIDN'T HOLD YOU PRISONER.
I'M IMPATIENT AND DO THINGS IN HASTE...
...BUT YOU... YOU'RE THE EXACT OPPOSITE.
WITH KIN, MY PATH IS CLEAR AND SMOOTH.
OH...
...I SEE.
YOUR CENTER IS CALM.

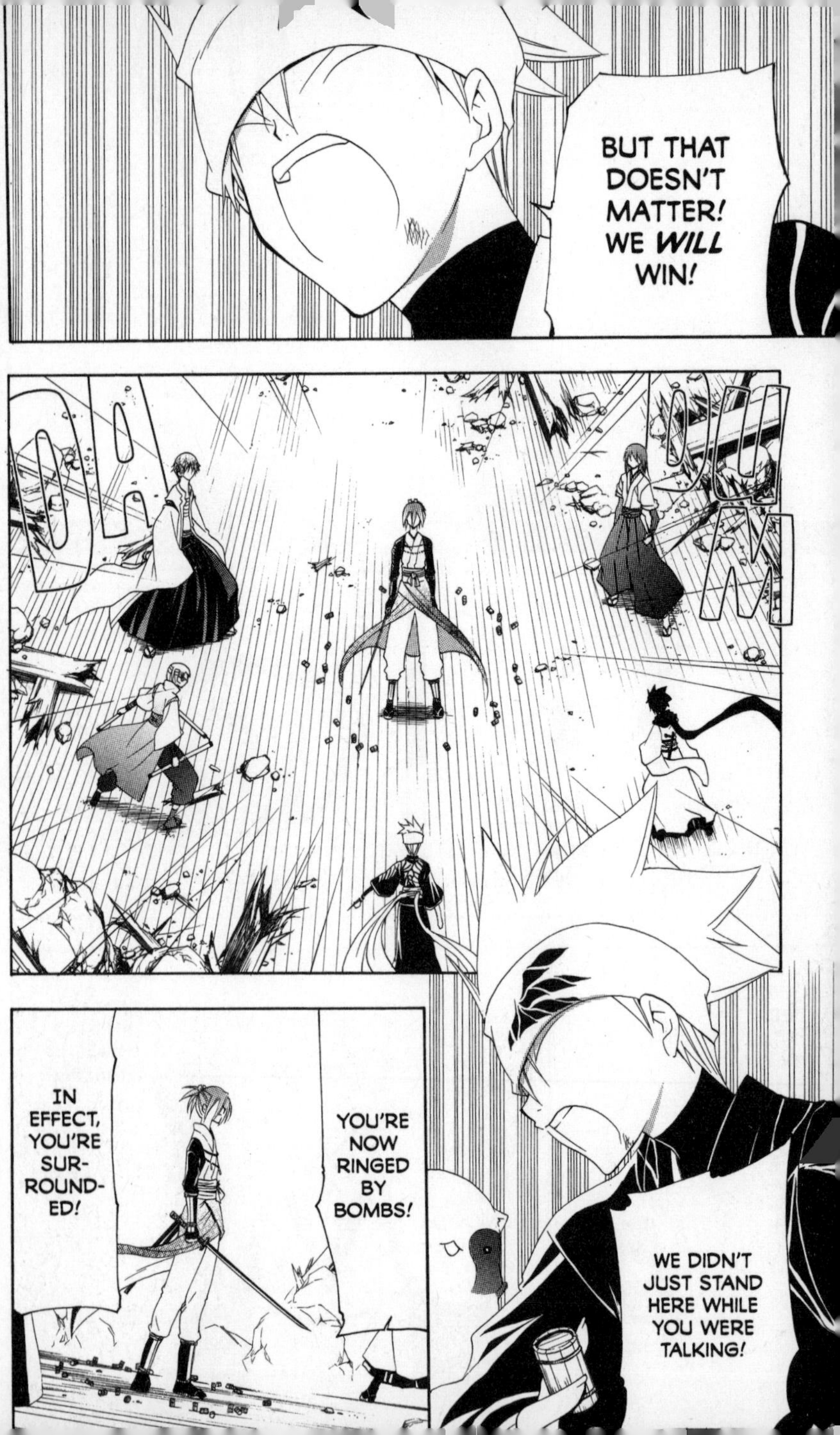
BUT THAT DOESN'T MATTER! WE *WILL* WIN!
WE DIDN'T JUST STAND HERE WHILE YOU WERE TALKING!
YOU'RE NOW RINGED BY BOMBS!
IN EFFECT, YOU'RE SUR-ROUND-ED!

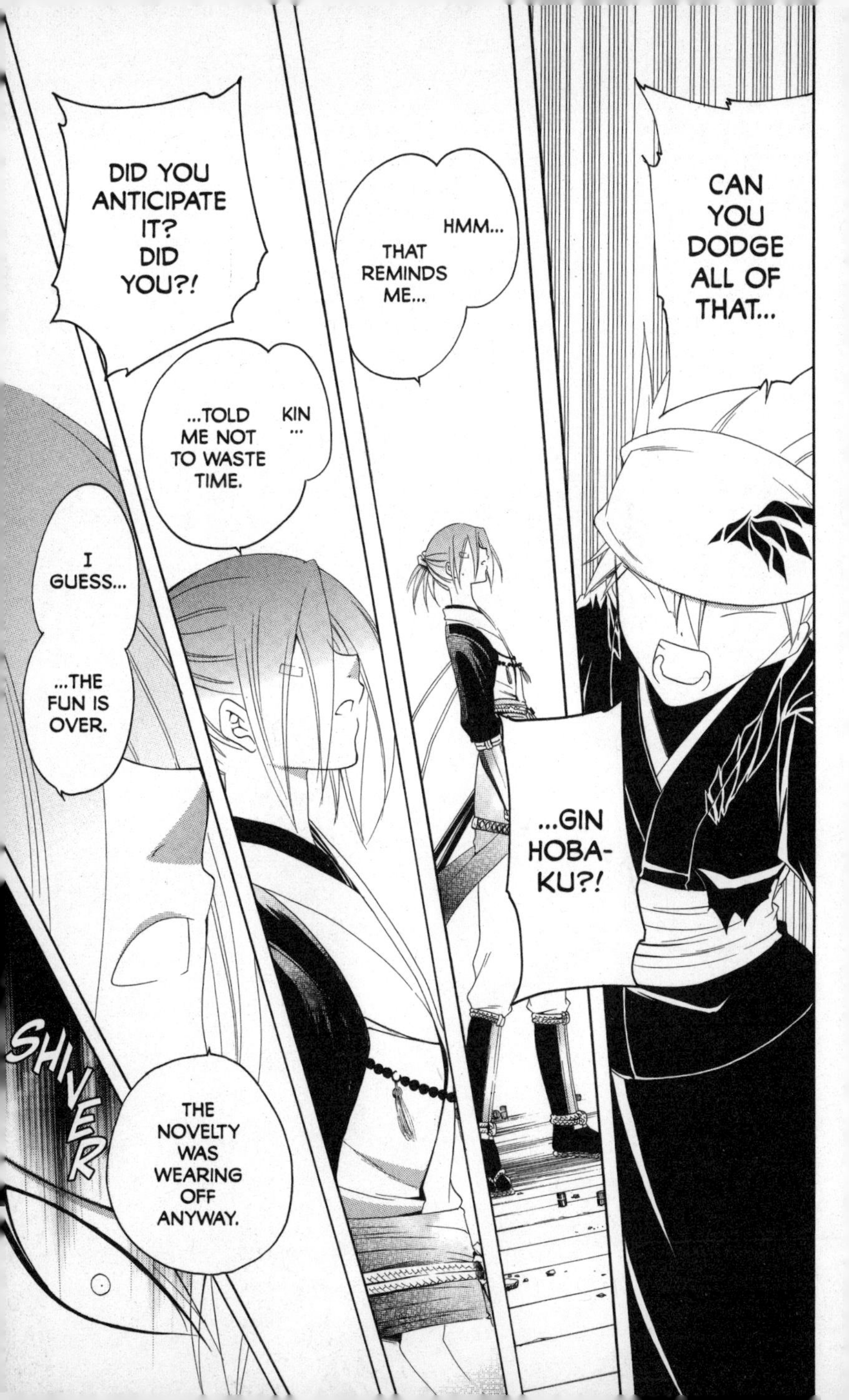
CAN YOU DODGE ALL OF THAT...
...GIN HOBAKU?!
HMM...
THAT REMINDS ME...
KIN...
...TOLD ME NOT TO WASTE TIME.
DID YOU ANTICIPATE IT? DID YOU?!
I GUESS...
...THE FUN IS OVER.
SHIVER
THE NOVELTY WAS WEARING OFF ANYWAY.

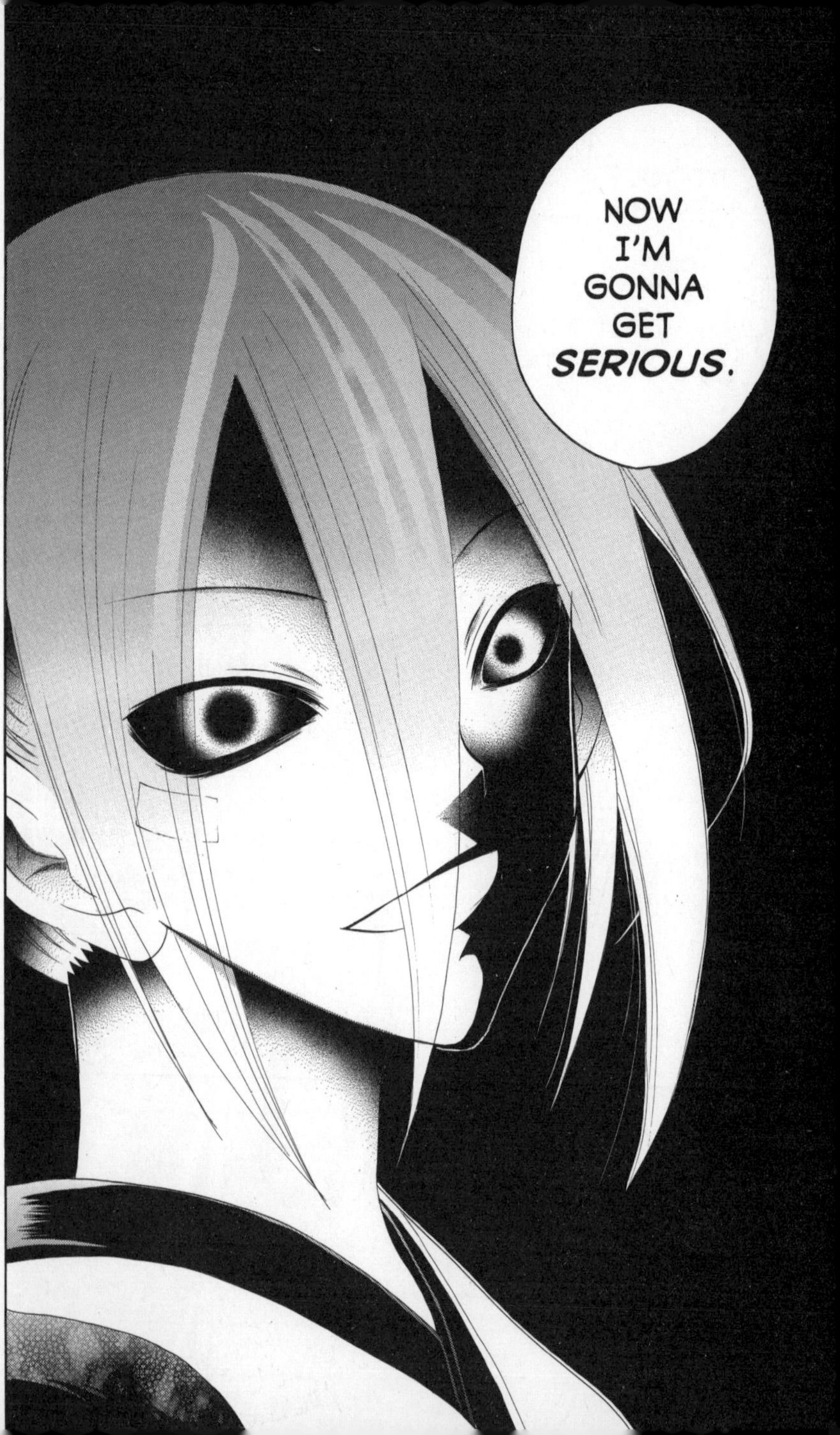
NOW I'M GONNA GET *SERIOUS*.

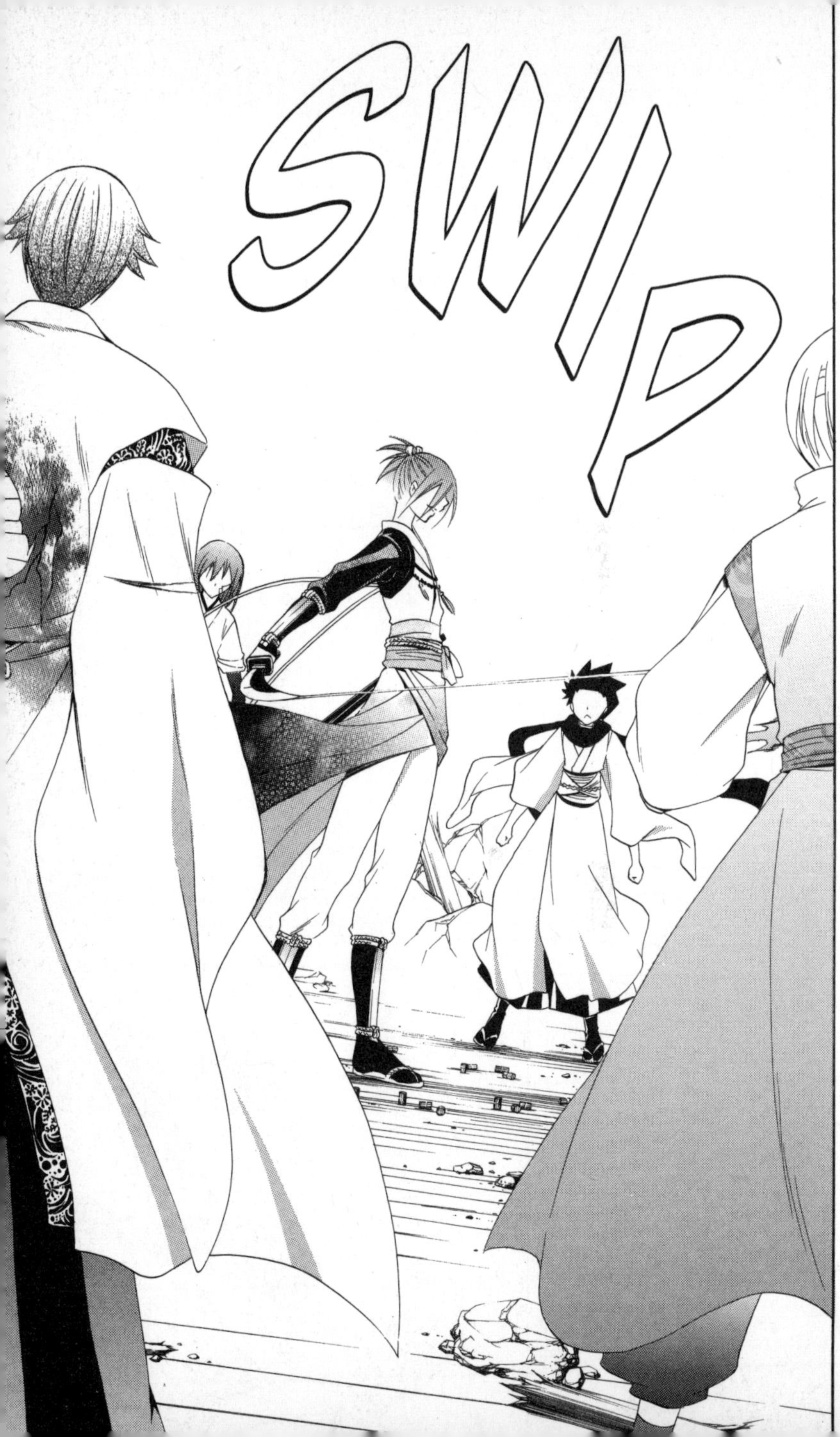
SWIP

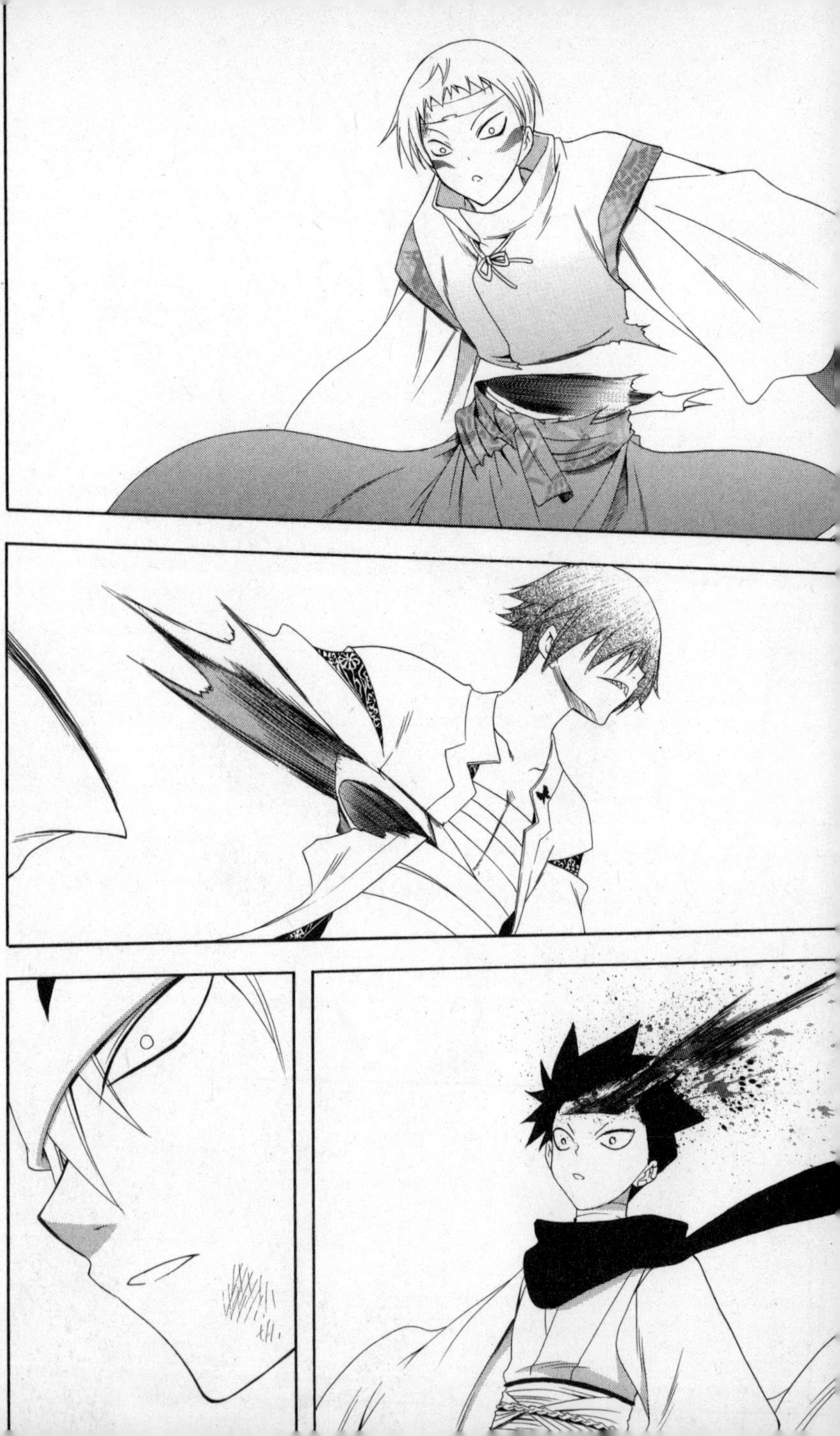

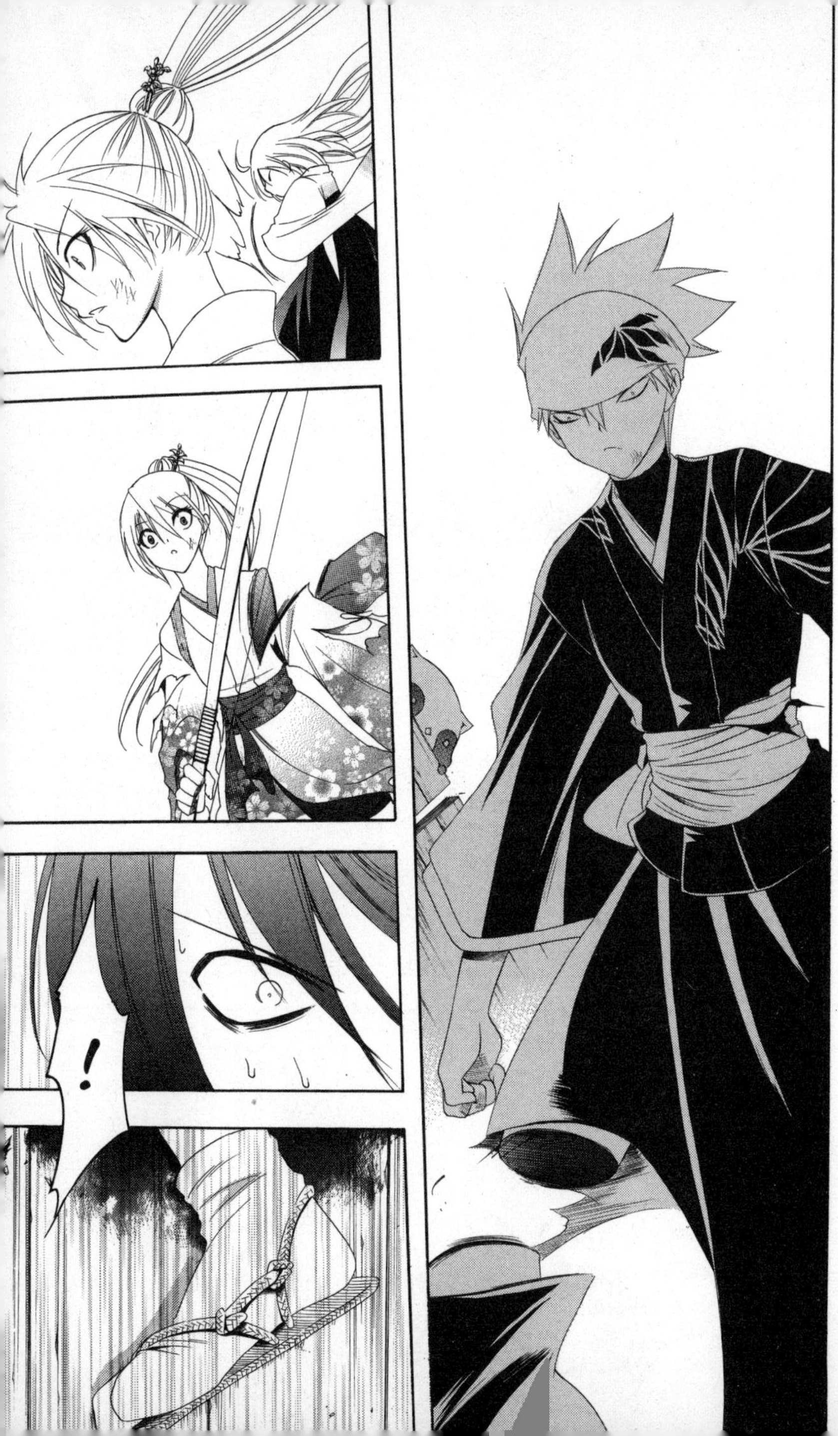
!

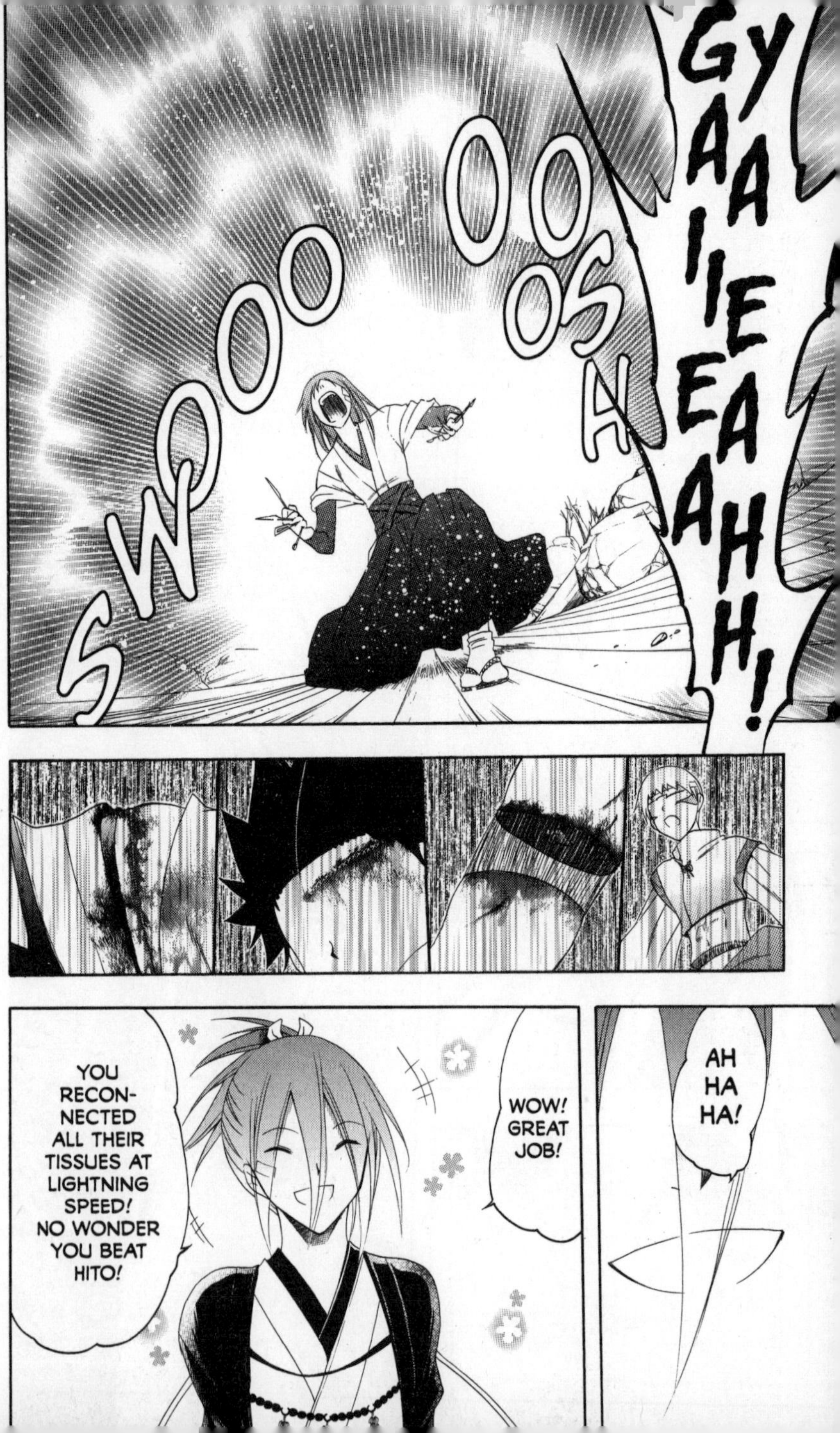
GYAAIIEEAAHH!
SWOOOOOOOSH
AH HA HA!
WOW! GREAT JOB!
YOU RECONNECTED ALL THEIR TISSUES AT LIGHTNING SPEED! NO WONDER YOU BEAT HITO!

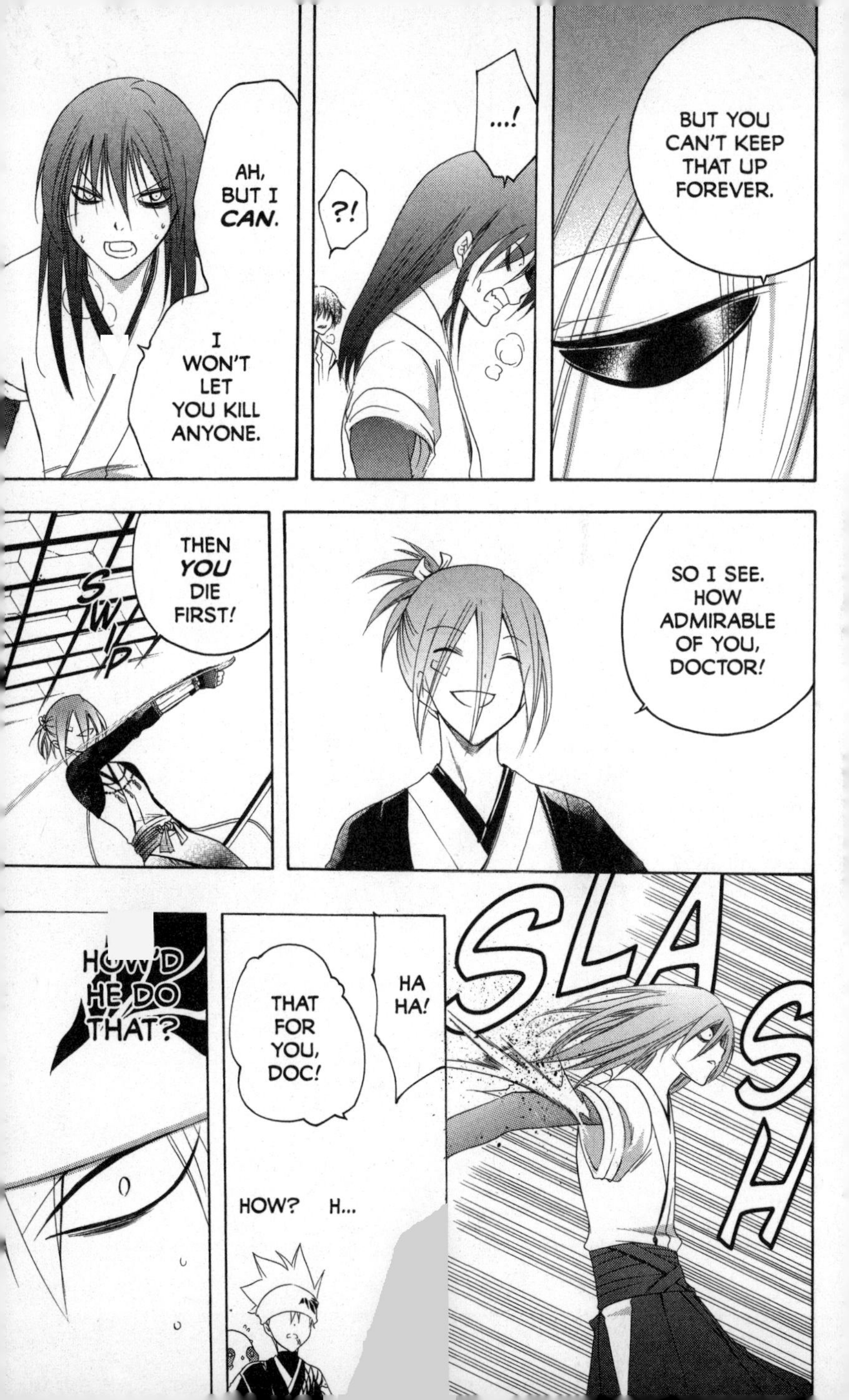
BUT YOU CAN'T KEEP THAT UP FOREVER.
...!
?!
AH, BUT I *CAN*.
I WON'T LET YOU KILL ANYONE.
SO I SEE. HOW ADMIRABLE OF YOU, DOCTOR!
THEN *YOU* DIE FIRST!
SWIP
SLASH
HA HA!
THAT FOR YOU, DOC!
HOW? H...
HOW'D HE DO THAT?

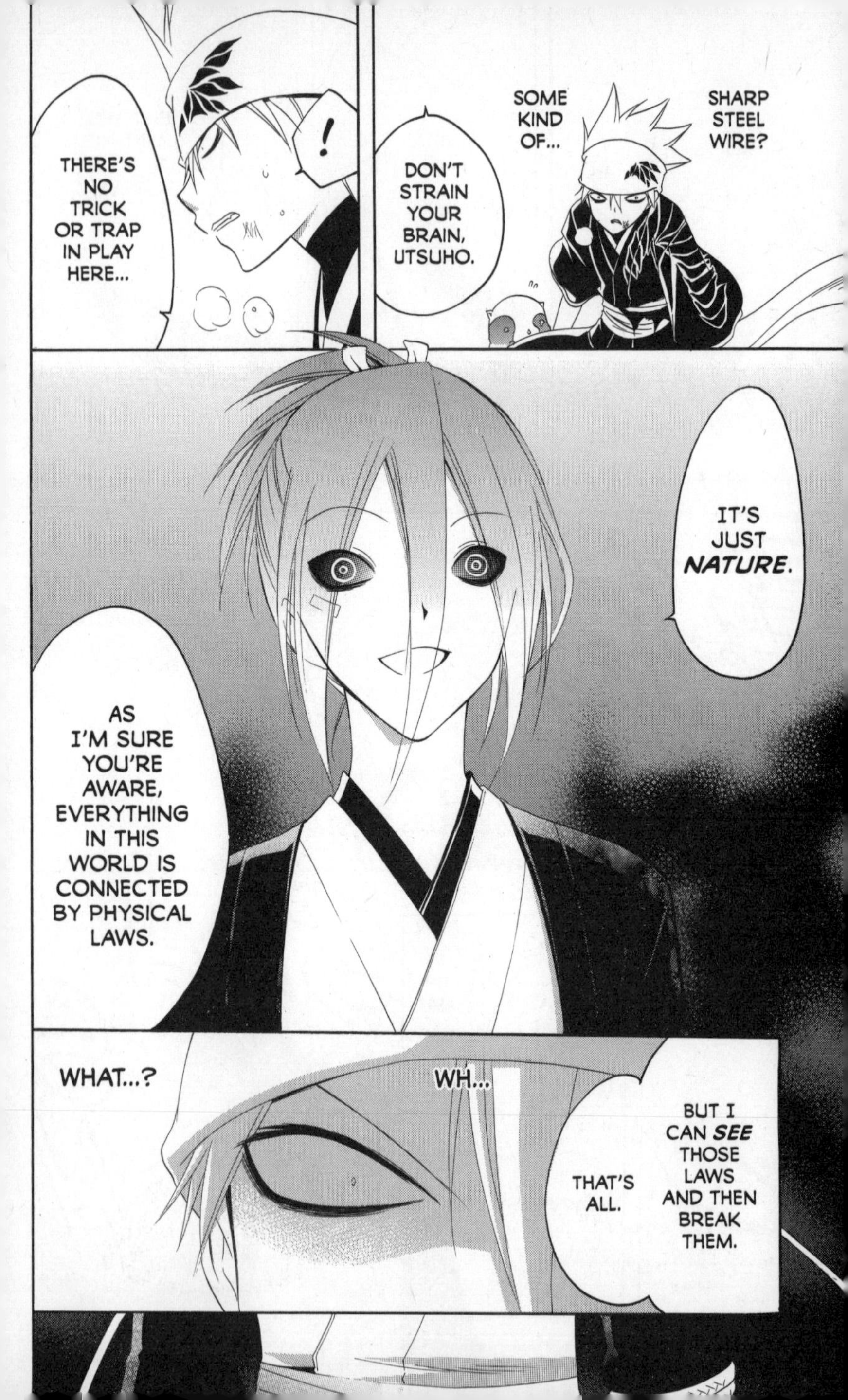

SOME KIND OF...
SHARP STEEL WIRE?
DON'T STRAIN YOUR BRAIN, UTSUHO.
!
THERE'S NO TRICK OR TRAP IN PLAY HERE...
IT'S JUST *NATURE*.
AS I'M SURE YOU'RE AWARE, EVERYTHING IN THIS WORLD IS CONNECTED BY PHYSICAL LAWS.
BUT I CAN *SEE* THOSE LAWS AND THEN BREAK THEM.
THAT'S ALL.
WH...
WHAT...?

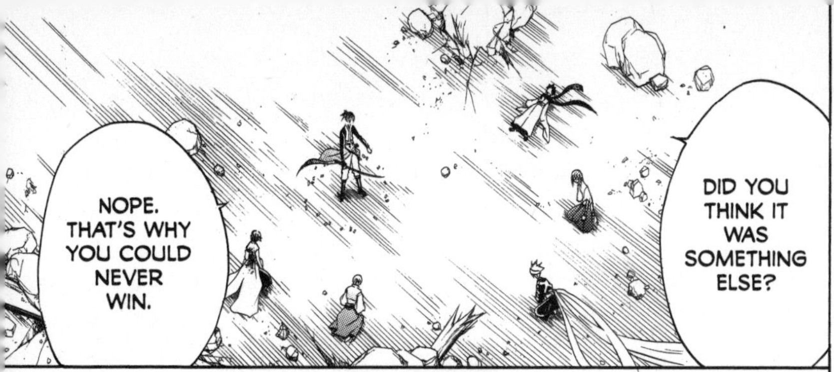
DID YOU THINK IT WAS SOMETHING ELSE?
NOPE. THAT'S WHY YOU COULD NEVER WIN.

Chapter 193 Nearer the Truth

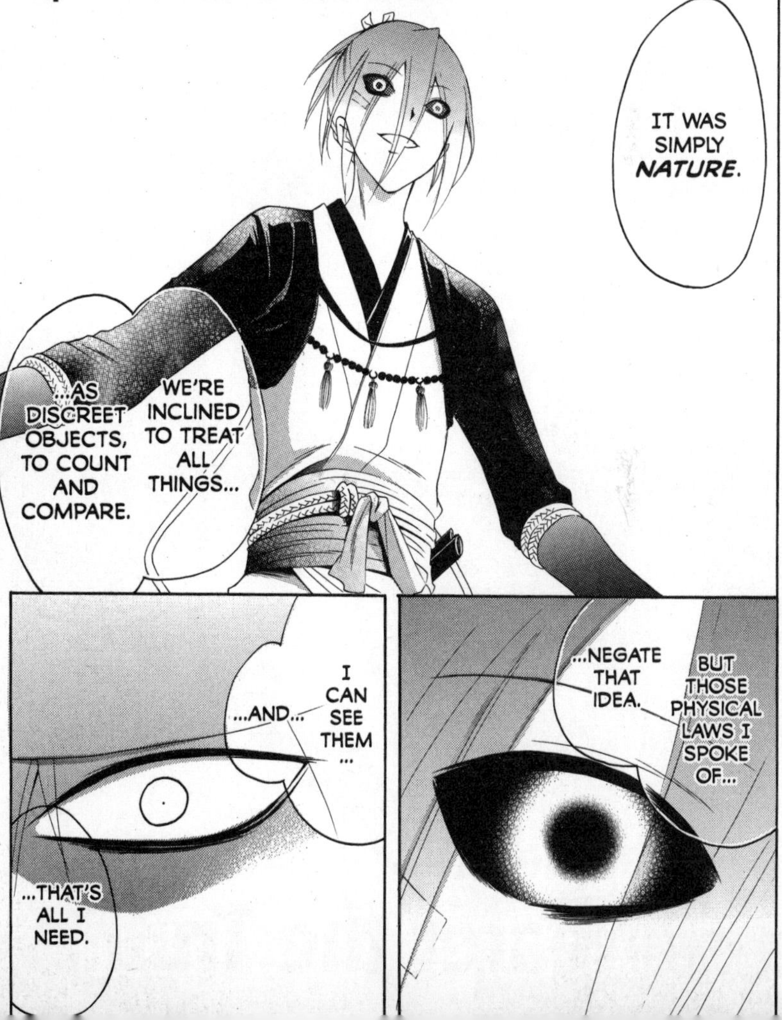
IT WAS SIMPLY *NATURE*.
WE'RE INCLINED TO TREAT ALL THINGS...
...AS DISCREET OBJECTS, TO COUNT AND COMPARE.
BUT THOSE PHYSICAL LAWS I SPOKE OF...
...NEGATE THAT IDEA.
I CAN SEE THEM...
...AND...
...THAT'S ALL I NEED.

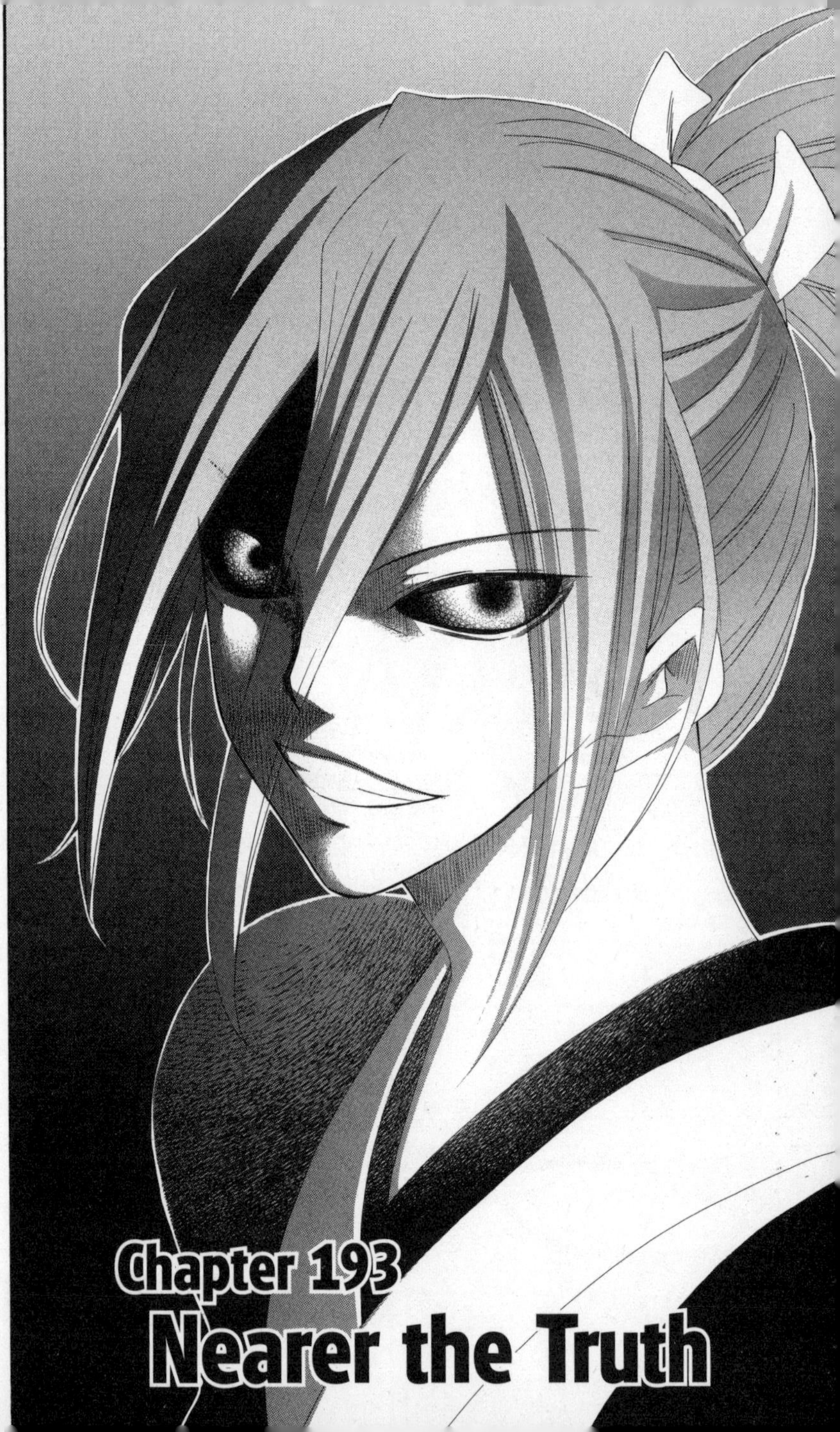
Chapter 193
Nearer the Truth

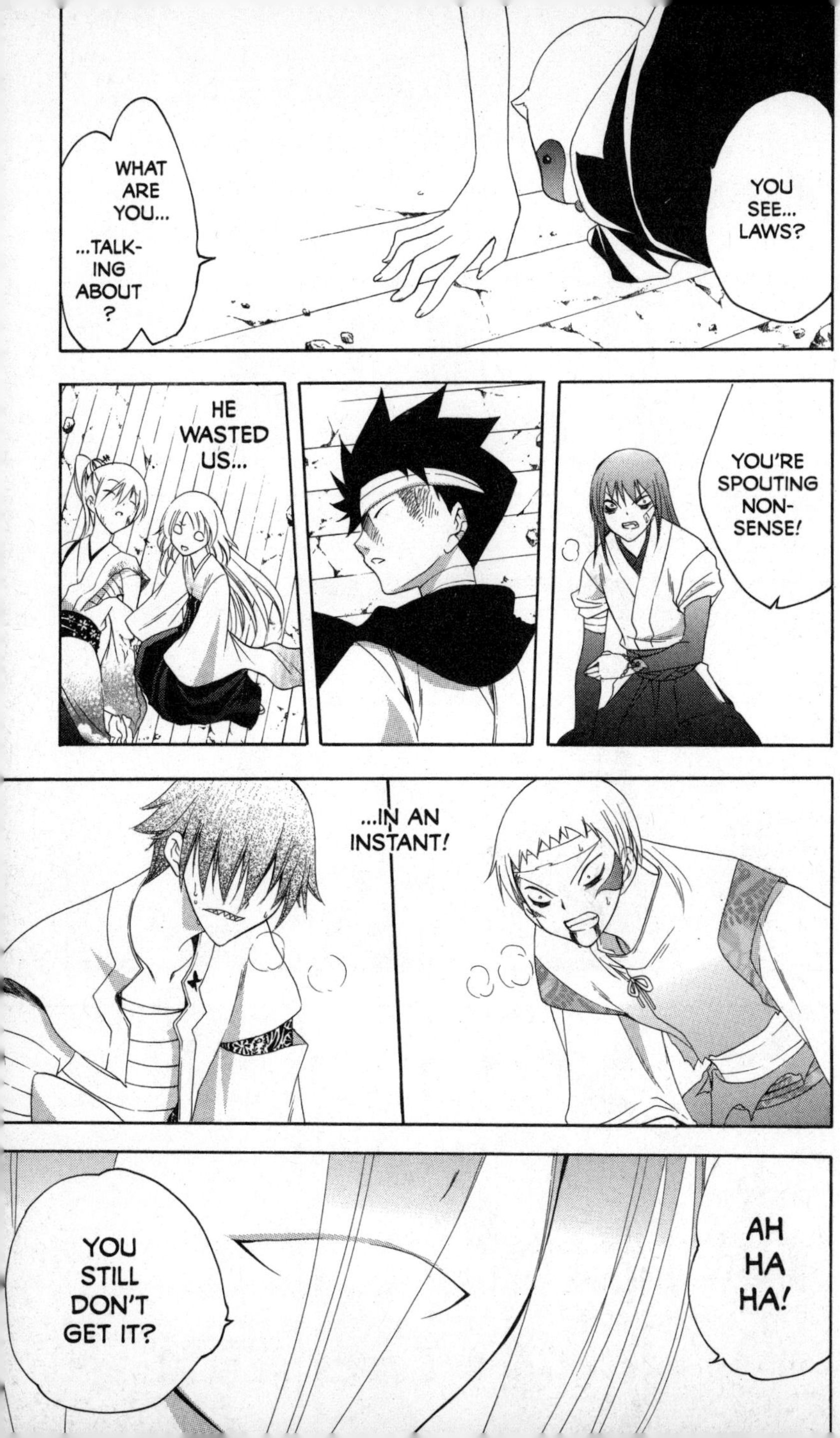
YOU SEE... LAWS?
WHAT ARE YOU... ...TALKING ABOUT?
YOU'RE SPOUTING NONSENSE!
HE WASTED US...
...IN AN INSTANT!
AH HA HA!
YOU STILL DON'T GET IT?

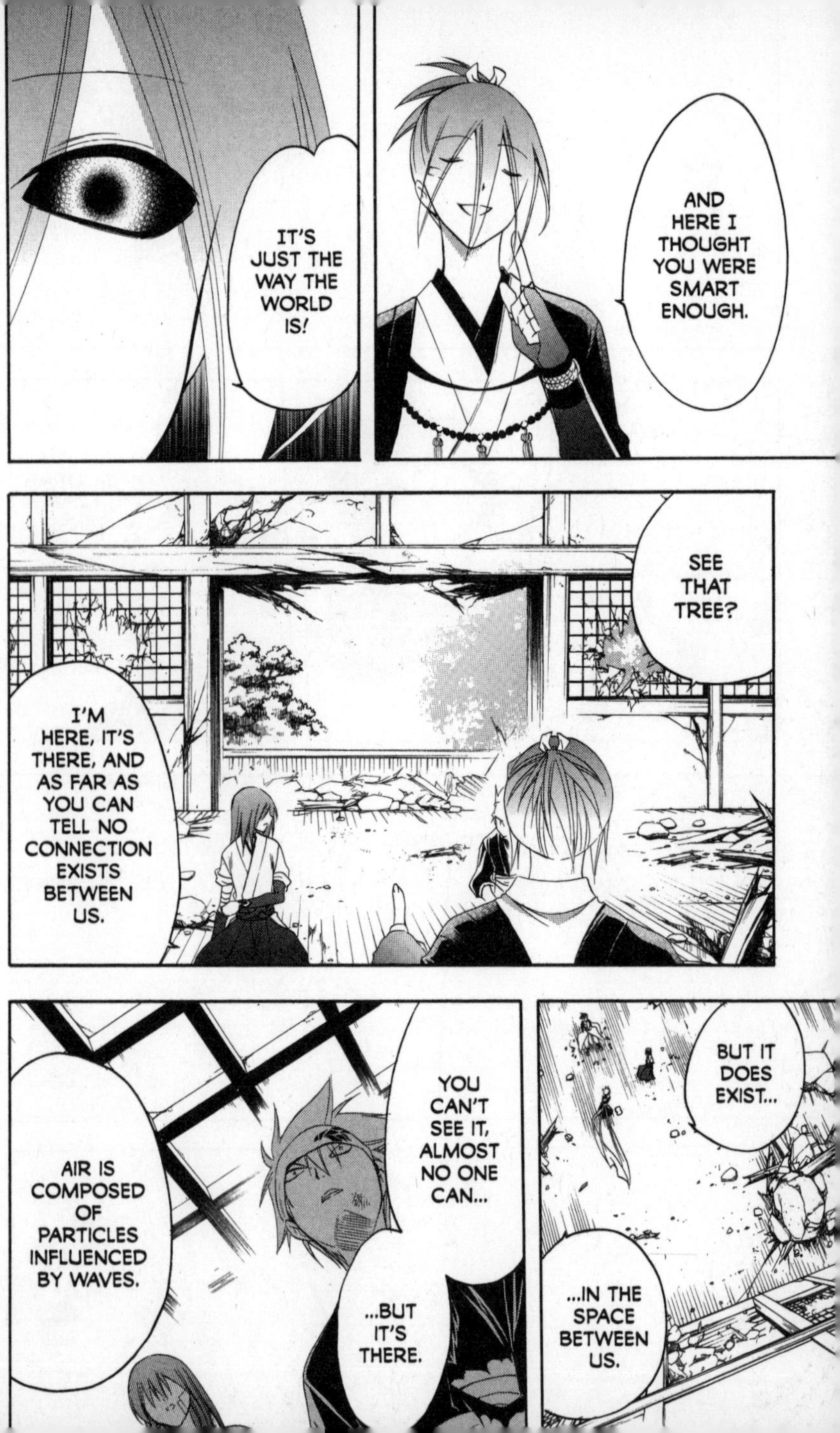
AND HERE I THOUGHT YOU WERE SMART ENOUGH.
IT'S JUST THE WAY THE WORLD IS!
SEE THAT TREE?
I'M HERE, IT'S THERE, AND AS FAR AS YOU CAN TELL NO CONNECTION EXISTS BETWEEN US.
BUT IT DOES EXIST...
...IN THE SPACE BETWEEN US.
YOU CAN'T SEE IT, ALMOST NO ONE CAN...
AIR IS COMPOSED OF PARTICLES INFLUENCED BY WAVES.
...BUT IT'S THERE.

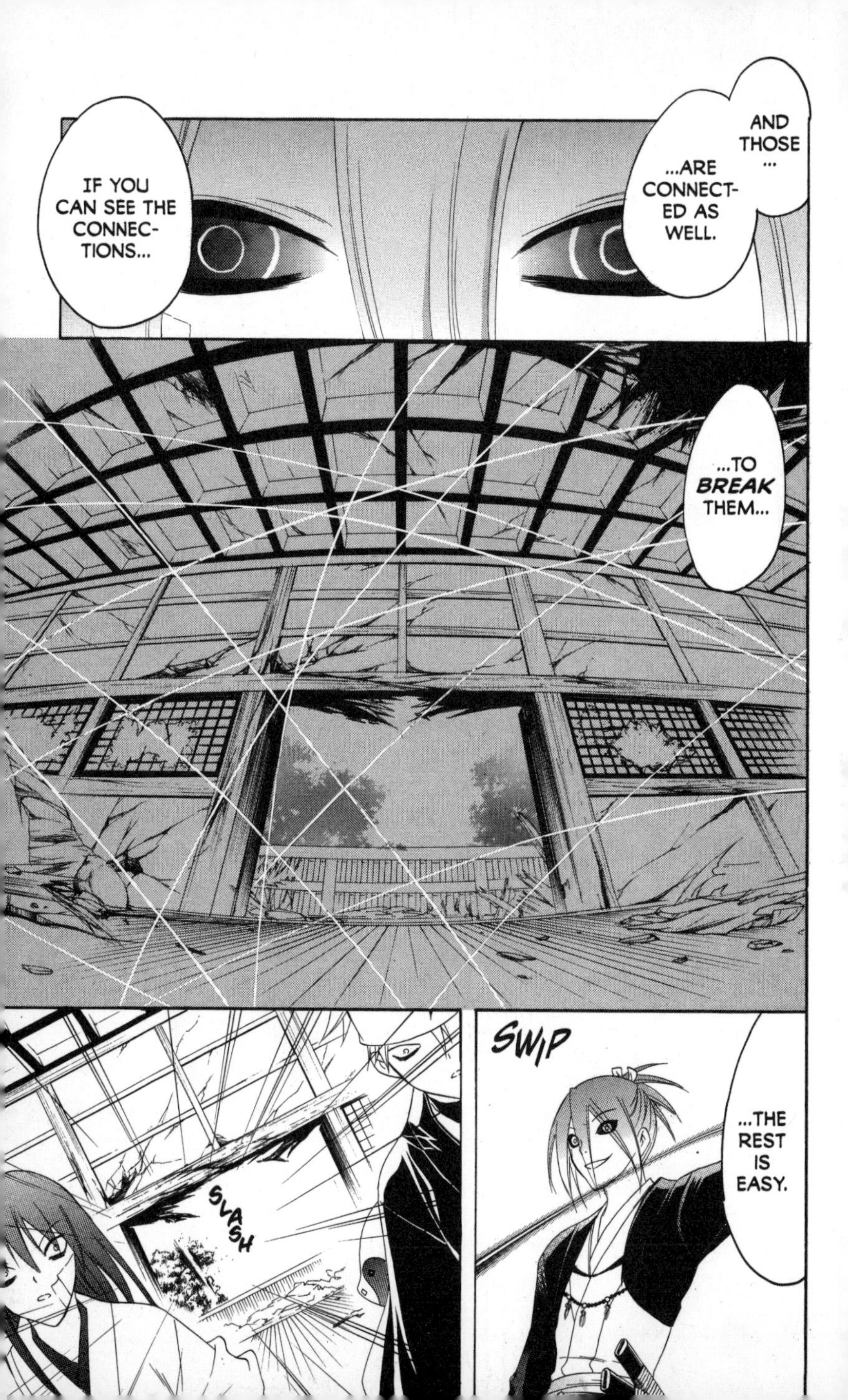
AND THOSE ...
...ARE CONNECTED AS WELL.
IF YOU CAN SEE THE CONNECTIONS...
...TO BREAK THEM...
SWIP
...THE REST IS EASY.
SLASH

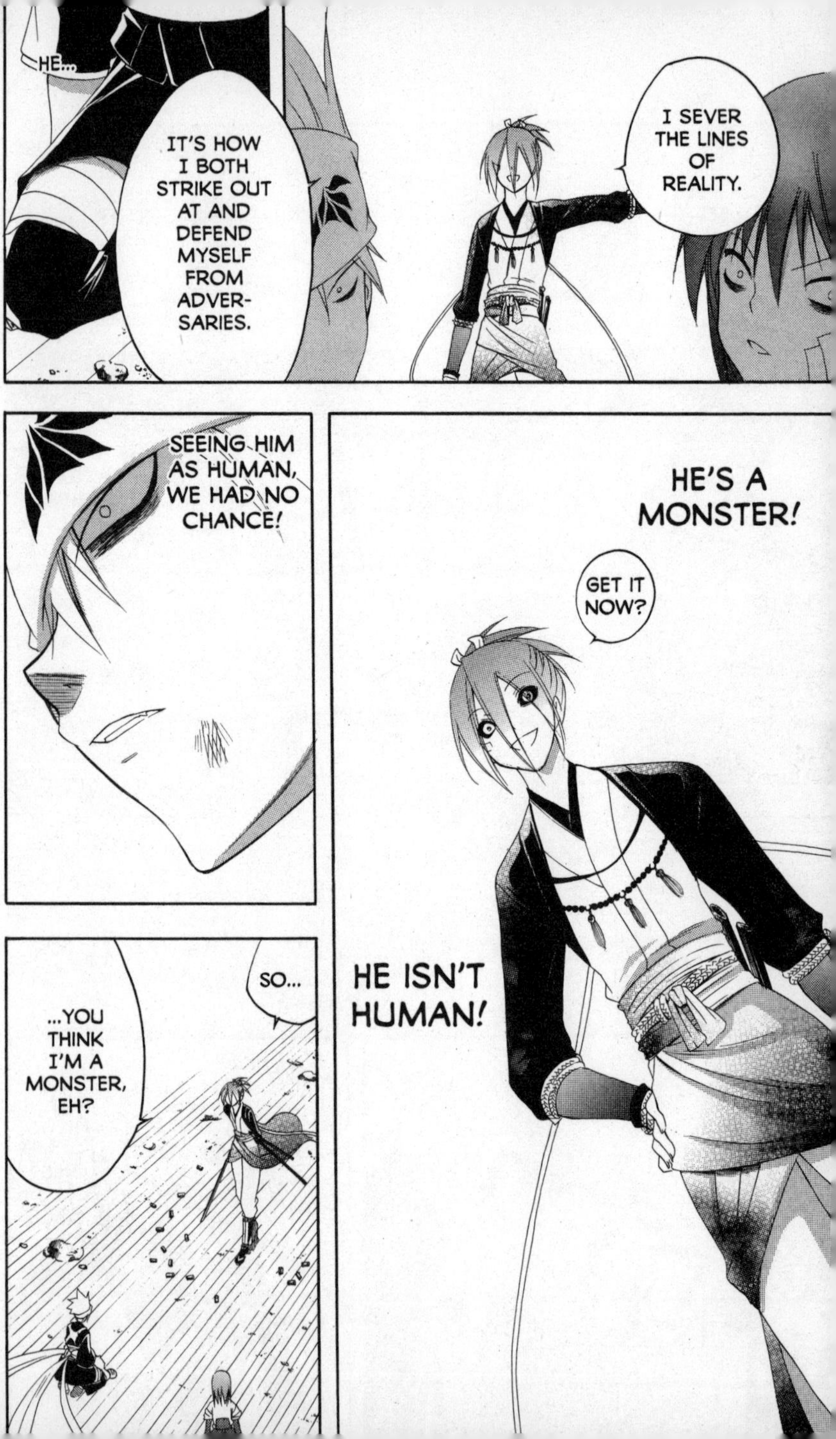
I SEVER THE LINES OF REALITY.
IT'S HOW I BOTH STRIKE OUT AT AND DEFEND MYSELF FROM ADVERSARIES.
HE...
HE'S A MONSTER!
GET IT NOW?
HE ISN'T HUMAN!
SEEING HIM AS HUMAN, WE HAD NO CHANCE!
SO...
...YOU THINK I'M A MONSTER, EH?

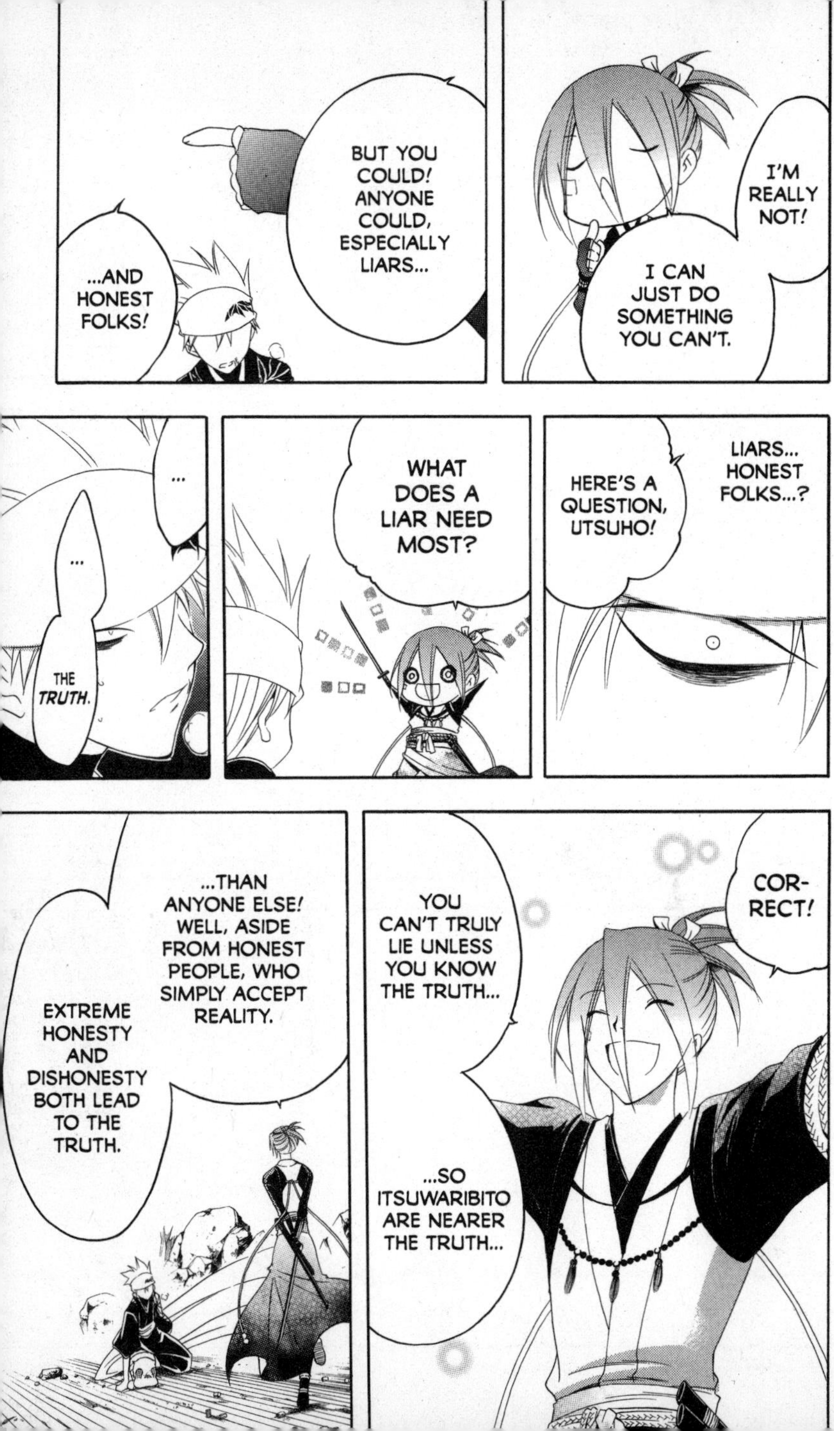
I'M REALLY NOT!
I CAN JUST DO SOMETHING YOU CAN'T.
BUT YOU COULD! ANYONE COULD, ESPECIALLY LIARS...
...AND HONEST FOLKS!
LIARS... HONEST FOLKS...?
HERE'S A QUESTION, UTSUHO!
WHAT DOES A LIAR NEED MOST?
...
...
THE *TRUTH*.
COR-RECT!
YOU CAN'T TRULY LIE UNLESS YOU KNOW THE TRUTH...
...SO ITSUWARIBITO ARE NEARER THE TRUTH...
...THAN ANYONE ELSE! WELL, ASIDE FROM HONEST PEOPLE, WHO SIMPLY ACCEPT REALITY.
EXTREME HONESTY AND DISHONESTY BOTH LEAD TO THE TRUTH.

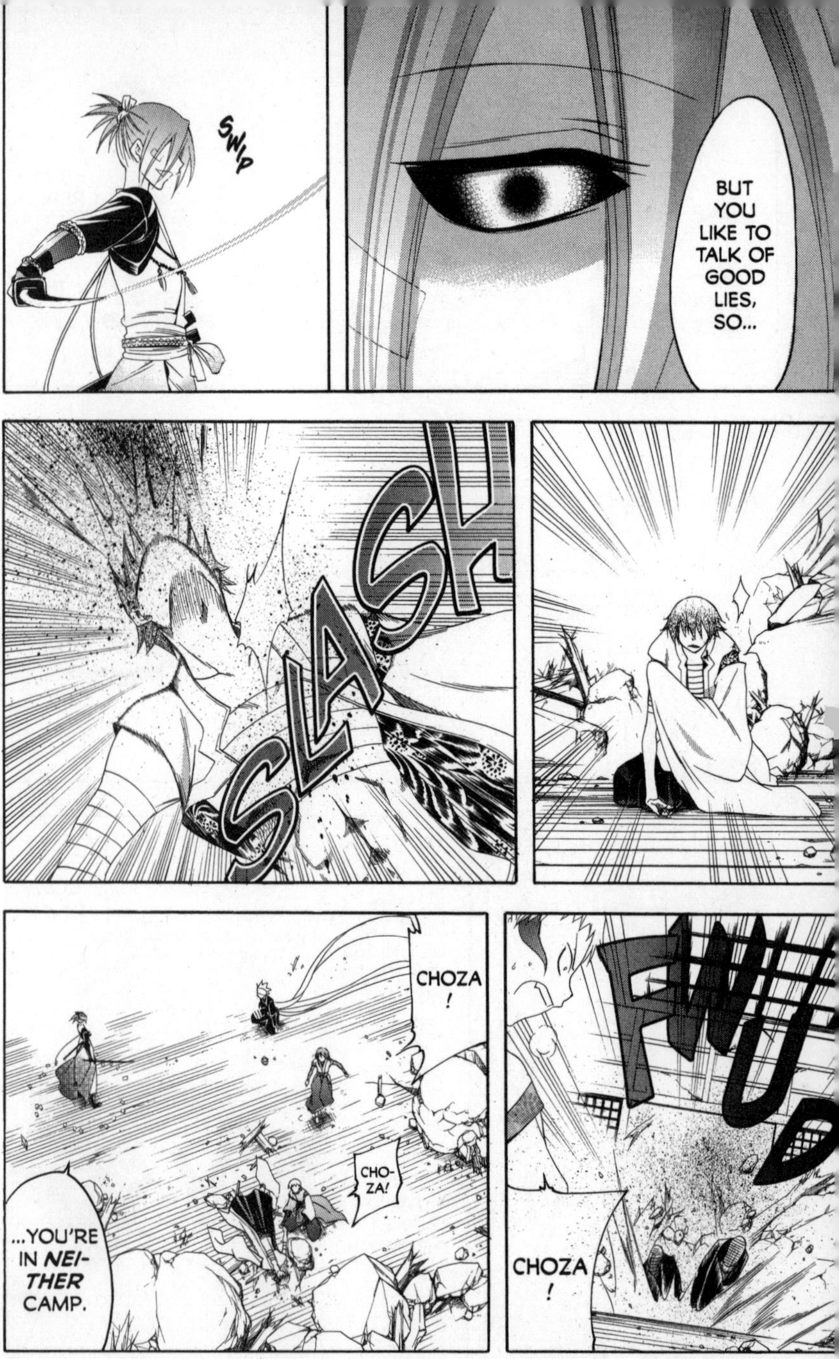
BUT YOU LIKE TO TALK OF GOOD LIES, SO...
SWIP
SLASH
FWUD
CHOZA!
CHOZA!
CHO-ZA!
...YOU'RE IN *NEI-THER* CAMP.

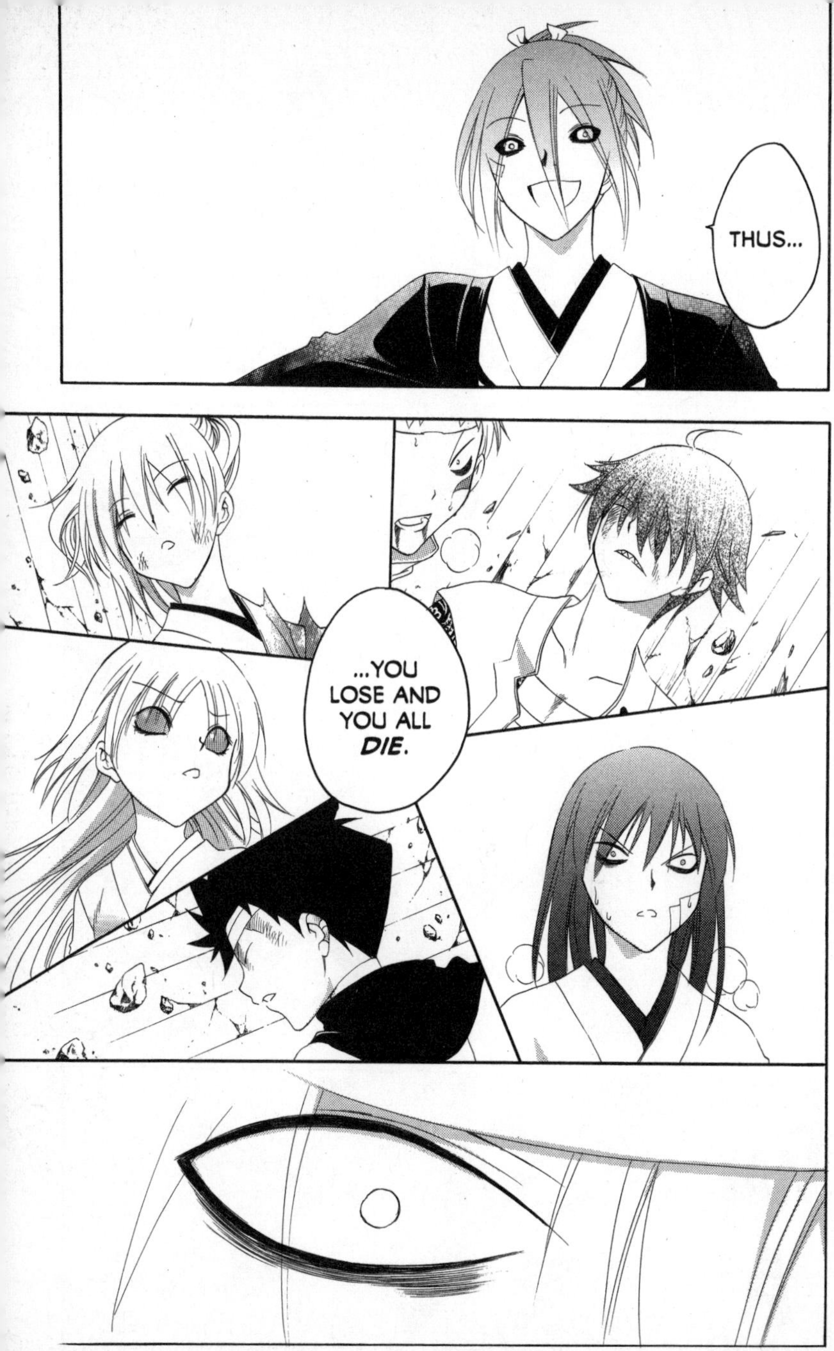
THUS...
...YOU LOSE AND YOU ALL *DIE*.

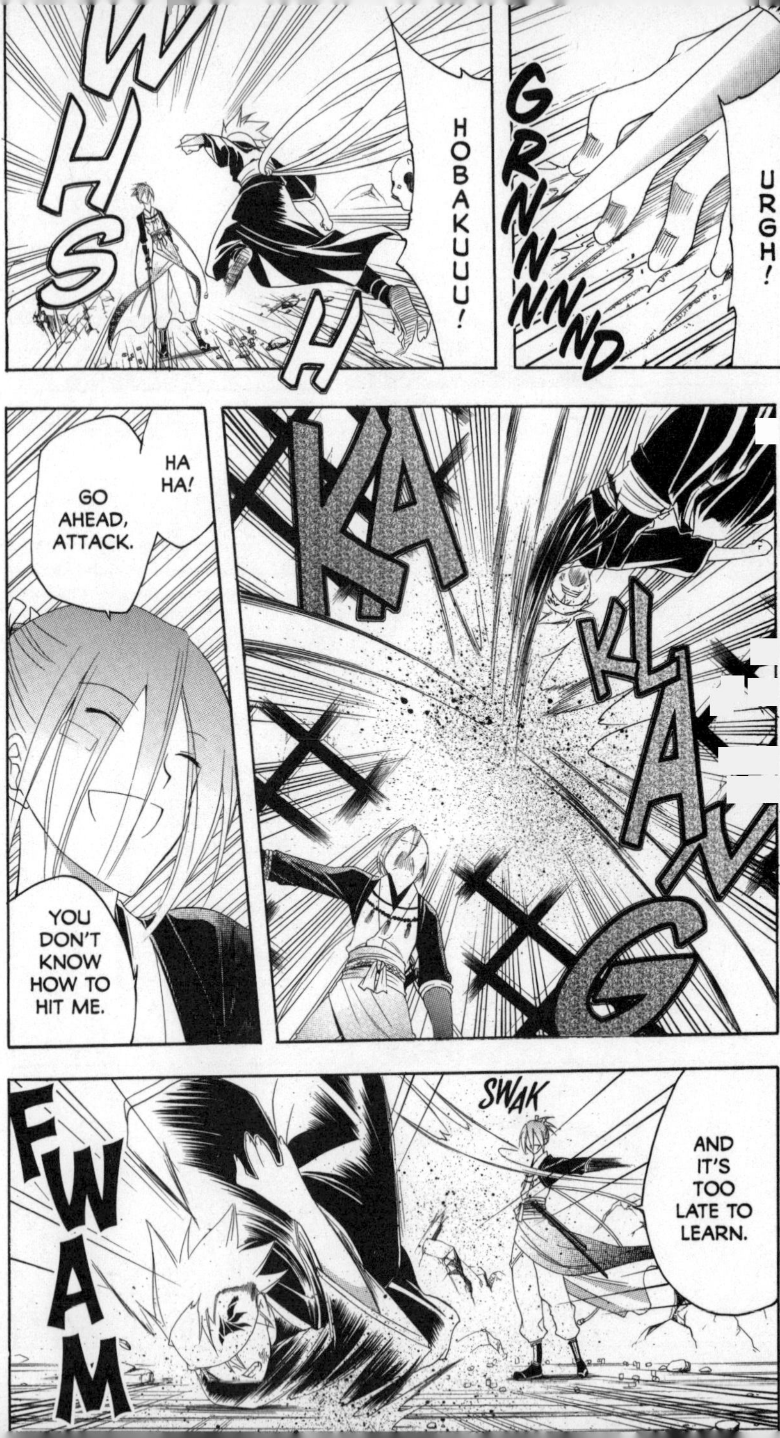
URGH!
GRNNNND
HOBAKUUU!
WHSH
KA
KLANG
HA HA!
GO AHEAD, ATTACK.
YOU DON'T KNOW HOW TO HIT ME.
AND IT'S TOO LATE TO LEARN.
SWAK
FWAM

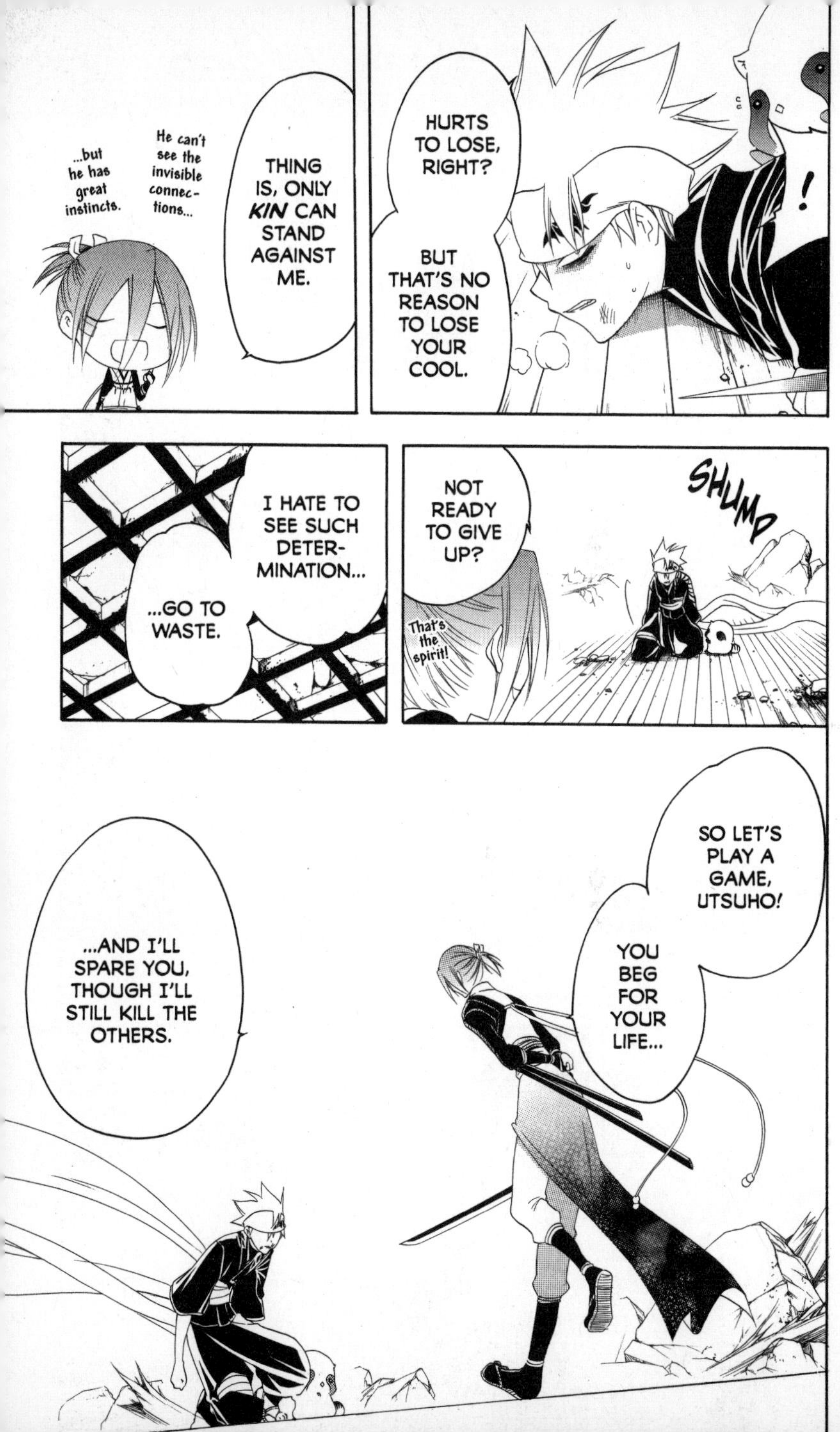
HURTS TO LOSE, RIGHT?
BUT THAT'S NO REASON TO LOSE YOUR COOL.
!
THING IS, ONLY *KIN* CAN STAND AGAINST ME.
He can't see the invisible connections...
...but he has great instincts.
SHUMP
NOT READY TO GIVE UP?
That's the spirit!
I HATE TO SEE SUCH DETERMINATION...
...GO TO WASTE.
SO LET'S PLAY A GAME, UTSUHO!
YOU BEG FOR YOUR LIFE...
...AND I'LL SPARE YOU, THOUGH I'LL STILL KILL THE OTHERS.

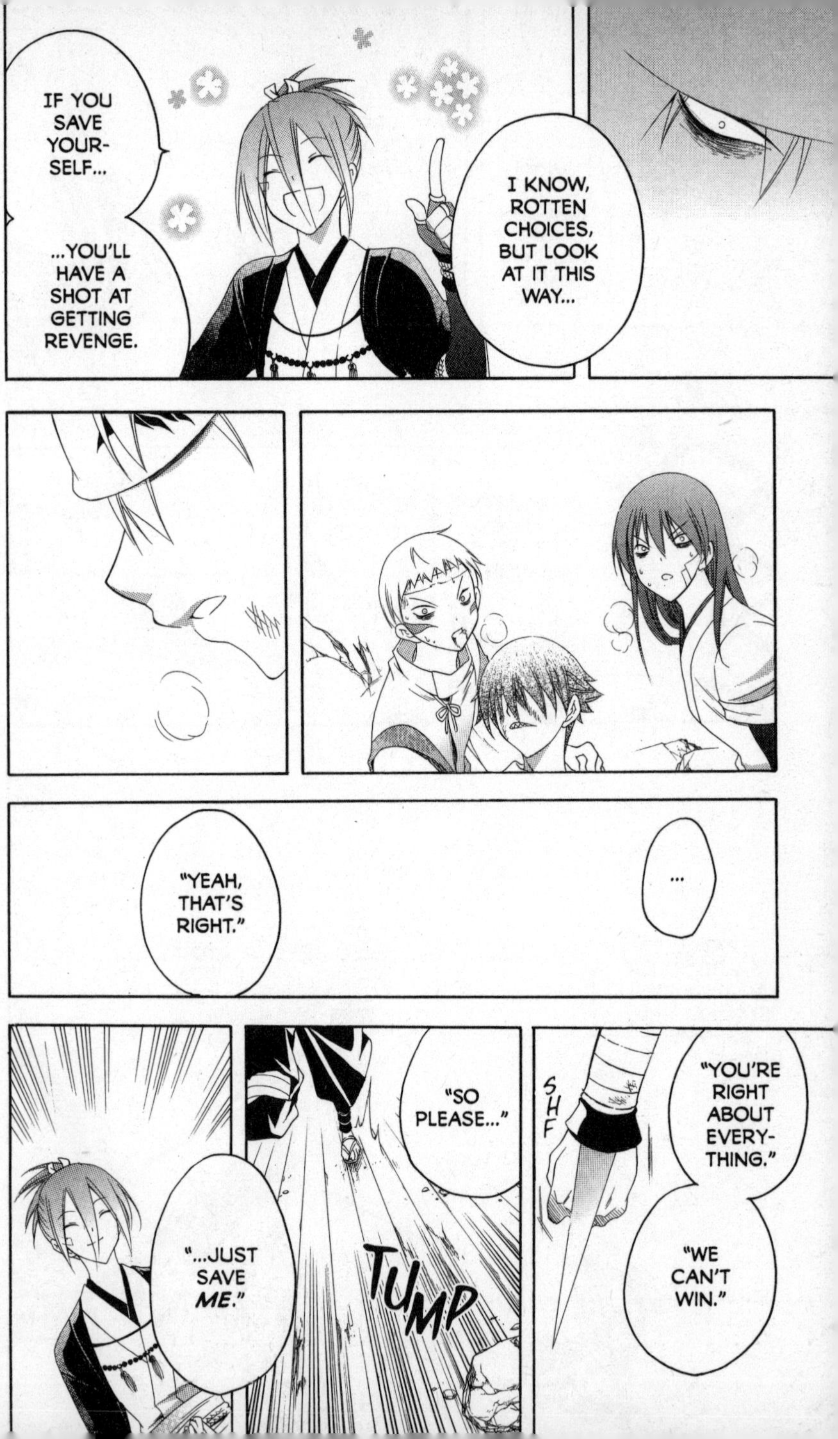
I KNOW, ROTTEN CHOICES, BUT LOOK AT IT THIS WAY...
IF YOU SAVE YOURSELF...
...YOU'LL HAVE A SHOT AT GETTING REVENGE.
...
"YEAH, THAT'S RIGHT."
SHF
"YOU'RE RIGHT ABOUT EVERYTHING."
"WE CAN'T WIN."
"SO PLEASE..."
TUMP
"...JUST SAVE *ME*."

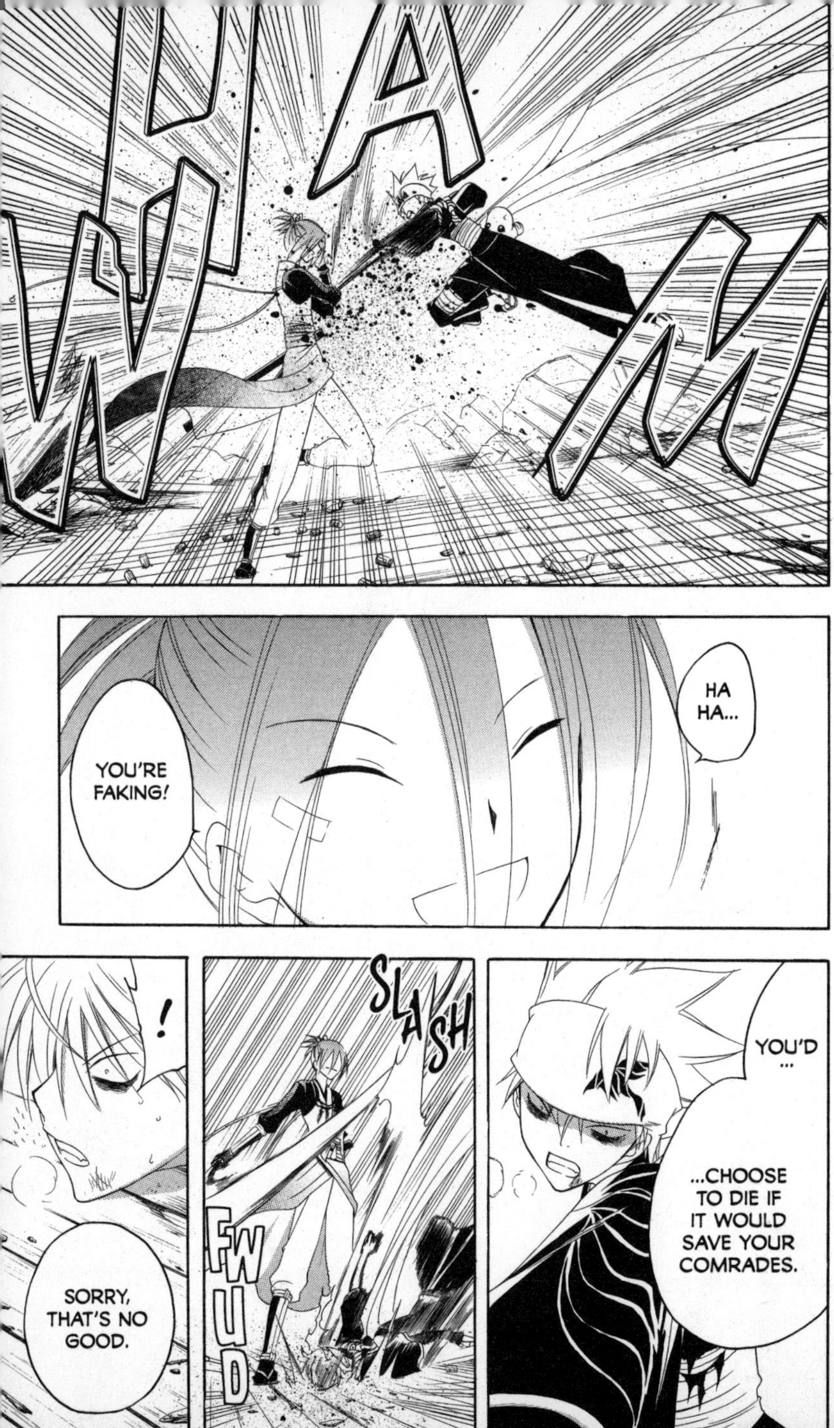
WHAM
HA HA...
YOU'RE FAKING!
YOU'D ...
...CHOOSE TO DIE IF IT WOULD SAVE YOUR COMRADES.
SLASH
FWUD
!
SORRY, THAT'S NO GOOD.

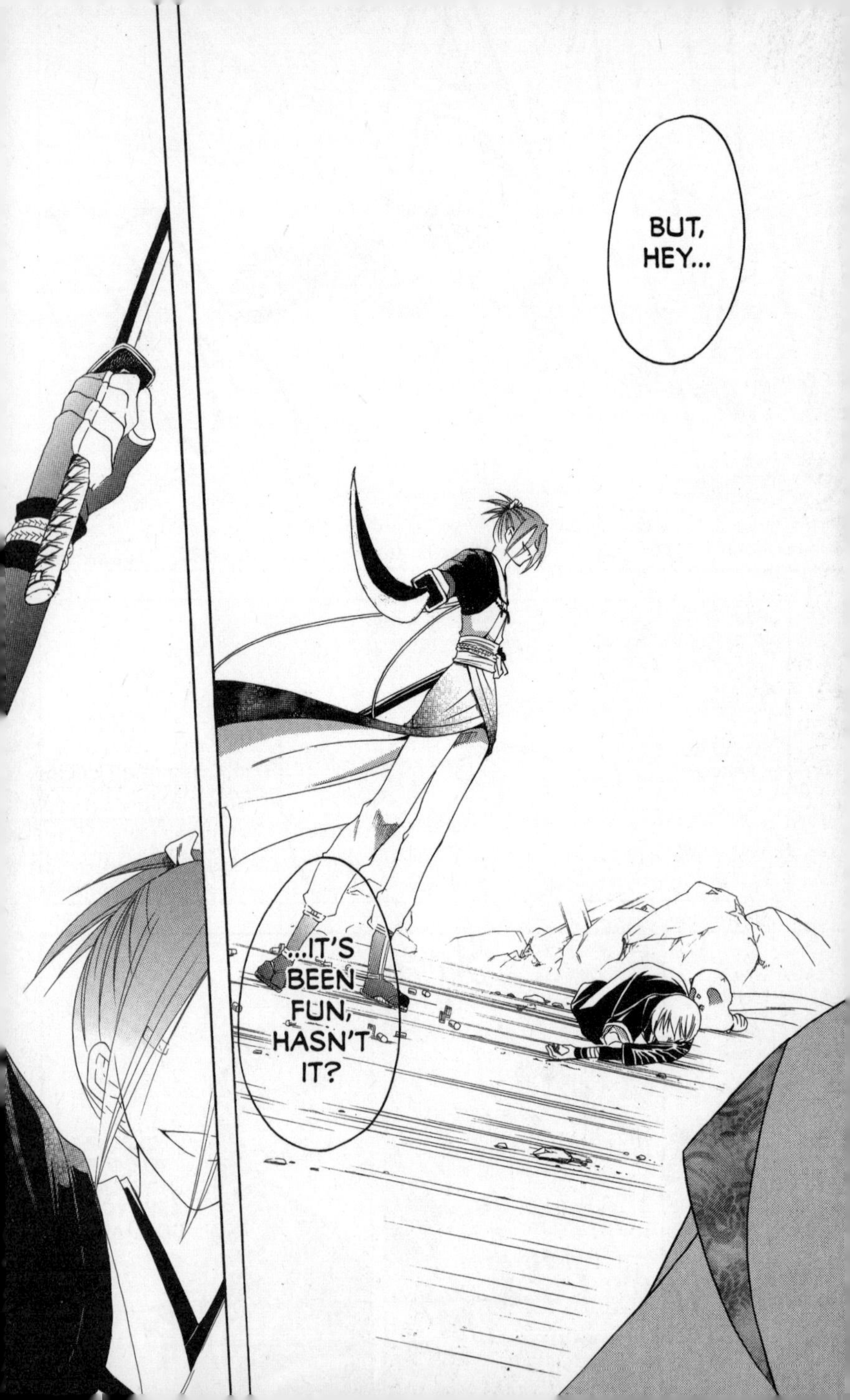
BUT, HEY...
...IT'S BEEN FUN, HASN'T IT?

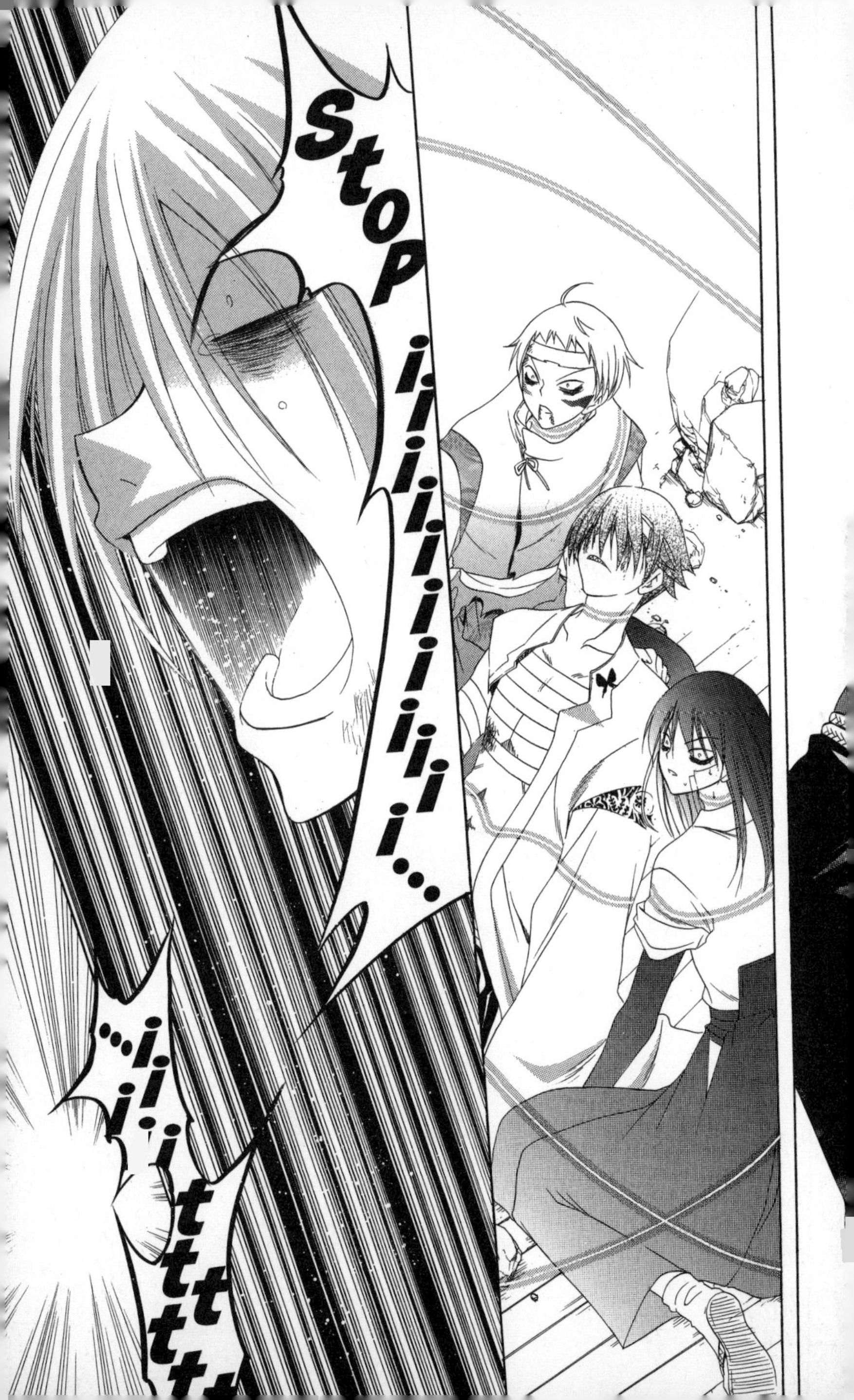
Stopiiiiiiiiiiii...
...iiiitttttt

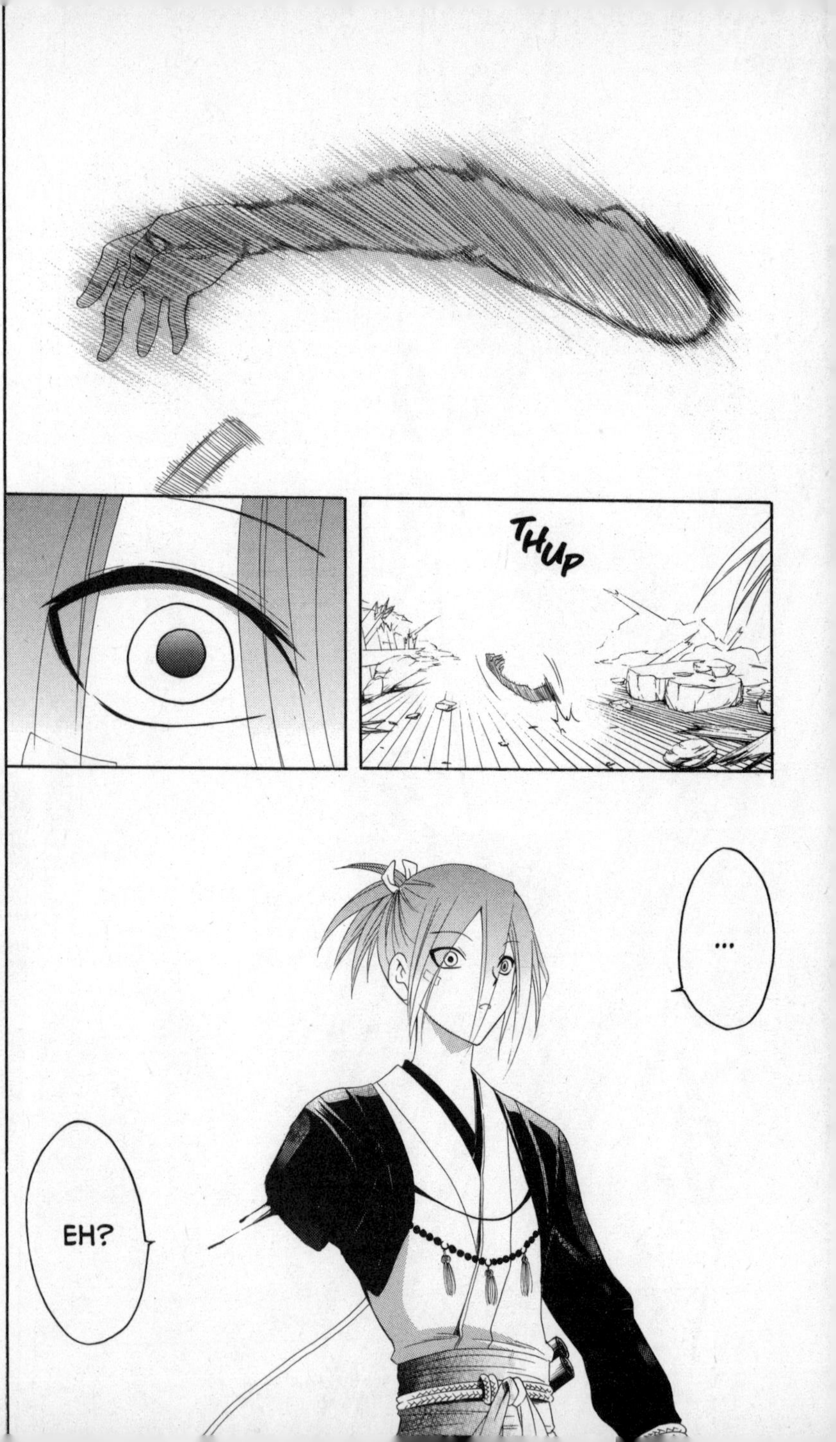
THUP
...
EH?

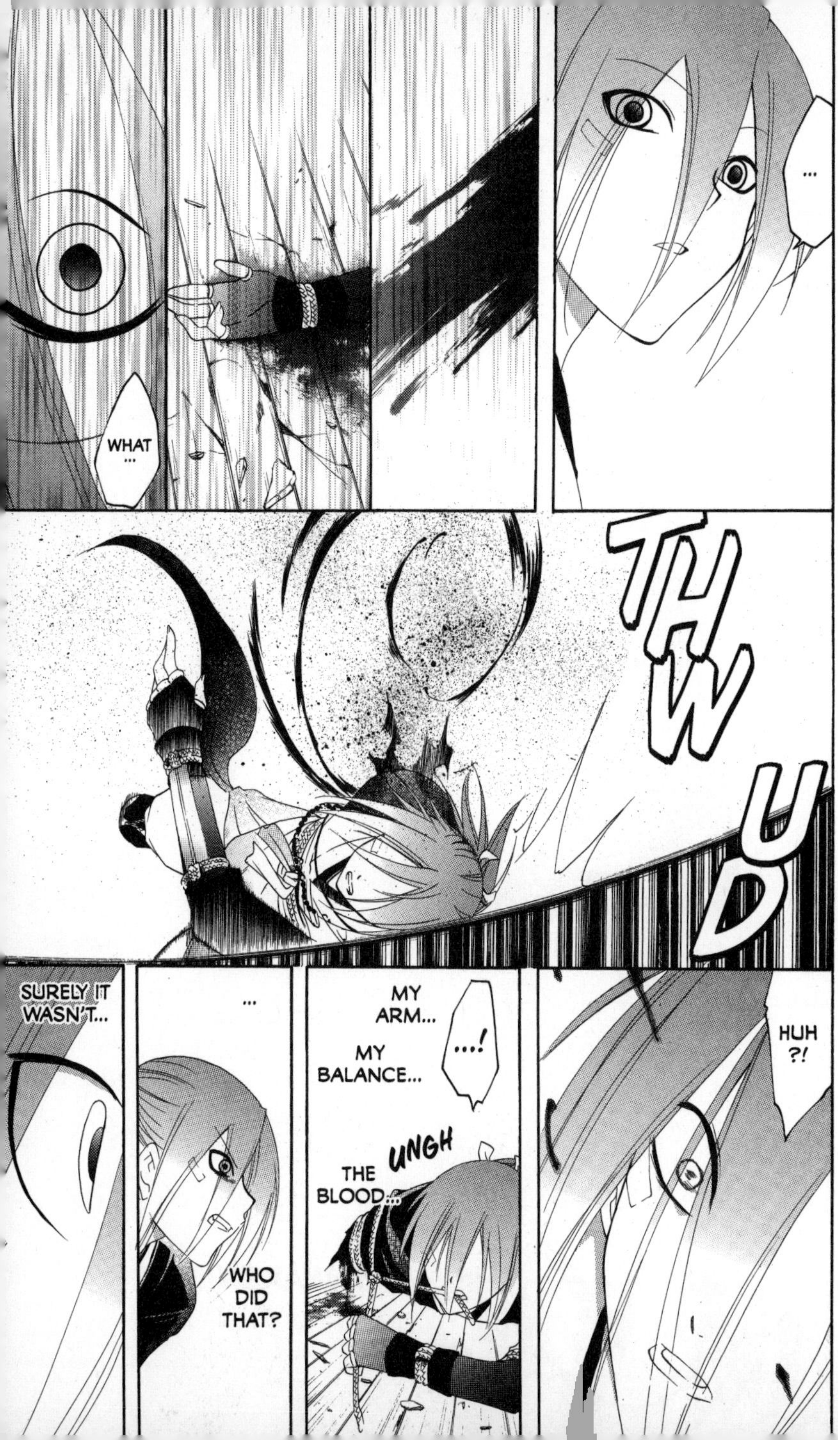
...
WHAT ...
THWUD
HUH ?!
...!
MY ARM...
MY BALANCE...
UNGH
THE BLOOD...
...
WHO DID THAT?
SURELY IT WASN'T...

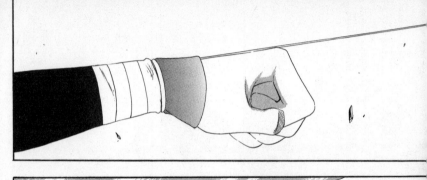

HAS
HE...

...AWAKENED?

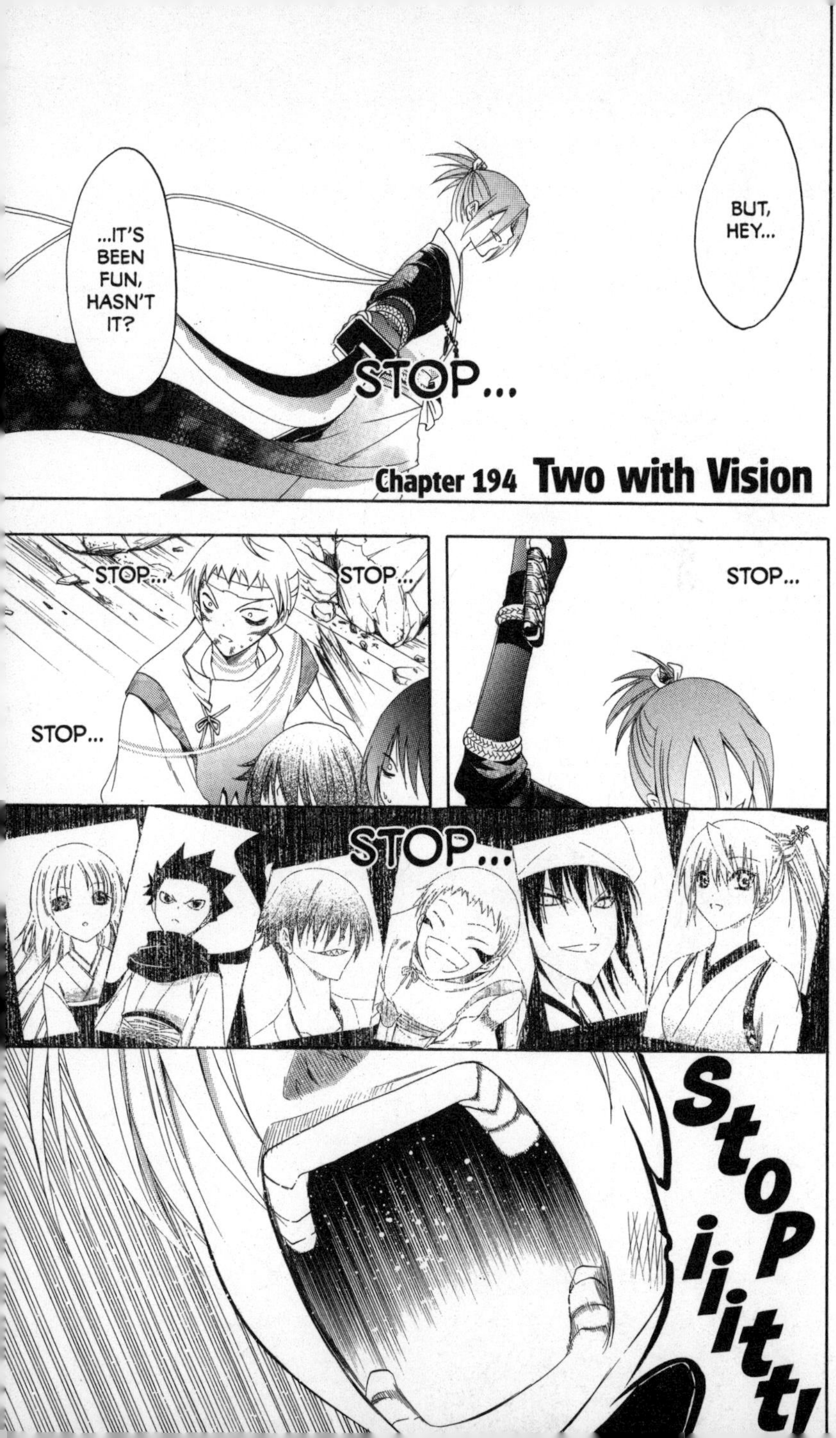
BUT, HEY...
...IT'S BEEN FUN, HASN'T IT?
STOP...
Chapter 194 Two with Vision
STOP...
STOP...
STOP...
STOP...
STOP...
STOPiiitt!

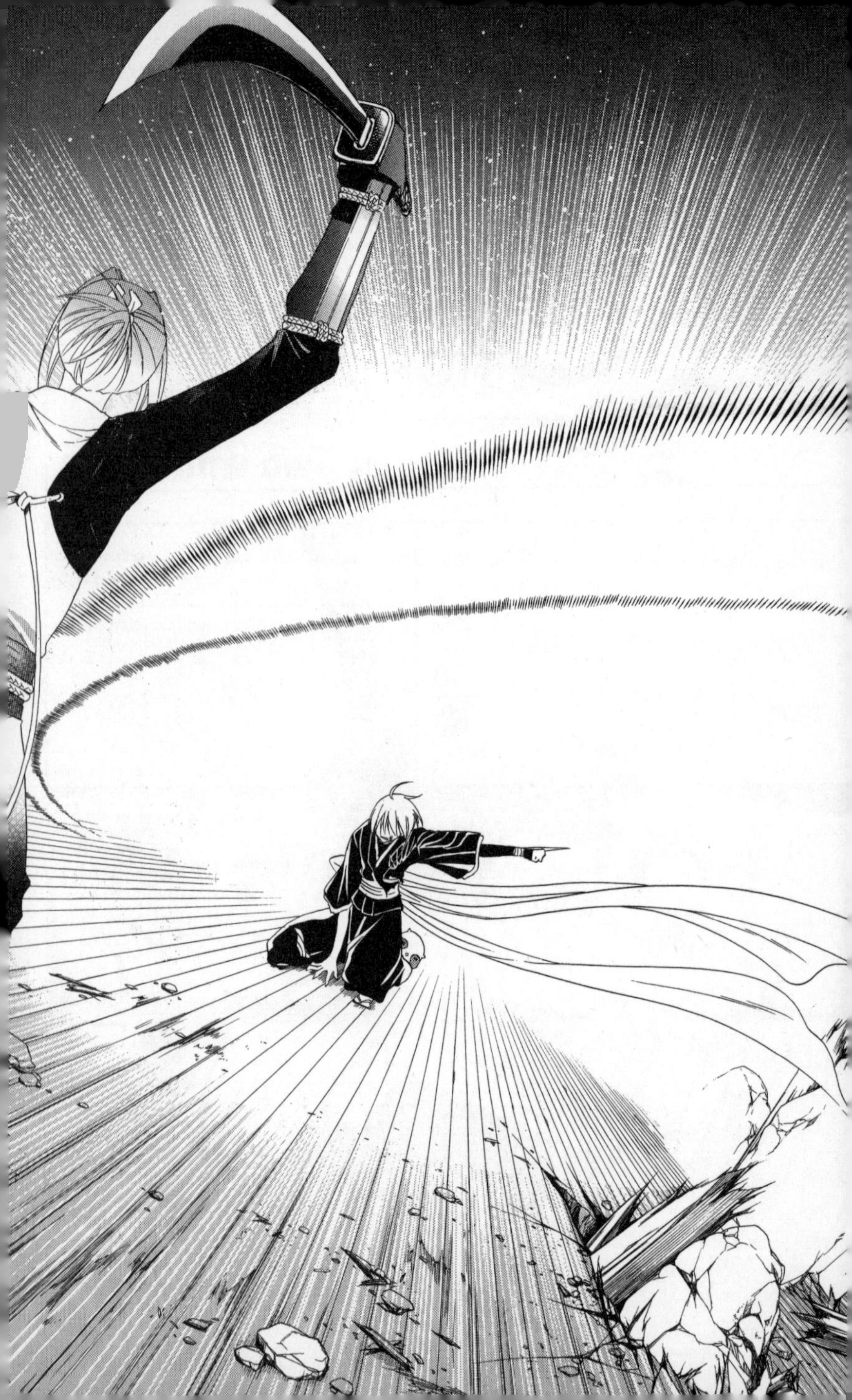

Chapter 194
Two with Vision

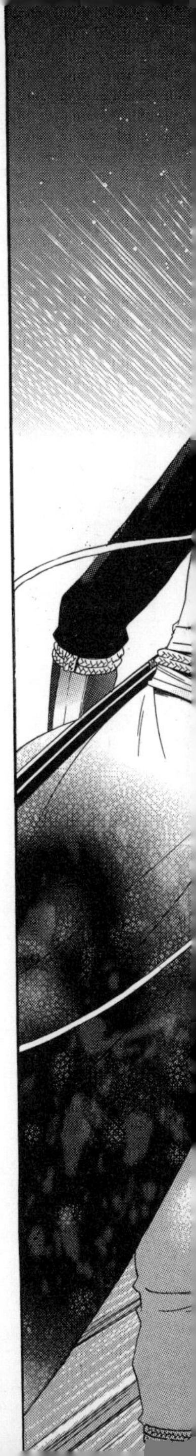

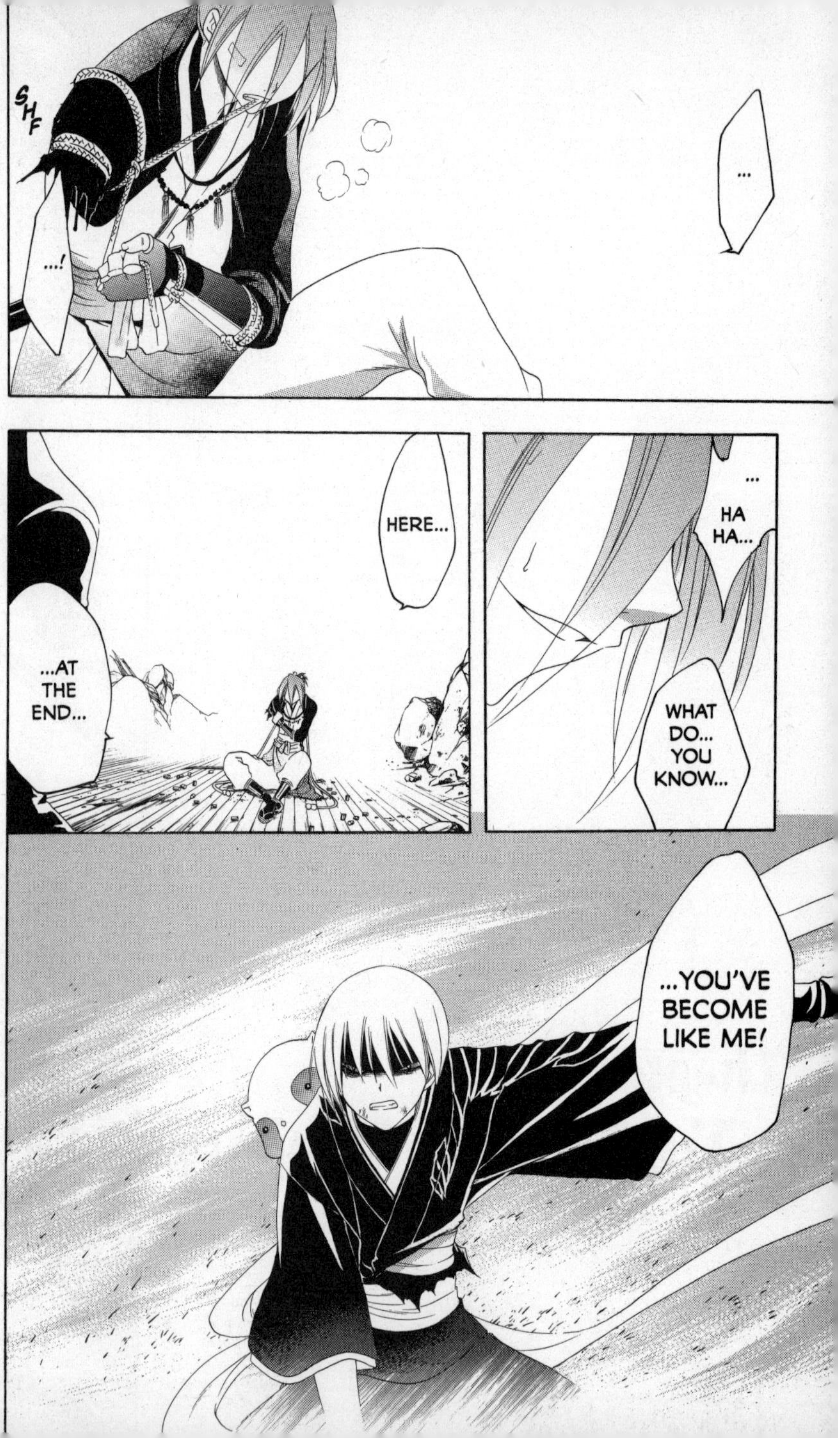
...
SHF
...!
... HA HA...
WHAT DO... YOU KNOW...
HERE...
...AT THE END...
...YOU'VE BECOME LIKE ME!

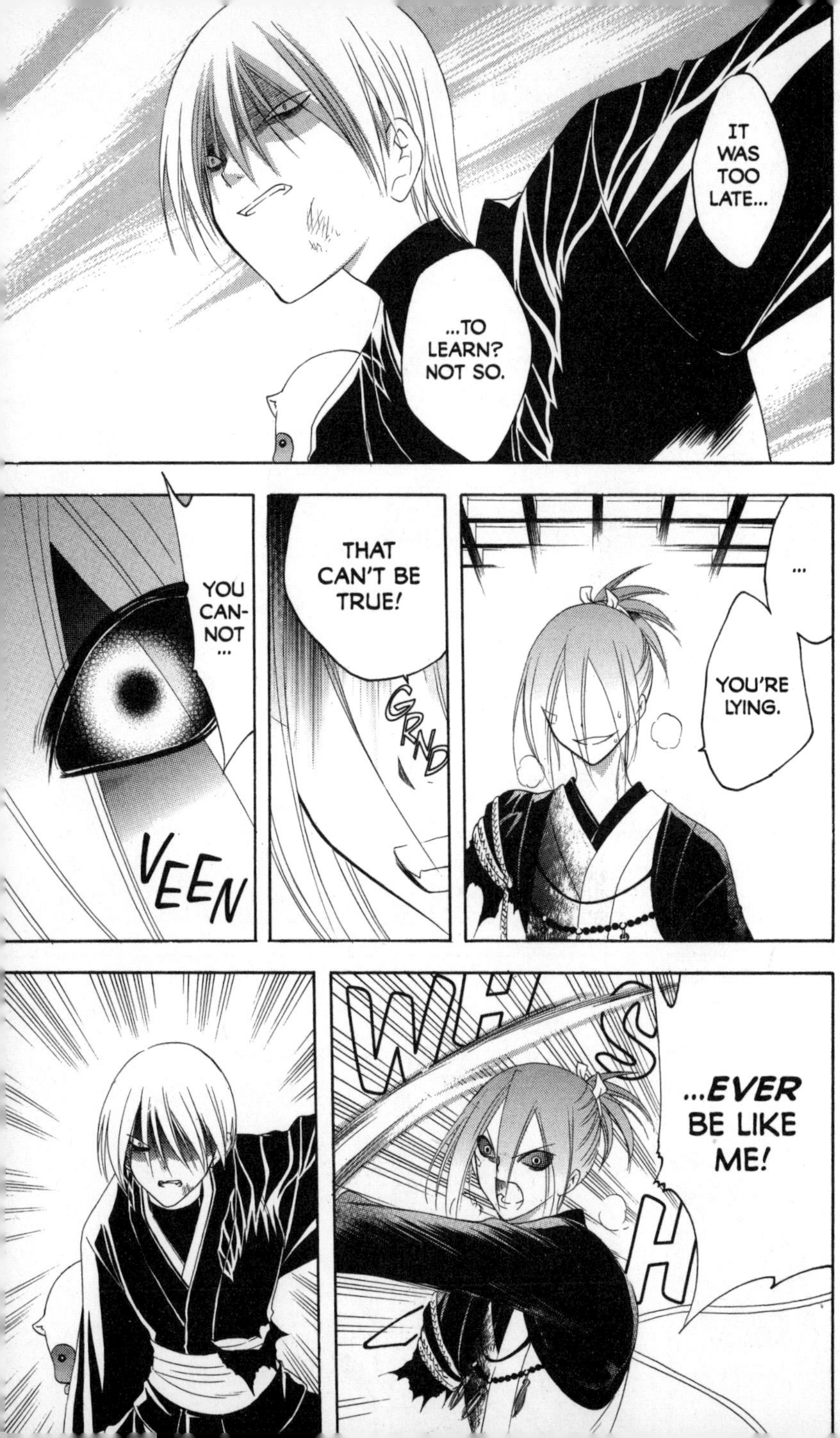
IT WAS TOO LATE...
...TO LEARN? NOT SO.
...
YOU'RE LYING.
THAT CAN'T BE TRUE!
GRND
YOU CAN-NOT ...
VEEN
...EVER BE LIKE ME!

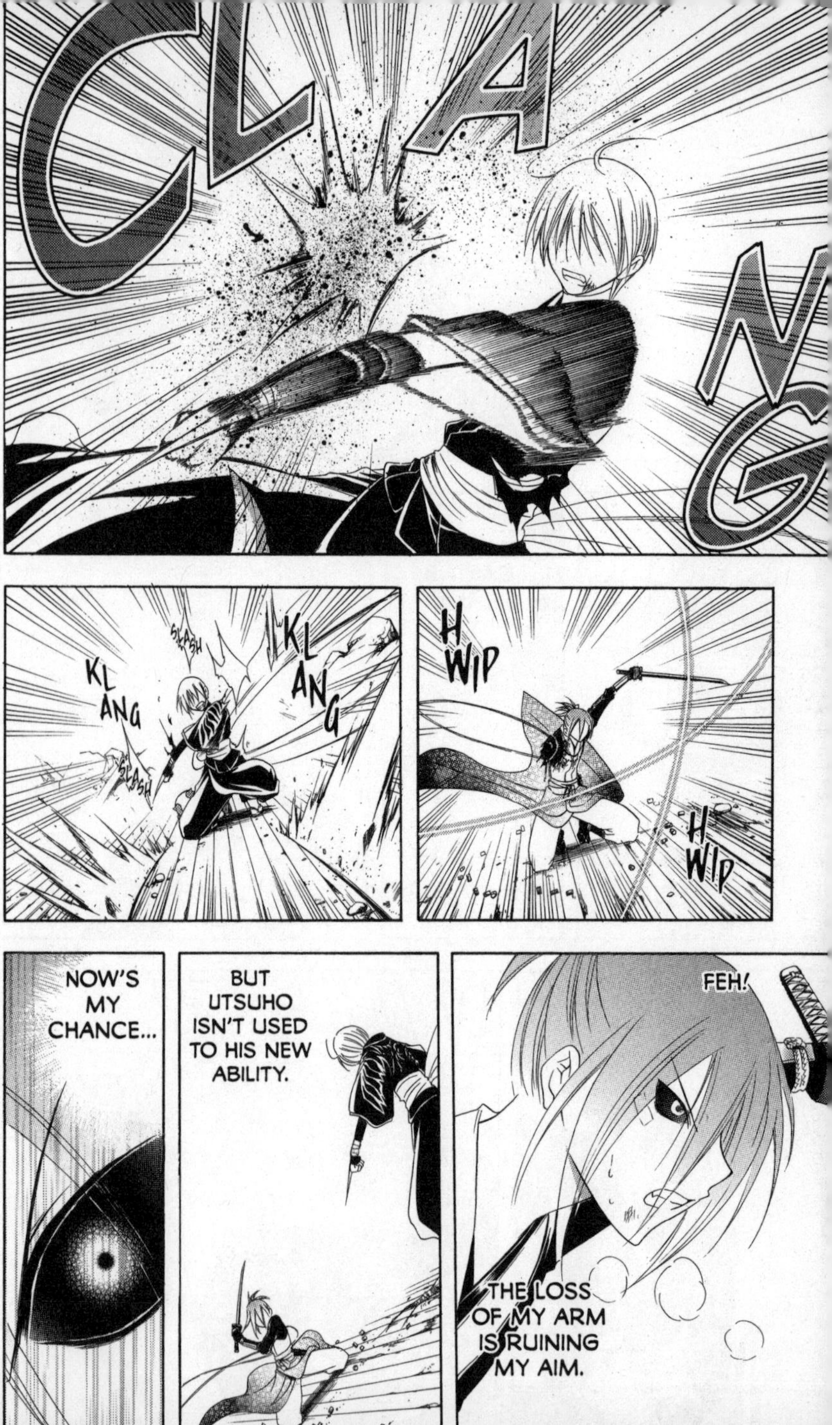
CLANG
HWIP
HWIP
KLANG
SLASH
KLANG
SLASH
FEH!
THE LOSS OF MY ARM IS RUINING MY AIM.
BUT UTSUHO ISN'T USED TO HIS NEW ABILITY.
NOW'S MY CHANCE...

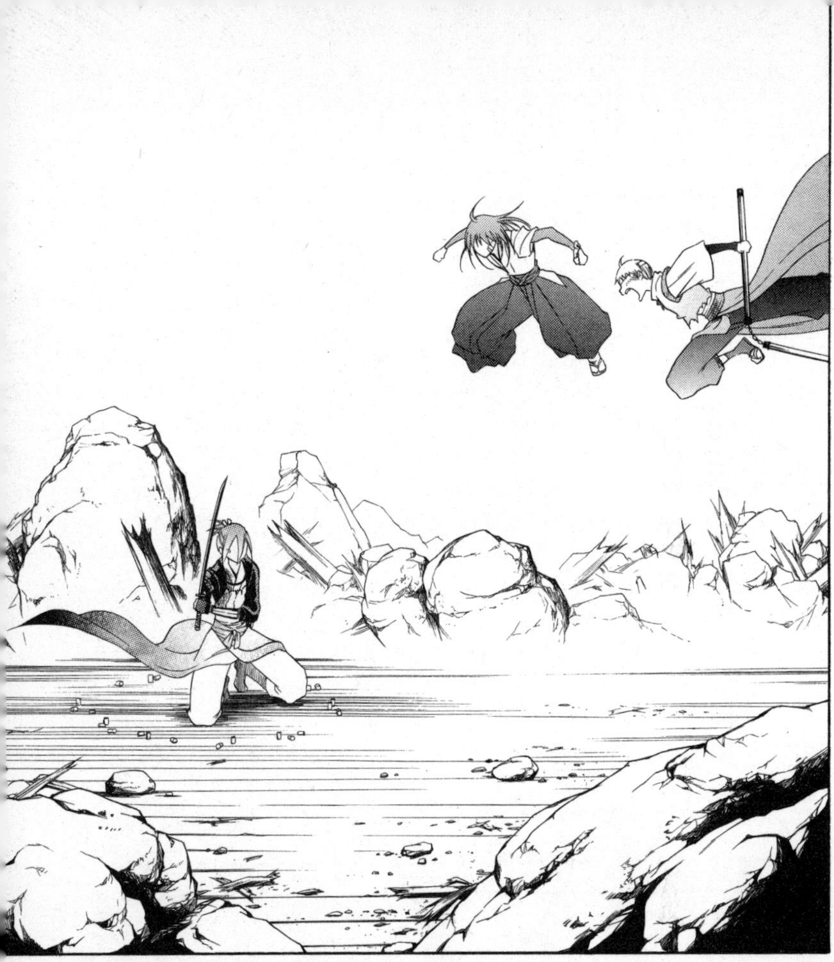

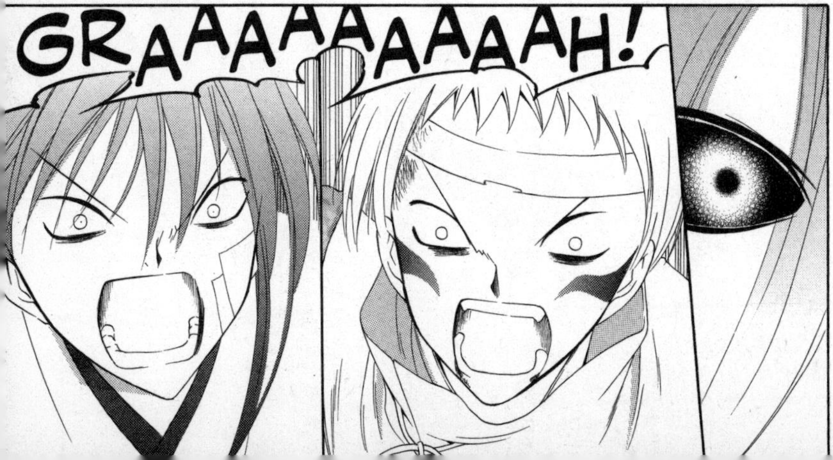
GRAAAAAAAAAAH!

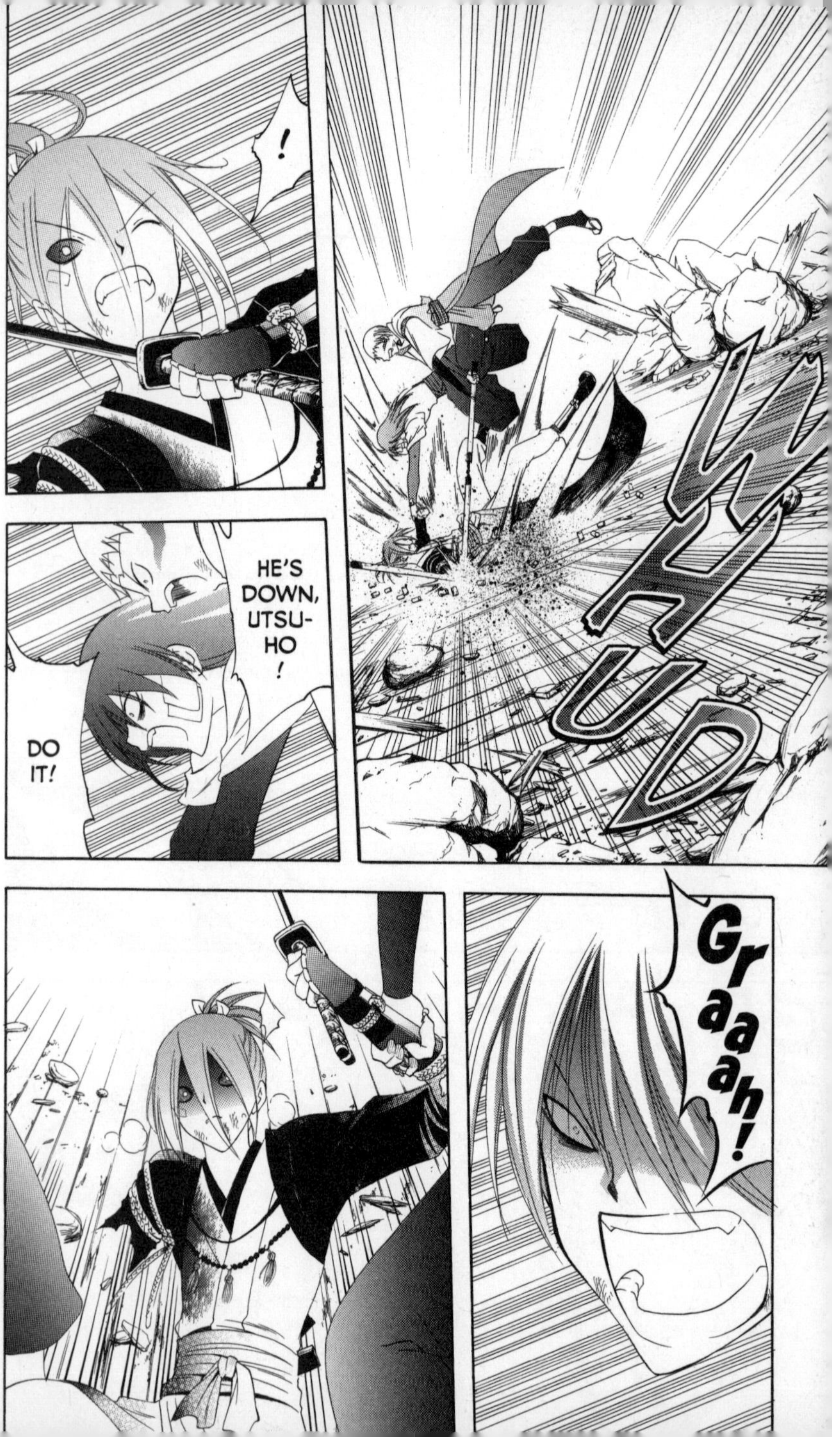
THUD
!
HE'S DOWN, UTSU-HO!
DO IT!
Graaah!

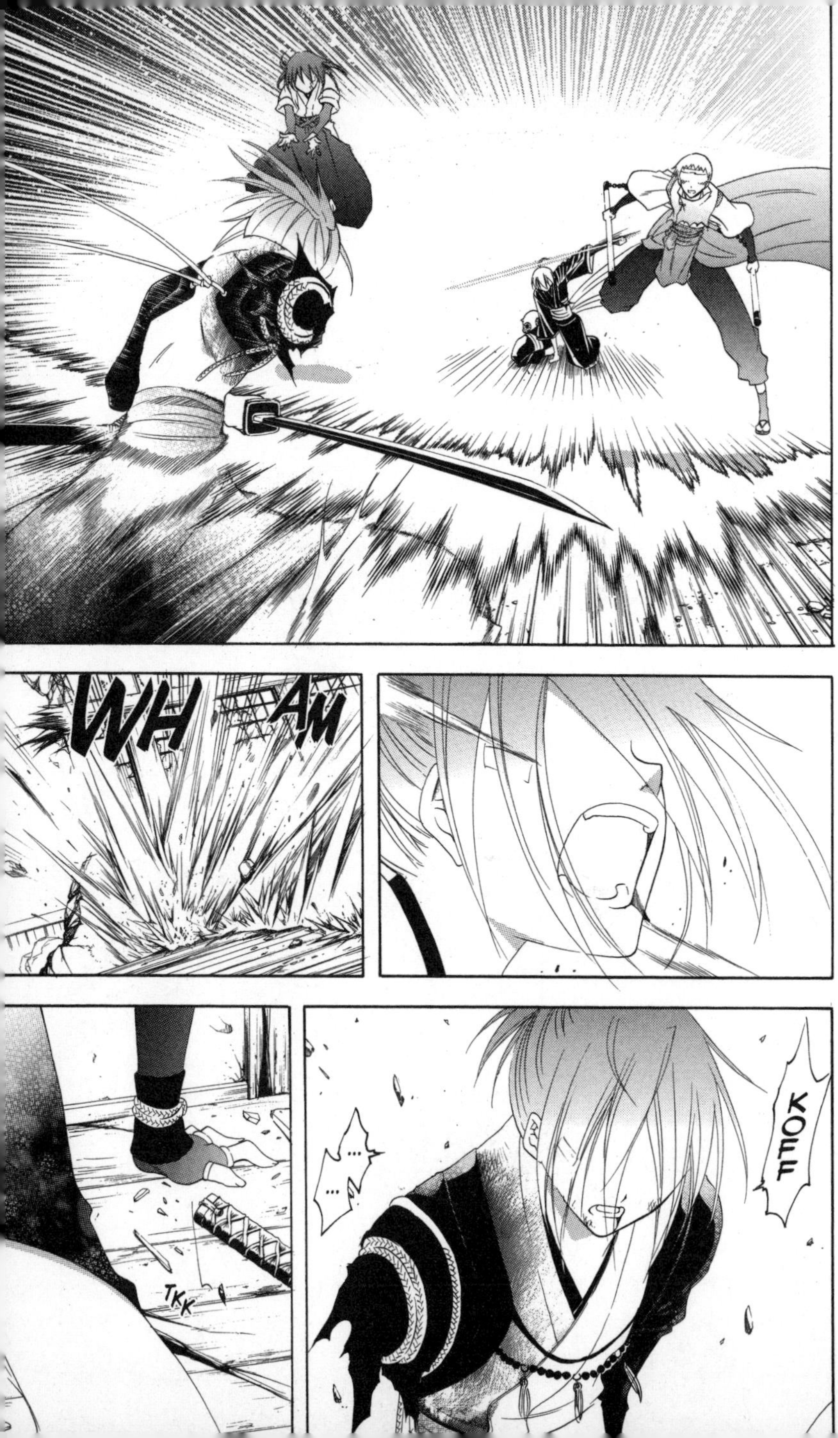
WHAM
KOFF
...
...
TKK

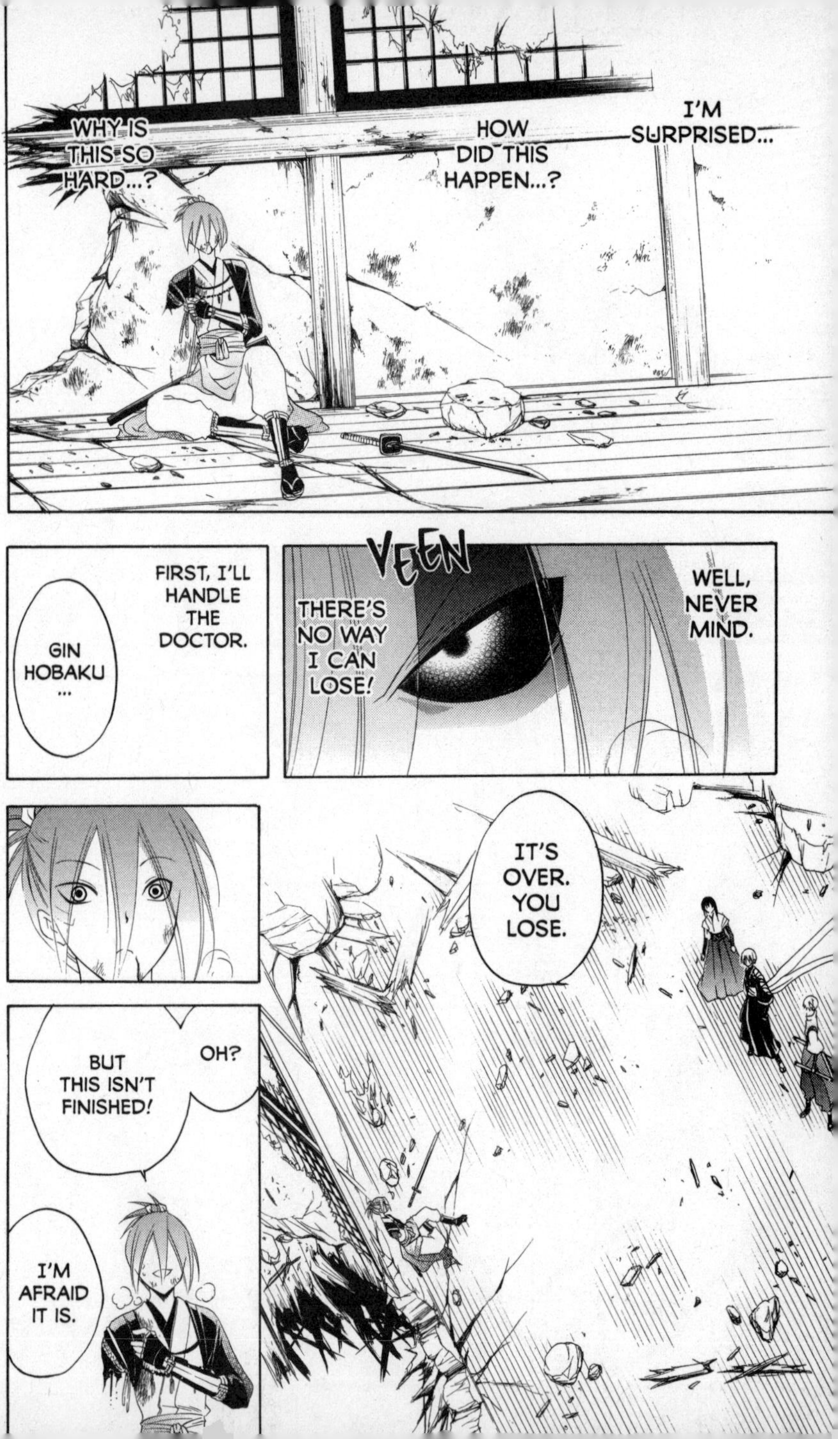
I'M SURPRISED...
HOW DID THIS HAPPEN...?
WHY IS THIS SO HARD...?
WELL, NEVER MIND.
VEEN
THERE'S NO WAY I CAN LOSE!
FIRST, I'LL HANDLE THE DOCTOR.
GIN HOBAKU ...
IT'S OVER. YOU LOSE.
OH?
BUT THIS ISN'T FINISHED!
I'M AFRAID IT IS.

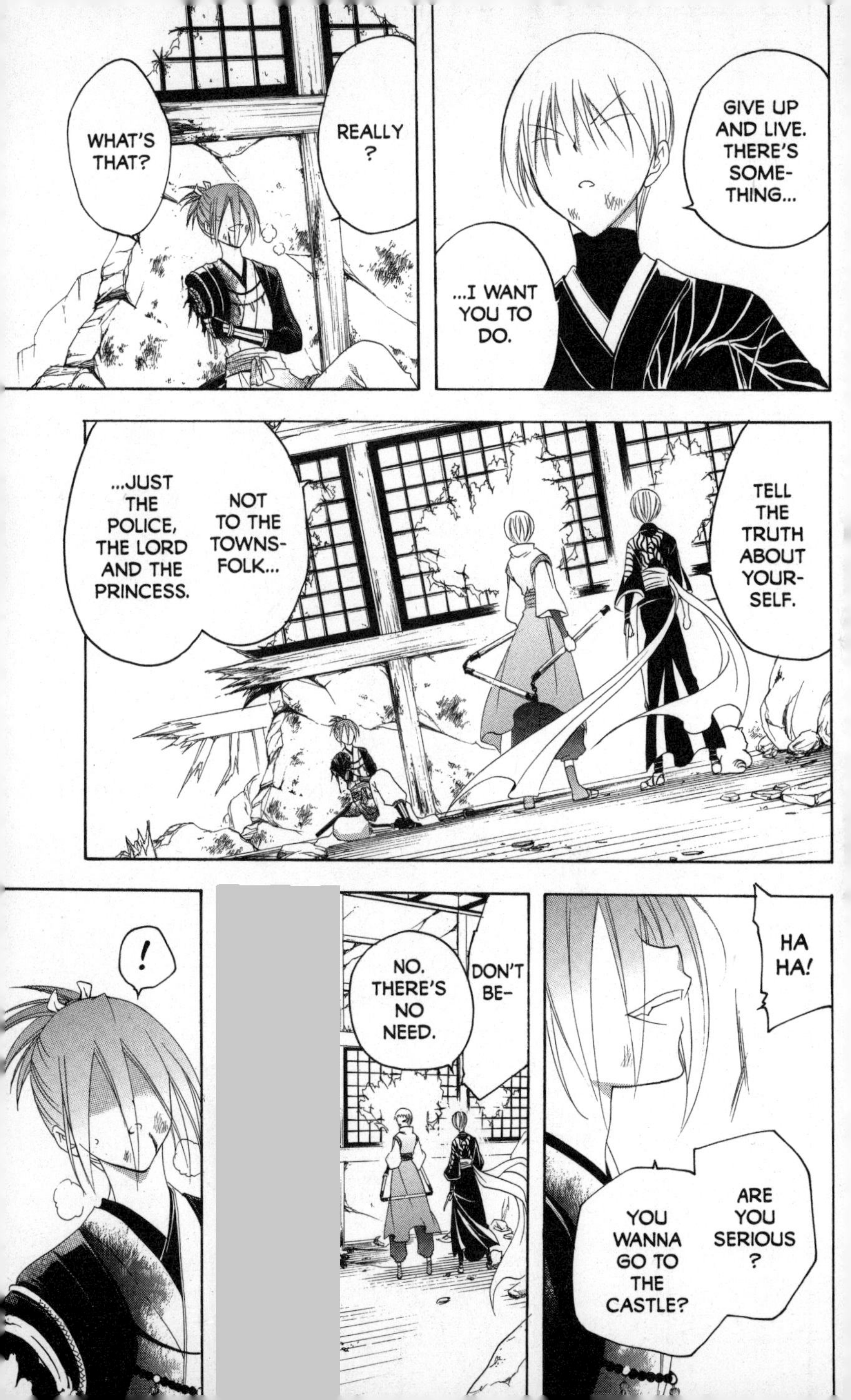
GIVE UP AND LIVE. THERE'S SOME-THING...
...I WANT YOU TO DO.
REALLY?
WHAT'S THAT?
TELL THE TRUTH ABOUT YOUR-SELF.
NOT TO THE TOWNS-FOLK...
...JUST THE POLICE, THE LORD AND THE PRINCESS.
HA HA!
ARE YOU SERIOUS?
YOU WANNA GO TO THE CASTLE?
DON'T BE-
NO. THERE'S NO NEED.
!

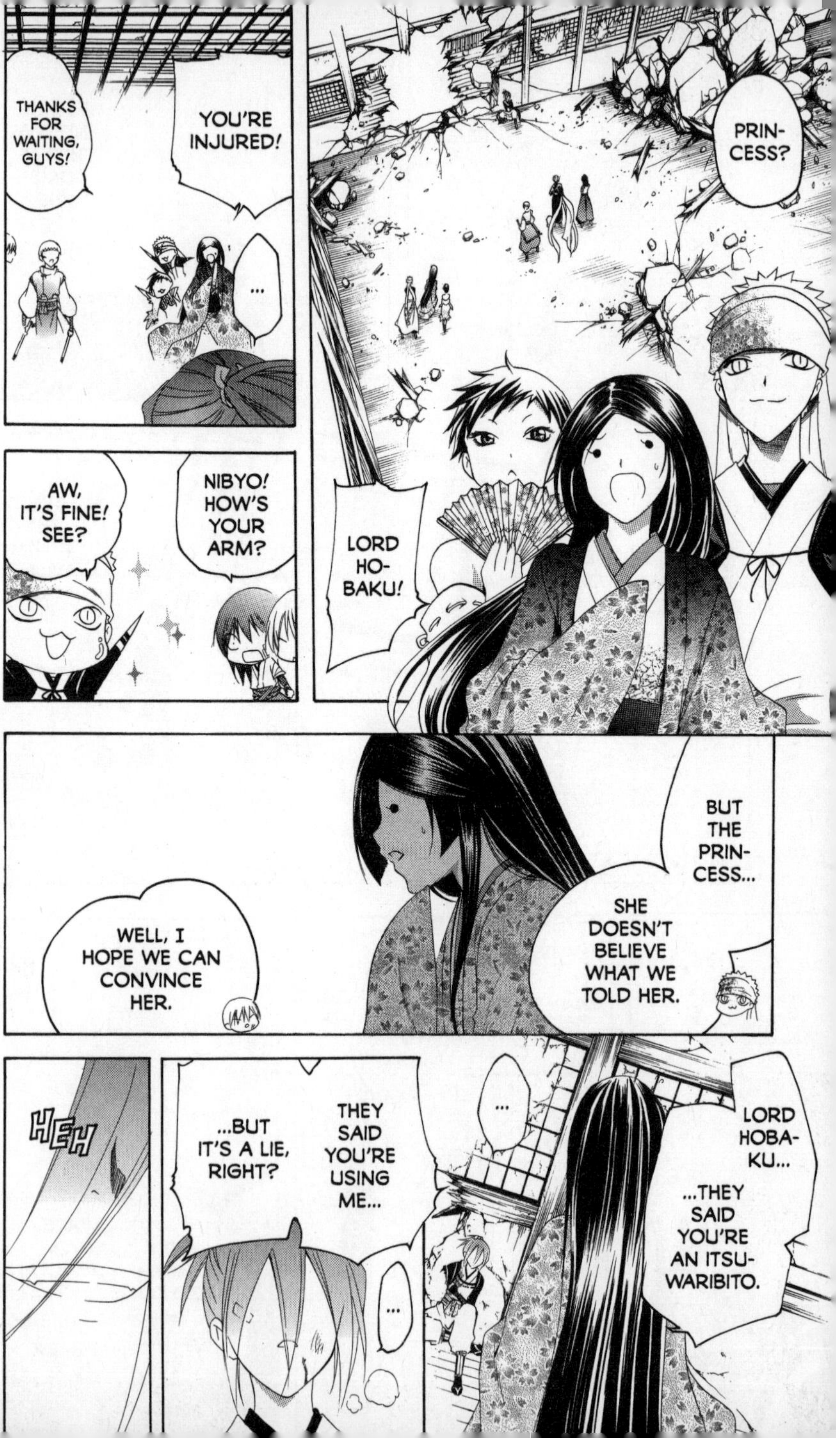
PRIN-CESS?
LORD HO-BAKU!
YOU'RE INJURED!
THANKS FOR WAITING, GUYS!
...
NIBYO! HOW'S YOUR ARM?
AW, IT'S FINE! SEE?
BUT THE PRIN-CESS...
SHE DOESN'T BELIEVE WHAT WE TOLD HER.
WELL, I HOPE WE CAN CONVINCE HER.
LORD HOBA-KU...
...THEY SAID YOU'RE AN ITSU-WARIBITO.
...
THEY SAID YOU'RE USING ME...
...BUT IT'S A LIE, RIGHT?
...
HEH

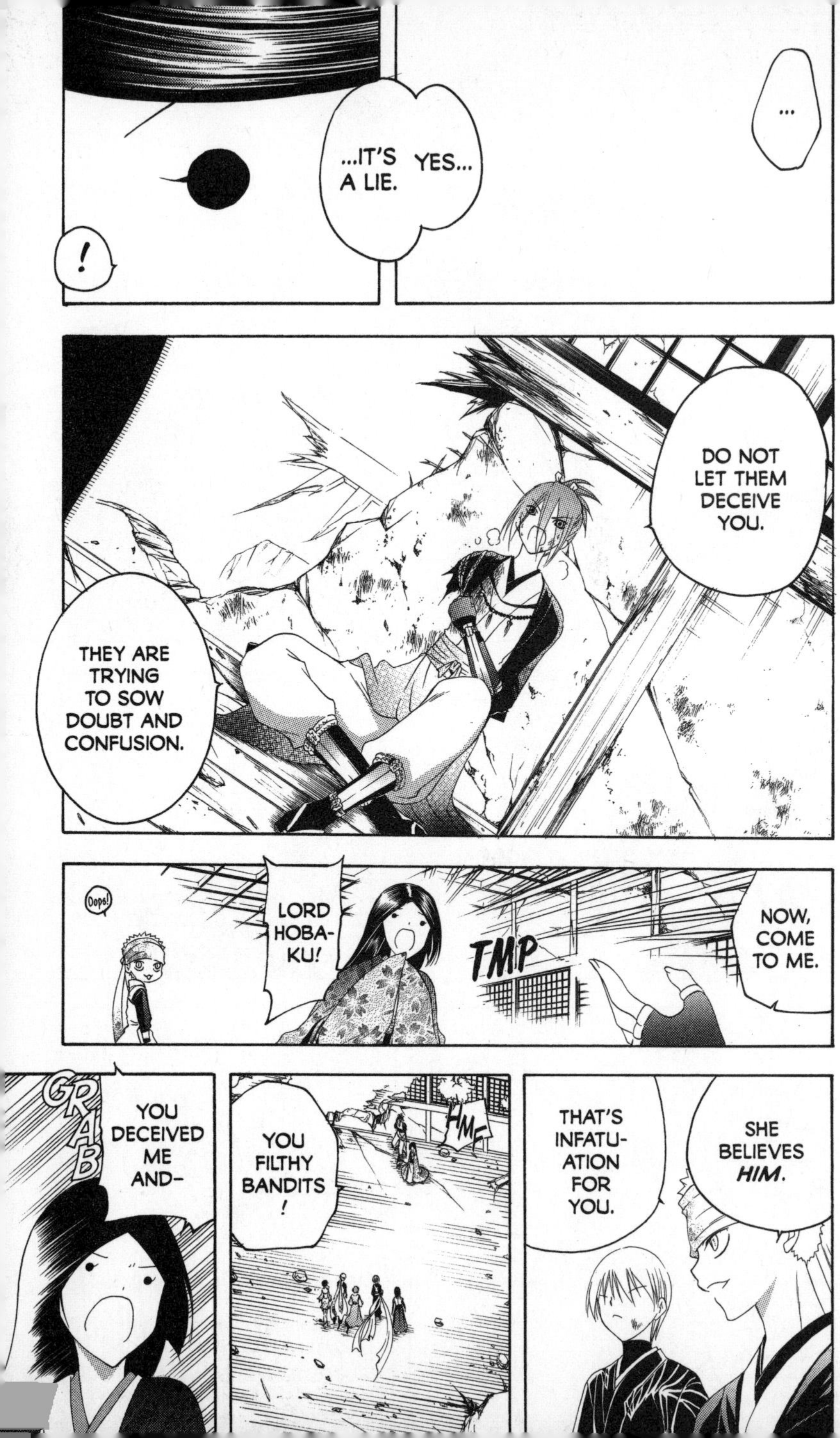
...
YES...
...IT'S A LIE.
!
DO NOT LET THEM DECEIVE YOU.
THEY ARE TRYING TO SOW DOUBT AND CONFUSION.
NOW, COME TO ME.
TMP
LORD HOBA-KU!
Oops!
SHE BELIEVES *HIM*.
THAT'S INFATU-ATION FOR YOU.
HMF
YOU FILTHY BANDITS!
YOU DECEIVED ME AND–
GRAB

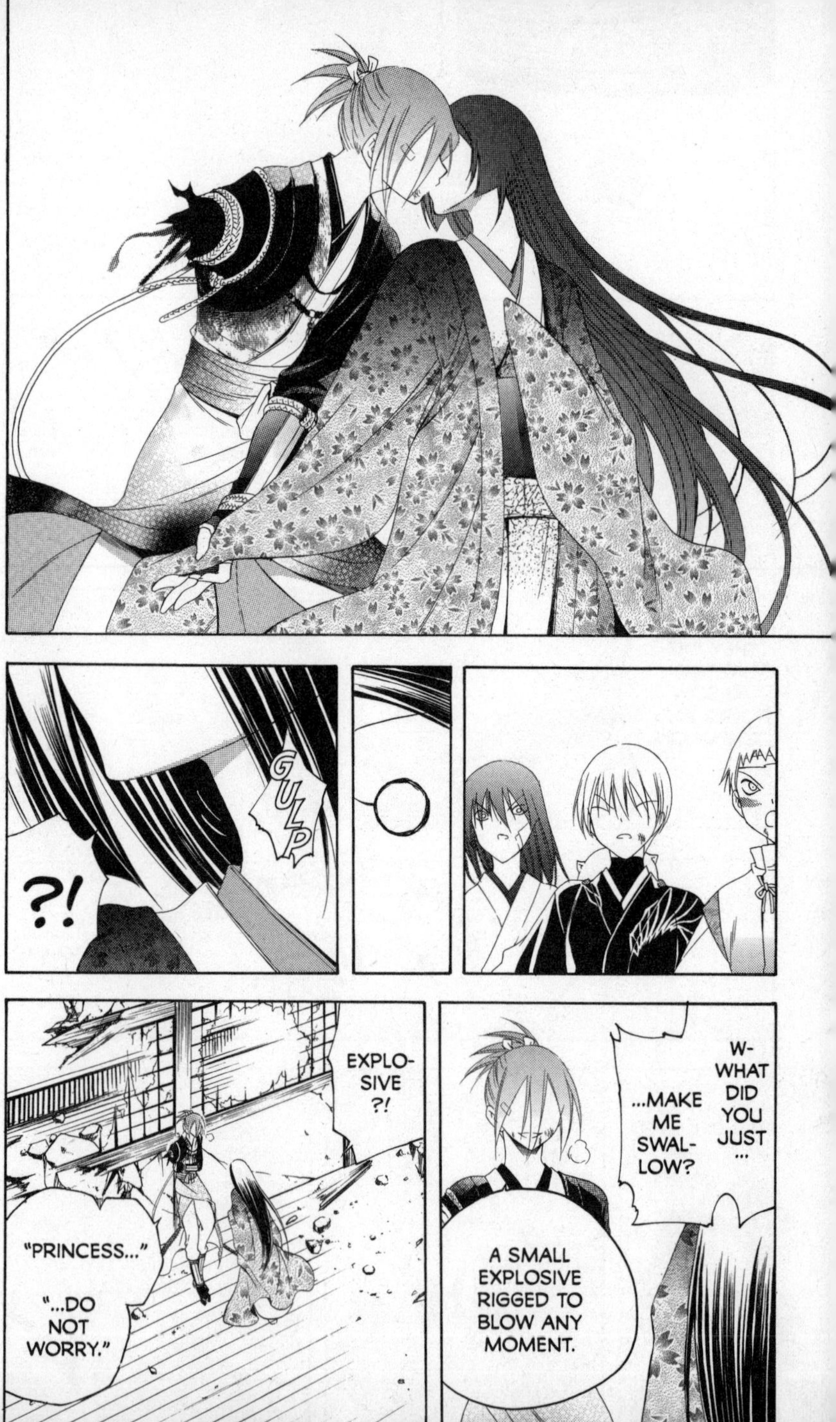
GULP
?!
W-WHAT DID YOU JUST...
...MAKE ME SWALLOW?
A SMALL EXPLOSIVE RIGGED TO BLOW ANY MOMENT.
EXPLOSIVE?!
"PRINCESS..."
"...DO NOT WORRY."

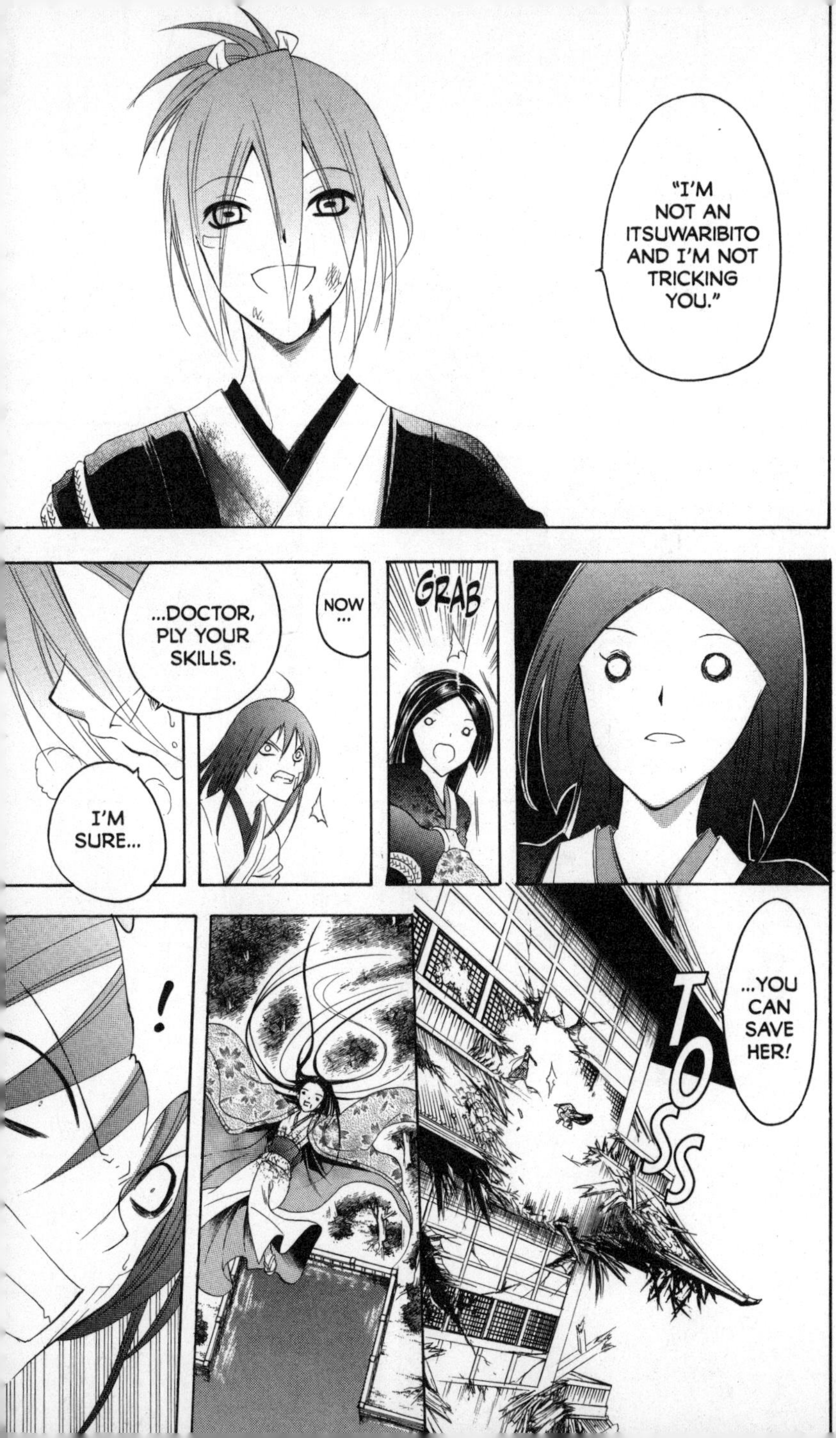
"I'M NOT AN ITSUWARIBITO AND I'M NOT TRICKING YOU."
GRAB
NOW ...
...DOCTOR, PLY YOUR SKILLS.
I'M SURE...
...YOU CAN SAVE HER!
TOSS
!

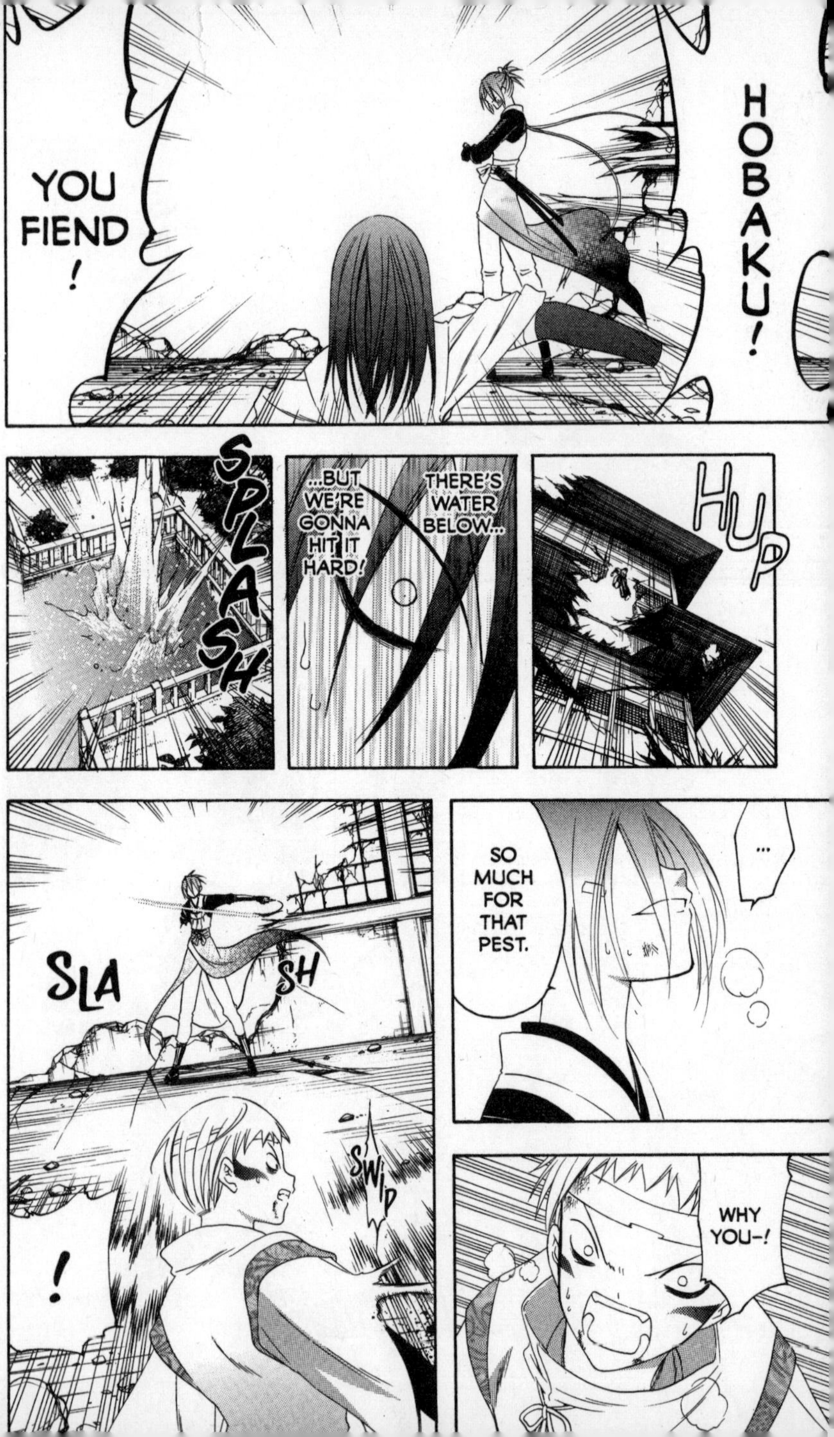
HOBAKU!
YOU FIEND!
HUP
THERE'S WATER BELOW...
...BUT WE'RE GONNA HIT IT HARD!
SPLASH
...
SO MUCH FOR THAT PEST.
WHY YOU-!
SLASH
SWIP
!

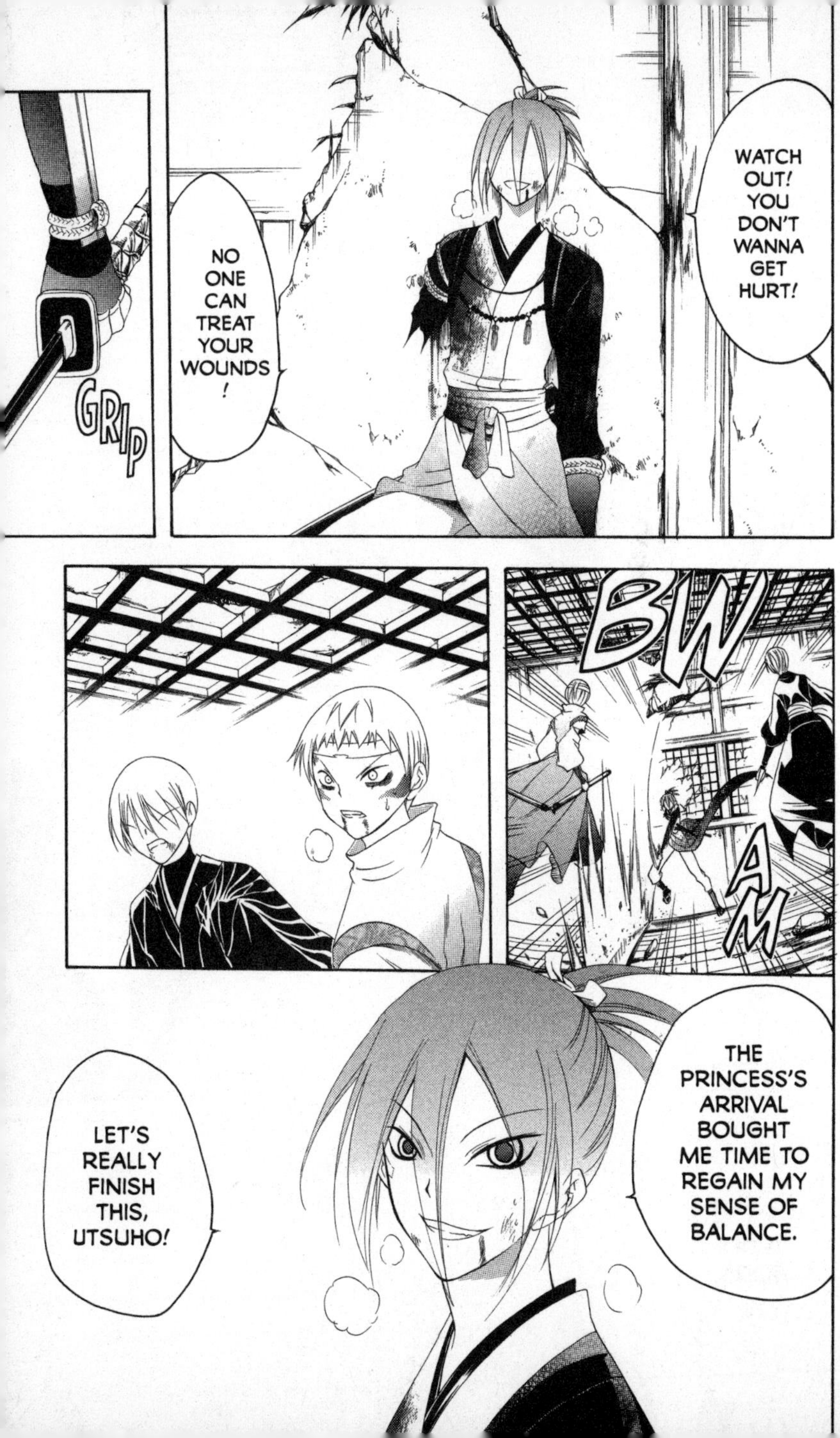
WATCH OUT! YOU DON'T WANNA GET HURT!
NO ONE CAN TREAT YOUR WOUNDS!
GRIP
BWAM
THE PRINCESS'S ARRIVAL BOUGHT ME TIME TO REGAIN MY SENSE OF BALANCE.
LET'S REALLY FINISH THIS, UTSUHO!

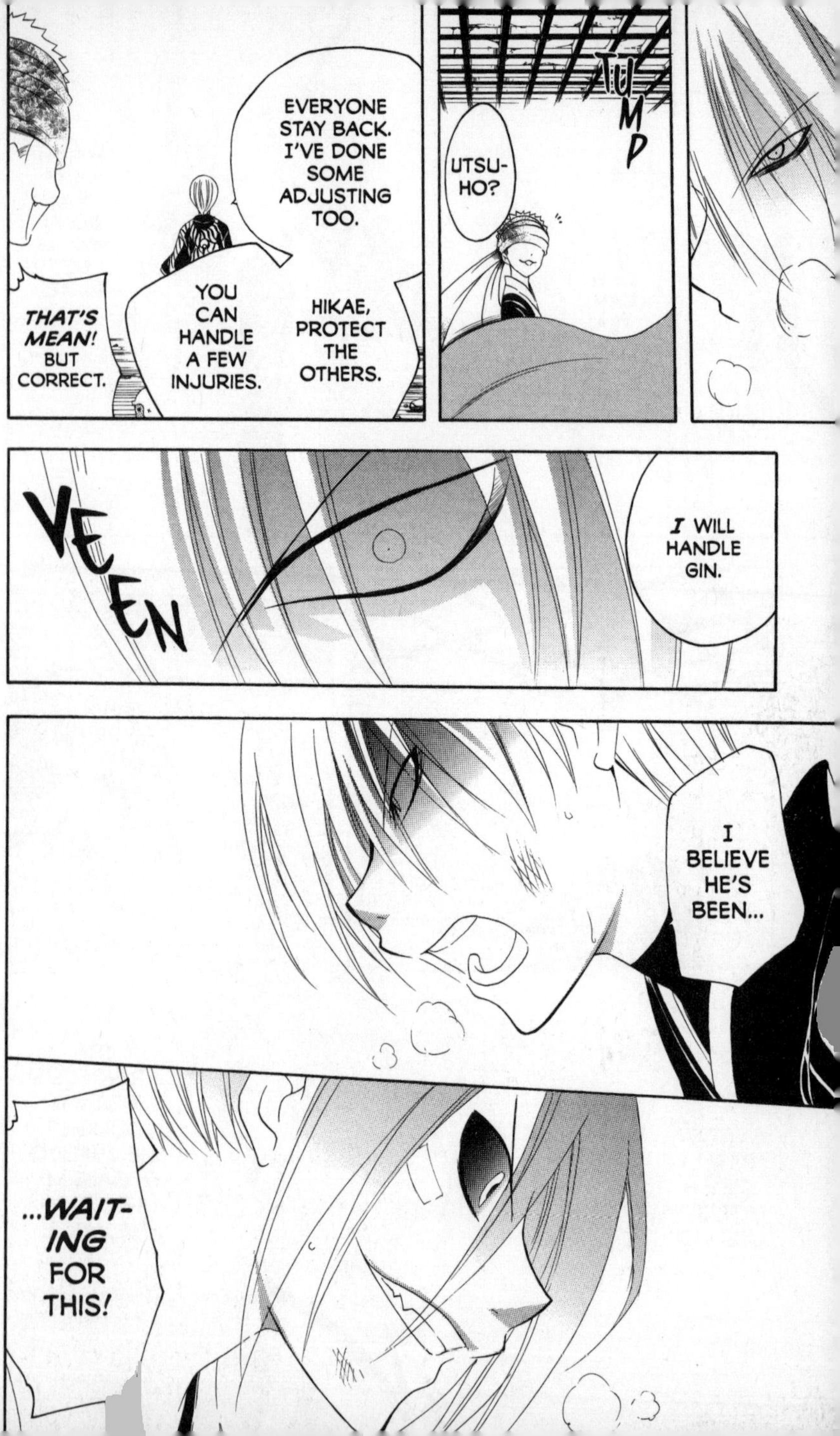
TUMP
UTSU-HO?
EVERYONE STAY BACK. I'VE DONE SOME ADJUSTING TOO.
HIKAE, PROTECT THE OTHERS.
YOU CAN HANDLE A FEW INJURIES.
THAT'S MEAN! BUT CORRECT.
I WILL HANDLE GIN.
VEEN
I BELIEVE HE'S BEEN...
...*WAIT-ING* FOR THIS!

Chapter 195
Liars and Honest People

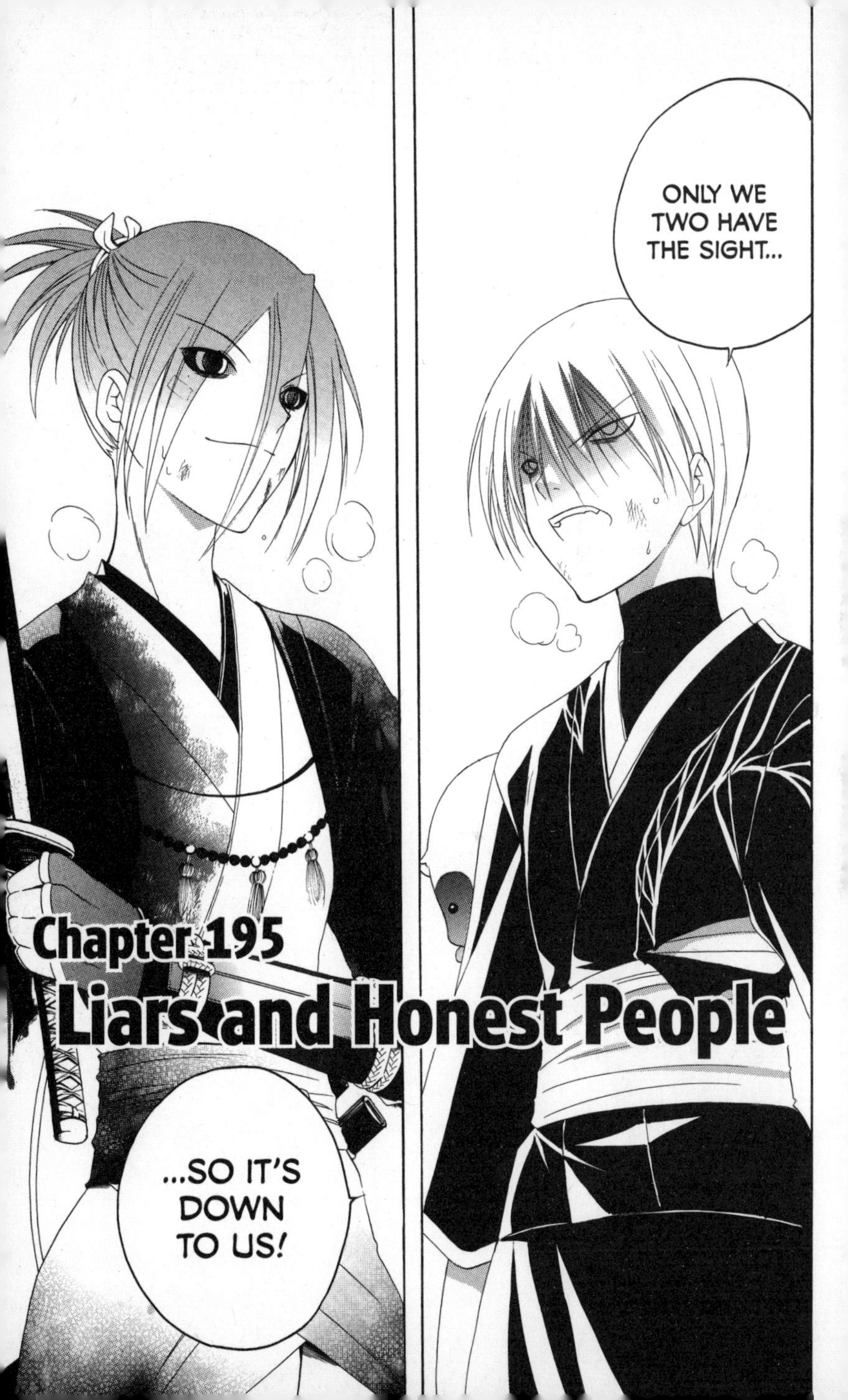
ONLY WE TWO HAVE THE SIGHT...
...SO IT'S DOWN TO US!

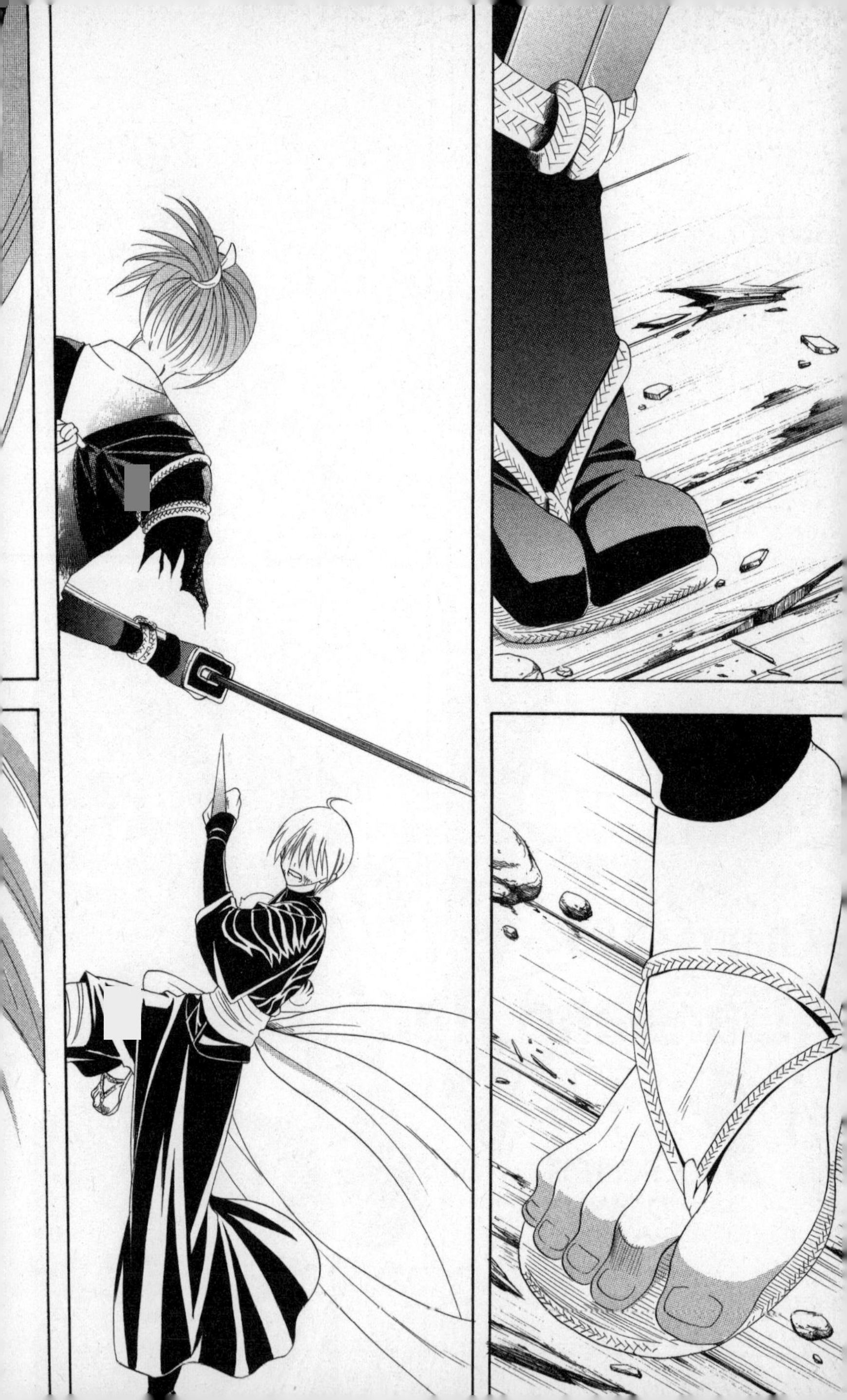

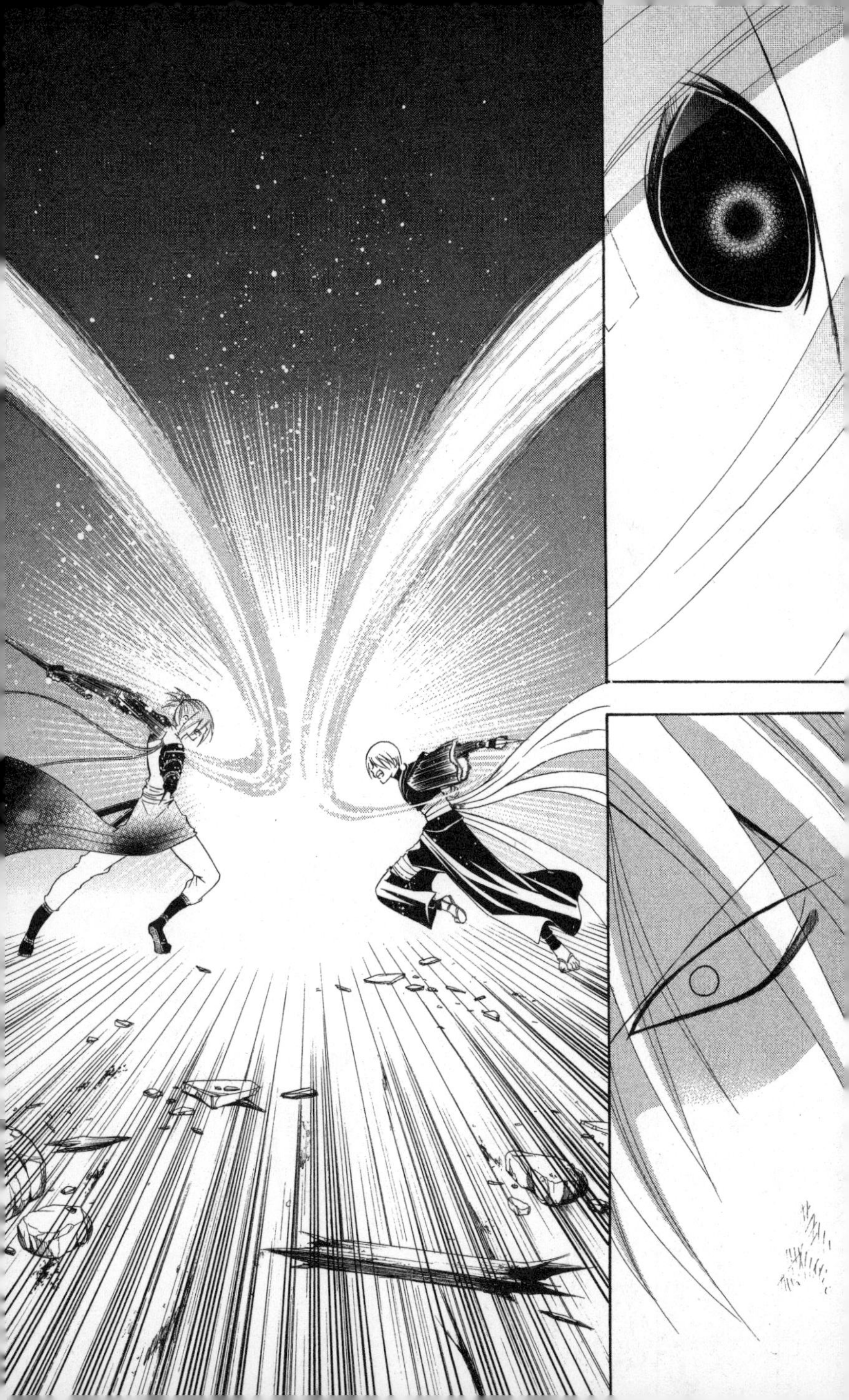

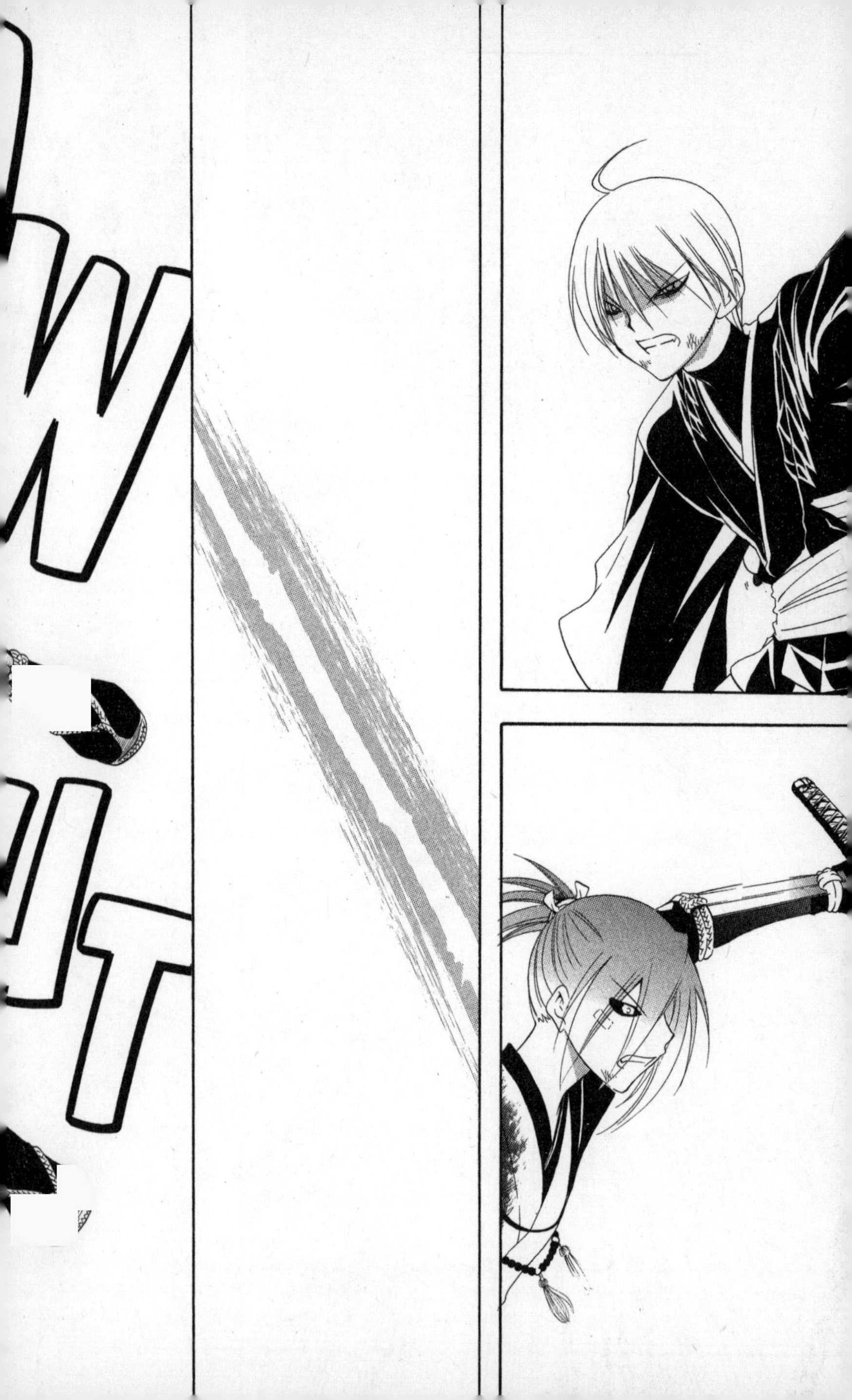

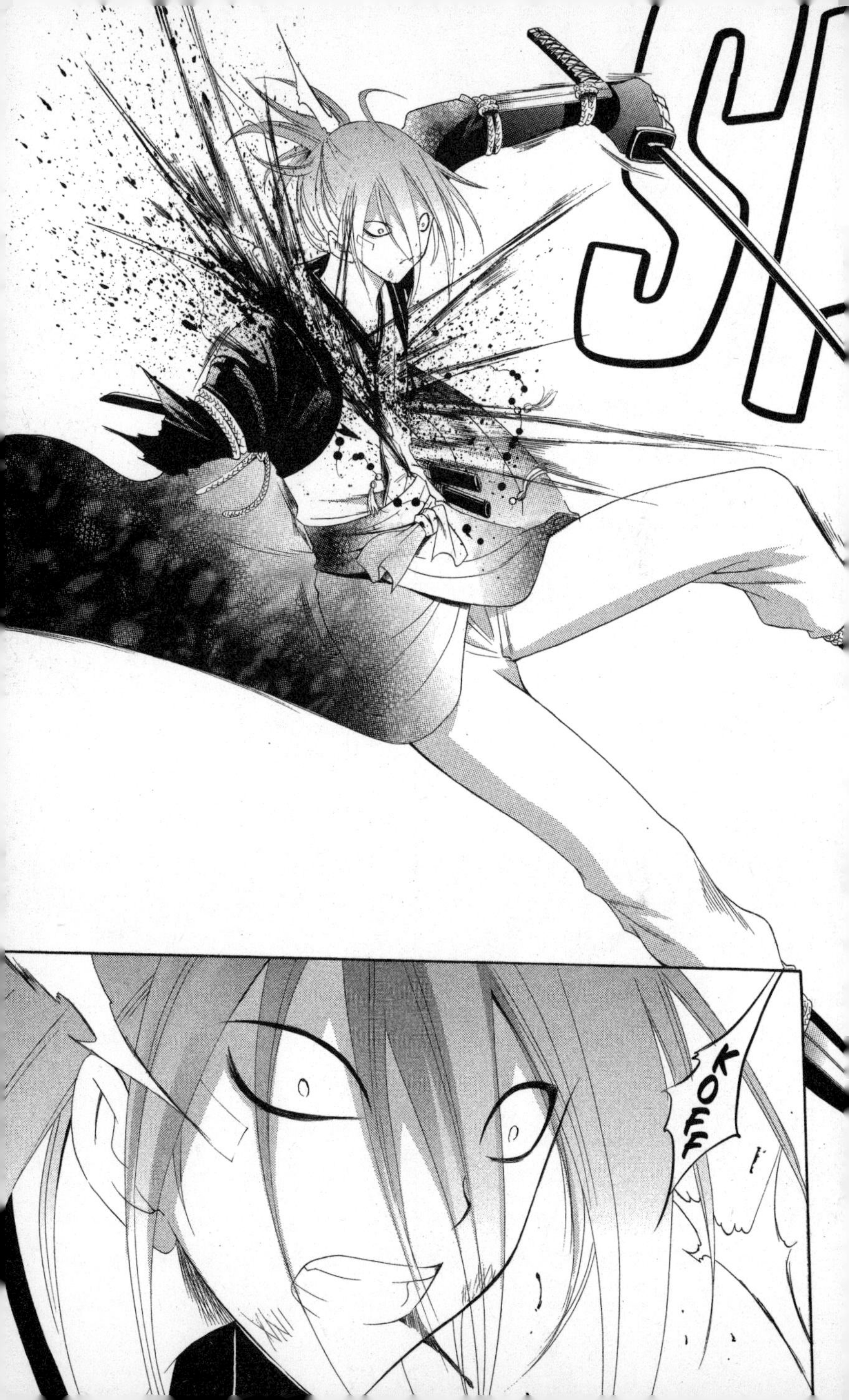
KOFF

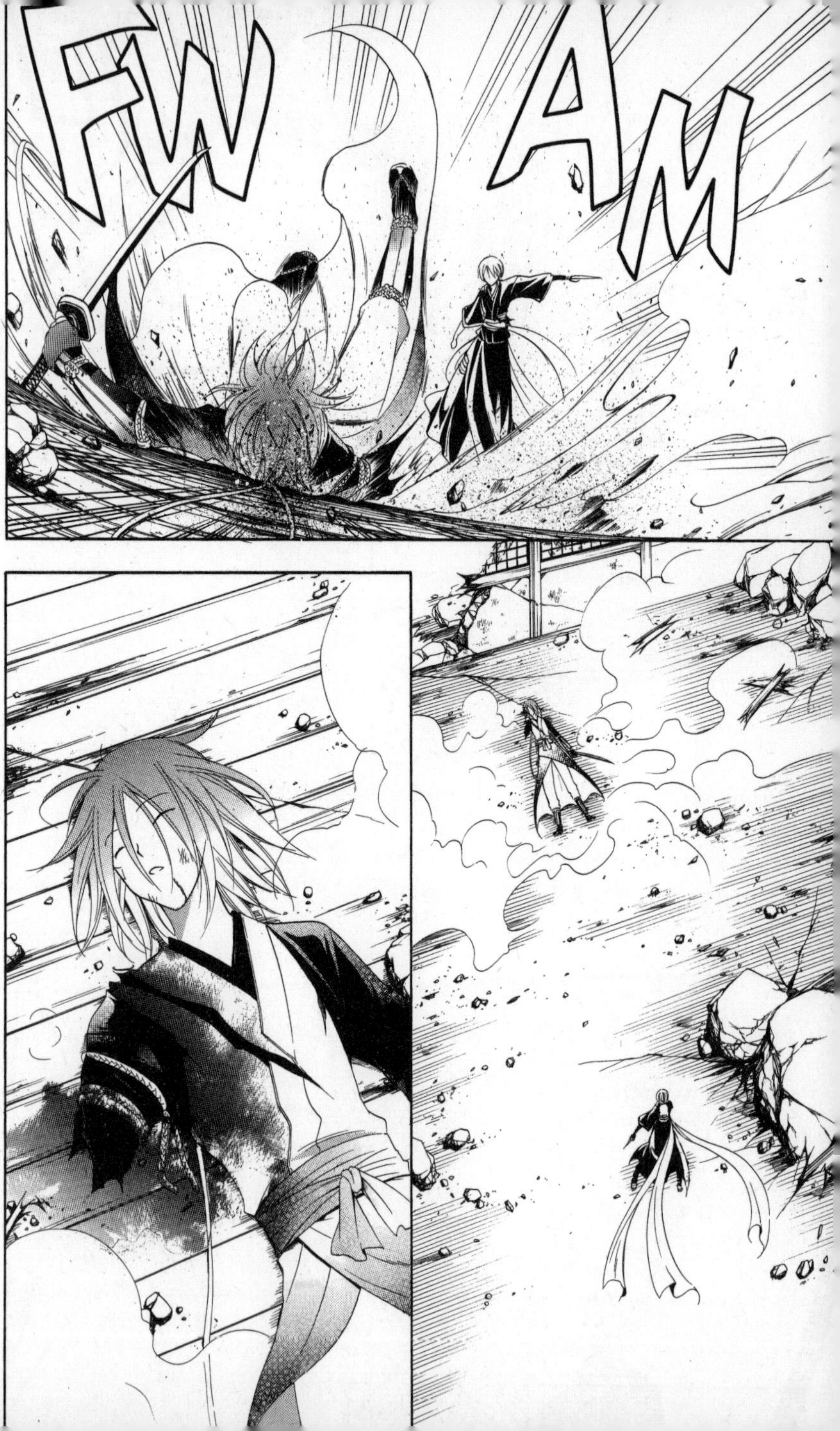
FWAM

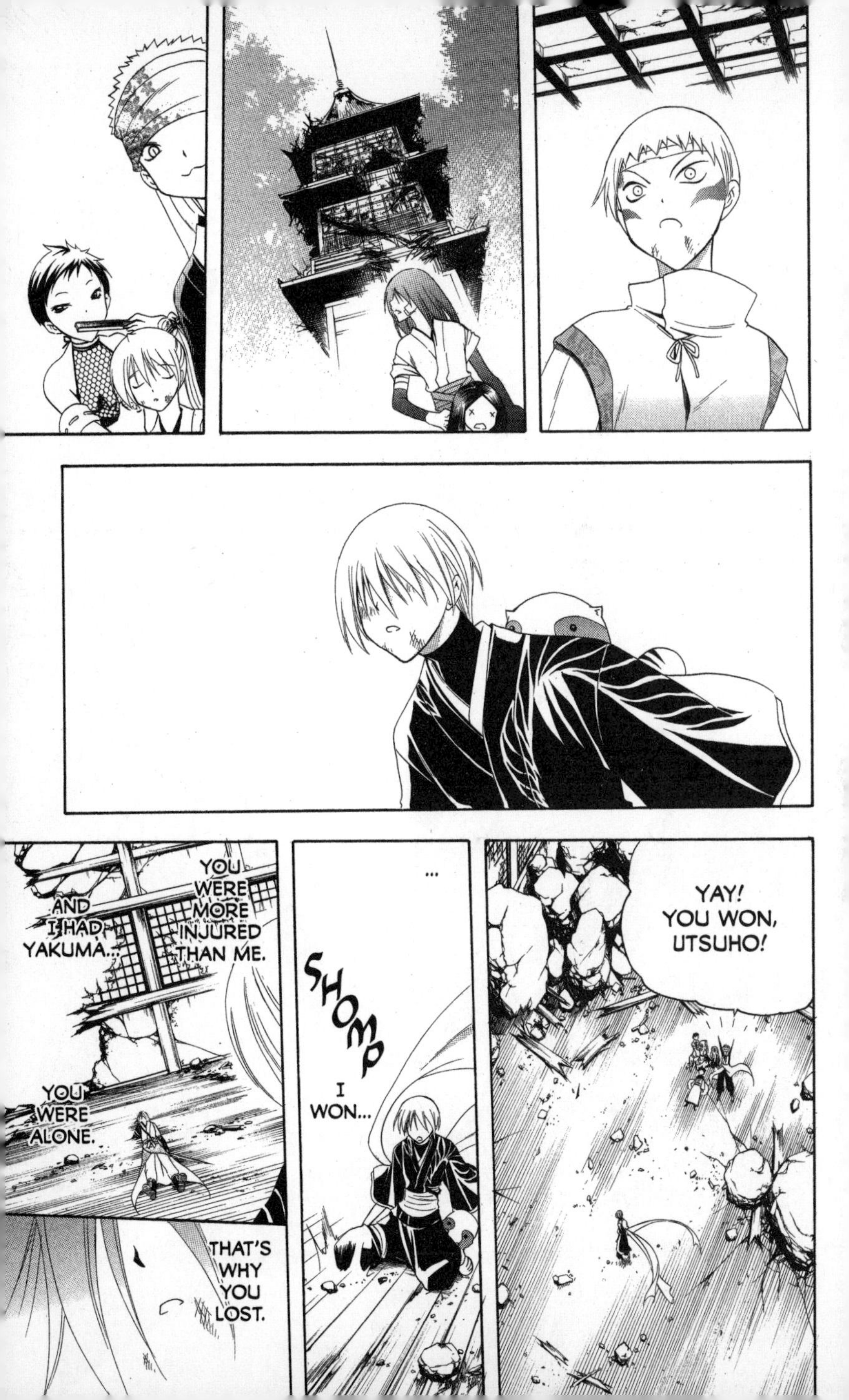
YAY! YOU WON, UTSUHO!
...
SHOMP
I WON...
YOU WERE MORE INJURED THAN ME.
AND I HAD YAKUMA...
YOU WERE ALONE.
THAT'S WHY YOU LOST.

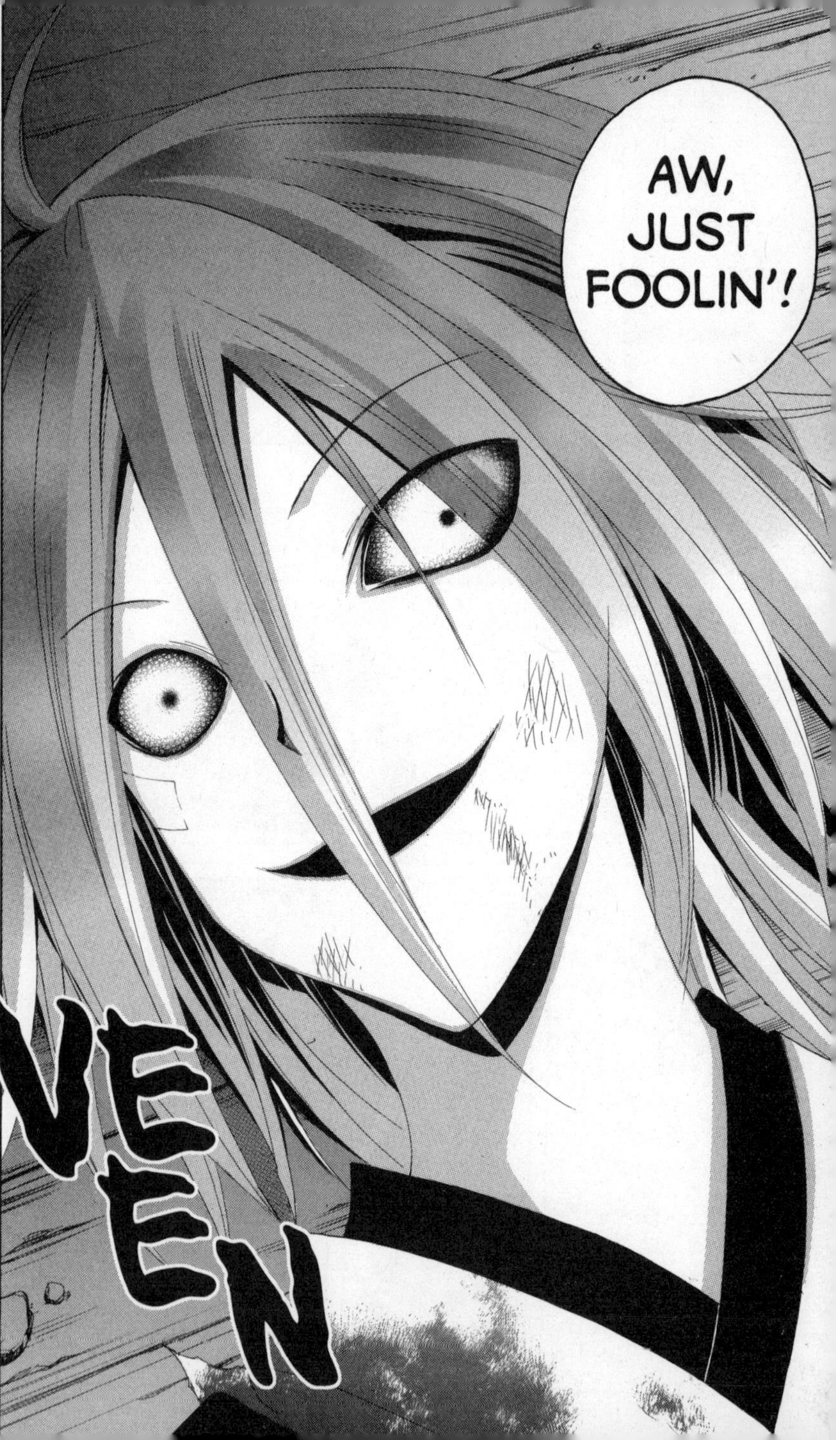
AW, JUST FOOLIN'!
VEEN

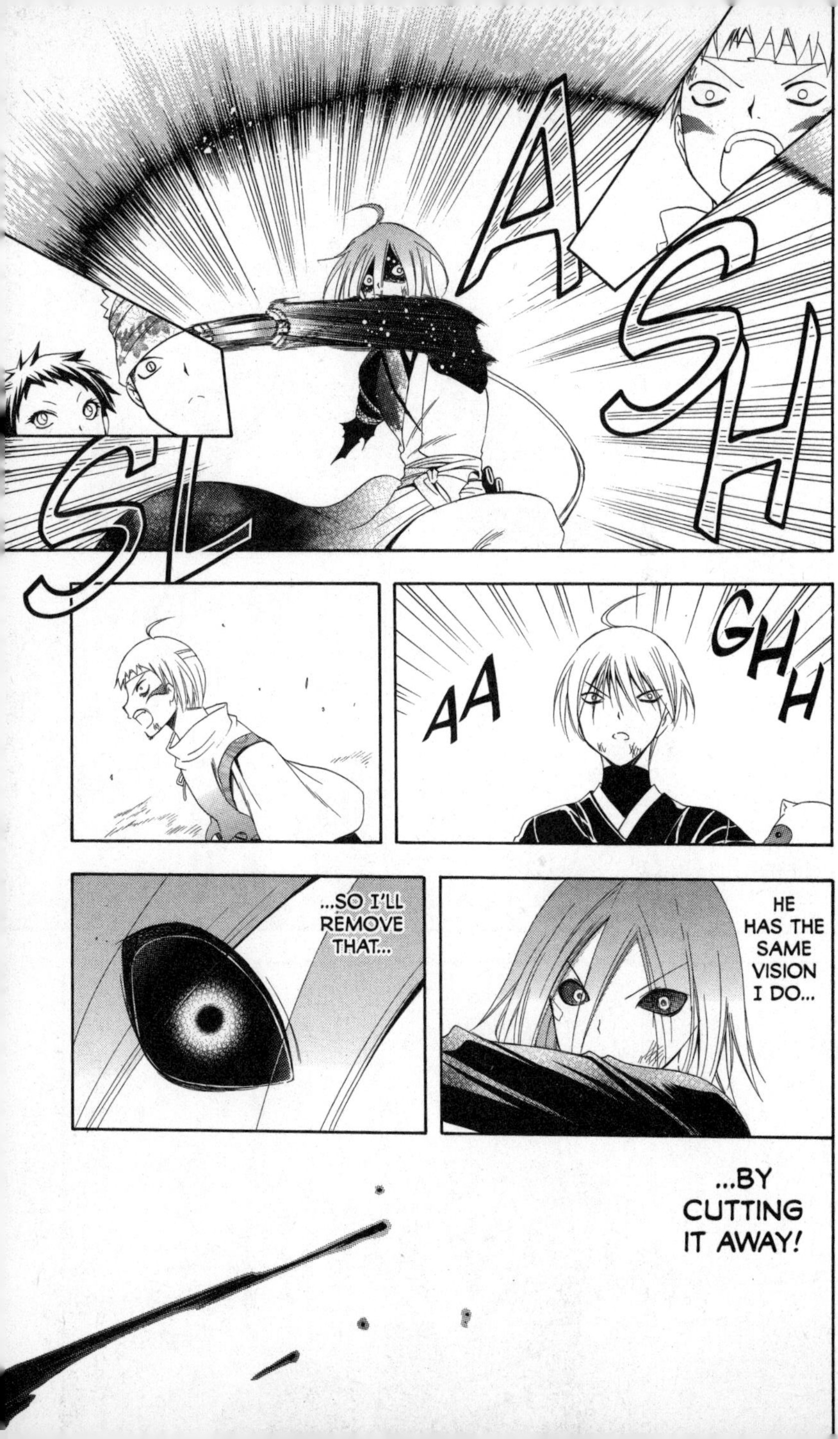
SL
ASH
AA
GHH
HE HAS THE SAME VISION I DO...
...SO I'LL REMOVE THAT...
...BY CUTTING IT AWAY!

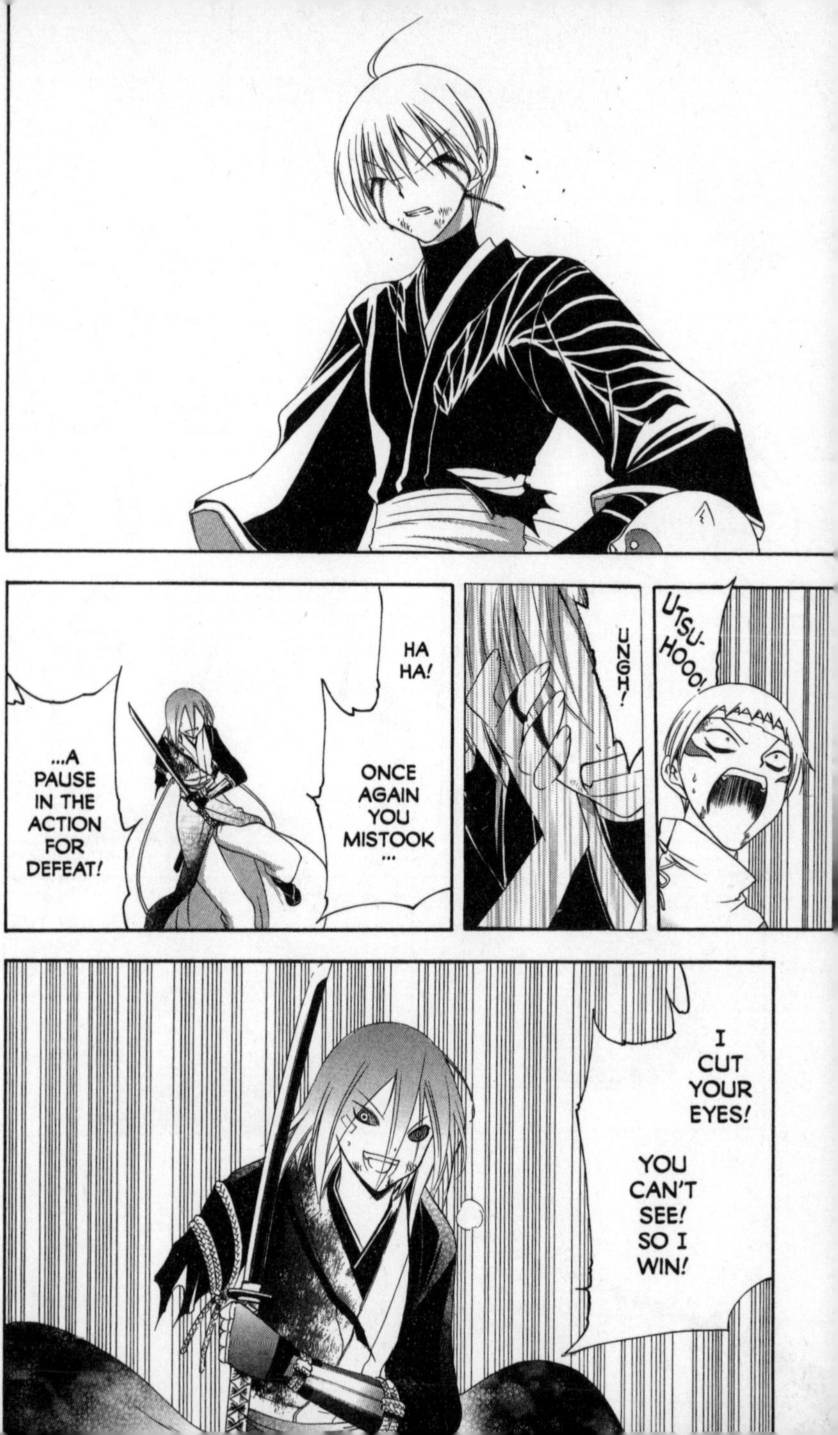
UTSU-HOOOO!
UNGH!
HA HA!
ONCE AGAIN YOU MISTOOK...
...A PAUSE IN THE ACTION FOR DEFEAT!
I CUT YOUR EYES!
YOU CAN'T SEE! SO I WIN!

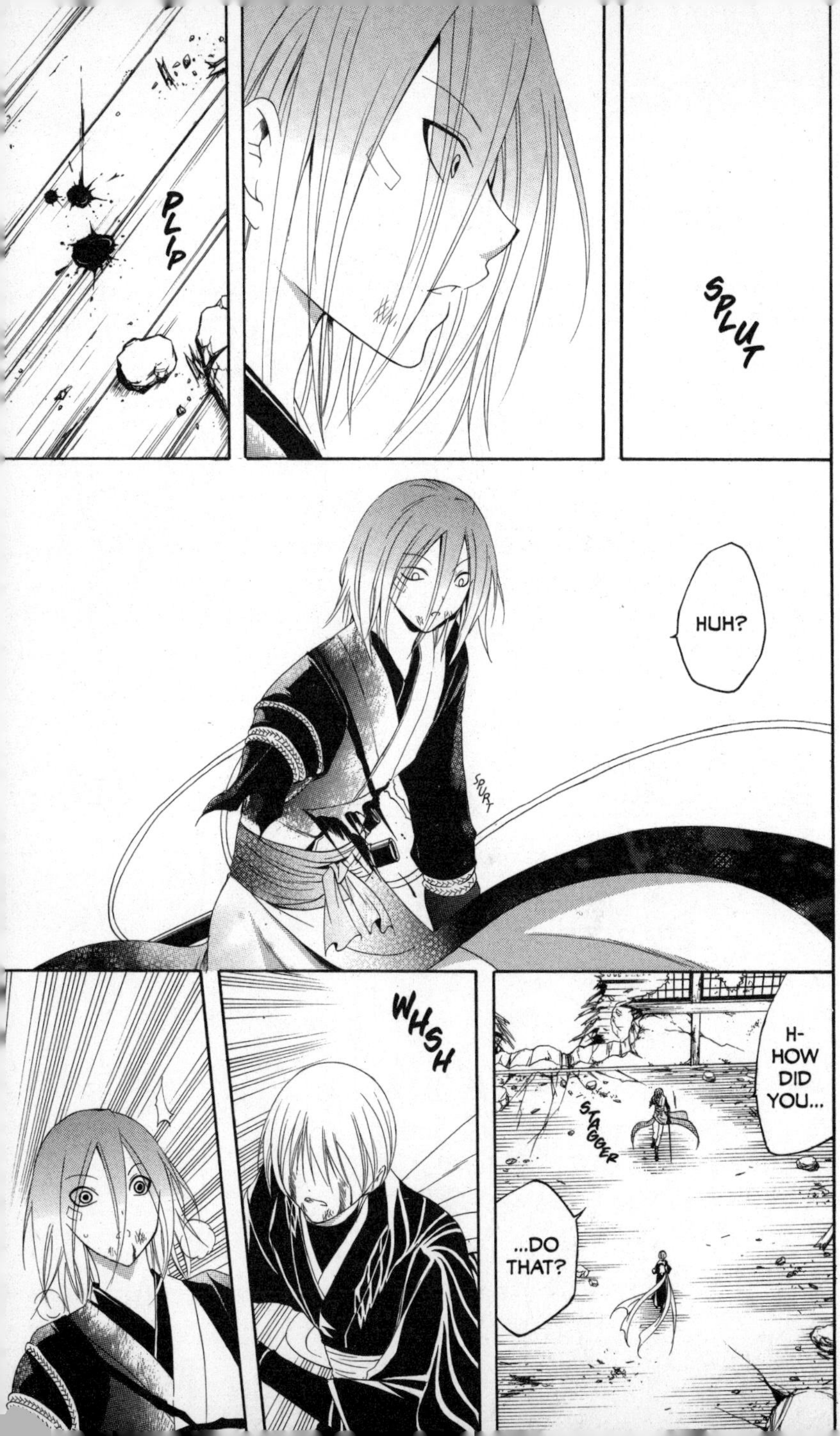
SPLUT
PLIP
HUH?
SPURT
H- HOW DID YOU...
STAGGER
...DO THAT?
WHSH

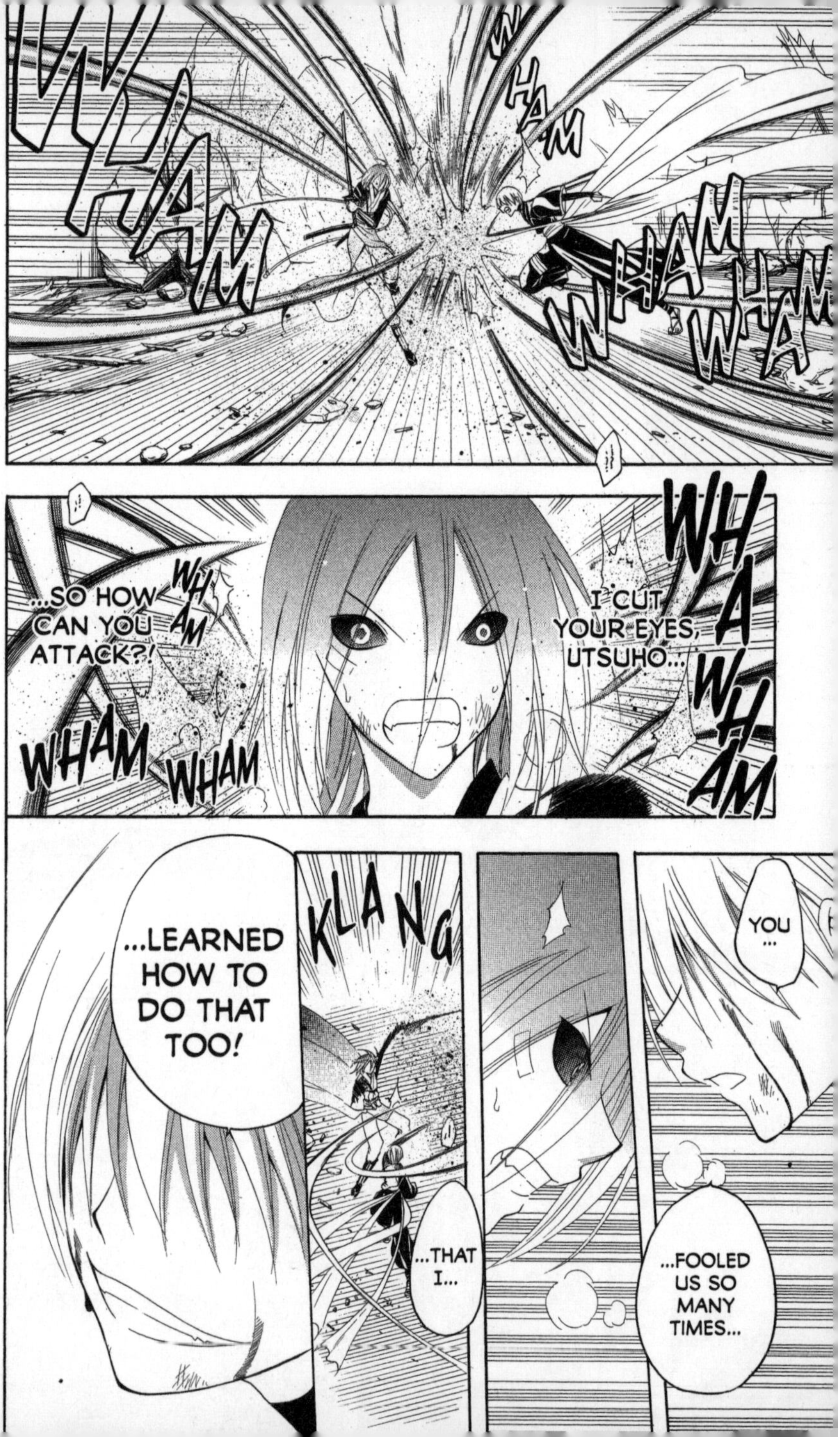
WHAM
WHAM WHAM
WHAM WHAM
WHAM
WHAM WHAM
I CUT YOUR EYES, UTSUHO...
WHAM
...SO HOW CAN YOU ATTACK?!
WHAM WHAM
YOU ...
...FOOLED US SO MANY TIMES...
KLANG
...THAT I...
...LEARNED HOW TO DO THAT TOO!

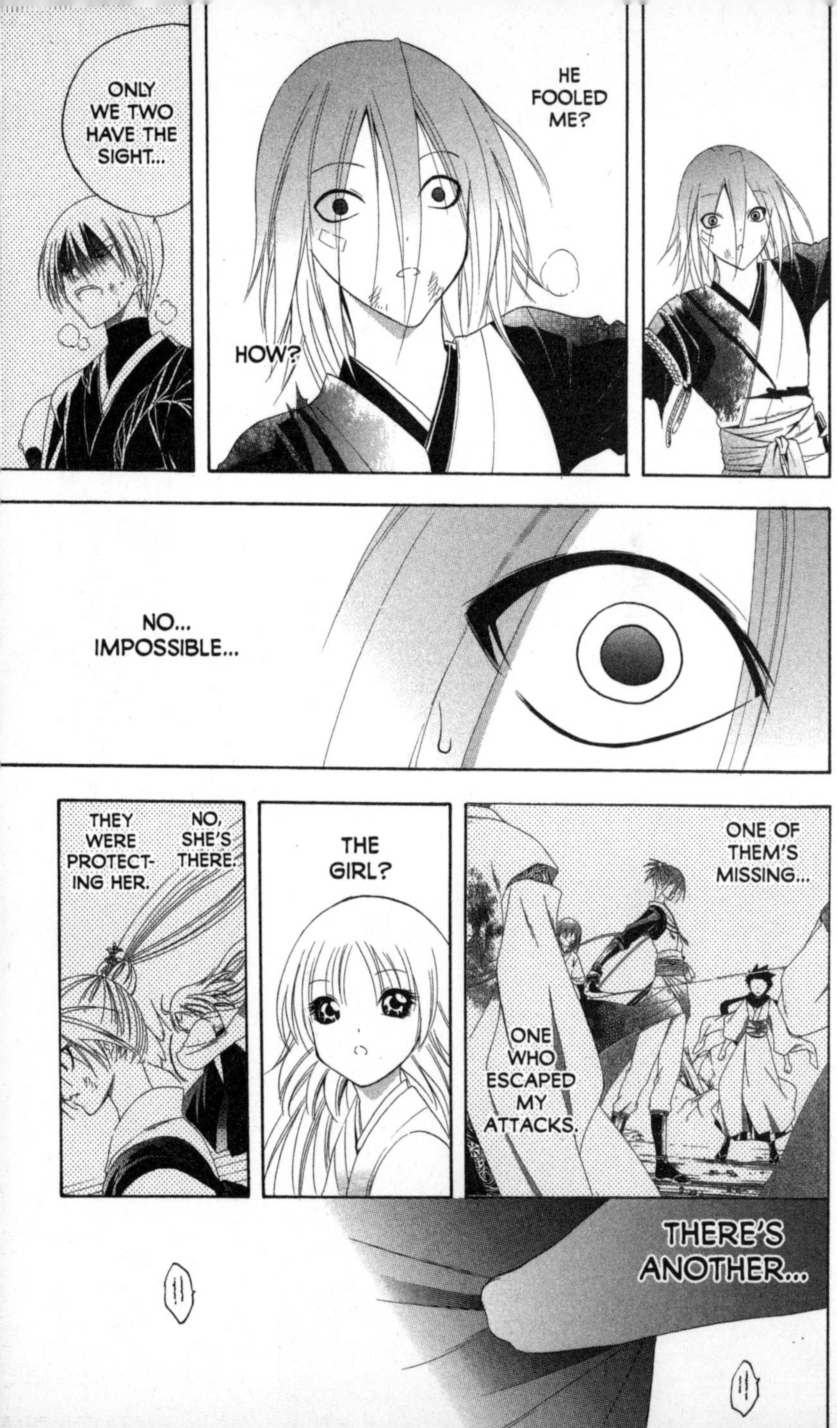
HE FOOLED ME?
HOW?
ONLY WE TWO HAVE THE SIGHT...
NO... IMPOSSIBLE...
ONE OF THEM'S MISSING...
ONE WHO ESCAPED MY ATTACKS.
THE GIRL?
NO, SHE'S THERE.
THEY WERE PROTECTING HER.
THERE'S ANOTHER...
!!
!!

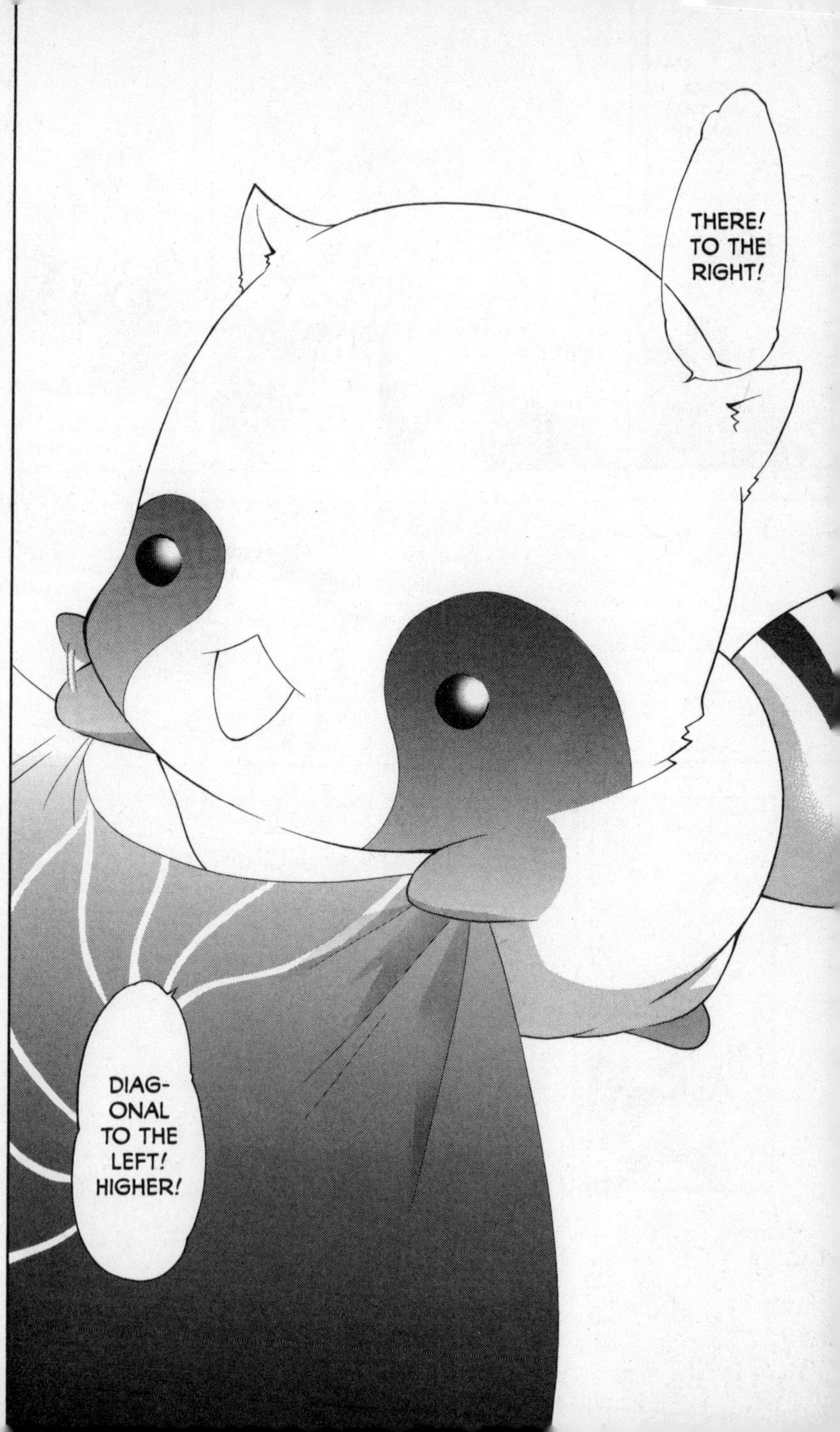
THERE! TO THE RIGHT!
DIAG-ONAL TO THE LEFT! HIGHER!

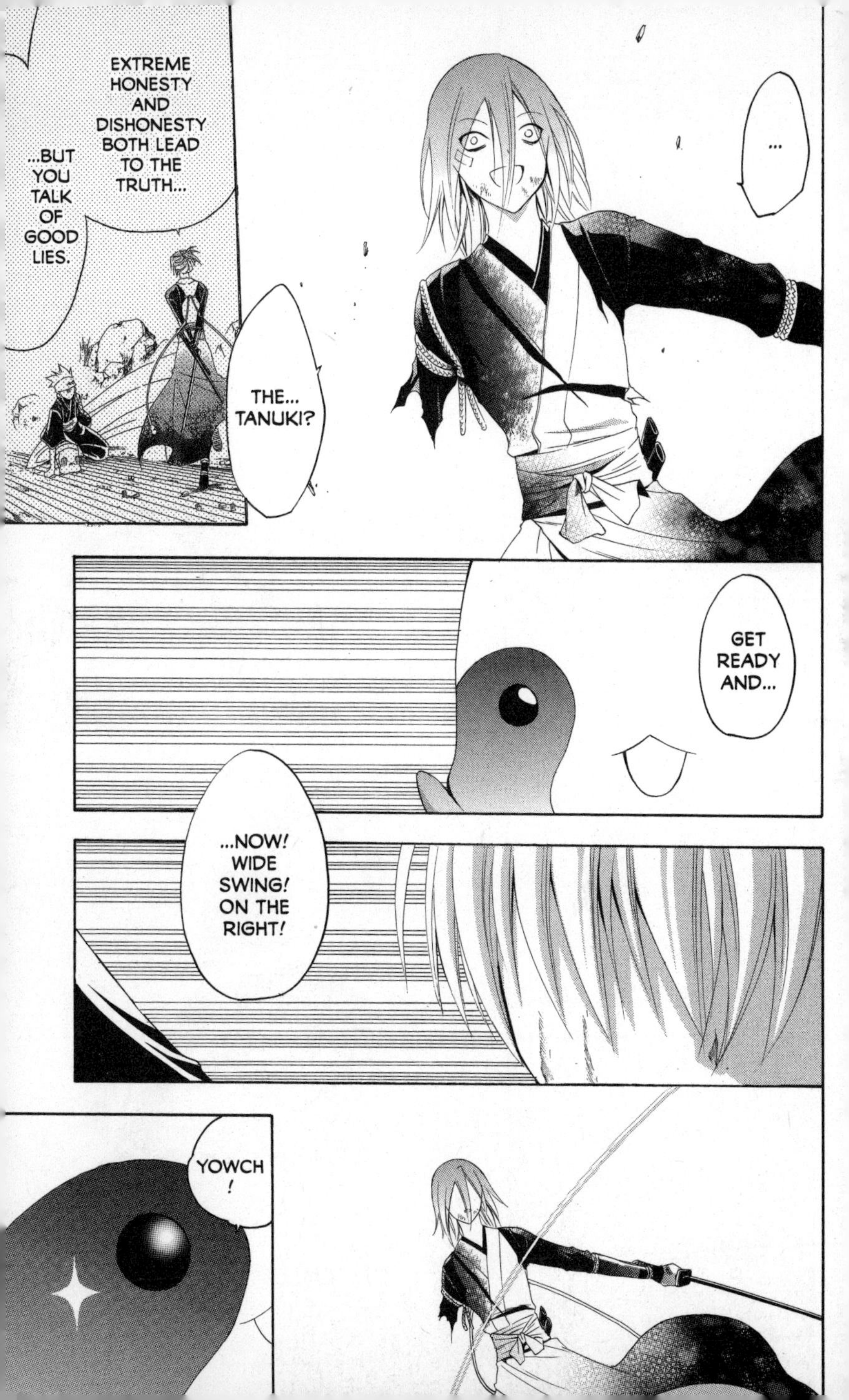
...
THE... TANUKI?
EXTREME HONESTY AND DISHONESTY BOTH LEAD TO THE TRUTH...
...BUT YOU TALK OF GOOD LIES.
GET READY AND...
...NOW! WIDE SWING! ON THE RIGHT!
YOWCH!

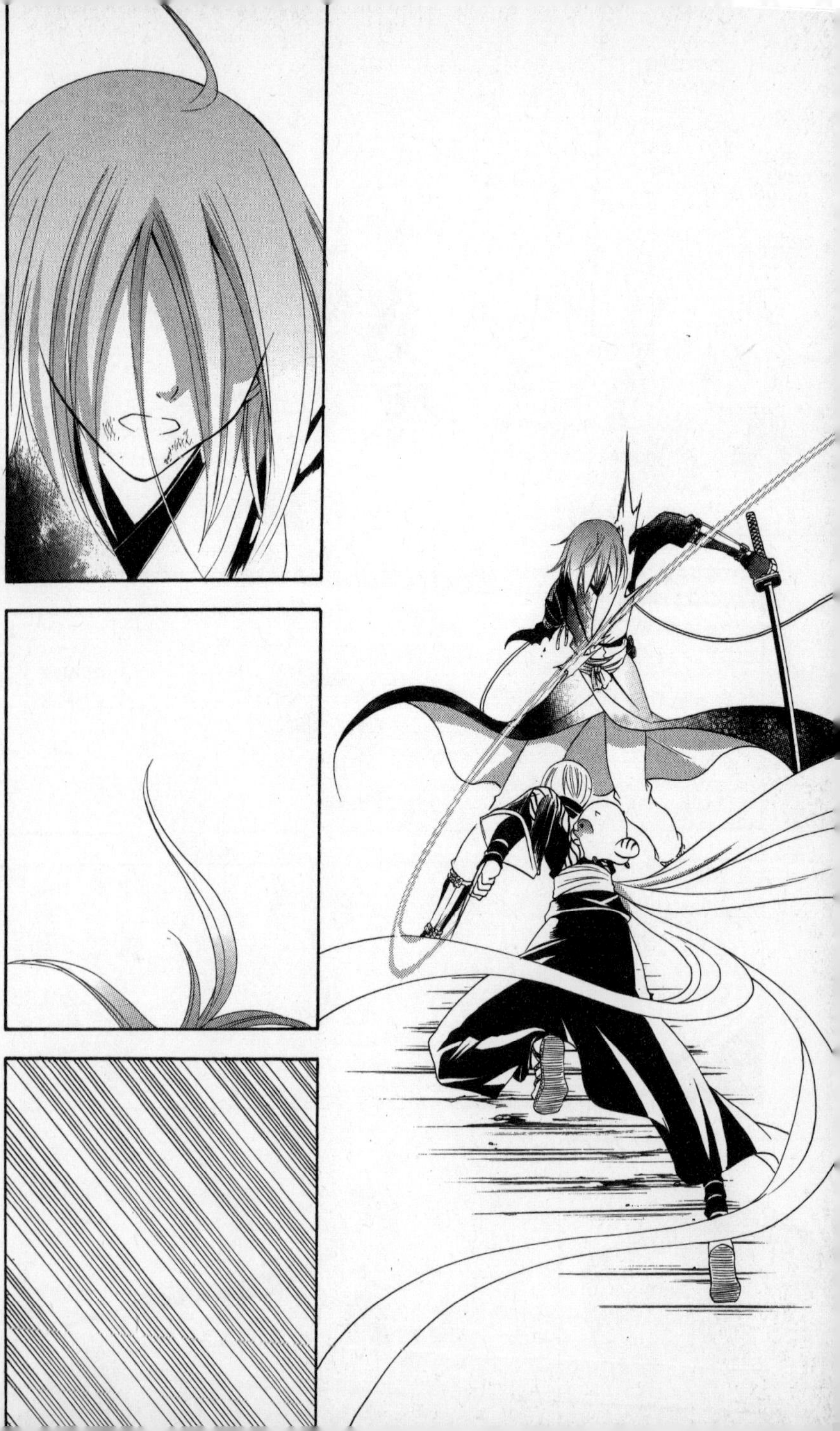

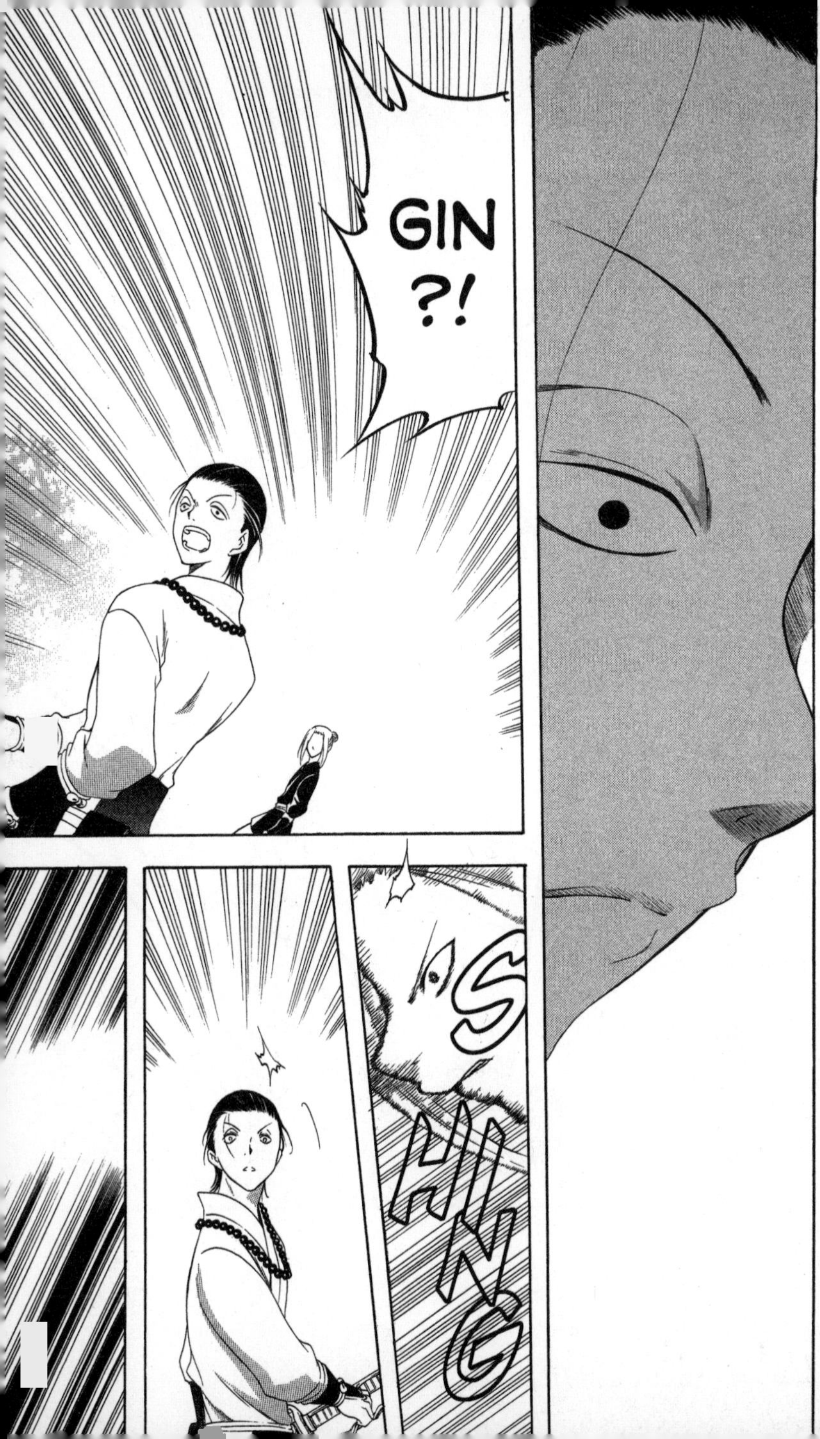
GIN ?!
SHING

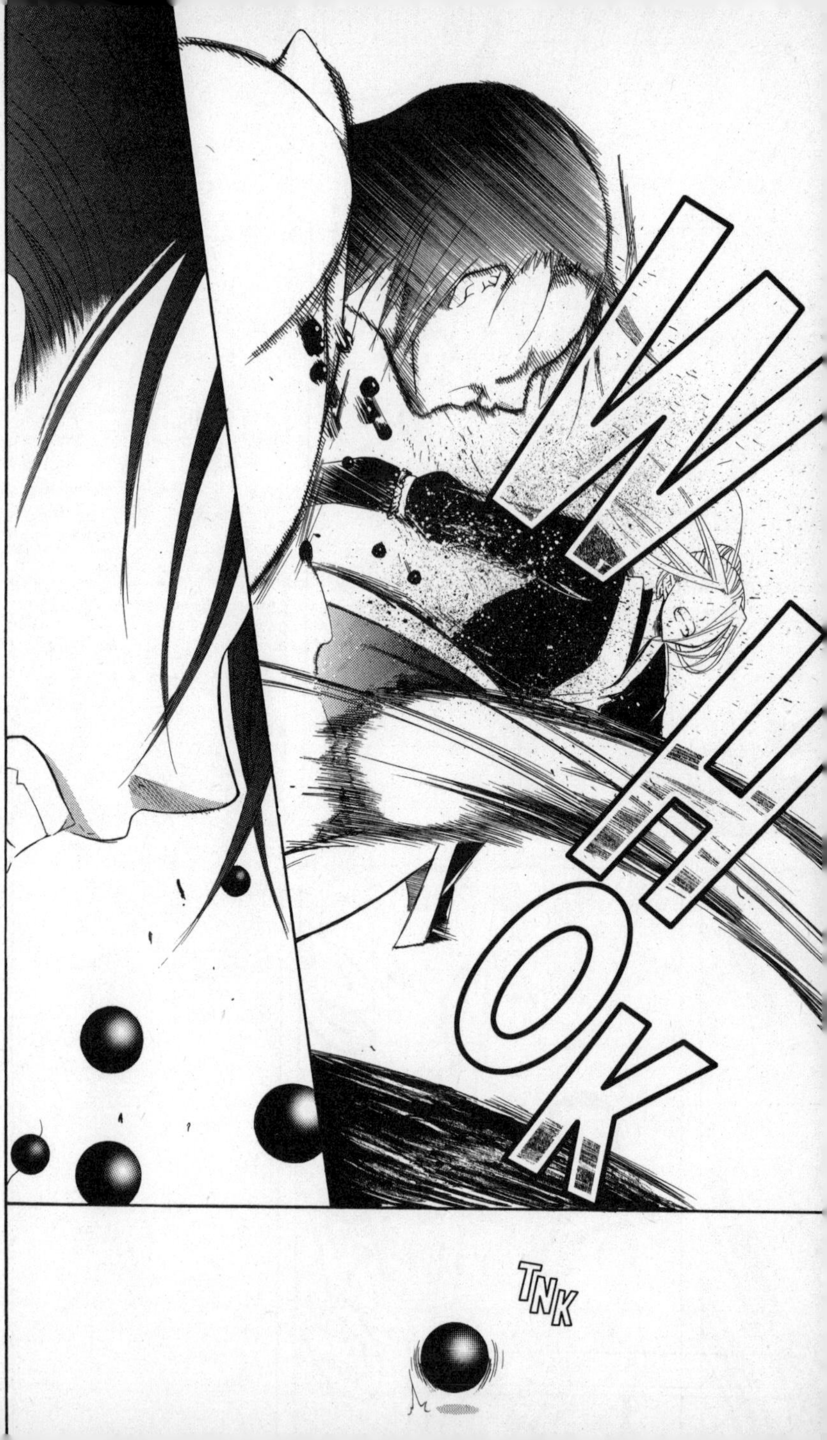
WHOK
TNK

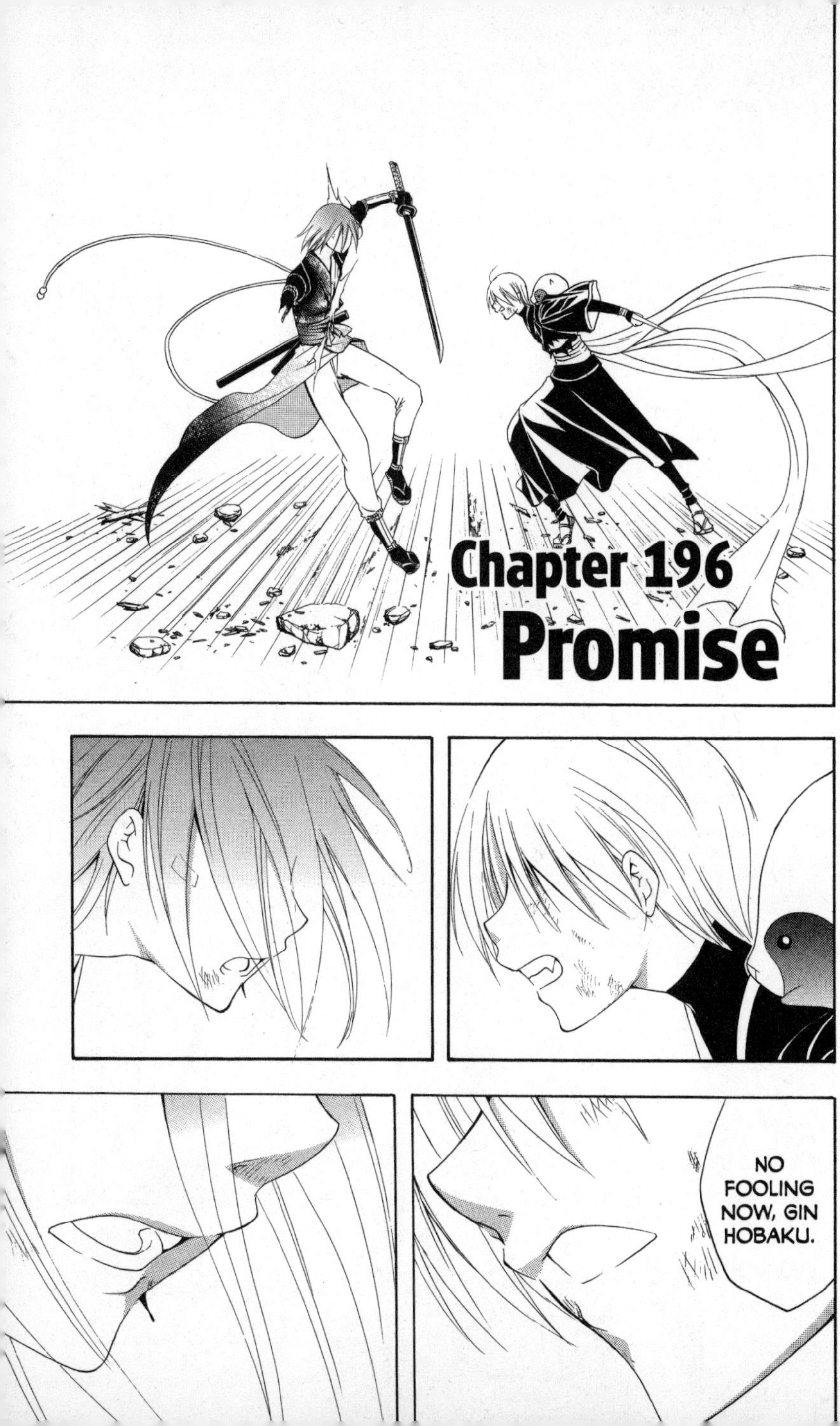
Chapter 196
Promise
NO FOOLING NOW, GIN HOBAKU.

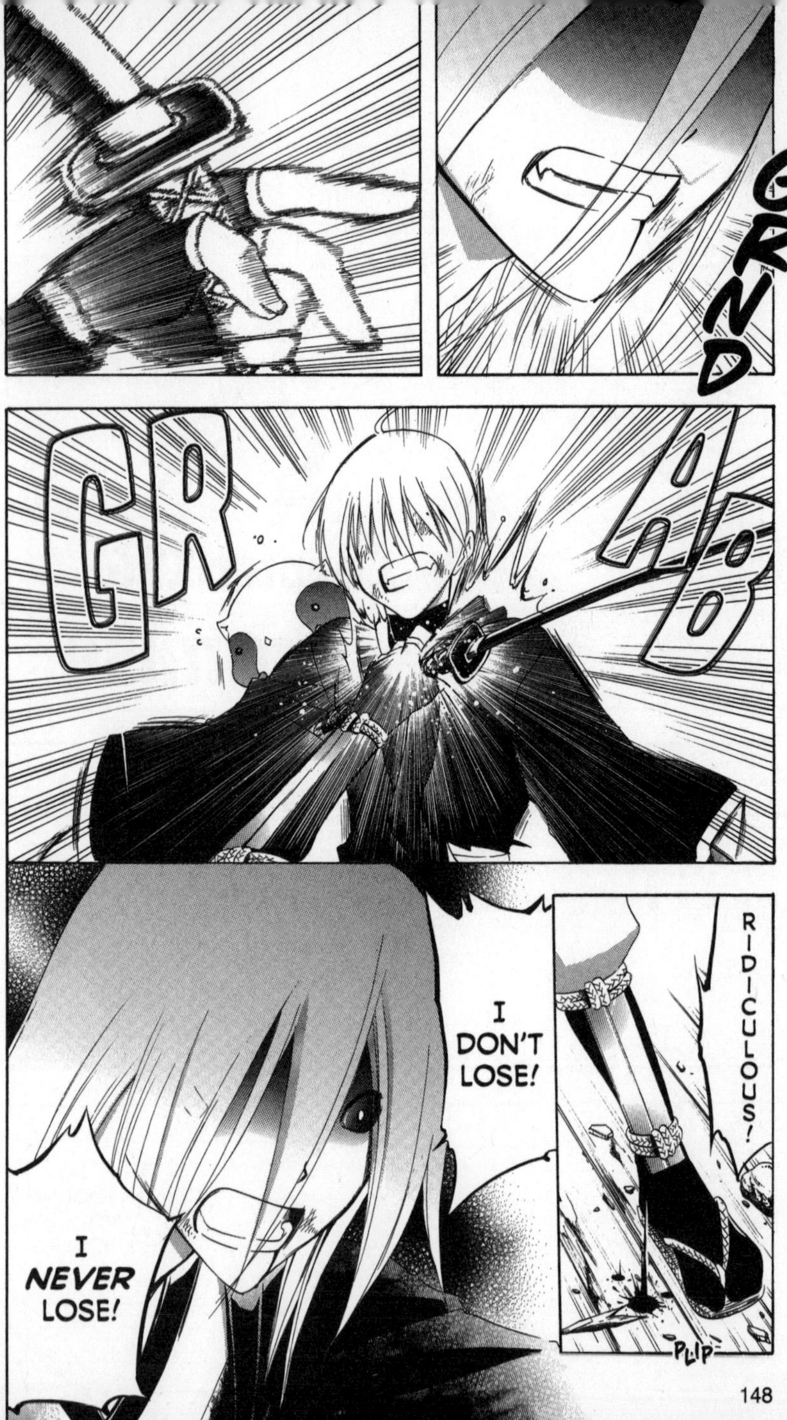
GRND
GRAB
RIDICULOUS!
PLIP
I DON'T LOSE!
I NEVER LOSE!

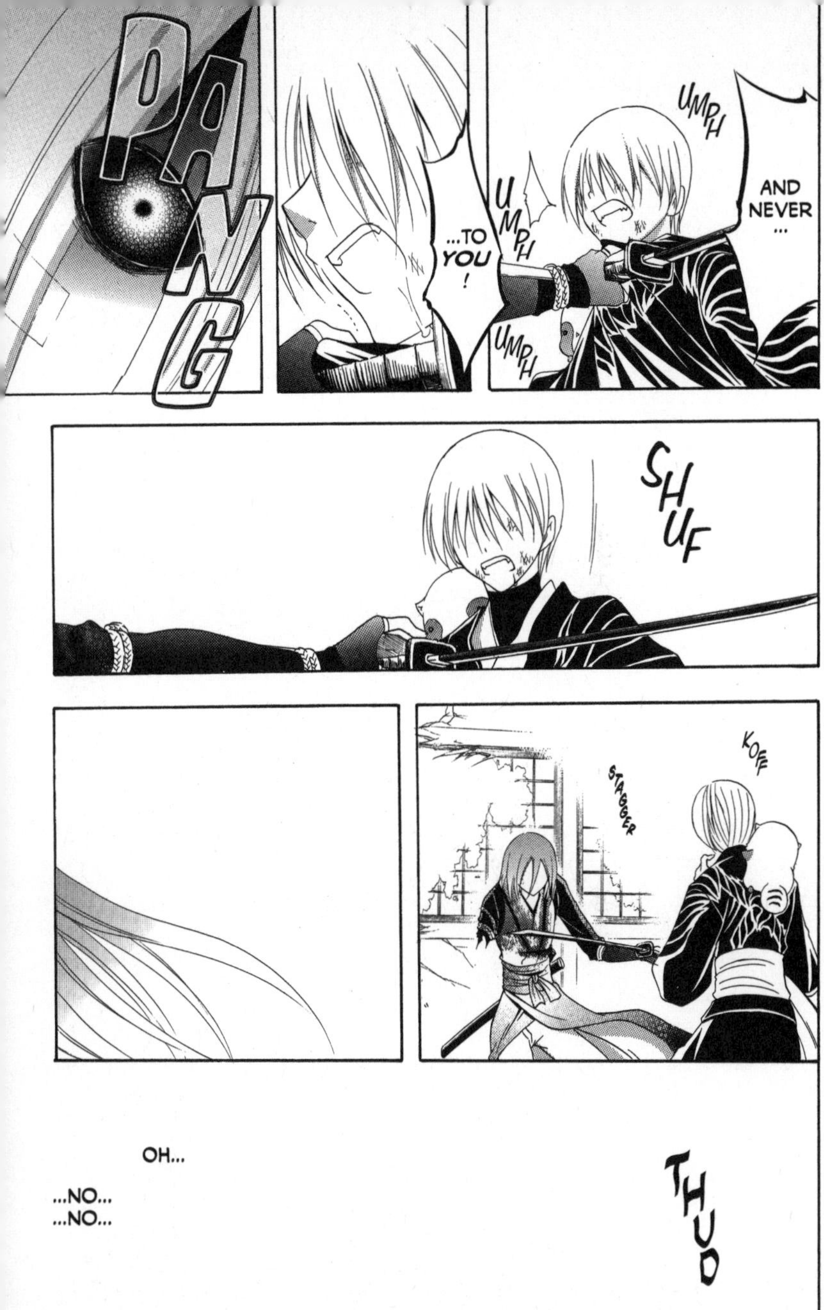
UMPH
AND NEVER...
UMPH
UMPH
...TO YOU!
PANG
SHUF
KOFF
STAGGER
THUD
OH...
...NO...
...NO...

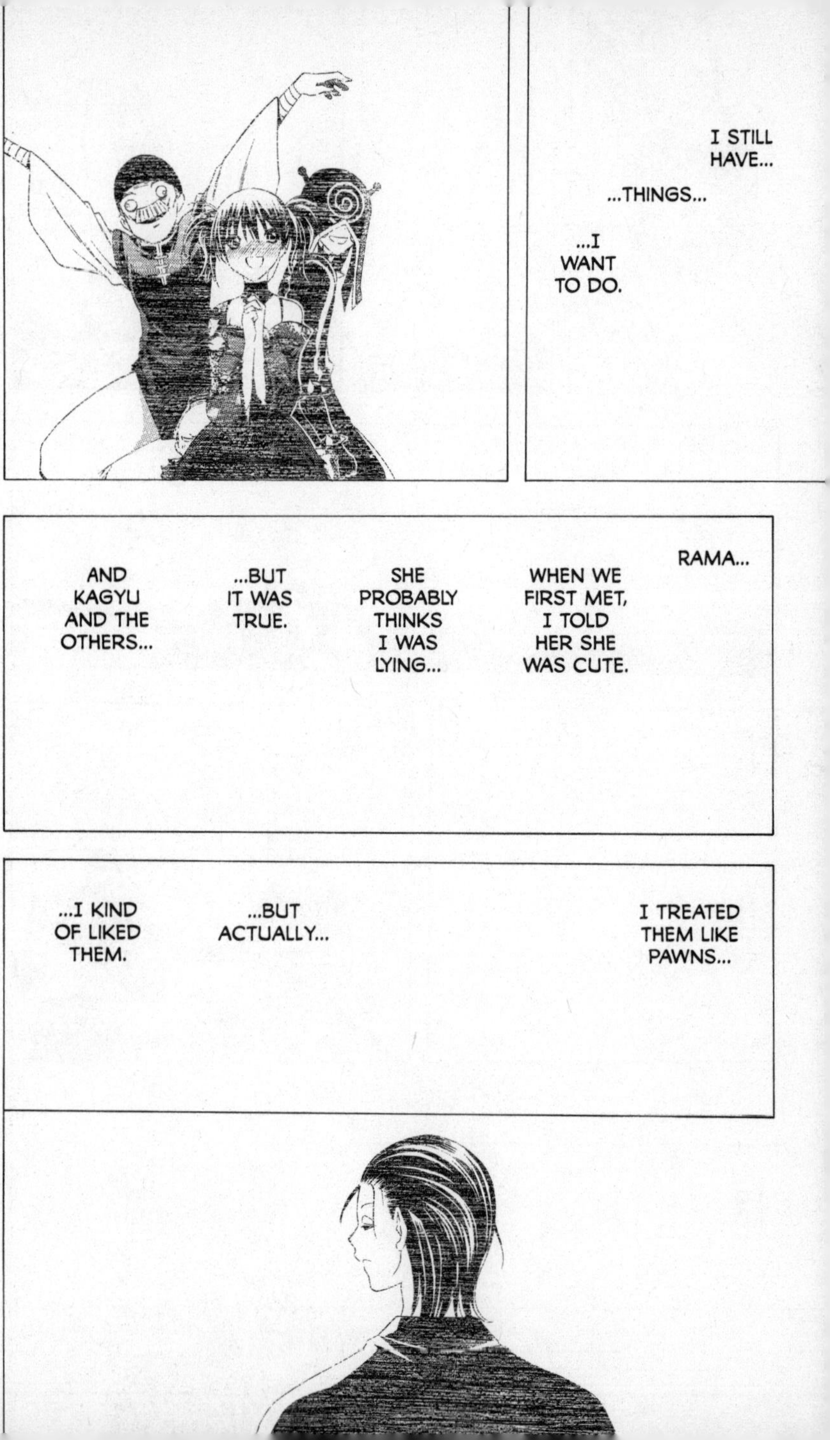
I STILL HAVE...
...THINGS...
...I WANT TO DO.
RAMA...
WHEN WE FIRST MET, I TOLD HER SHE WAS CUTE.
SHE PROBABLY THINKS I WAS LYING...
...BUT IT WAS TRUE.
AND KAGYU AND THE OTHERS...
I TREATED THEM LIKE PAWNS...
...BUT ACTUALLY...
...I KIND OF LIKED THEM.

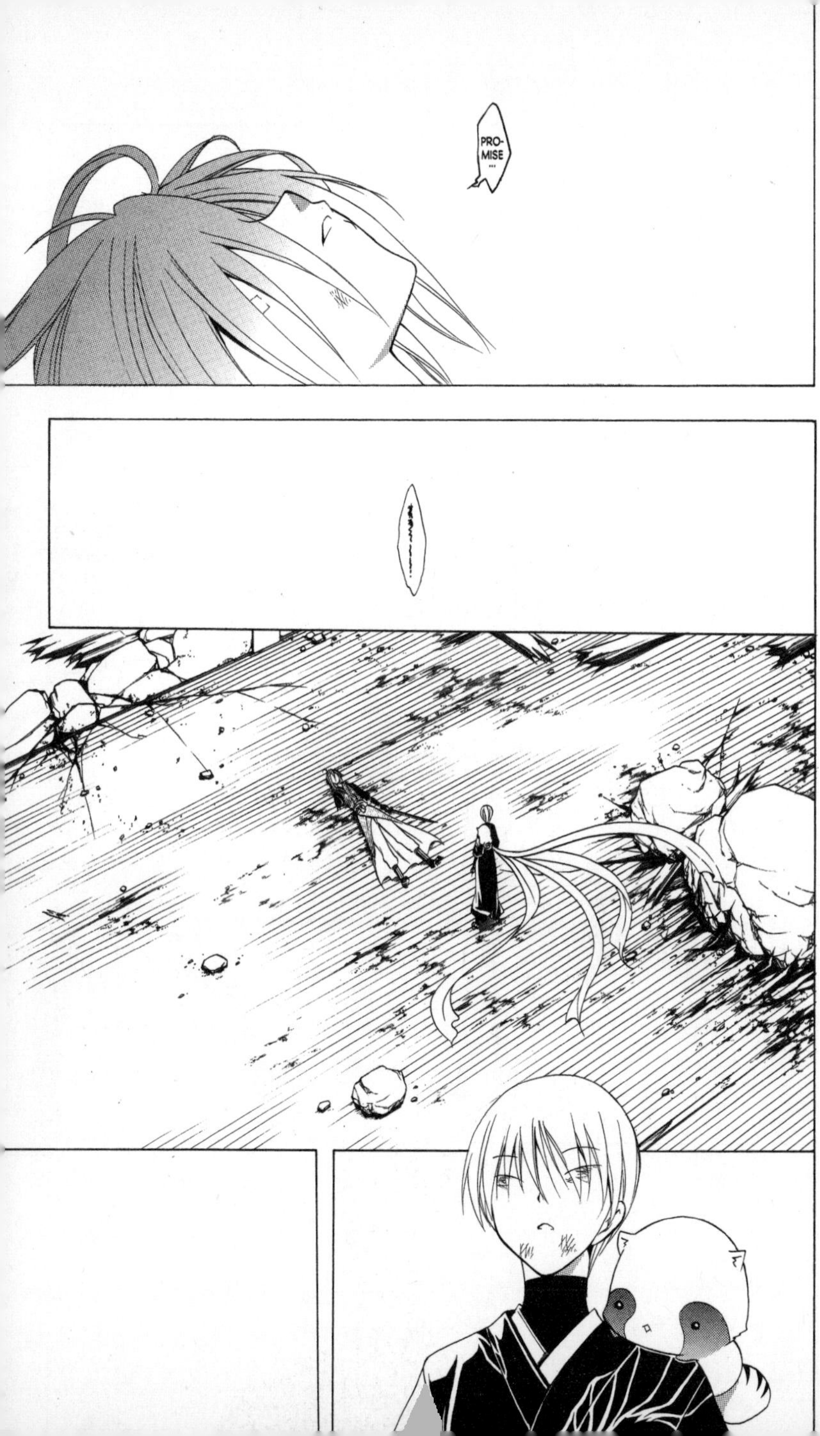
PRO-MISE ...

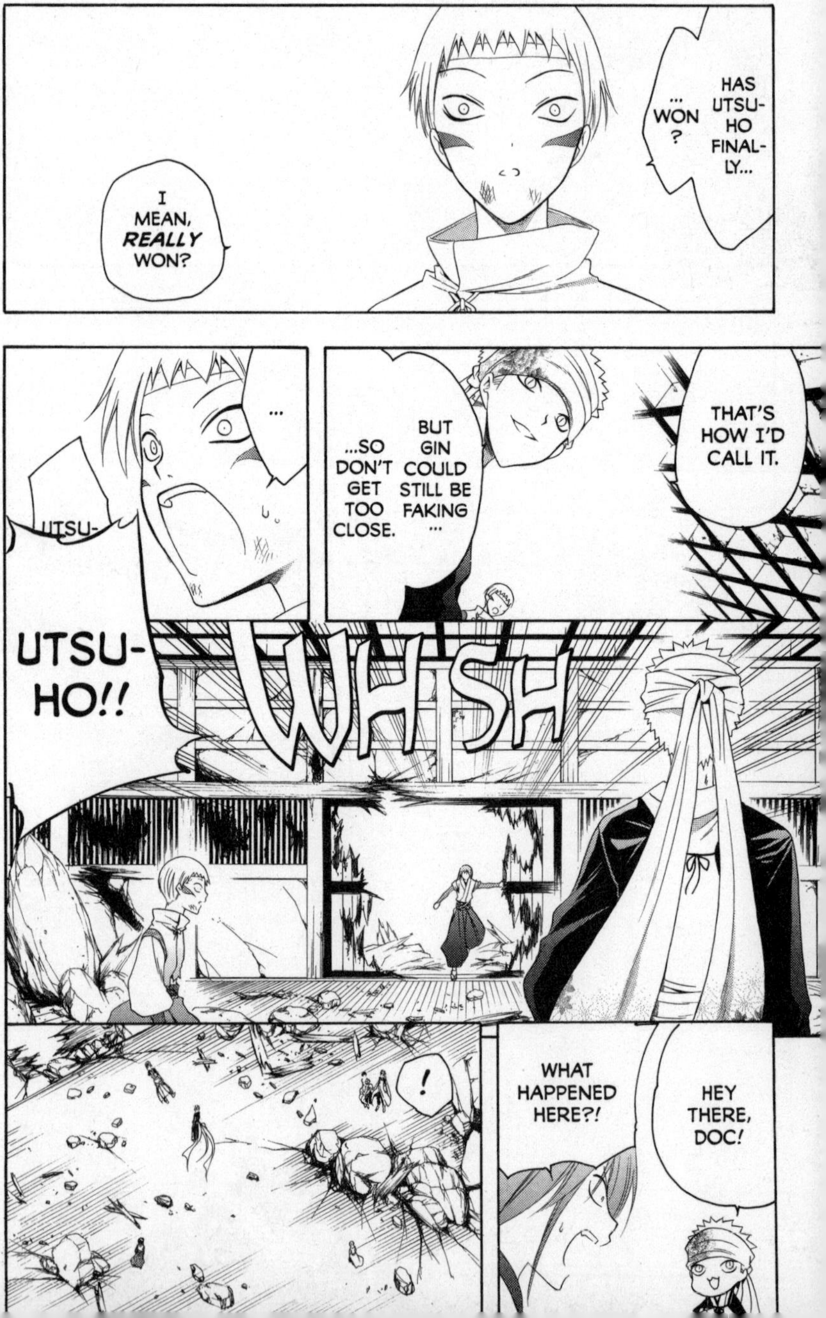
HAS UTSU-HO FINAL-LY...
... WON ?
I MEAN, *REALLY* WON?
THAT'S HOW I'D CALL IT.
BUT GIN COULD STILL BE FAKING ...
...SO DON'T GET TOO CLOSE.
...
UTSU-
WHSH
UTSU-HO!!
HEY THERE, DOC!
WHAT HAPPENED HERE?!
!

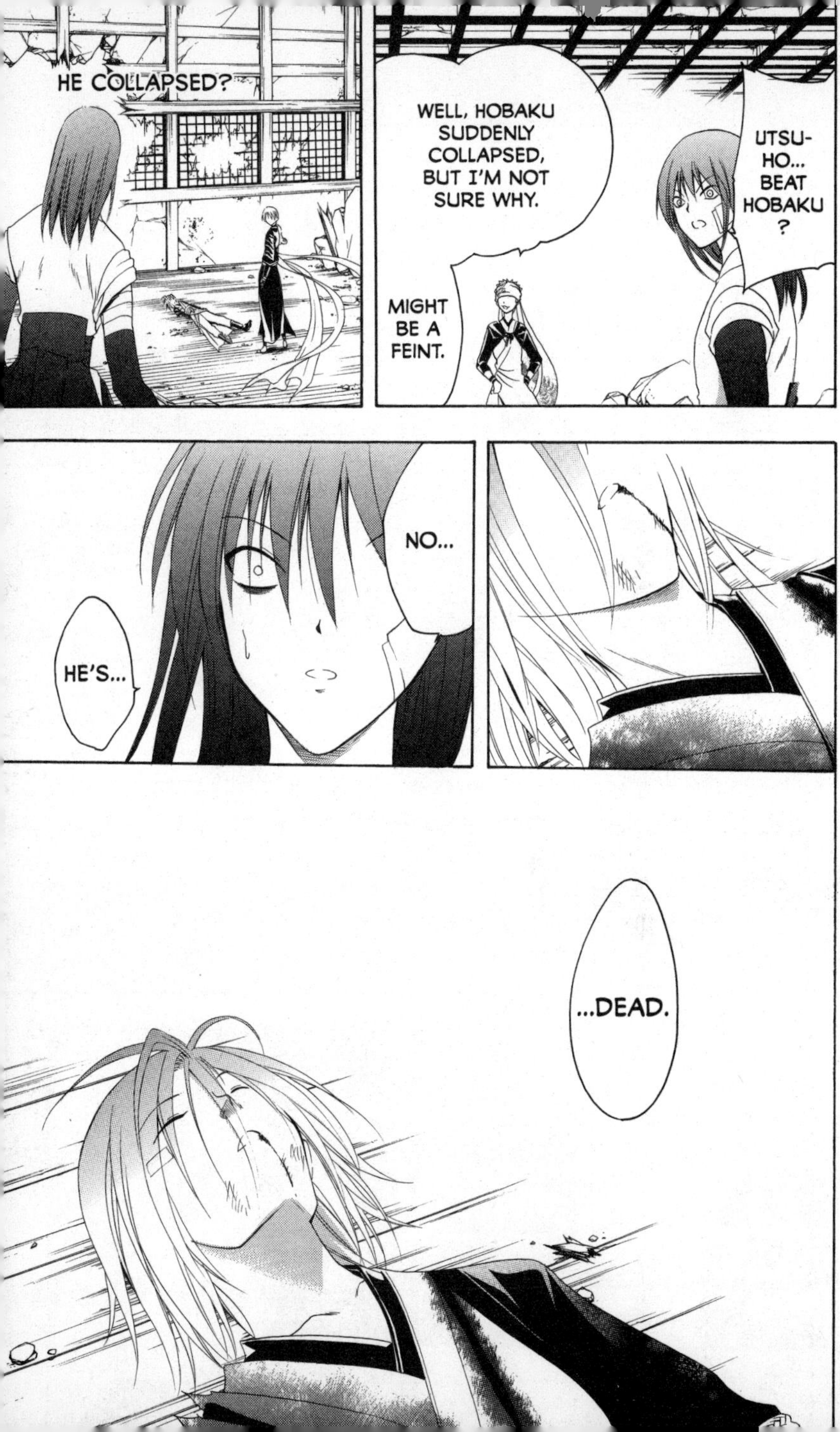
UTSU-HO... BEAT HOBAKU?
WELL, HOBAKU SUDDENLY COLLAPSED, BUT I'M NOT SURE WHY.
MIGHT BE A FEINT.
HE COLLAPSED?
NO...
HE'S...
...DEAD.

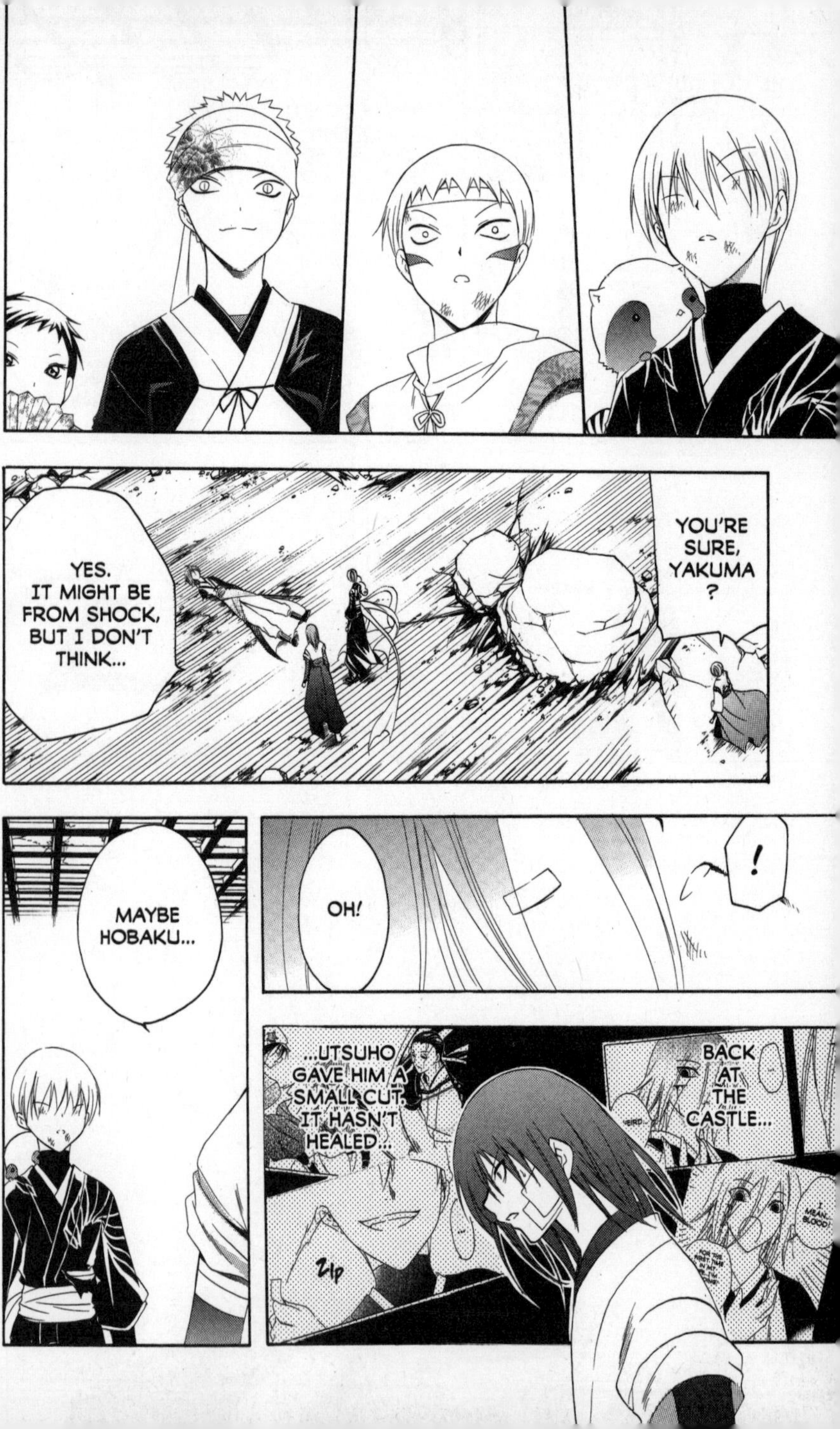
YOU'RE SURE, YAKUMA?
YES. IT MIGHT BE FROM SHOCK, BUT I DON'T THINK...
!
OH!
BACK AT THE CASTLE...
...UTSUHO GAVE HIM A SMALL CUT. IT HASN'T HEALED...
ZIP
MAYBE HOBAKU...

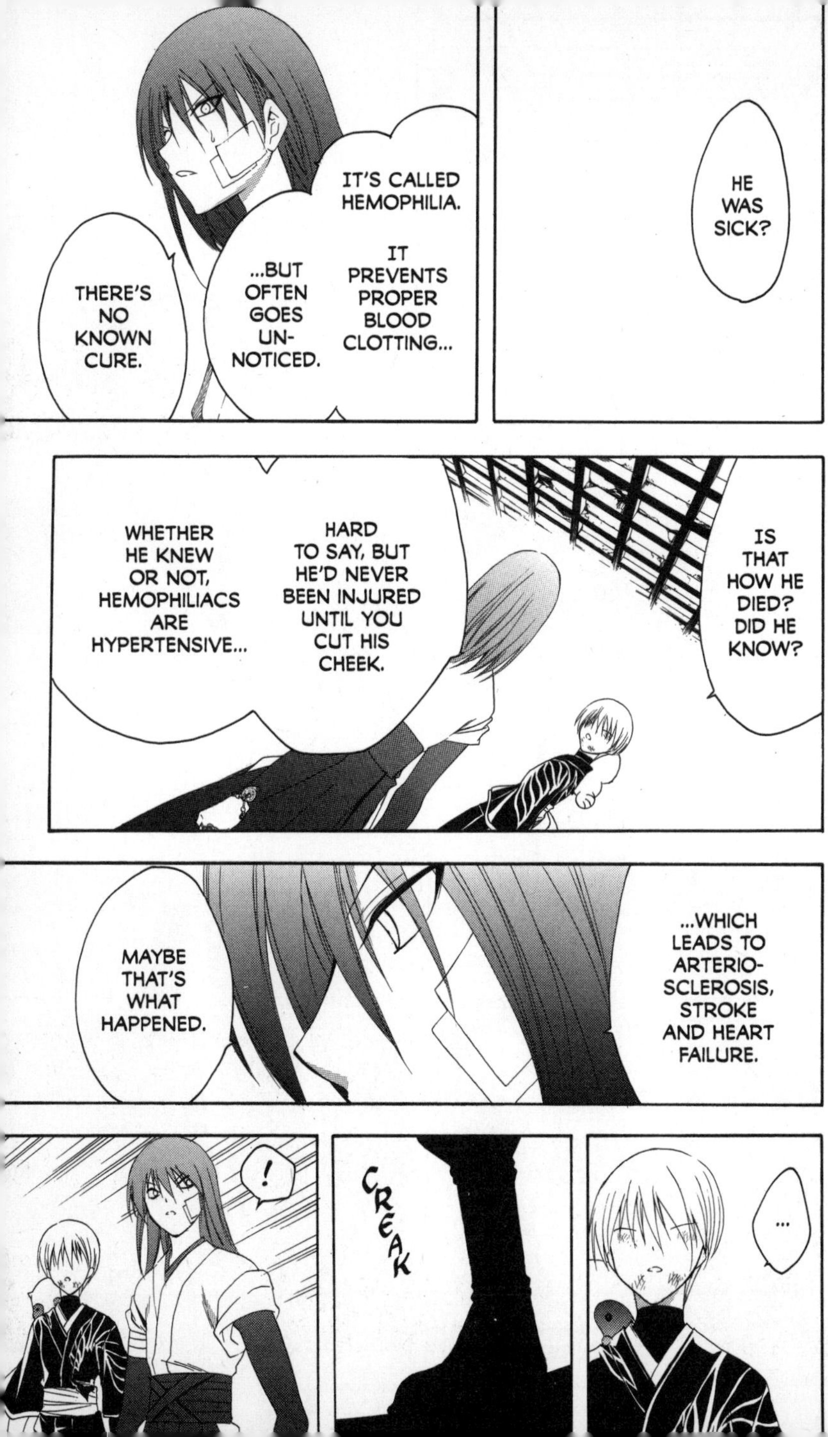
HE WAS SICK?
IT'S CALLED HEMOPHILIA.
IT PREVENTS PROPER BLOOD CLOTTING...
...BUT OFTEN GOES UN-NOTICED.
THERE'S NO KNOWN CURE.
IS THAT HOW HE DIED? DID HE KNOW?
HARD TO SAY, BUT HE'D NEVER BEEN INJURED UNTIL YOU CUT HIS CHEEK.
WHETHER HE KNEW OR NOT, HEMOPHILIACS ARE HYPERTENSIVE...
...WHICH LEADS TO ARTERIO-SCLEROSIS, STROKE AND HEART FAILURE.
MAYBE THAT'S WHAT HAPPENED.
...
CREAK
!

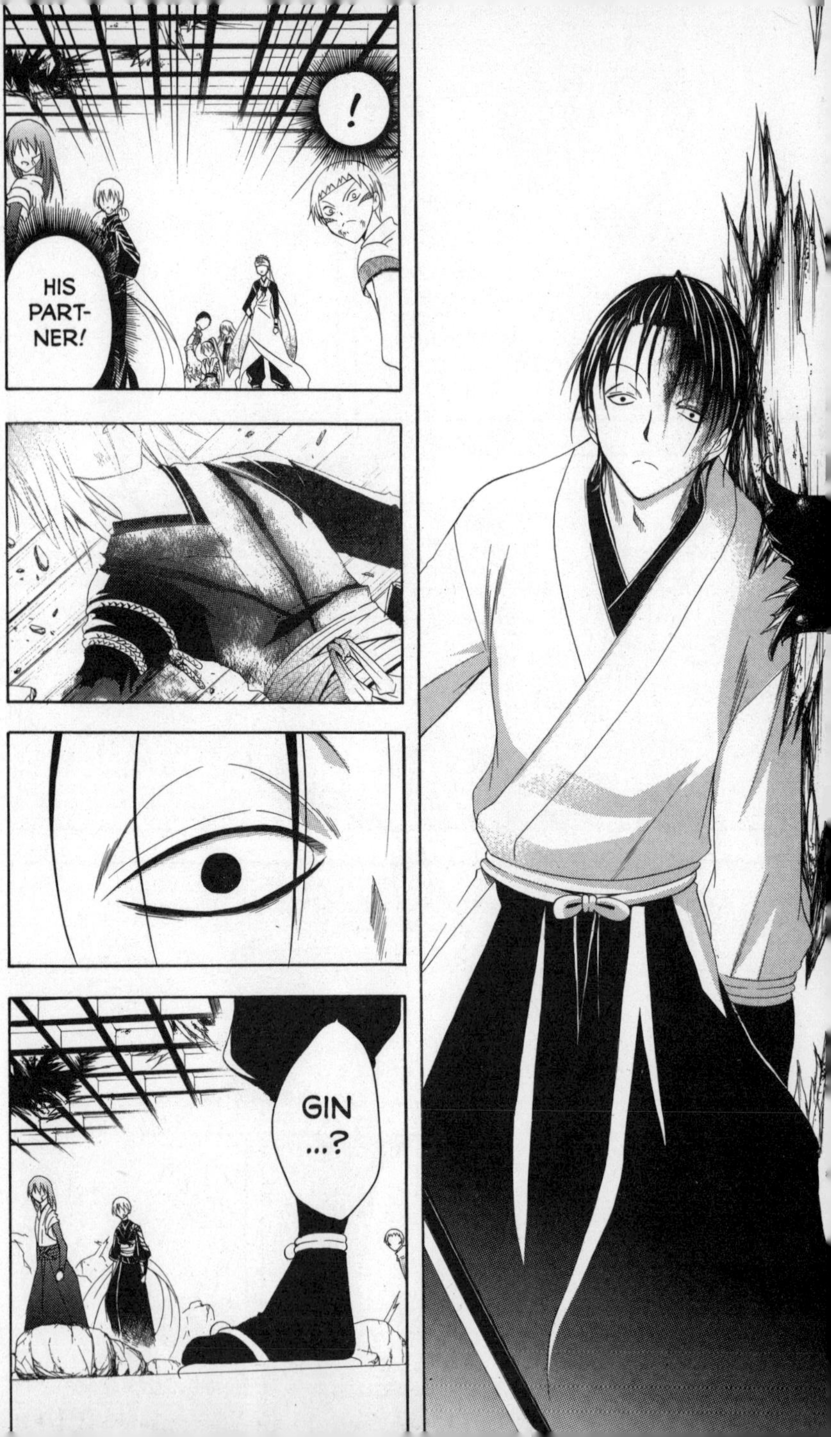
!
HIS PARTNER!
GIN ...?

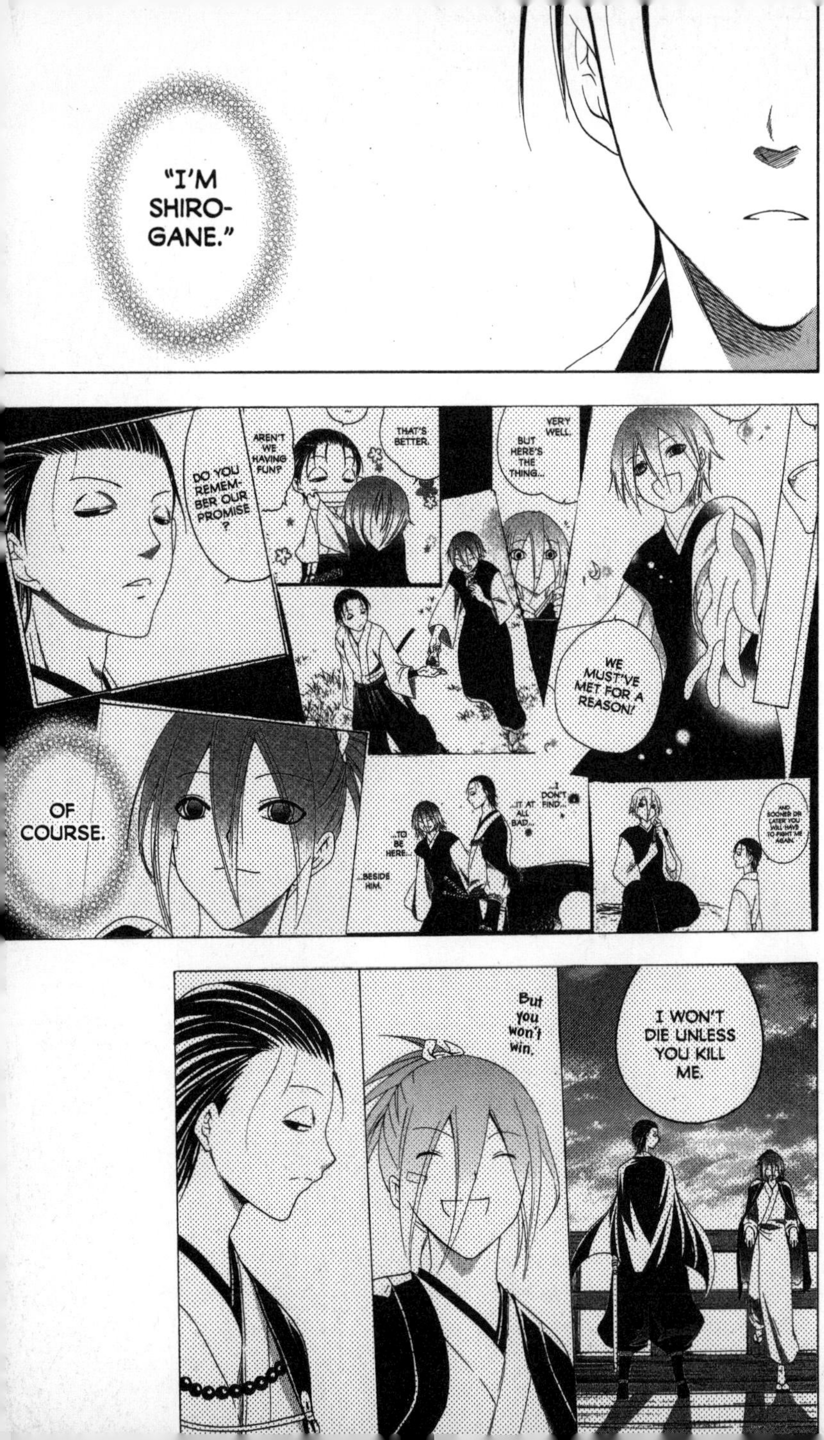
"I'M SHIRO-GANE."
VERY WELL.
BUT HERE'S THE THING...
WE MUST'VE MET FOR A REASON!
THAT'S BETTER.
AREN'T WE HAVING FUN?
DO YOU REMEMBER OUR PROMISE?
AND SOONER OR LATER YOU WILL HAVE TO FIGHT ME AGAIN.
...I DON'T FIND...
...IT AT ALL BAD...
...TO BE HERE...
...BESIDE HIM.
OF COURSE.
I WON'T DIE UNLESS YOU KILL ME.
But you won't win.

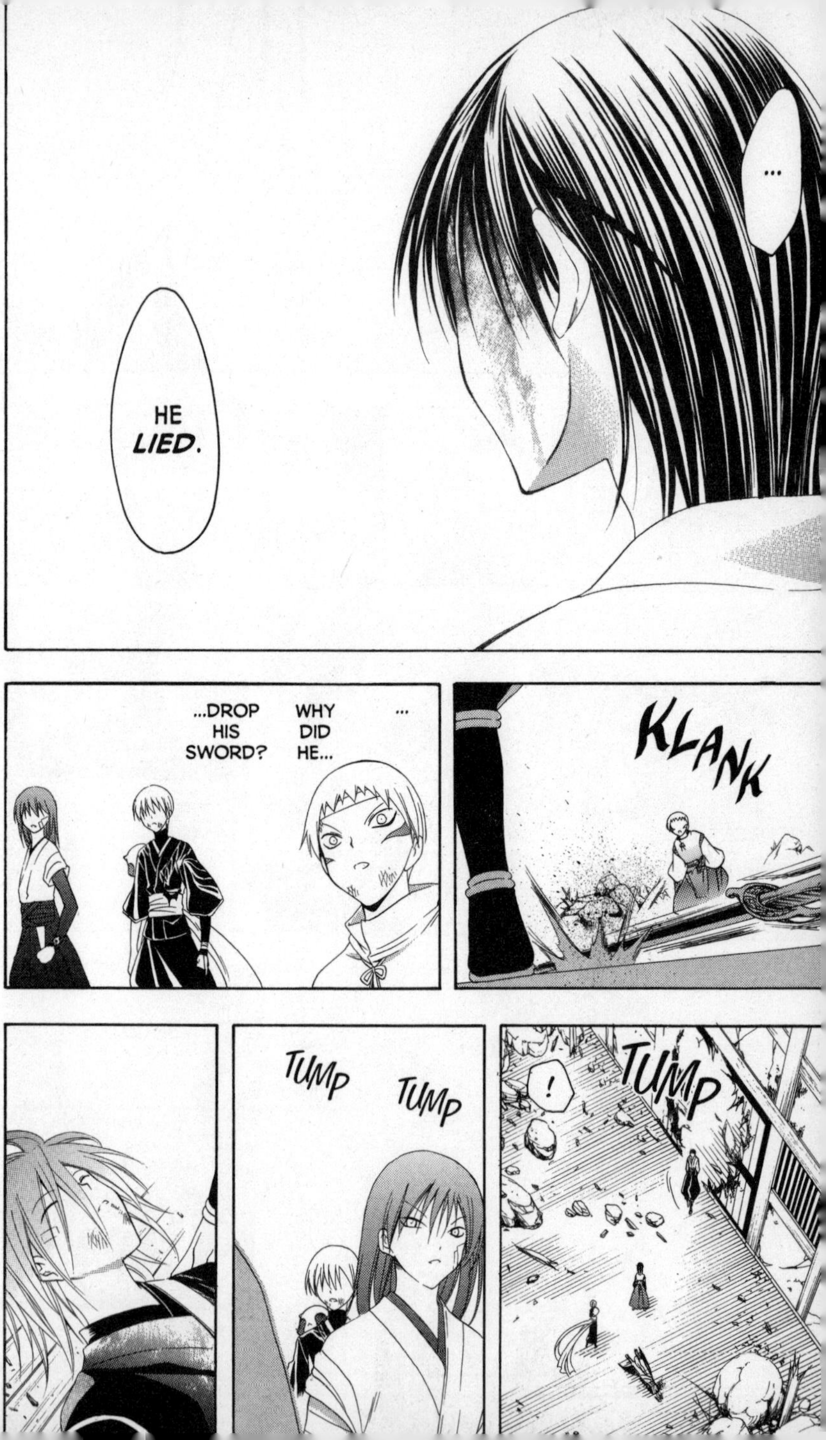
...
HE LIED.
KLANK
...
WHY DID HE...
...DROP HIS SWORD?
TUMP
!
TUMP
TUMP

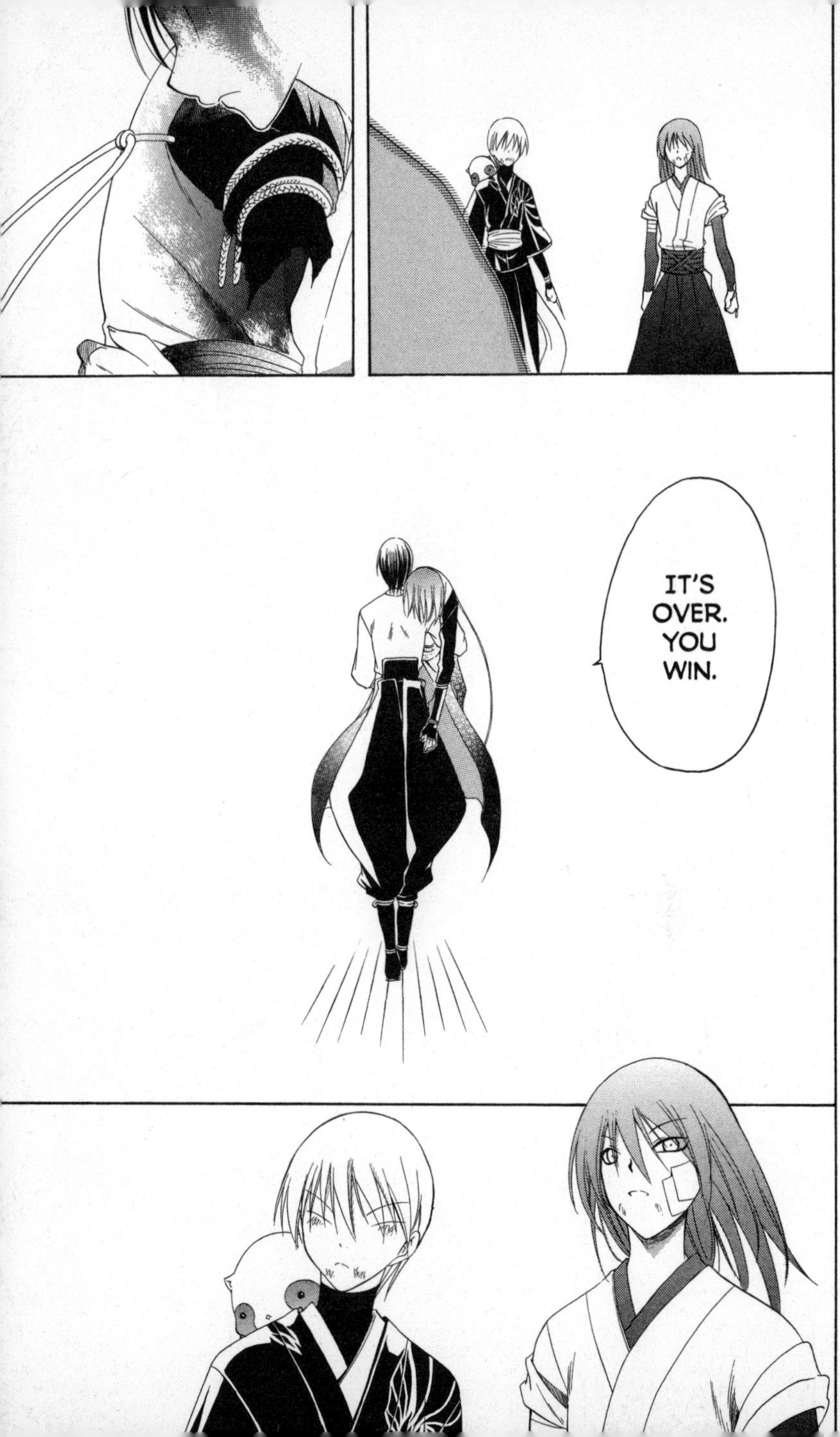
IT'S OVER. YOU WIN.

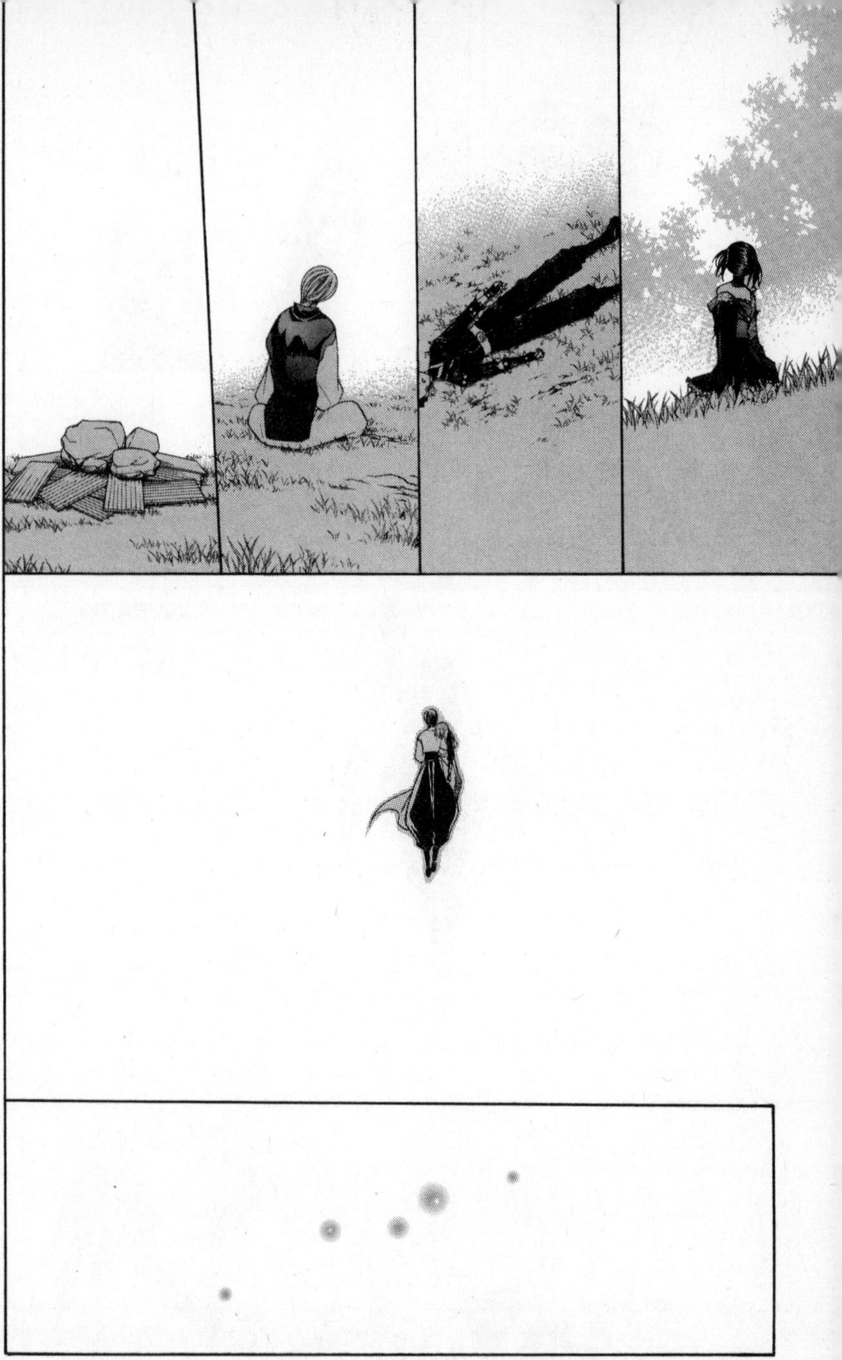

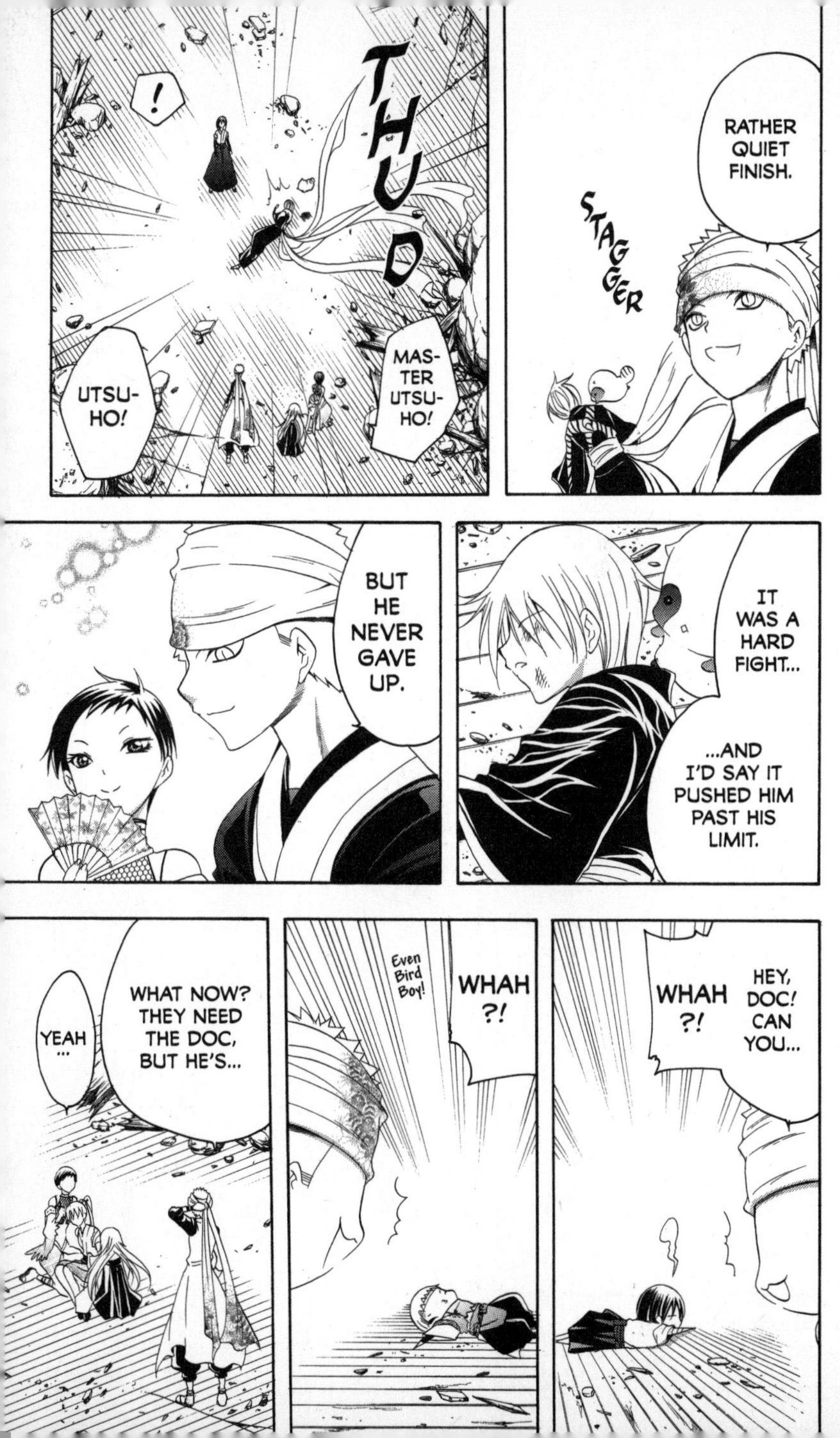
RATHER QUIET FINISH.
STAGGER
THUD
!
MASTER UTSUHO!
UTSUHO!
IT WAS A HARD FIGHT...
...AND I'D SAY IT PUSHED HIM PAST HIS LIMIT.
BUT HE NEVER GAVE UP.
HEY, DOC! CAN YOU...
WHAH ?!
WHAH ?!
Even Bird Boy!
WHAT NOW? THEY NEED THE DOC, BUT HE'S...
YEAH...

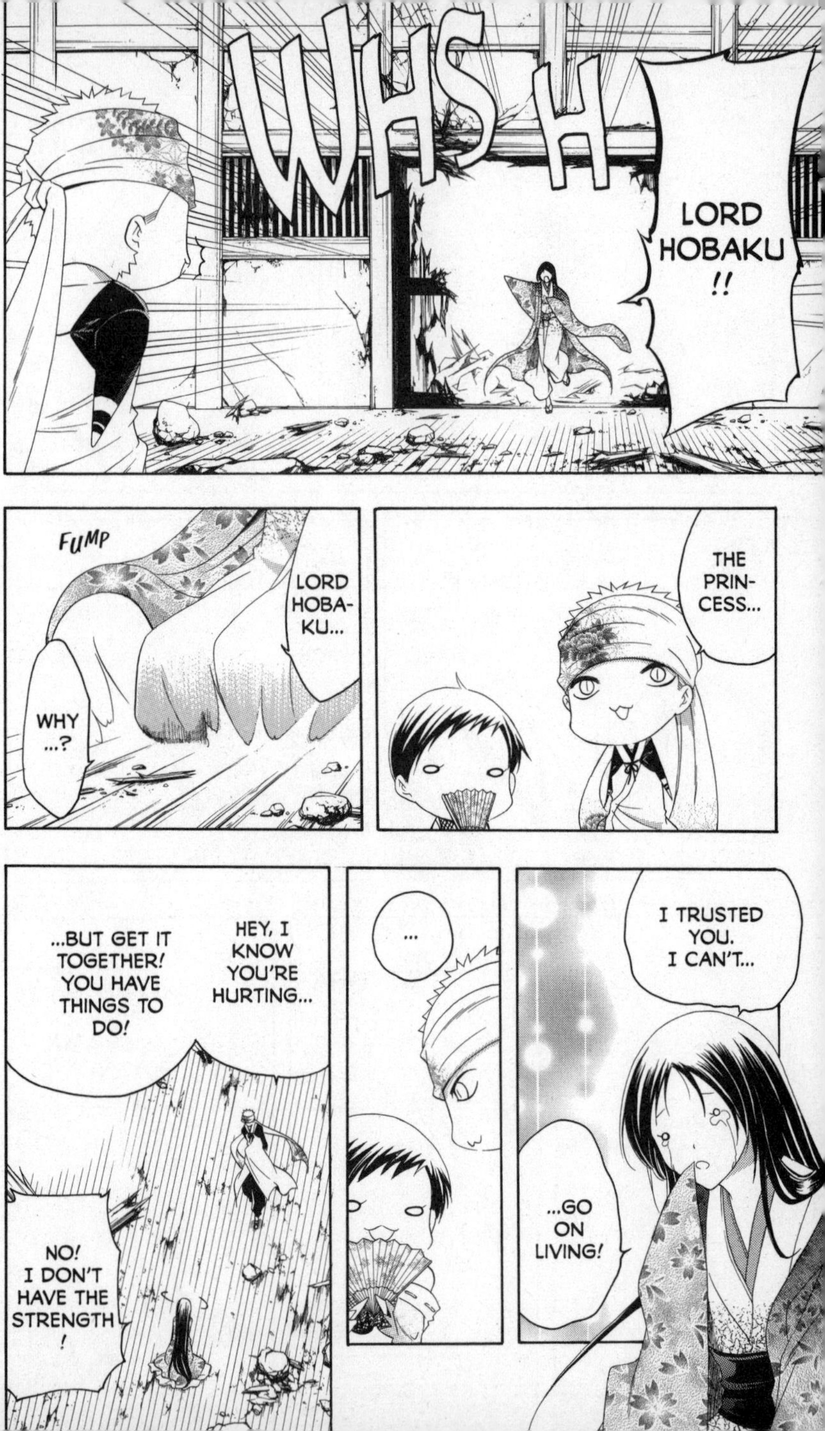
WHSH
LORD HOBAKU !!
THE PRINCESS...
FUMP
LORD HOBAKU...
WHY...?
I TRUSTED YOU. I CAN'T...
...GO ON LIVING!
...
HEY, I KNOW YOU'RE HURTING...
...BUT GET IT TOGETHER! YOU HAVE THINGS TO DO!
NO! I DON'T HAVE THE STRENGTH!

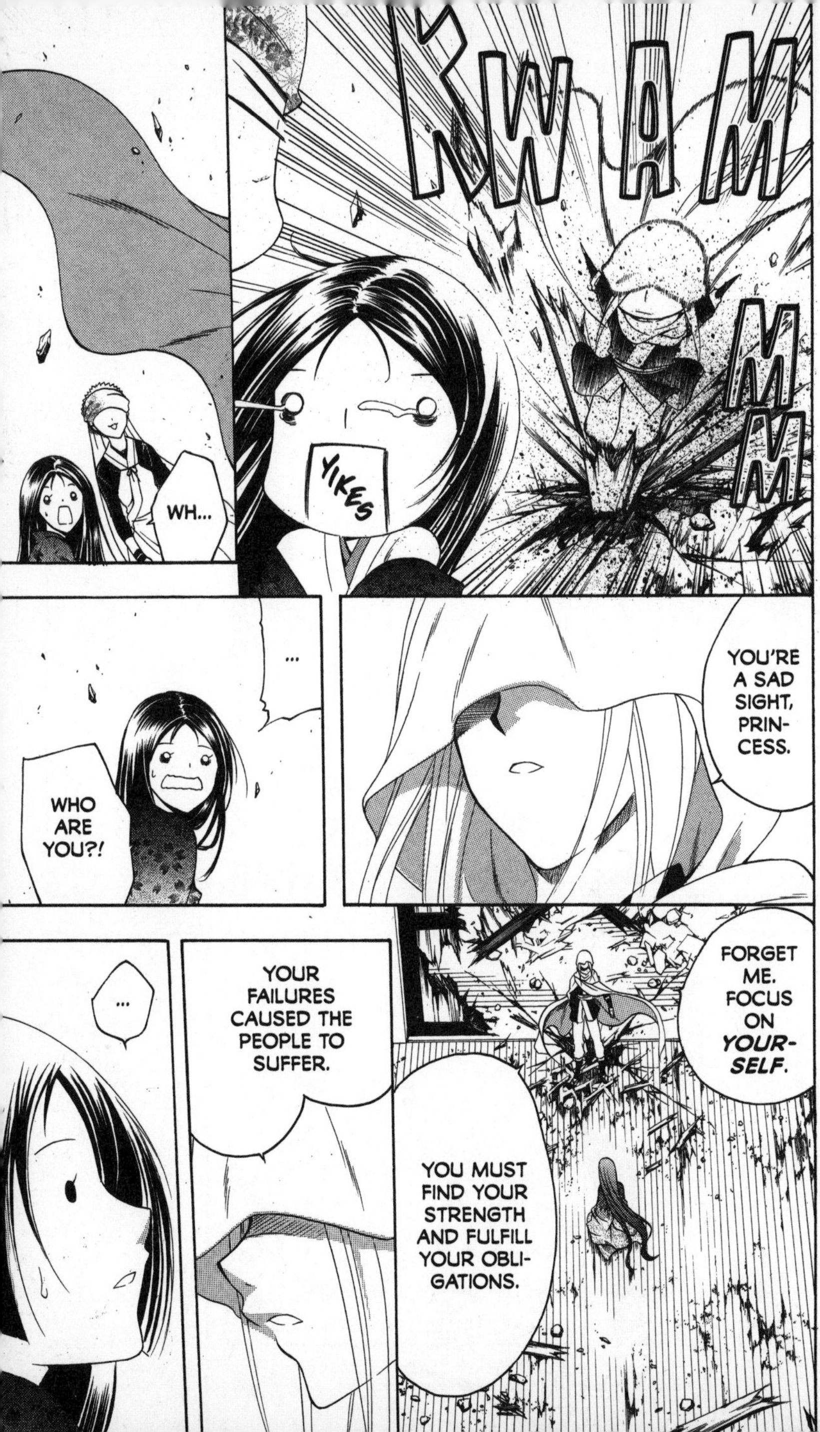
KWAM
MMM
YIKES
WH...
YOU'RE A SAD SIGHT, PRIN-CESS.
...
WHO ARE YOU?!
FORGET ME. FOCUS ON *YOUR-SELF*.
YOUR FAILURES CAUSED THE PEOPLE TO SUFFER.
YOU MUST FIND YOUR STRENGTH AND FULFILL YOUR OBLI-GATIONS.
...

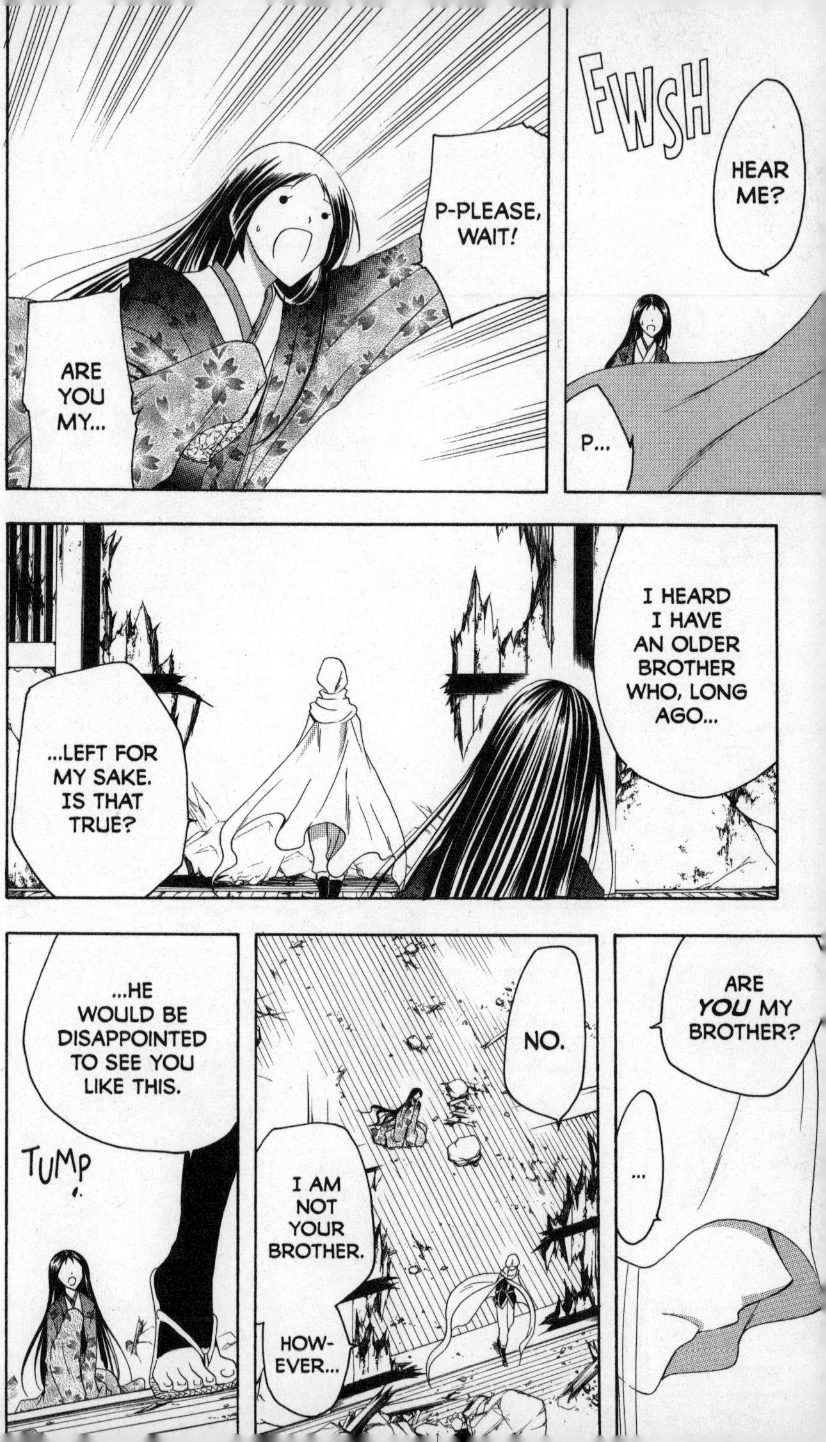
HEAR ME?
FWSH
P...
P-PLEASE, WAIT!
ARE YOU MY...
I HEARD I HAVE AN OLDER BROTHER WHO, LONG AGO...
...LEFT FOR MY SAKE. IS THAT TRUE?
ARE *YOU* MY BROTHER?
...
NO.
I AM NOT YOUR BROTHER.
HOW-EVER...
...HE WOULD BE DISAPPOINTED TO SEE YOU LIKE THIS.
TUMP

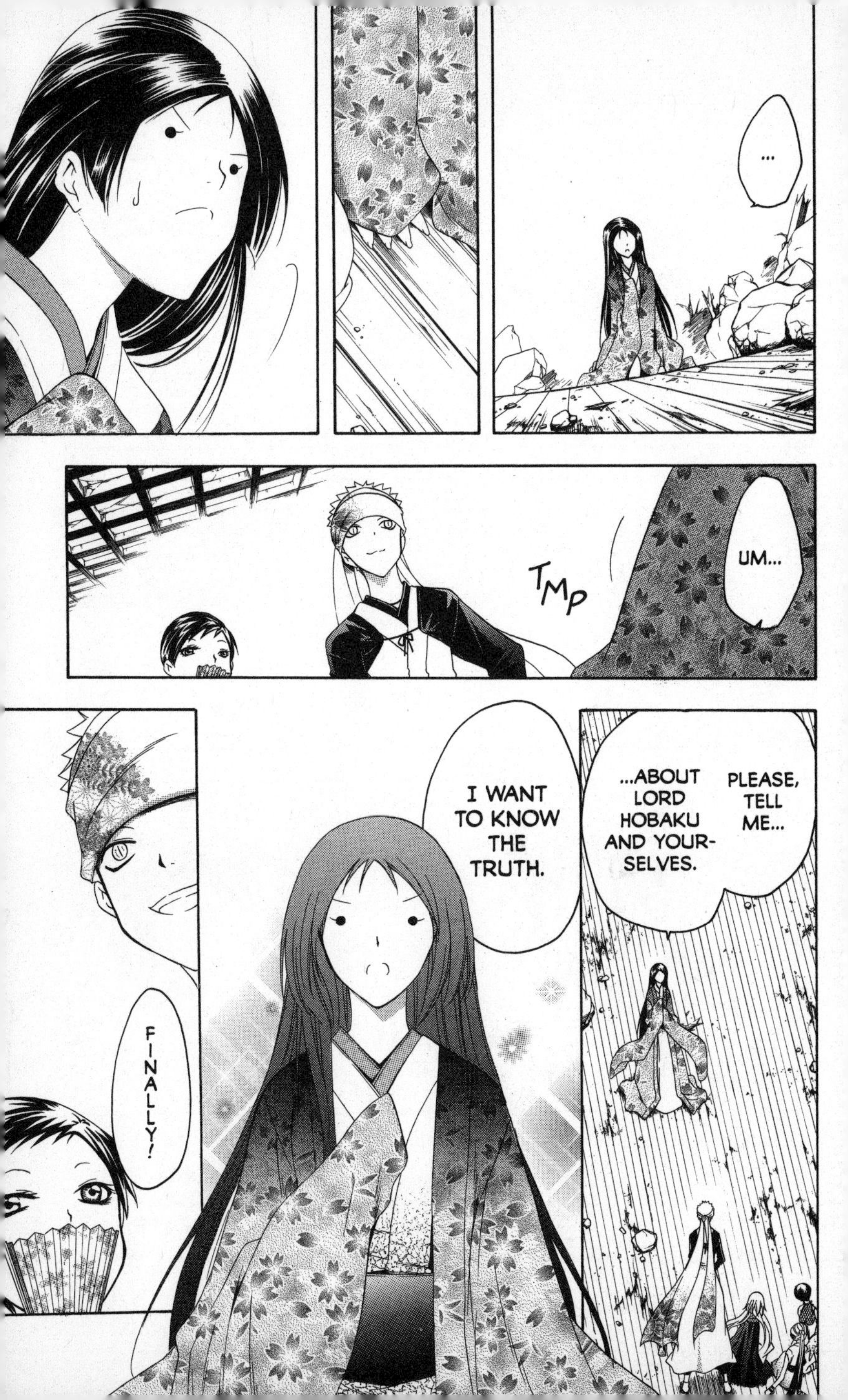
...
UM...
TMP
PLEASE, TELL ME...
...ABOUT LORD HOBAKU AND YOURSELVES.
I WANT TO KNOW THE TRUTH.
FINALLY!

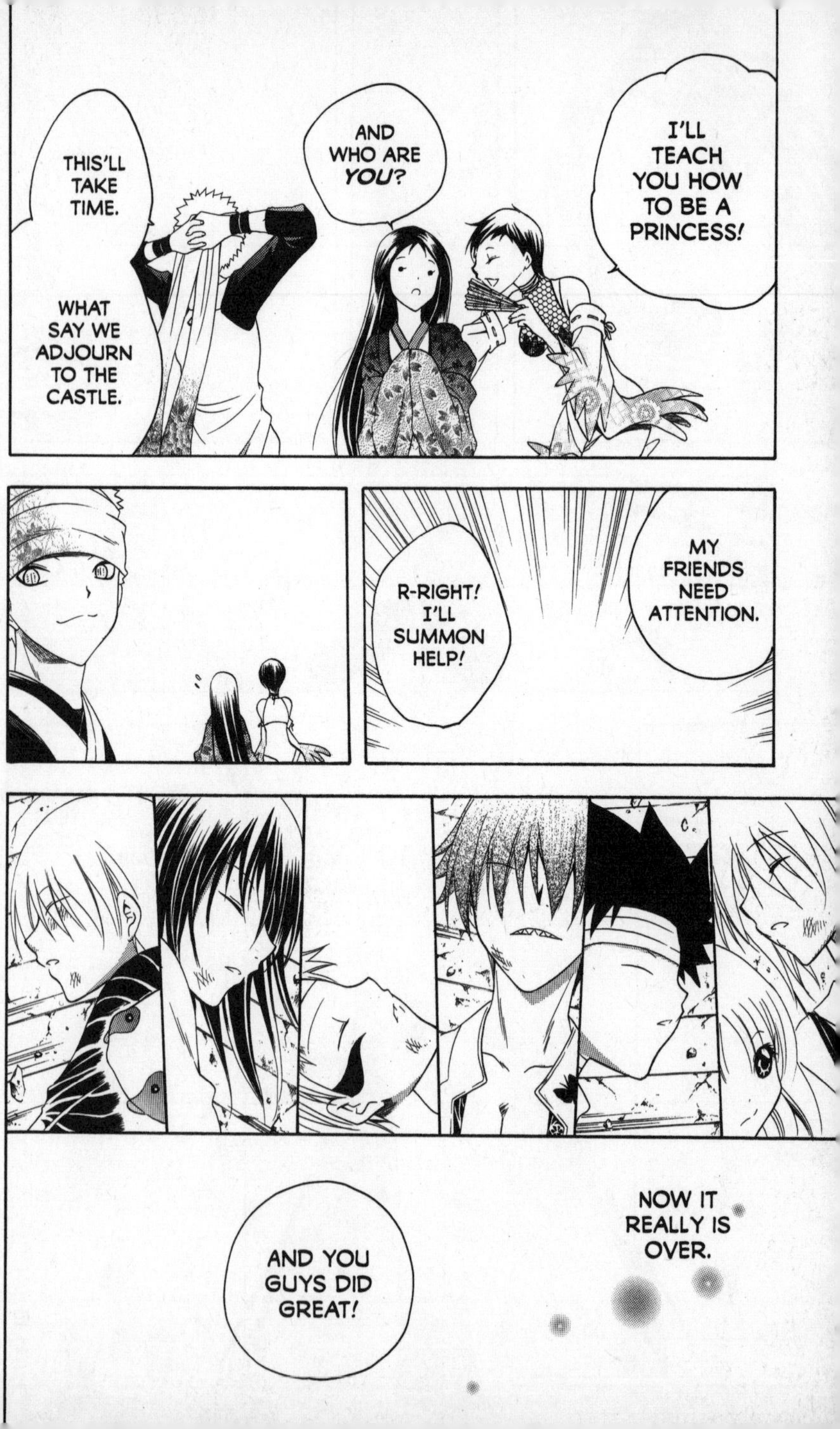
I'LL TEACH YOU HOW TO BE A PRINCESS!
AND WHO ARE *YOU*?
THIS'LL TAKE TIME.
WHAT SAY WE ADJOURN TO THE CASTLE.
MY FRIENDS NEED ATTENTION.
R-RIGHT! I'LL SUMMON HELP!
NOW IT REALLY IS OVER.
AND YOU GUYS DID GREAT!

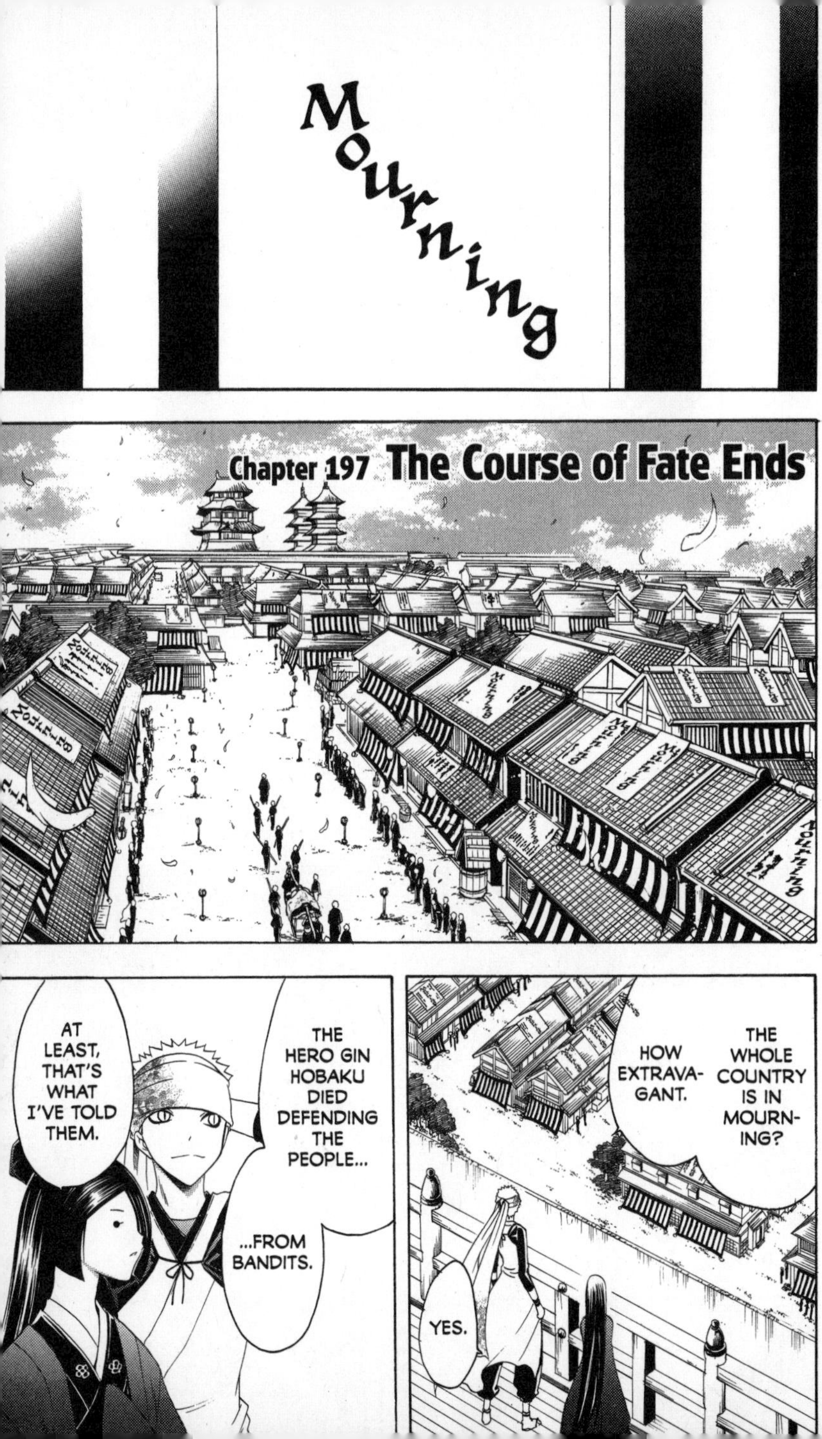
Mourning
Chapter 197 The Course of Fate Ends
THE WHOLE COUNTRY IS IN MOURNING?
HOW EXTRAVAGANT.
YES.
THE HERO GIN HOBAKU DIED DEFENDING THE PEOPLE...
...FROM BANDITS.
AT LEAST, THAT'S WHAT I'VE TOLD THEM.

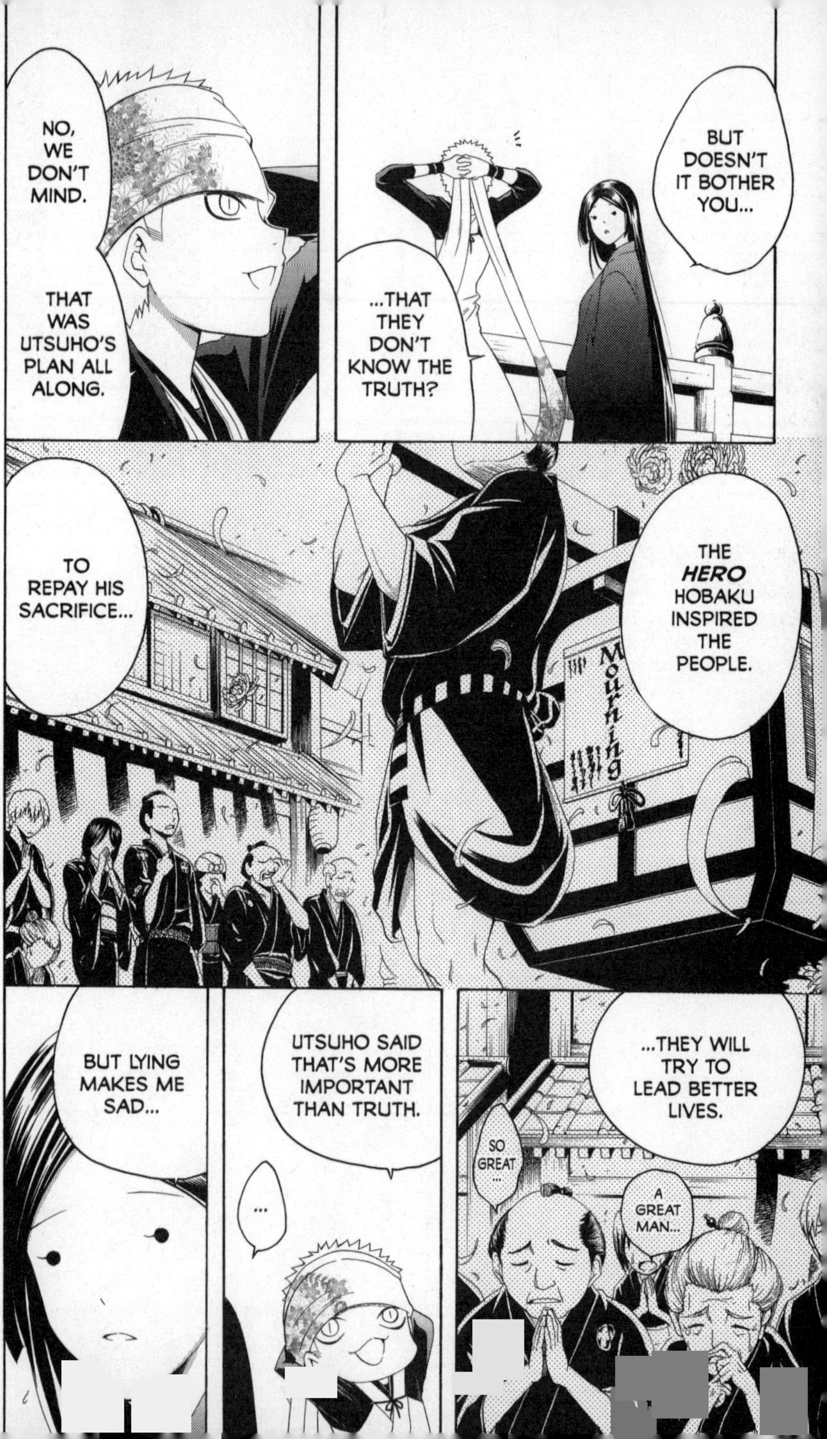
BUT DOESN'T IT BOTHER YOU...
...THAT THEY DON'T KNOW THE TRUTH?
NO, WE DON'T MIND.
THAT WAS UTSUHO'S PLAN ALL ALONG.
THE *HERO* HOBAKU INSPIRED THE PEOPLE.
Mourning
TO REPAY HIS SACRIFICE...
...THEY WILL TRY TO LEAD BETTER LIVES.
A GREAT MAN...
SO GREAT...
UTSUHO SAID THAT'S MORE IMPORTANT THAN TRUTH.
...
BUT LYING MAKES ME SAD...

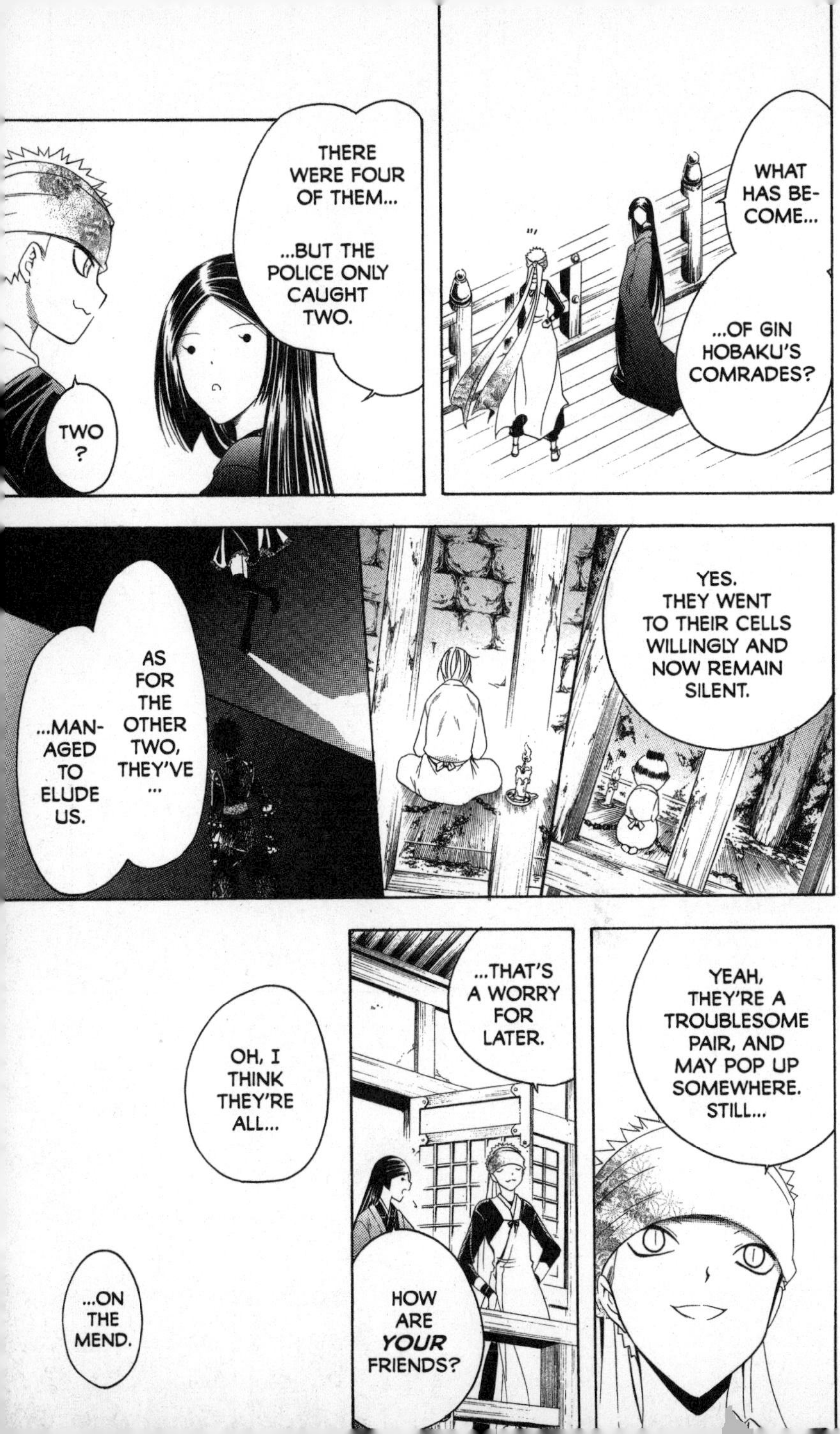
WHAT HAS BE-COME...
...OF GIN HOBAKU'S COMRADES?
THERE WERE FOUR OF THEM...
...BUT THE POLICE ONLY CAUGHT TWO.
TWO?
YES. THEY WENT TO THEIR CELLS WILLINGLY AND NOW REMAIN SILENT.
AS FOR THE OTHER TWO, THEY'VE...
...MAN-AGED TO ELUDE US.
YEAH, THEY'RE A TROUBLESOME PAIR, AND MAY POP UP SOMEWHERE. STILL...
...THAT'S A WORRY FOR LATER.
HOW ARE *YOUR* FRIENDS?
OH, I THINK THEY'RE ALL...
...ON THE MEND.

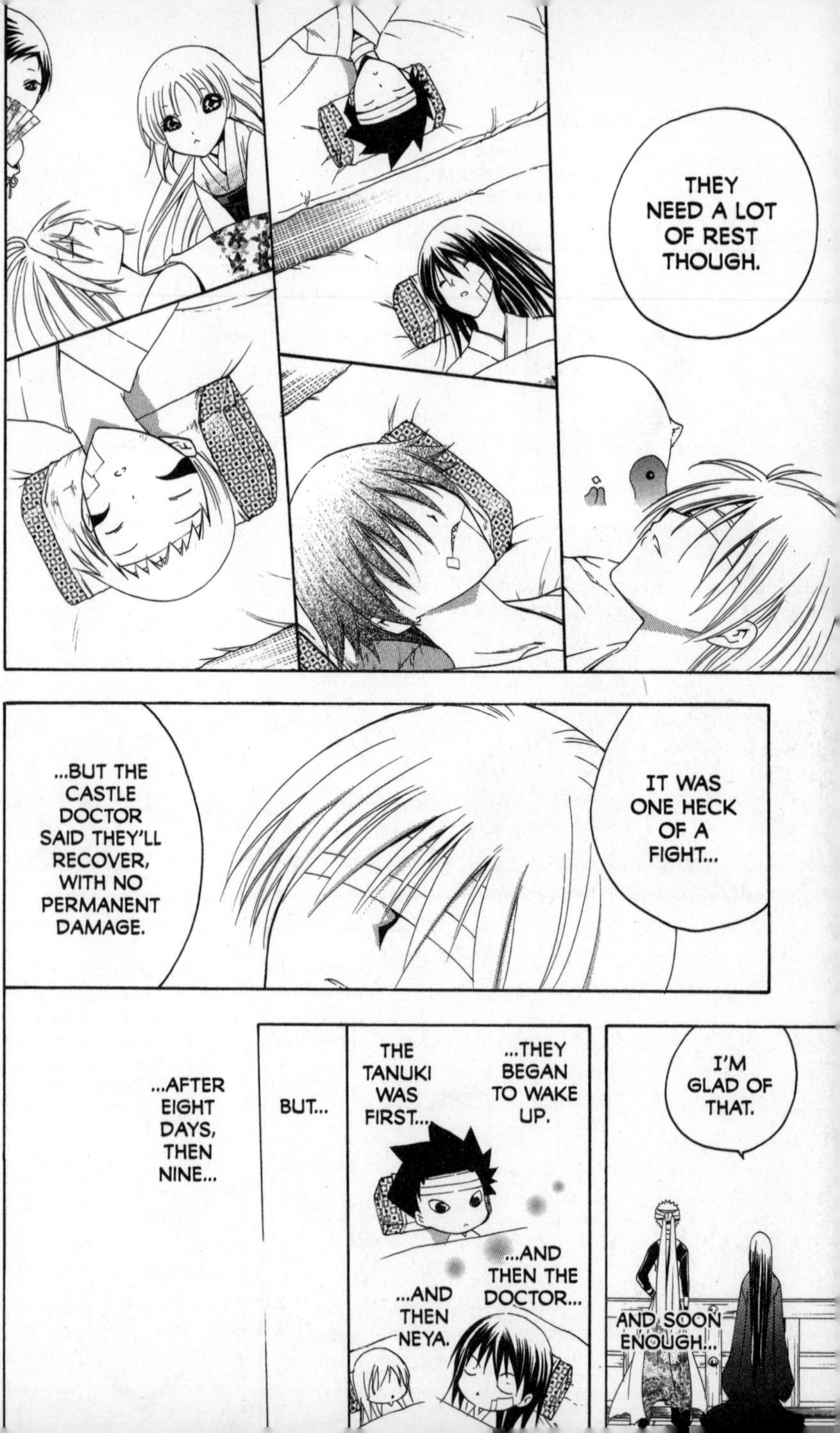
THEY NEED A LOT OF REST THOUGH.
IT WAS ONE HECK OF A FIGHT...
...BUT THE CASTLE DOCTOR SAID THEY'LL RECOVER, WITH NO PERMANENT DAMAGE.
I'M GLAD OF THAT.
AND SOON ENOUGH...
...THEY BEGAN TO WAKE UP.
THE TANUKI WAS FIRST...
...AND THEN THE DOCTOR...
...AND THEN NEYA.
BUT...
...AFTER EIGHT DAYS, THEN NINE...

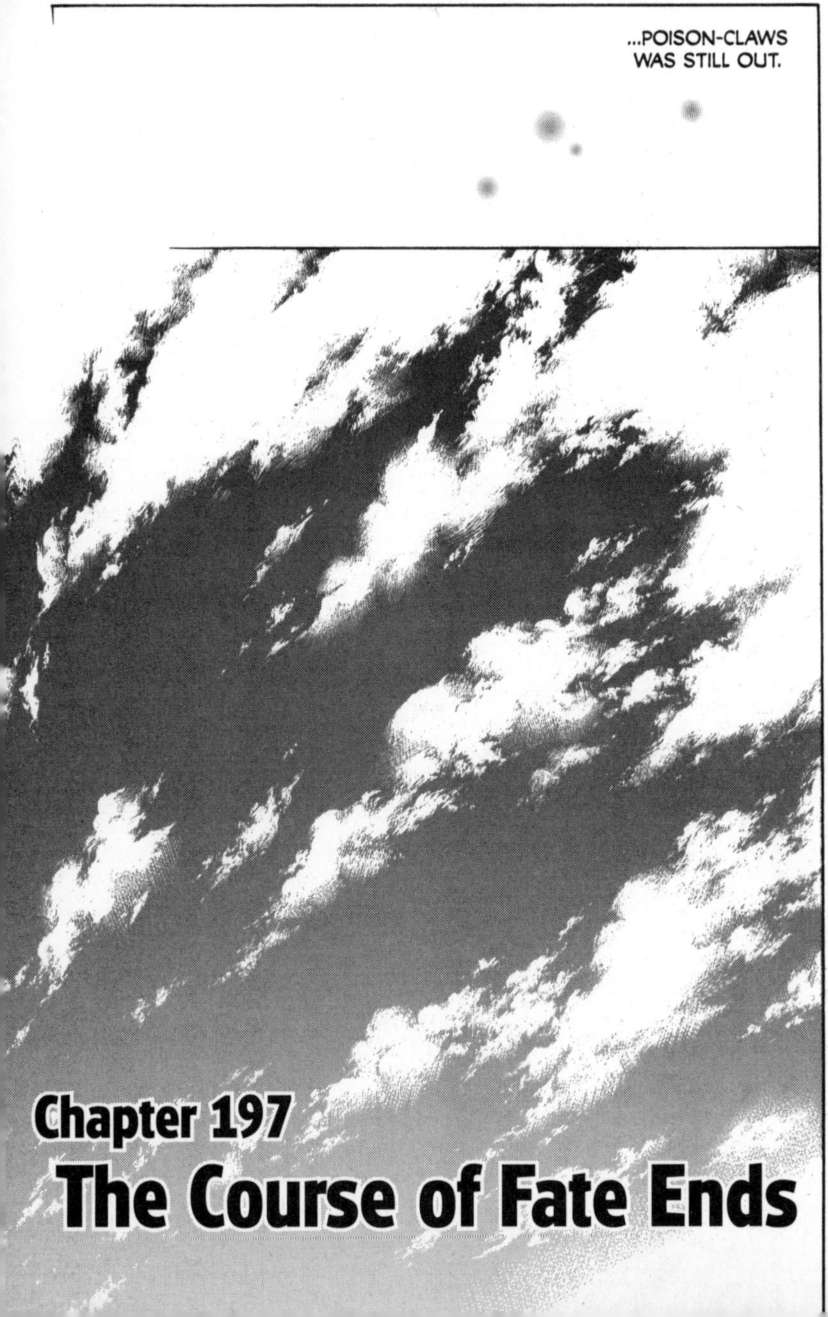
...POISON-CLAWS WAS STILL OUT.
Chapter 197
The Course of Fate Ends

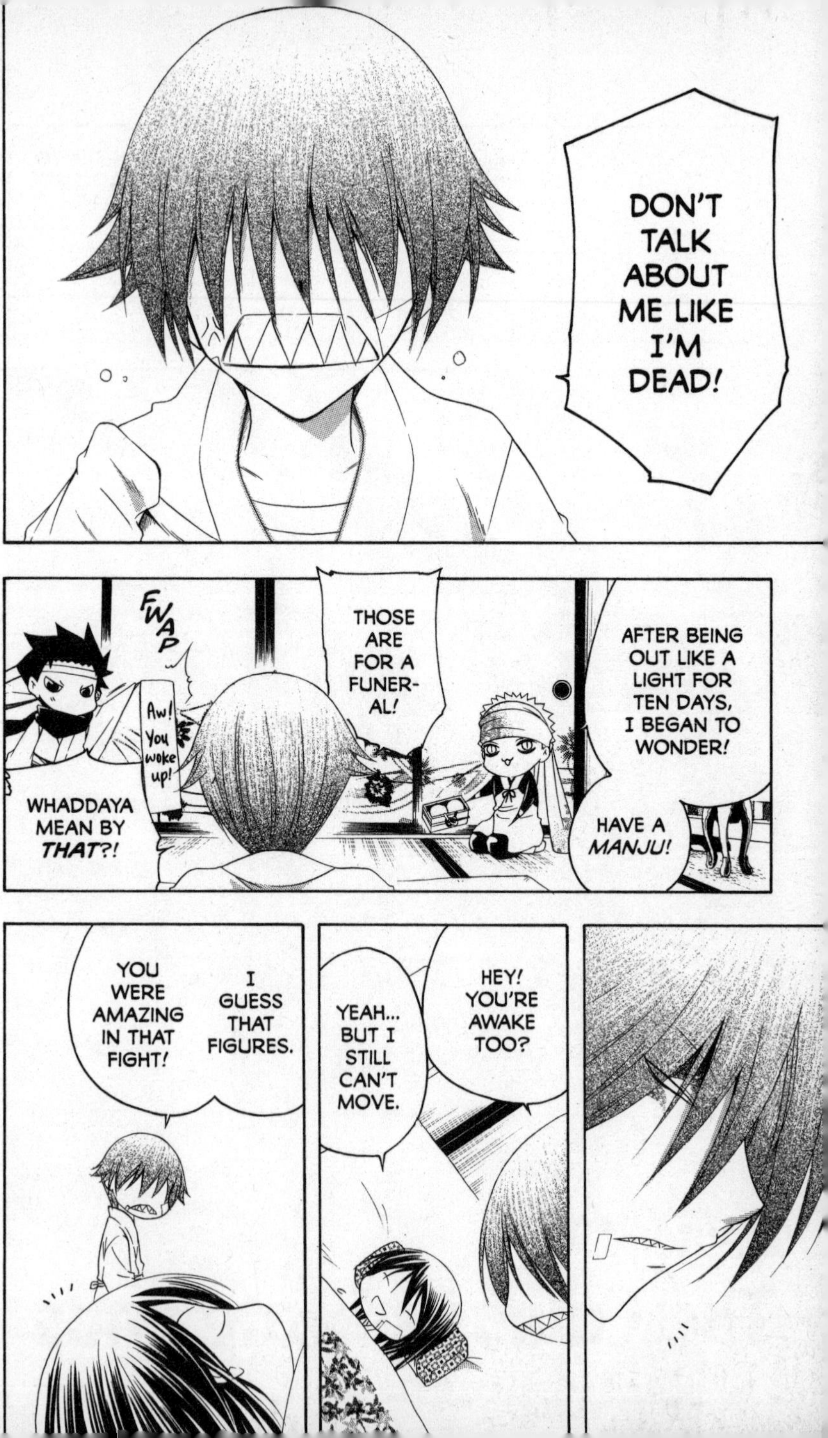
DON'T TALK ABOUT ME LIKE I'M DEAD!
AFTER BEING OUT LIKE A LIGHT FOR TEN DAYS, I BEGAN TO WONDER!
HAVE A *MANJU*!
THOSE ARE FOR A FUNER-AL!
FWAP
Aw! You woke up!
WHADDAYA MEAN BY *THAT*?!
HEY! YOU'RE AWAKE TOO?
YEAH... BUT I STILL CAN'T MOVE.
I GUESS THAT FIGURES.
YOU WERE AMAZING IN THAT FIGHT!

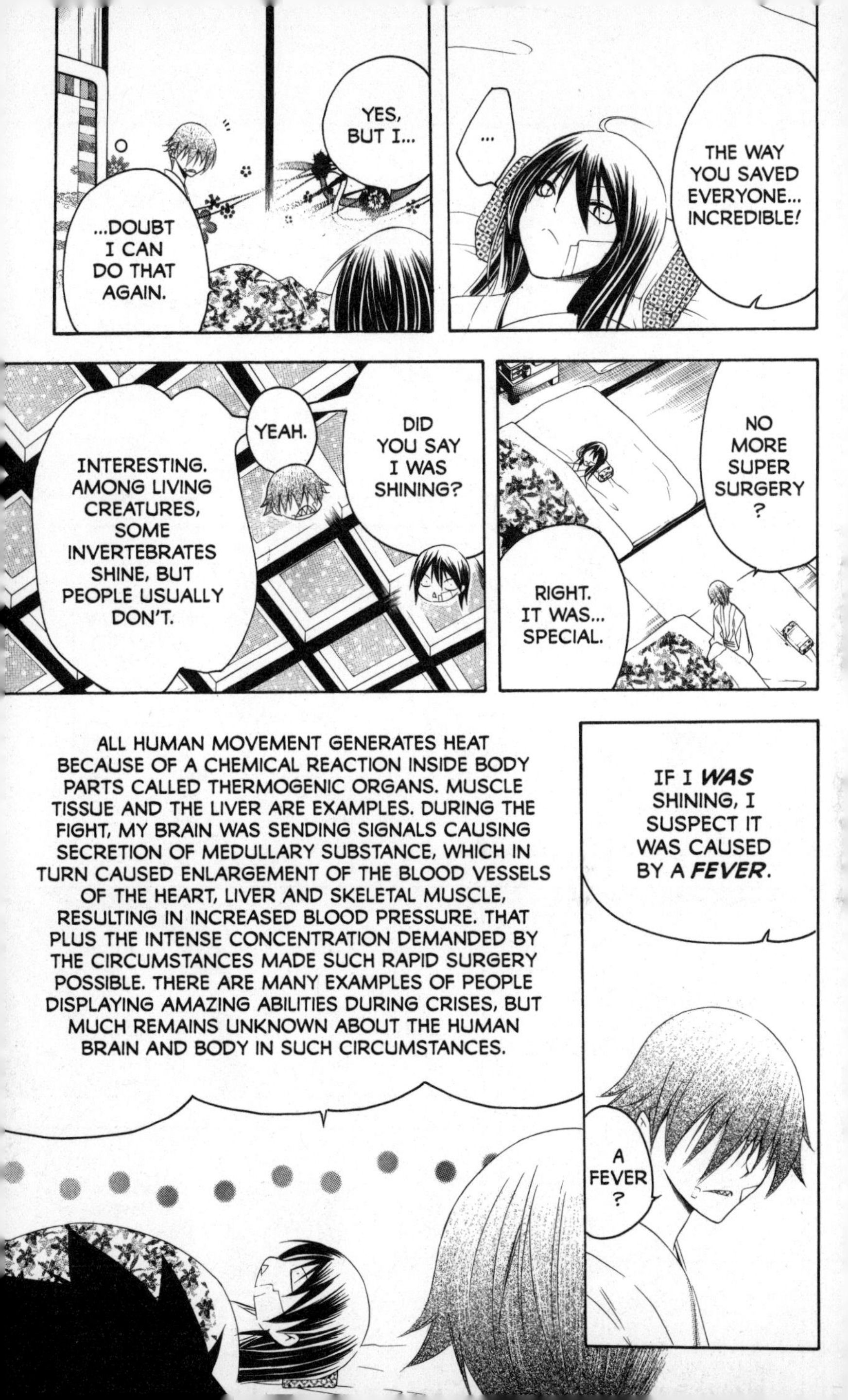
THE WAY YOU SAVED EVERYONE... INCREDIBLE!
...
YES, BUT I...
...DOUBT I CAN DO THAT AGAIN.
NO MORE SUPER SURGERY?
RIGHT. IT WAS... SPECIAL.
DID YOU SAY I WAS SHINING?
YEAH.
INTERESTING. AMONG LIVING CREATURES, SOME INVERTEBRATES SHINE, BUT PEOPLE USUALLY DON'T.
IF I ***WAS*** SHINING, I SUSPECT IT WAS CAUSED BY A ***FEVER***.
A FEVER?
ALL HUMAN MOVEMENT GENERATES HEAT BECAUSE OF A CHEMICAL REACTION INSIDE BODY PARTS CALLED THERMOGENIC ORGANS. MUSCLE TISSUE AND THE LIVER ARE EXAMPLES. DURING THE FIGHT, MY BRAIN WAS SENDING SIGNALS CAUSING SECRETION OF MEDULLARY SUBSTANCE, WHICH IN TURN CAUSED ENLARGEMENT OF THE BLOOD VESSELS OF THE HEART, LIVER AND SKELETAL MUSCLE, RESULTING IN INCREASED BLOOD PRESSURE. THAT PLUS THE INTENSE CONCENTRATION DEMANDED BY THE CIRCUMSTANCES MADE SUCH RAPID SURGERY POSSIBLE. THERE ARE MANY EXAMPLES OF PEOPLE DISPLAYING AMAZING ABILITIES DURING CRISES, BUT MUCH REMAINS UNKNOWN ABOUT THE HUMAN BRAIN AND BODY IN SUCH CIRCUMSTANCES.

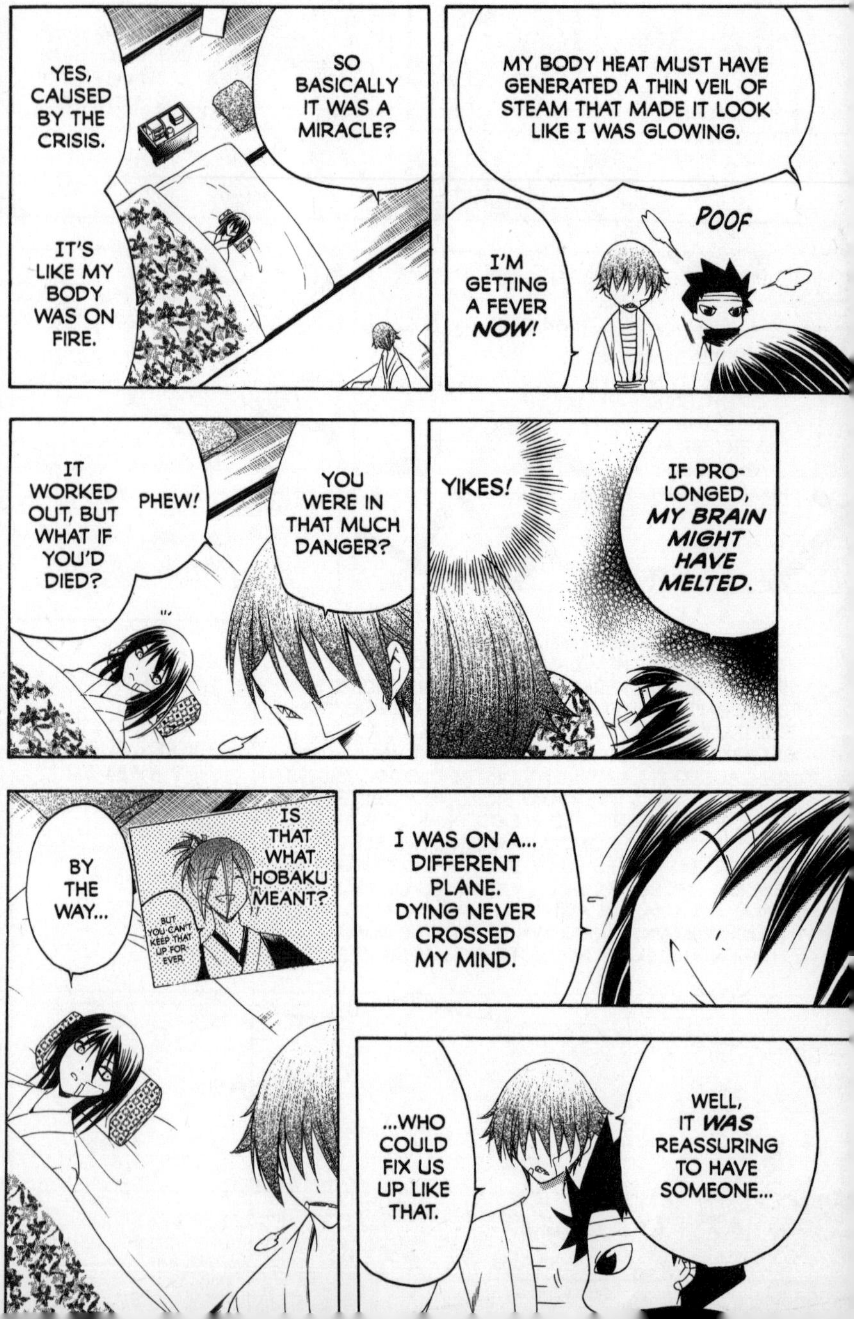
MY BODY HEAT MUST HAVE GENERATED A THIN VEIL OF STEAM THAT MADE IT LOOK LIKE I WAS GLOWING.
POOF
I'M GETTING A FEVER *NOW*!
SO BASICALLY IT WAS A MIRACLE?
YES, CAUSED BY THE CRISIS.
IT'S LIKE MY BODY WAS ON FIRE.
IF PRO-LONGED, *MY BRAIN MIGHT HAVE MELTED*.
YIKES!
YOU WERE IN THAT MUCH DANGER?
PHEW!
IT WORKED OUT, BUT WHAT IF YOU'D DIED?
I WAS ON A... DIFFERENT PLANE. DYING NEVER CROSSED MY MIND.
WELL, IT *WAS* REASSURING TO HAVE SOMEONE...
...WHO COULD FIX US UP LIKE THAT.
IS THAT WHAT HOBAKU MEANT?
BUT YOU CAN'T KEEP THAT UP FOREVER.
BY THE WAY...

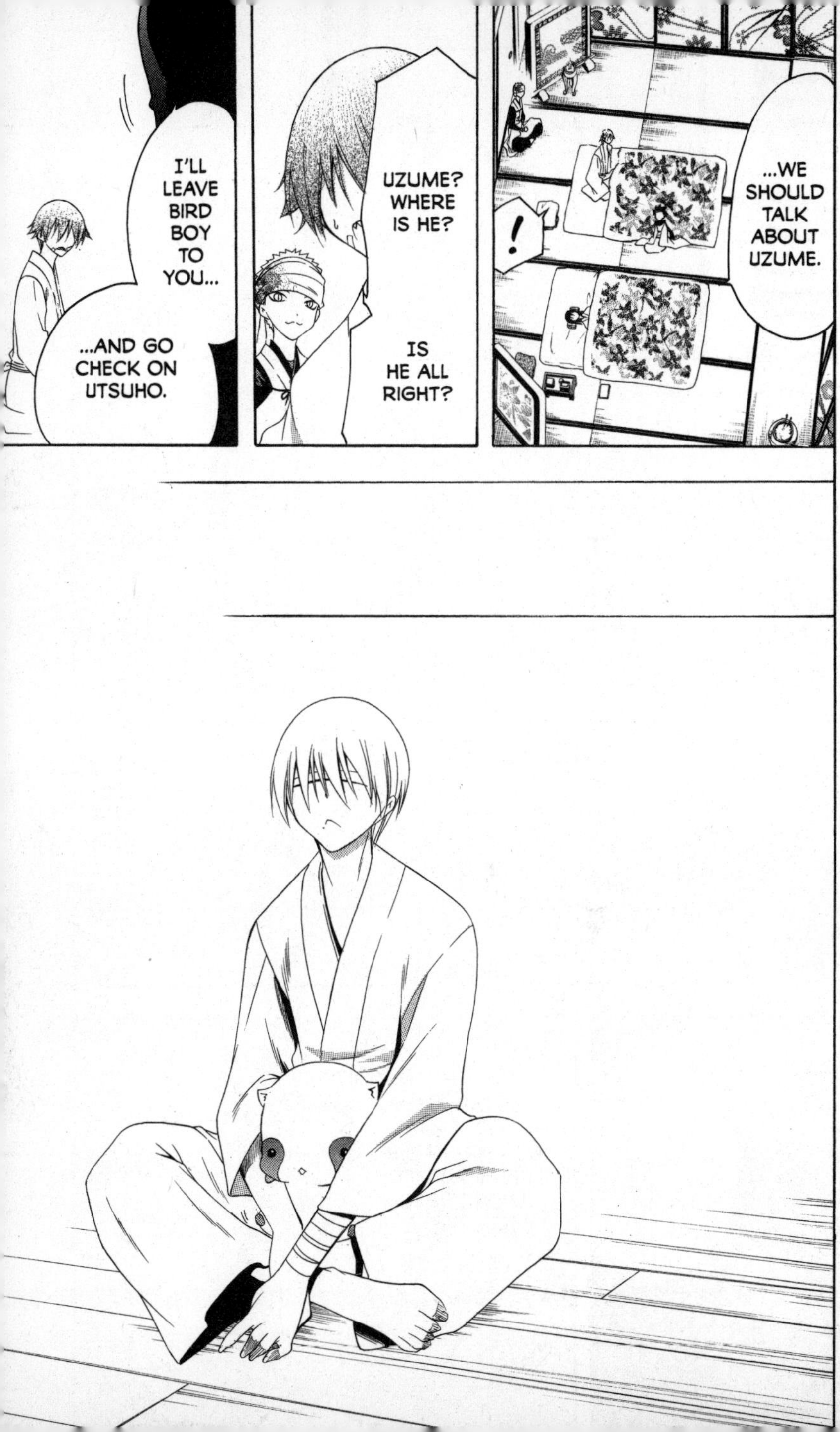
...WE SHOULD TALK ABOUT UZUME.
!
UZUME? WHERE IS HE?
IS HE ALL RIGHT?
I'LL LEAVE BIRD BOY TO YOU...
...AND GO CHECK ON UTSUHO.

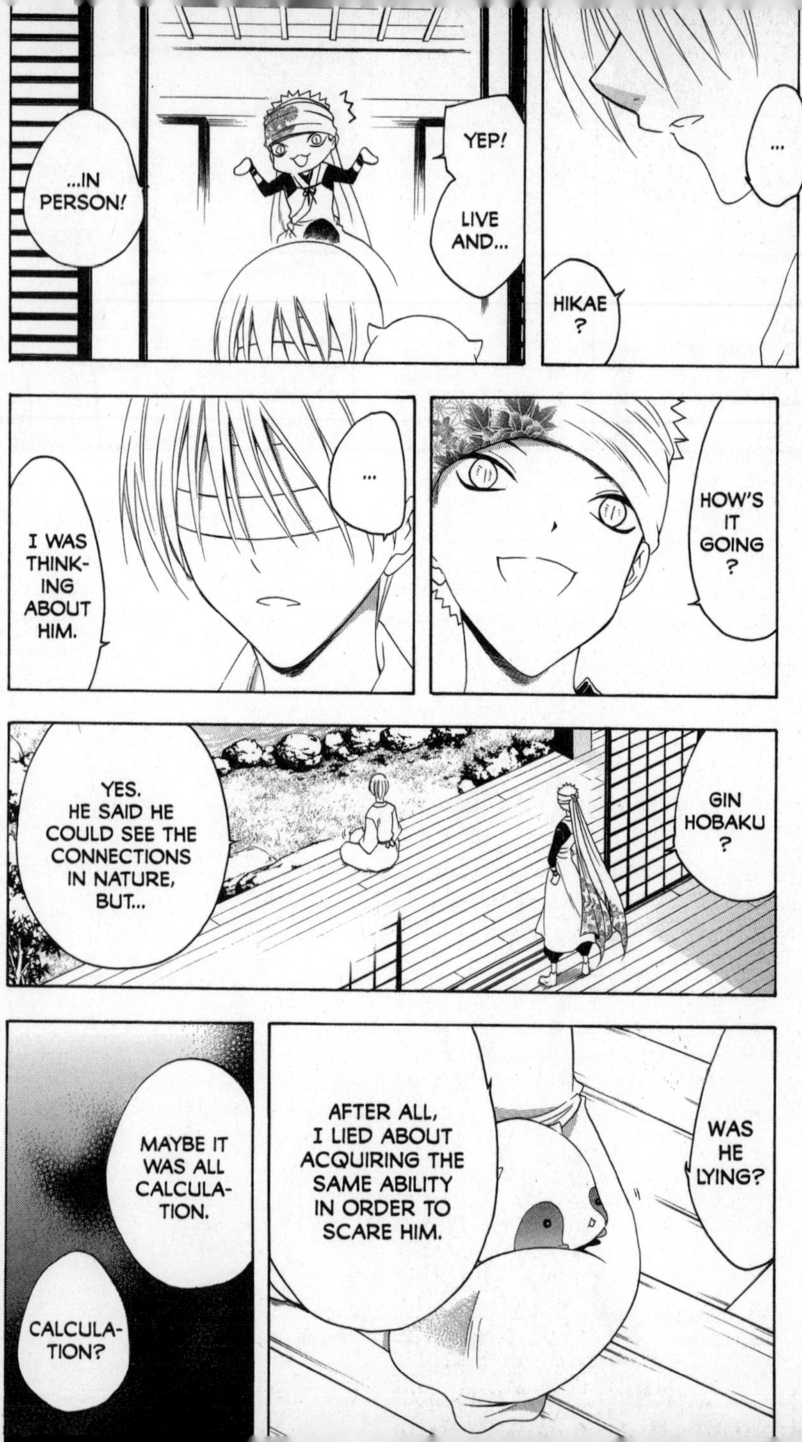
...
HIKAE?
YEP! LIVE AND...
...IN PERSON!
HOW'S IT GOING?
...
I WAS THINKING ABOUT HIM.
GIN HOBAKU?
YES. HE SAID HE COULD SEE THE CONNECTIONS IN NATURE, BUT...
WAS HE LYING?
AFTER ALL, I LIED ABOUT ACQUIRING THE SAME ABILITY IN ORDER TO SCARE HIM.
MAYBE IT WAS ALL CALCULATION.
CALCULATION?

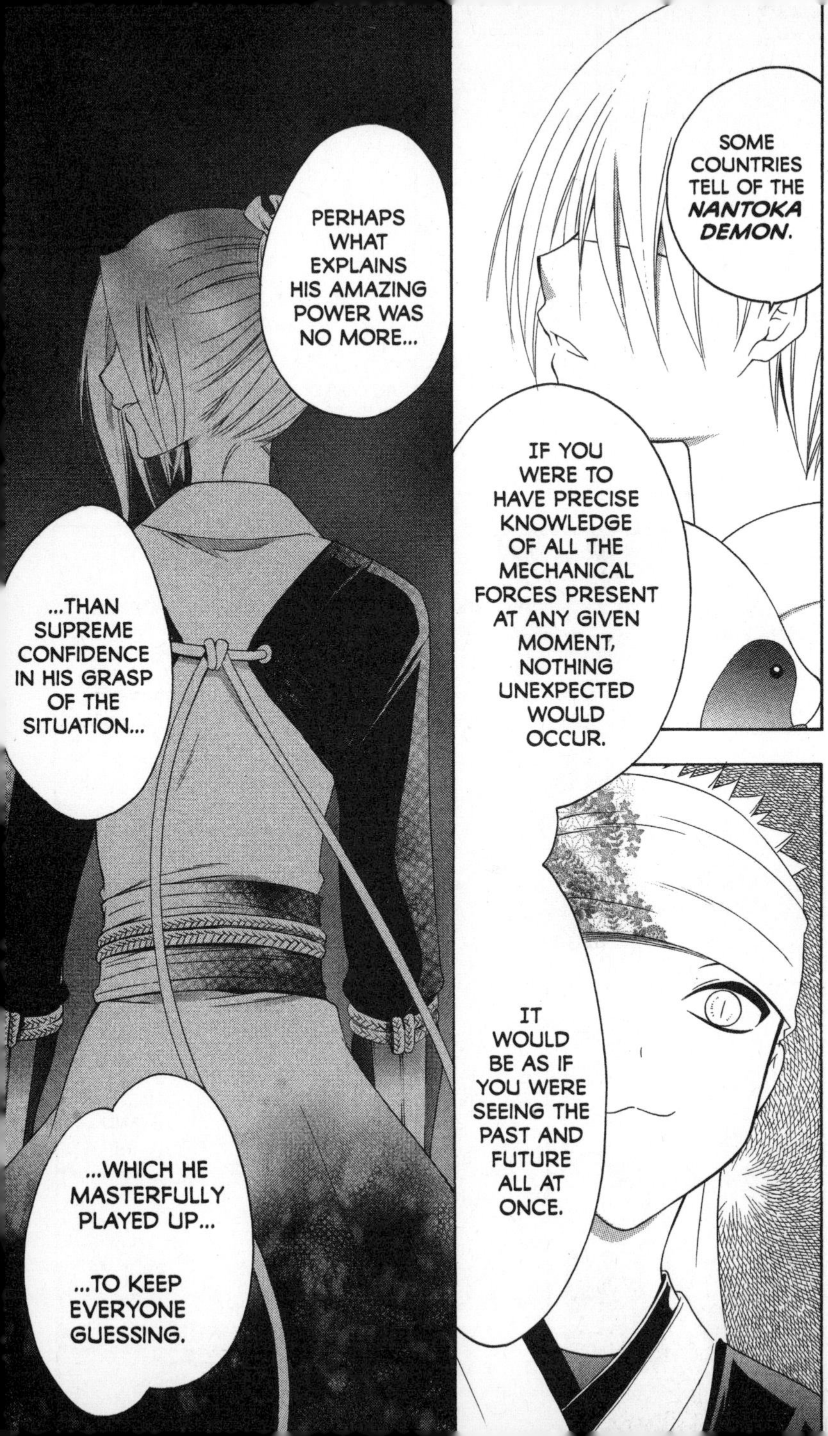
SOME COUNTRIES TELL OF THE *NANTOKA DEMON*.
IF YOU WERE TO HAVE PRECISE KNOWLEDGE OF ALL THE MECHANICAL FORCES PRESENT AT ANY GIVEN MOMENT, NOTHING UNEXPECTED WOULD OCCUR.
IT WOULD BE AS IF YOU WERE SEEING THE PAST AND FUTURE ALL AT ONCE.
PERHAPS WHAT EXPLAINS HIS AMAZING POWER WAS NO MORE...
...THAN SUPREME CONFIDENCE IN HIS GRASP OF THE SITUATION...
...WHICH HE MASTERFULLY PLAYED UP...
...TO KEEP EVERYONE GUESSING.

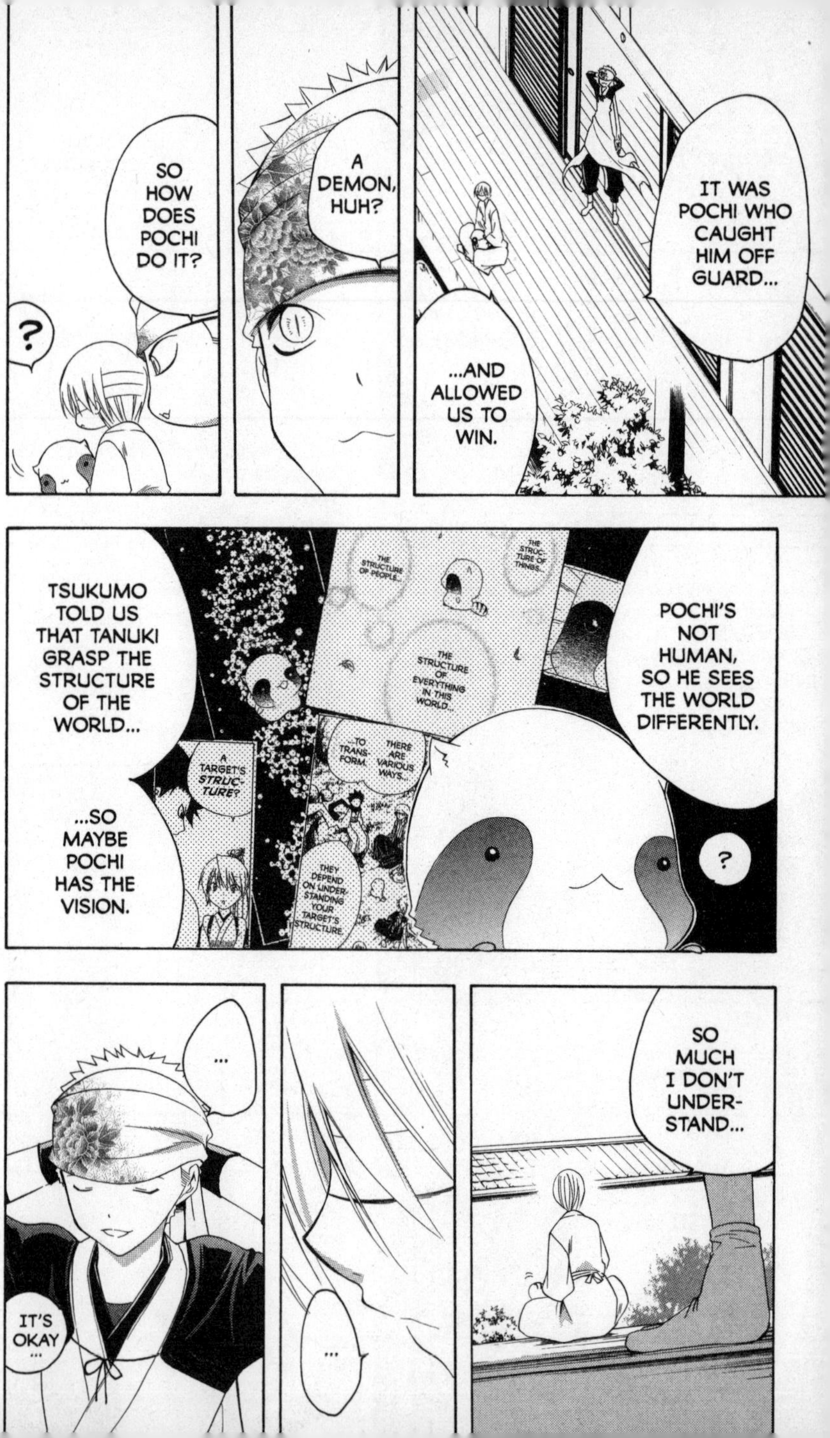
IT WAS POCHI WHO CAUGHT HIM OFF GUARD...
...AND ALLOWED US TO WIN.
A DEMON, HUH?
SO HOW DOES POCHI DO IT?
?
POCHI'S NOT HUMAN, SO HE SEES THE WORLD DIFFERENTLY.
?
THE STRUCTURE OF THINGS...
THE STRUCTURE OF PEOPLE...
THE STRUCTURE OF EVERYTHING IN THIS WORLD...
THERE ARE VARIOUS WAYS...
...TO TRANSFORM.
THEY DEPEND ON UNDERSTANDING YOUR TARGET'S STRUCTURE
A TARGET'S STRUCTURE?
TSUKUMO TOLD US THAT TANUKI GRASP THE STRUCTURE OF THE WORLD...
...SO MAYBE POCHI HAS THE VISION.
SO MUCH I DON'T UNDERSTAND...
...
...
IT'S OKAY...

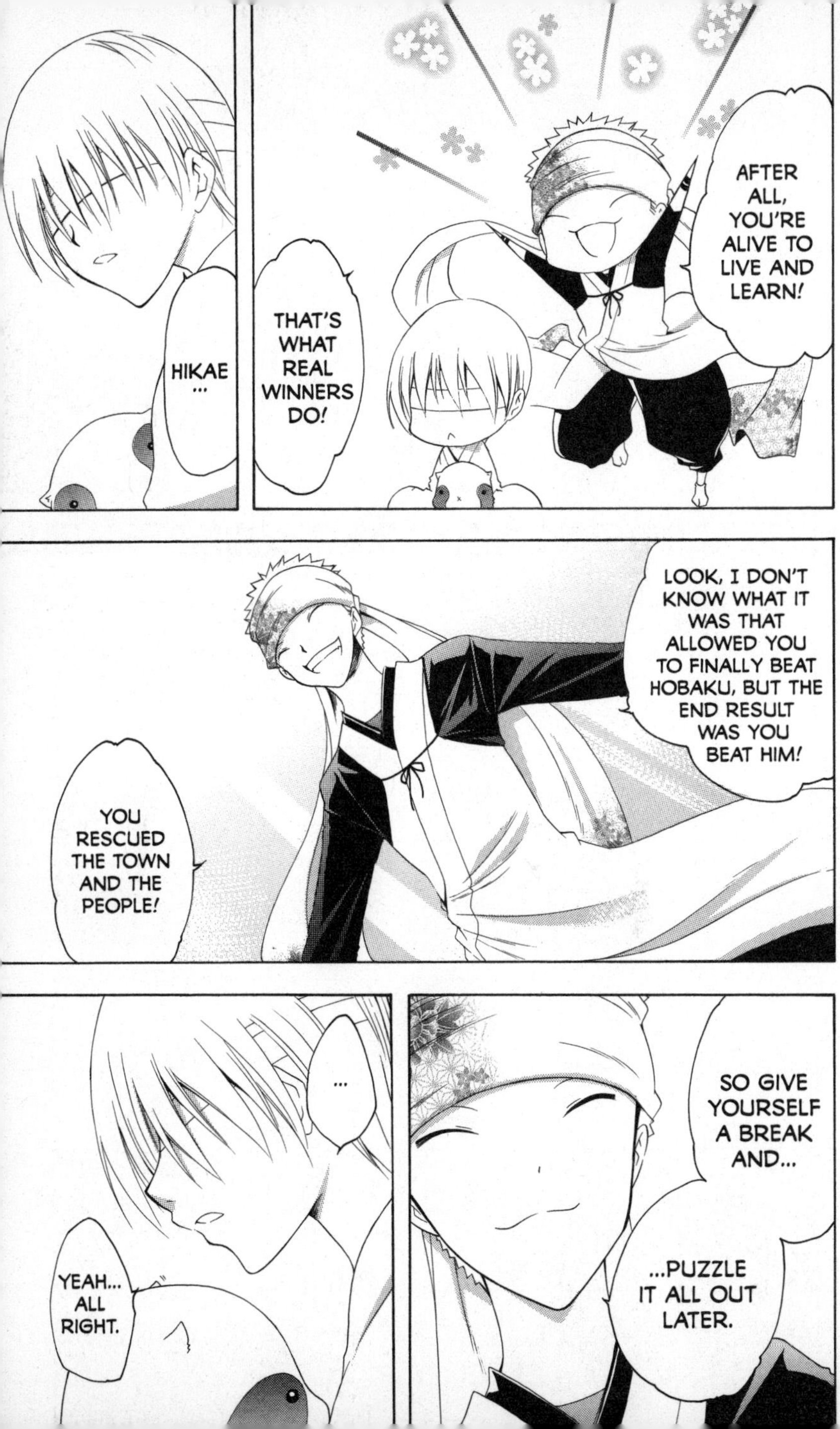
AFTER ALL, YOU'RE ALIVE TO LIVE AND LEARN!
THAT'S WHAT REAL WINNERS DO!
HIKAE ...
LOOK, I DON'T KNOW WHAT IT WAS THAT ALLOWED YOU TO FINALLY BEAT HOBAKU, BUT THE END RESULT WAS YOU BEAT HIM!
YOU RESCUED THE TOWN AND THE PEOPLE!
SO GIVE YOURSELF A BREAK AND...
...PUZZLE IT ALL OUT LATER.
...
YEAH... ALL RIGHT.

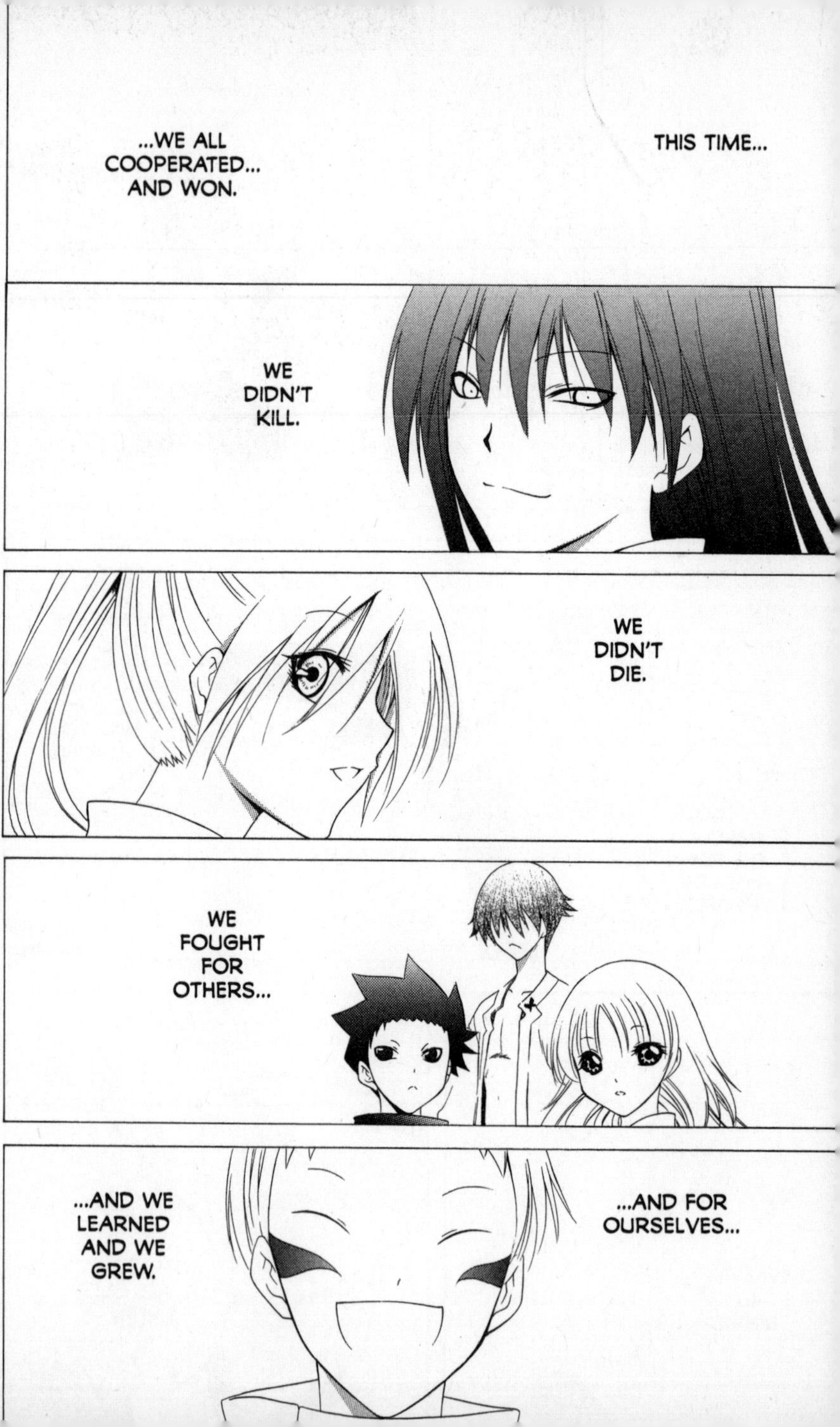
THIS TIME...
...WE ALL COOPERATED... AND WON.
WE DIDN'T KILL.
WE DIDN'T DIE.
WE FOUGHT FOR OTHERS...
...AND FOR OURSELVES...
...AND WE LEARNED AND WE GREW.

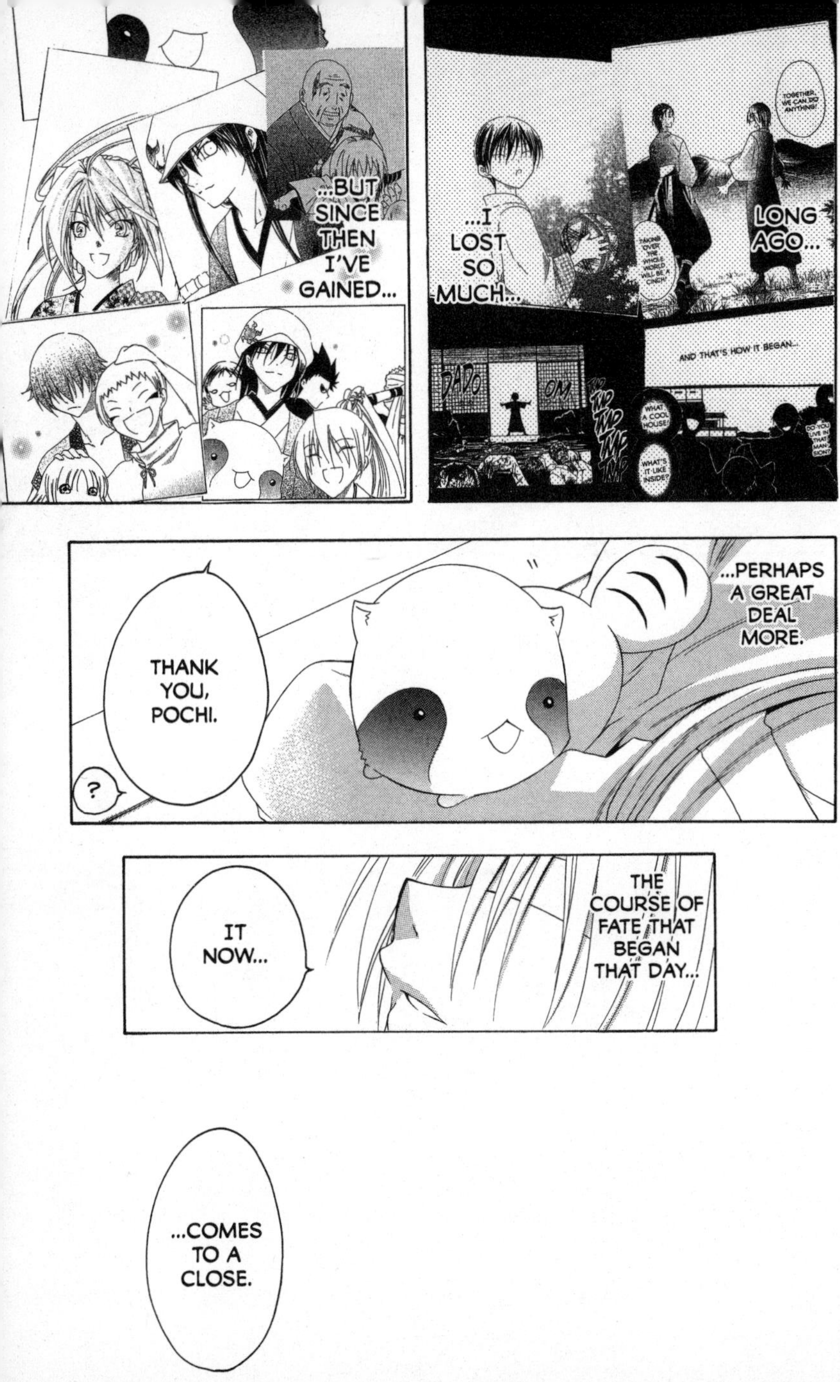

LONG AGO...
TOGETHER, WE CAN DO ANYTHING!
TAKING OVER THE WHOLE WORLD WILL BE A CINCH!
...I LOST SO MUCH...
AND THAT'S HOW IT BEGAN...
DO YOU LIVE IN THAT MANSION?
WHAT A COOL HOUSE!
WHAT'S IT LIKE INSIDE?
OM
DADO
...BUT SINCE THEN I'VE GAINED...
...PERHAPS A GREAT DEAL MORE.
THANK YOU, POCHI.
?
THE COURSE OF FATE THAT BEGAN THAT DAY...
IT NOW...
...COMES TO A CLOSE.

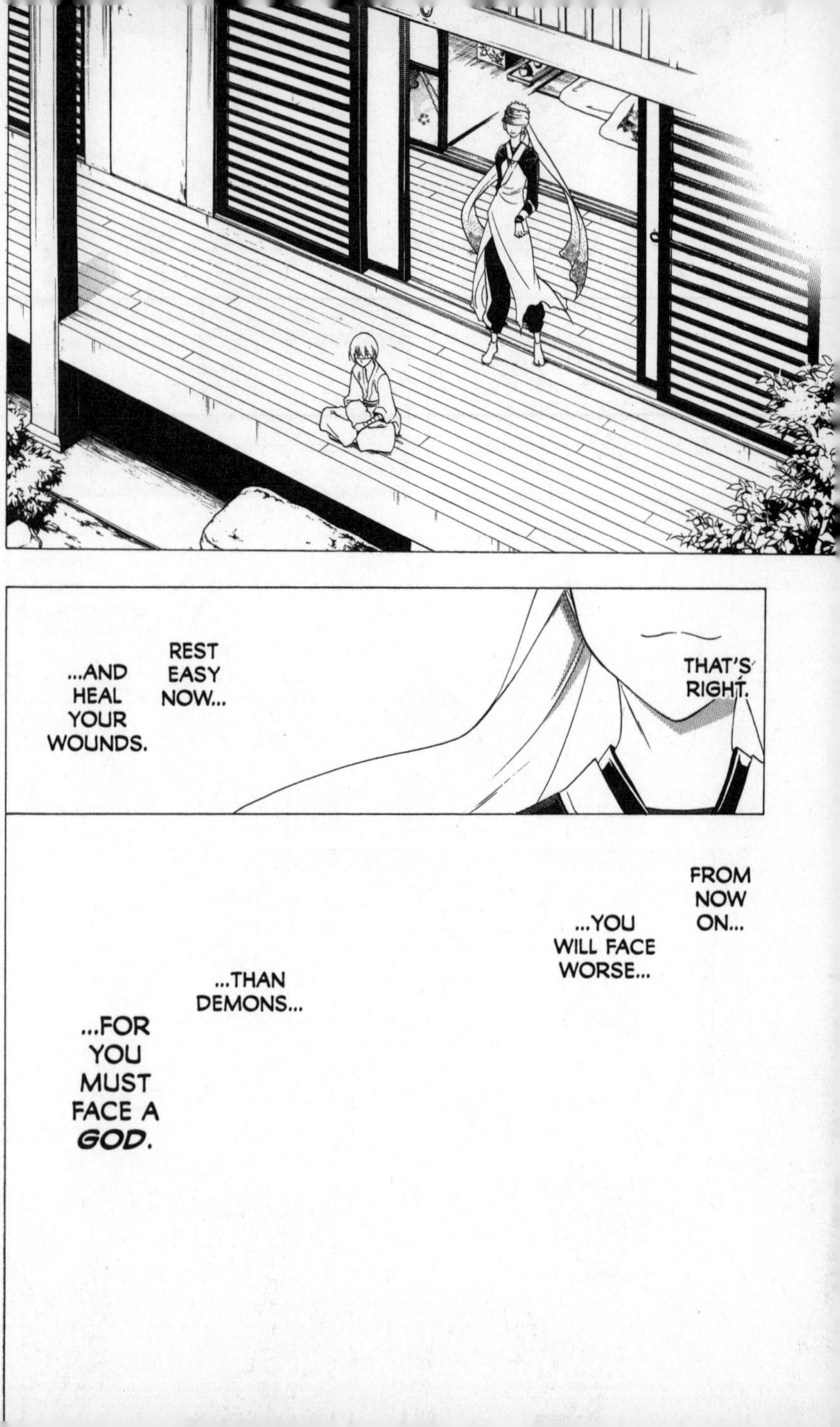
THAT'S RIGHT.
REST EASY NOW...
...AND HEAL YOUR WOUNDS.
FROM NOW ON...
...YOU WILL FACE WORSE...
...THAN DEMONS...
...FOR YOU MUST FACE A *GOD*.

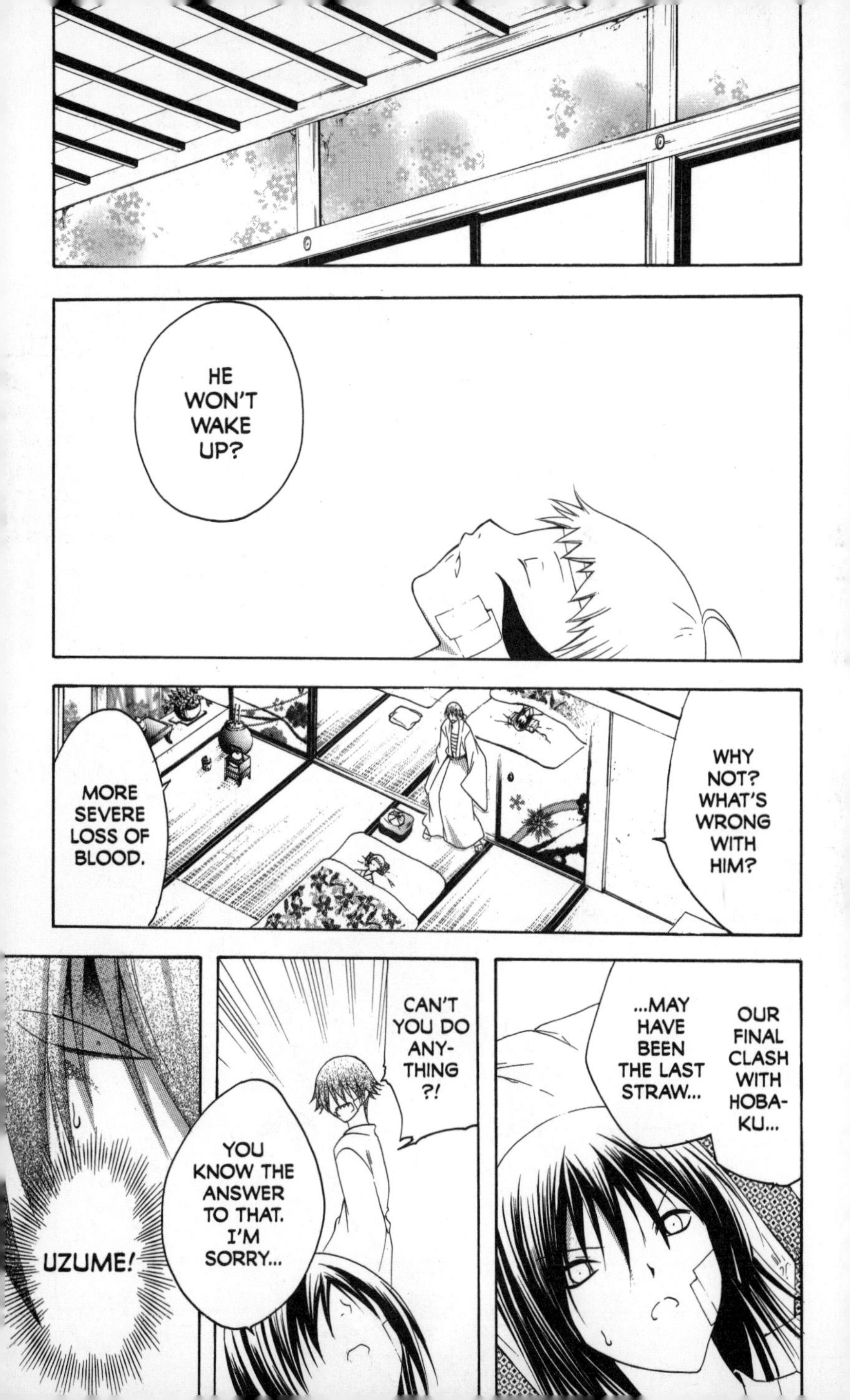
HE WON'T WAKE UP?
WHY NOT? WHAT'S WRONG WITH HIM?
MORE SEVERE LOSS OF BLOOD.
OUR FINAL CLASH WITH HOBA-KU...
...MAY HAVE BEEN THE LAST STRAW...
CAN'T YOU DO ANY-THING?!
YOU KNOW THE ANSWER TO THAT. I'M SORRY...
UZUME!

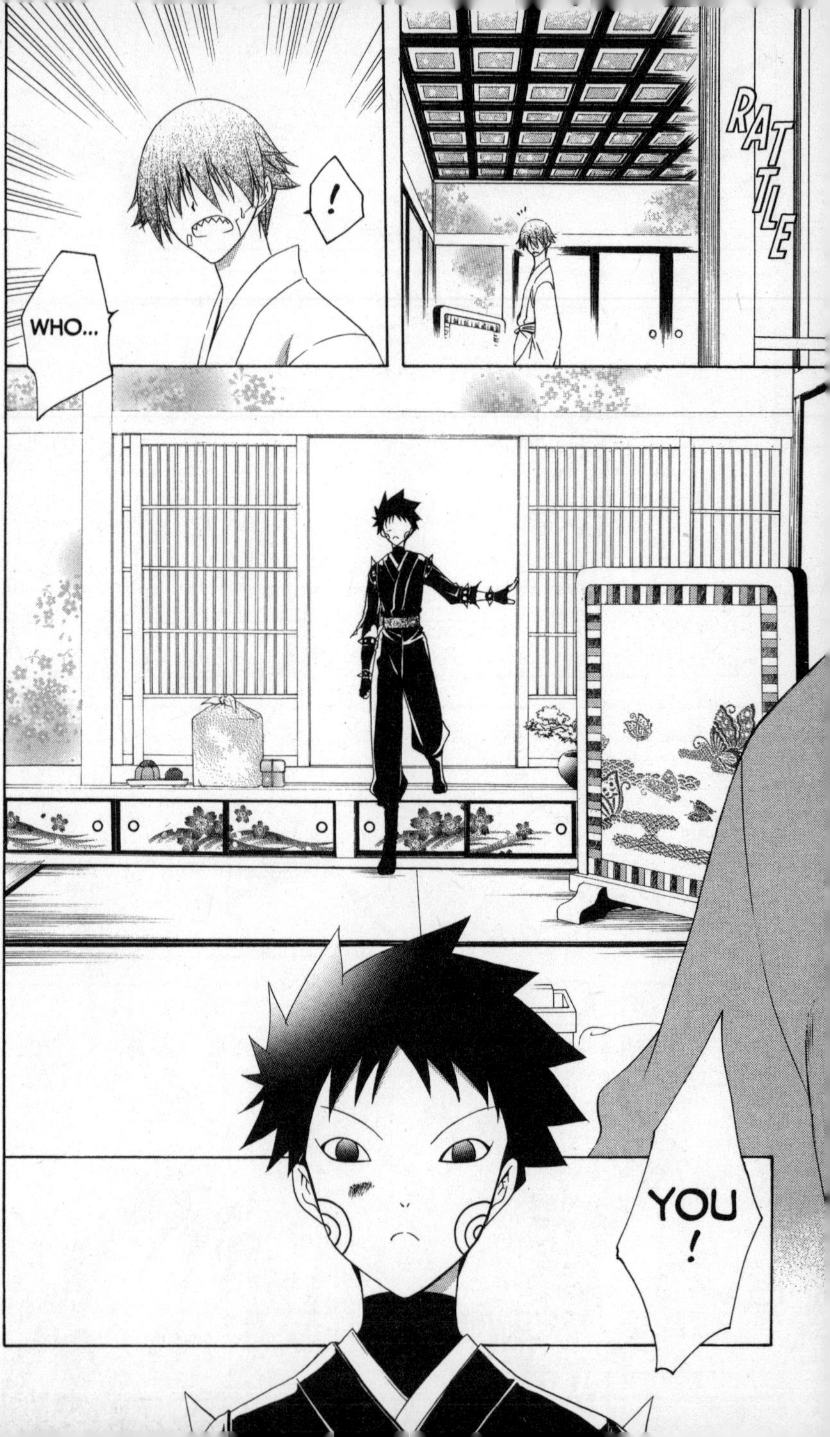
RATTLE
!
WHO...
YOU!

Bonus Manga

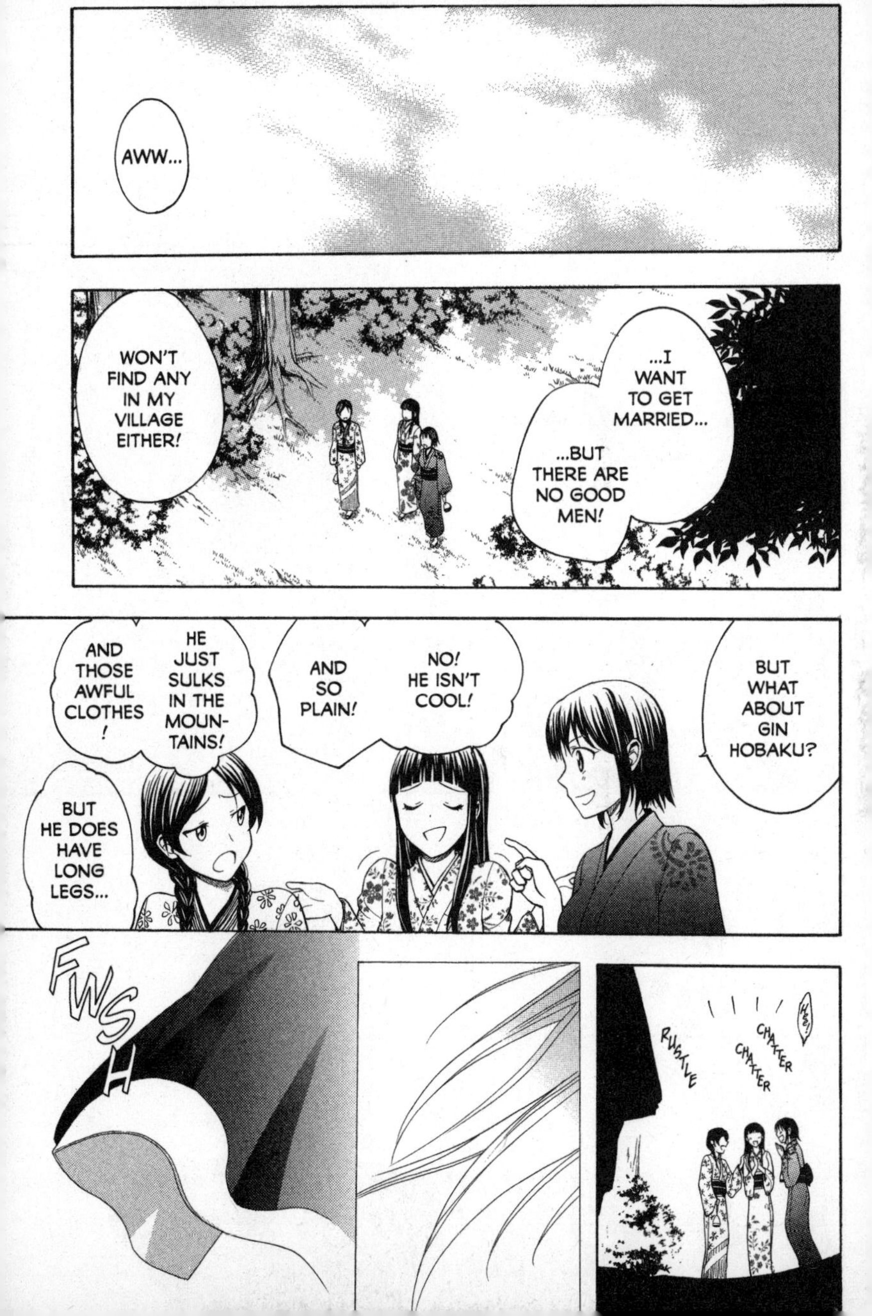
AWW...
...I WANT TO GET MARRIED...
...BUT THERE ARE NO GOOD MEN!
WON'T FIND ANY IN MY VILLAGE EITHER!
BUT WHAT ABOUT GIN HOBAKU?
NO! HE ISN'T COOL!
AND SO PLAIN!
HE JUST SULKS IN THE MOUNTAINS!
AND THOSE AWFUL CLOTHES!
BUT HE DOES HAVE LONG LEGS...
HEE!
CHATTER
CHATTER
RUSTLE
FWSH

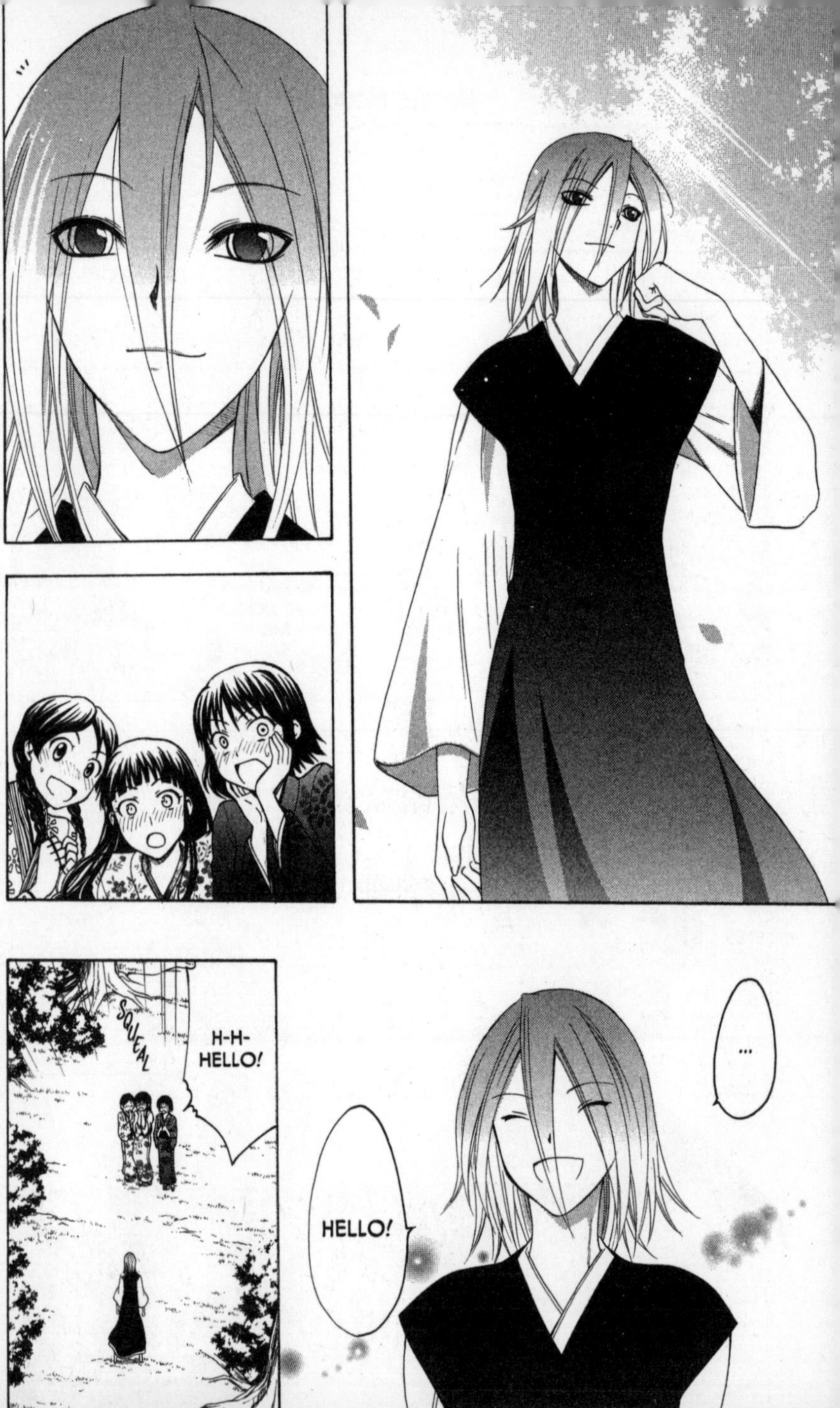
...
HELLO!
SQUEAL
H-H-HELLO!

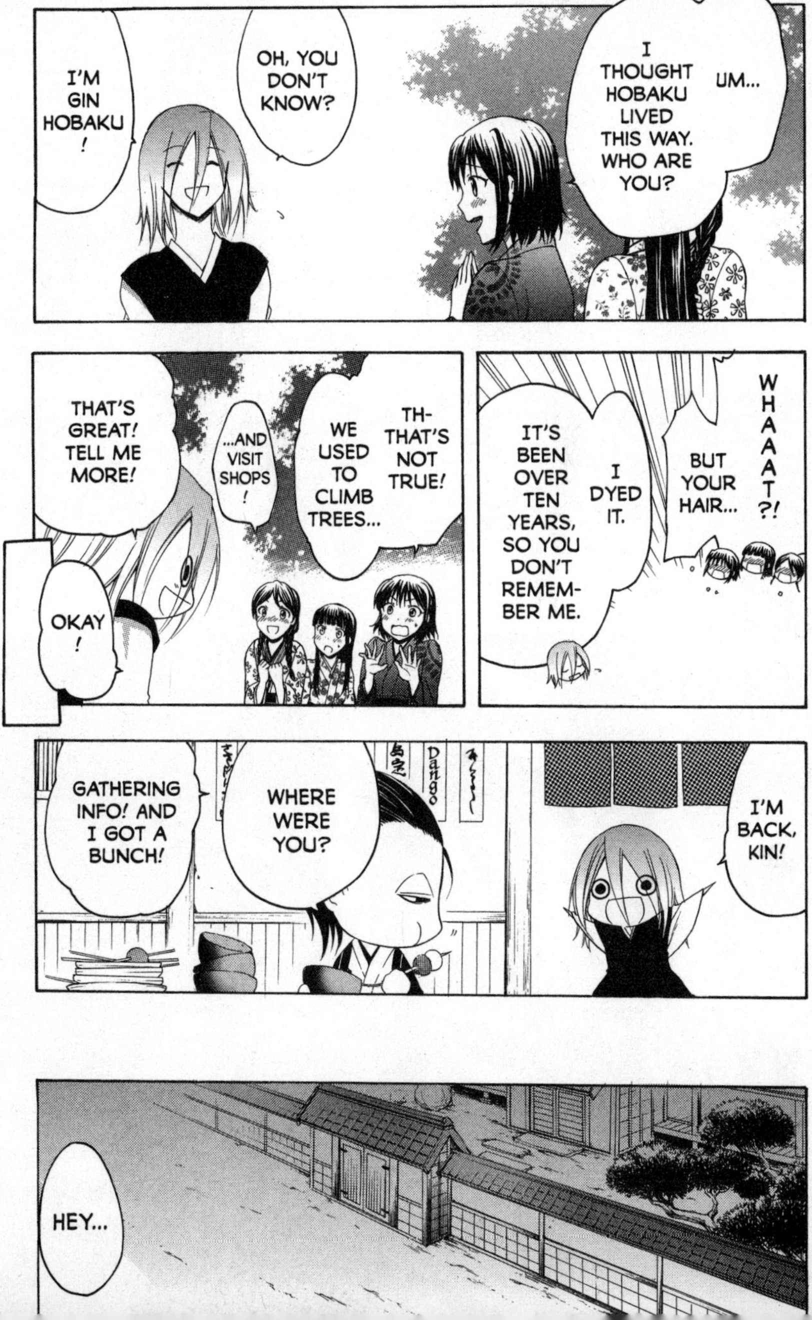
UM...
I THOUGHT HOBAKU LIVED THIS WAY. WHO ARE YOU?
OH, YOU DON'T KNOW?
I'M GIN HOBAKU!
WHAAAT?!
BUT YOUR HAIR...
I DYED IT.
IT'S BEEN OVER TEN YEARS, SO YOU DON'T REMEMBER ME.
TH-THAT'S NOT TRUE!
WE USED TO CLIMB TREES...
...AND VISIT SHOPS!
THAT'S GREAT! TELL ME MORE!
OKAY!
I'M BACK, KIN!
Dango
WHERE WERE YOU?
GATHERING INFO! AND I GOT A BUNCH!
HEY...

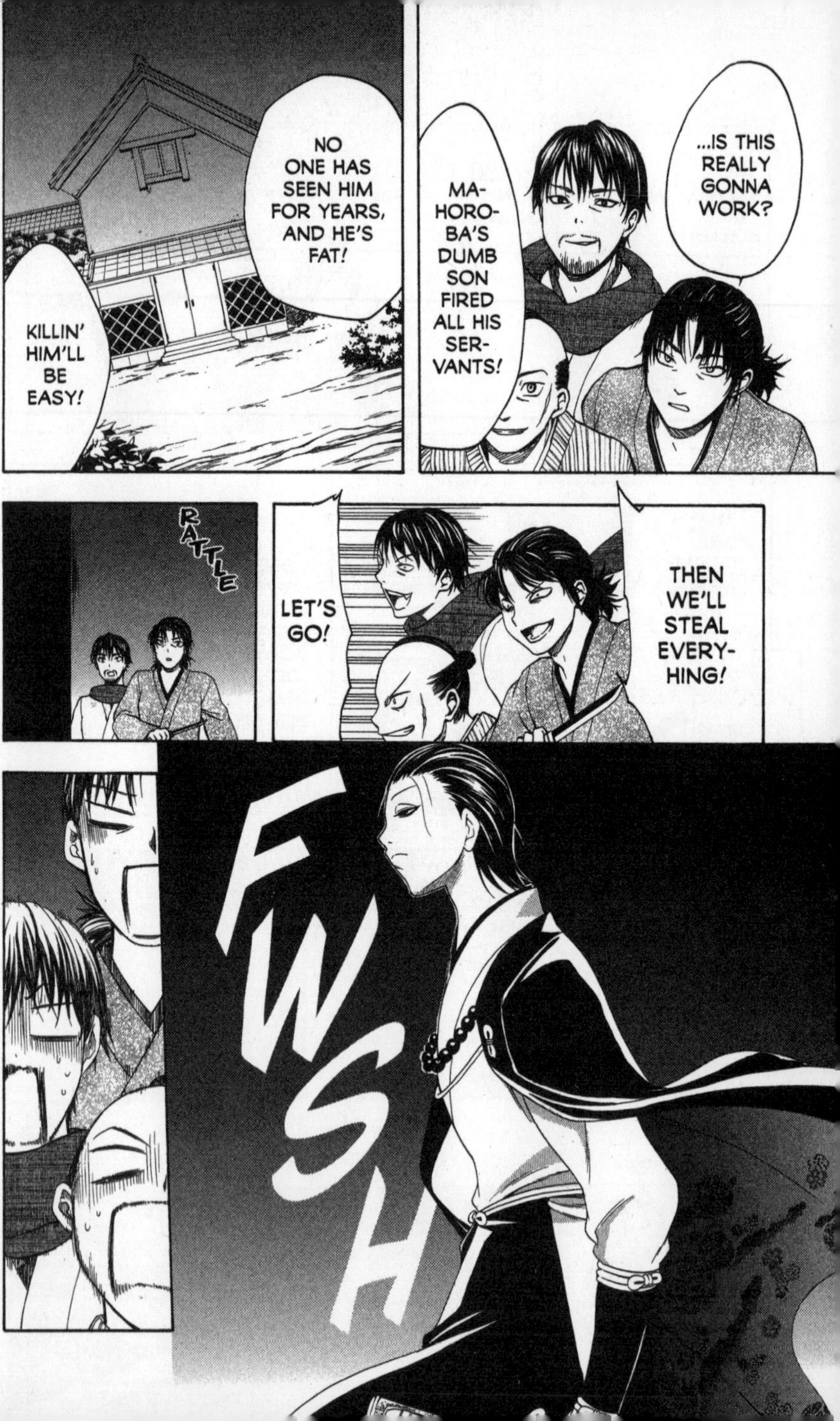
...IS THIS REALLY GONNA WORK?
MAHOROBA'S DUMB SON FIRED ALL HIS SERVANTS!
NO ONE HAS SEEN HIM FOR YEARS, AND HE'S FAT!
KILLIN' HIM'LL BE EASY!
THEN WE'LL STEAL EVERYTHING!
LET'S GO!
RATTLE
FWSH

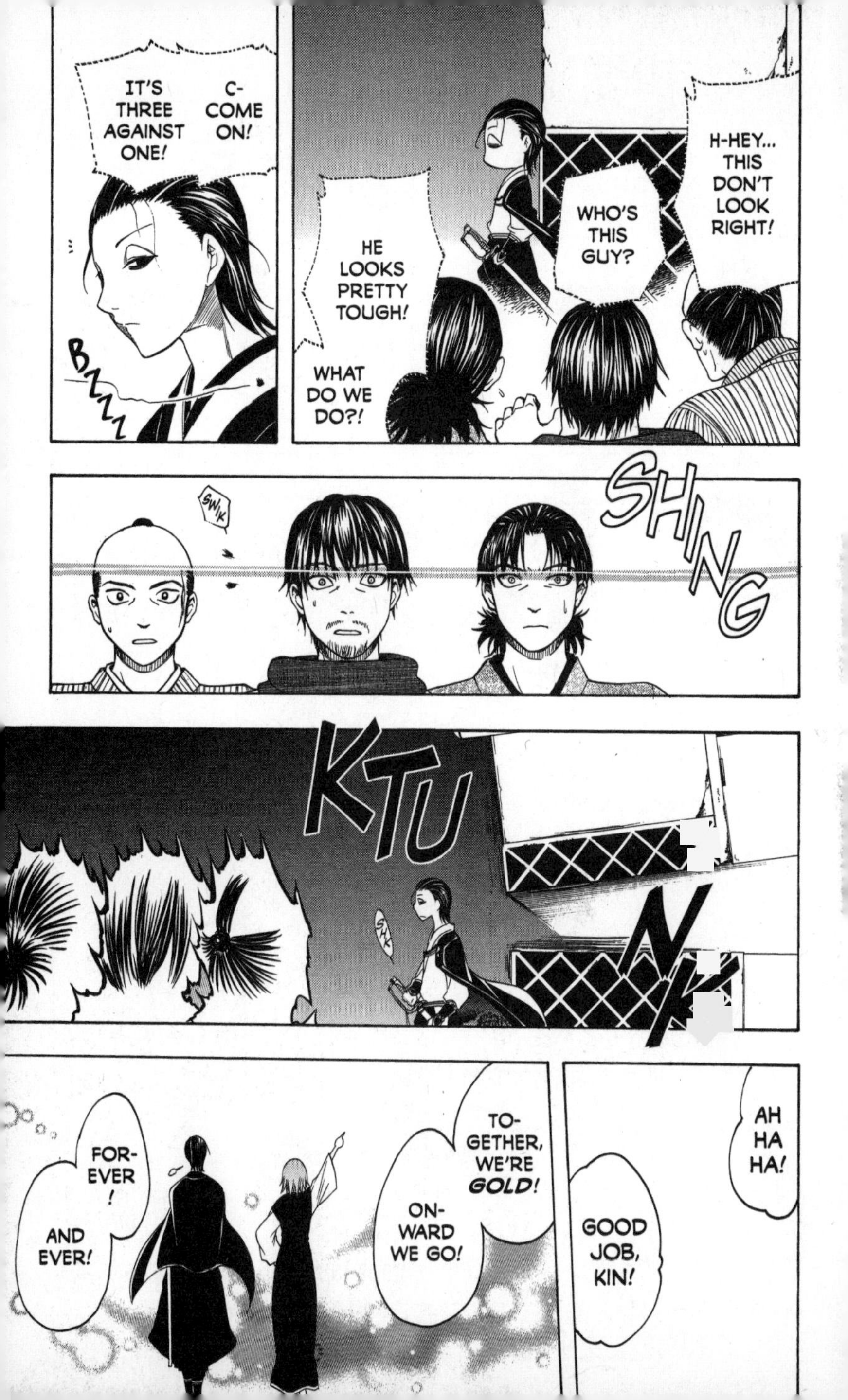
H-HEY... THIS DON'T LOOK RIGHT!
WHO'S THIS GUY?
HE LOOKS PRETTY TOUGH!
WHAT DO WE DO?!
C- COME ON!
IT'S THREE AGAINST ONE!
BZZZ
SHING
SWIK
KTUNK
SHK
AH HA HA!
GOOD JOB, KIN!
TOGETHER, WE'RE *GOLD*!
ONWARD WE GO!
FOREVER!
AND EVER!

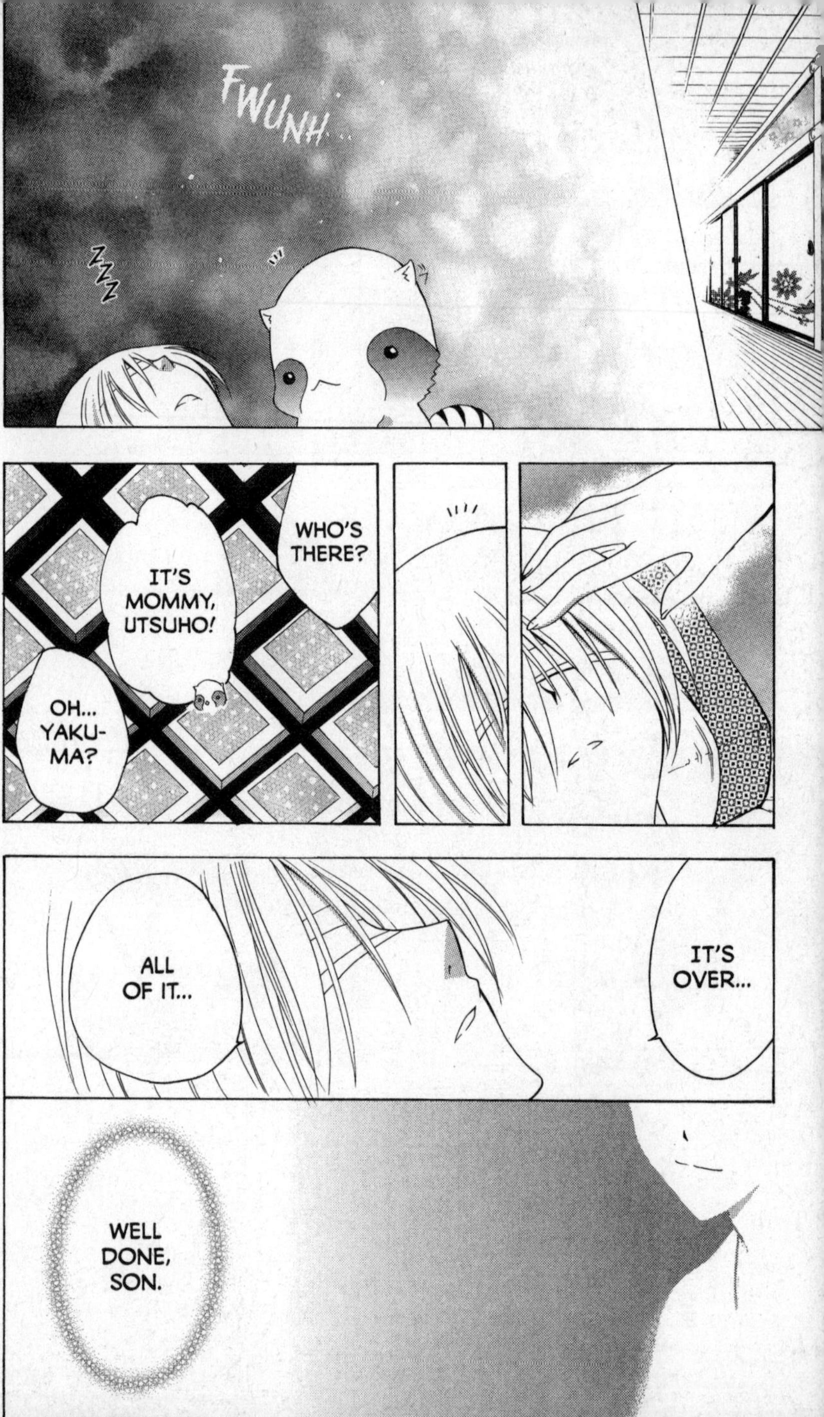
FWUNH...
ZZZ
WHO'S THERE?
IT'S MOMMY, UTSUHO!
OH... YAKU-MA?
IT'S OVER...
ALL OF IT...
WELL DONE, SON.

CONTINUED IN VOL. 21...

ITSUWARIBITO

Volume 20
Shonen Sunday Edition

Story and Art by
YUUKI IINUMA

ITSUWARIBITO ◆ UTSUHO ◆ Vol. 20
by Yuuki IINUMA
© 2009 Yuuki IINUMA
All rights reserved.
Original Japanese edition published by SHOGAKUKAN.
English translation rights in the United States of America and Canada
arranged with SHOGAKUKAN.

Translation/John Werry
Touch-up Art & Lettering/Susan Daigle-Leach
Design/Matt Hinrichs
Editor/Gary Leach

The stories, characters and incidents mentioned
in this publication are entirely fictional.

Printed in the U.S.A.

Published by VIZ Media, LLC
P.O. Box 77010
San Francisco, CA 94107

10 9 8 7 6 5 4 3 2 1
First printing, April 2017

www.viz.com   WWW.SHONENSUNDAY.COM

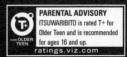

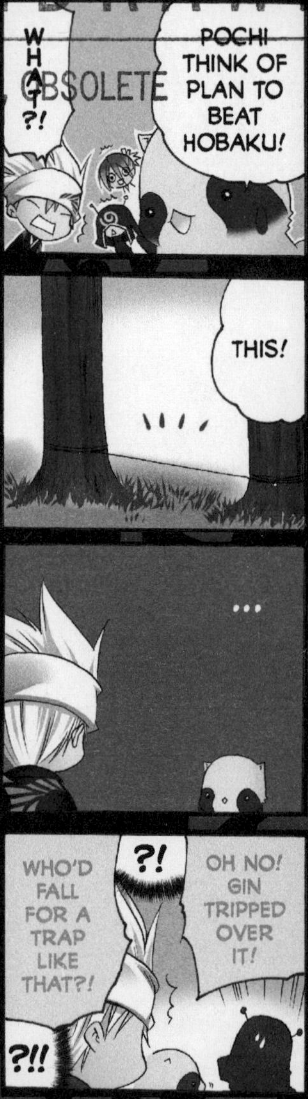
POCHI THINK OF PLAN TO BEAT HOBAKU!
WHAT?!
THIS!
...
?!
OH NO! GIN TRIPPED OVER IT!
WHO'D FALL FOR A TRAP LIKE THAT?!
?!!